Petitioners, Penitents, and Poets

Beihefte zur Zeitschrift für die alttestamentliche Wissenschaft

Herausgegeben von
John Barton, Reinhard G. Kratz, Nathan MacDonald,
Sara Milstein and Markus Witte

Volume 524

Petitioners, Penitents, and Poets

On Prayer and Praying in Second Temple Judaism

Edited by
Ariel Feldman and Timothy J. Sandoval

DE GRUYTER

ISBN 978-3-11-062040-5
e-ISBN (PDF) 978-3-11-062452-6
e-ISBN (EPUB) 978-3-11-062134-1
ISSN 0934-2575

Library of Congress Control Number: 2020939079

Bibliographic information published by the Deutsche Nationalbibliothek
The Deutsche Nationalbibliothek lists this publication in the Deutsche Nationalbibliografie; detailed bibliographic data are available on the Internet at http://dnb.dnb.de.

© 2020 Walter de Gruyter GmbH, Berlin/Boston
Typesetting: jürgen ullrich typosatz, Nördlingen
Printing and Binding: LSC Communications, United States

www.degruyter.com

Preface

The essays in *Petitioners, Penitents, and Poets: On Prayer and Praying in Second Temple Judaism* are revisions and expansions of papers delivered at a conference by the same name held at Brite Divinity School at Texas Christian University on May 21–22, 2019. We are grateful not only to colleagues who presented papers at this event and who have contributed to this volume, but also to others who made both the conference and the volume possible. Funds from the Cristol Endowment for Jewish Studies at Brite Divinity School and Texas Christian University provided the support for our small conference. The actual conference itself, however, would have seen no success without the invaluable logistical assistance of Ms. Reina Rodriguez and Mr. Marcus Hayes. Thanks are also due to Mr. Zachary Poppen who proofread several essays included in the volume prior to it being sent to press. We are especially appreciative of Professor Reinhard Kratz and the other editors of BZAW for accepting this book into their prestigious series, while Albrecht Döhnert and others at De Gruyter, as always, helpfully and professionally guided the project along.

Finally, although a somewhat belated gesture, we are happy to dedicate the volume to two of its contributors who have recently retired from their academic posts—Professors George J. Brooke and Carol A. Newsom. It is difficult to imagine two scholars from whom we have learned more.

Ariel Feldman and Timothy J. Sandoval

Table of Contents

Preface —— V

Abbreviations Including Frequently Cited Sources —— IX

Ariel Feldman and Timothy J. Sandoval
Introduction —— 1

Jonathan Kaplan
Pastiche, Hyperbole, and the Composition of Jonah's Prayer —— 27

Serge Frolov
Psalms: *Sitz im Leben* vs. *Sitz in der Literatur* —— 43

Carol A. Newsom
"If I had said …" (Ps 73:15): Retrospective Introspection
in Didactic Psalmody of the Second Temple Period —— 69

Timothy J. Sandoval
Agur's Words to God in Proverbs 30 and Prayerful Study
in the Second Temple Period —— 83

George J. Brooke
Patterns of Priesthood and Patterns of Prayer in the Dead Sea Scrolls —— 115

Charlotte Hempel
The Apotropaic Function of the Final Hymn in the Community Rules —— 131

Molly M. Zahn
The Absence of Prayer in the Temple Scroll —— 155

Ariel Feldman
On Amulets, Apotropaic Prayers, and Phylacteries:
The Contribution of Three New Texts from the Judean Desert —— 169

Matthias Henze
Prayer in 2 Baruch —— 199

John R. Levison
The Prayers of Eve in the Greek Life of Adam and Eve —— 219

Shelly Matthews
"I Have Prayed for You ... Strengthen Your Brothers" (Luke 22:32): Jesus's Proleptic Prayer for Peter and Other Gendered Tropes in Luke's War on Satan —— 231

Warren Carter
Praying the Lord's Prayer in (Some Sort of) *Tameion* (Matt 6:6) —— 247

Ancient Sources Index —— 267

Subject Index —— 279

Abbreviations Including Frequently Cited Sources

AB	Anchor Bible
ABD	*Anchor Bible Dictionary*. Edited by David Noel Freedman. 6 vols. New York: Doubleday, 1992.
AJEC	Ancient Judaism and Early Christianity
ANESSup	Ancient Near Eastern Studies Supplement Series
AYBRL	Anchor Yale Bible Reference Library
BAGD	Walter Bauer, William F. Arndt, F. Wilbur Gingrich, and Frederick W. Danker. *Greek-English Lexicon of the New Testament and Other Early Christian Literature*. 2nd ed. Chicago: University of Chicago Press, 1979.
BASOR	*Bulletin of the American Schools of Oriental Research*
BBET	Beiträge zur biblischen Exegese und Theologie
BDB	Francis Brown, S. R. Driver, and Charles A. Briggs, *The Brown-Driver-Briggs Hebrew and English Lexicon of the Old Testament*. Based on the lexicon of William Gesenius. Peabody: Hendrickson, 1994.
BETL	Bibliotheca Ephemeridum Theologicarum Lovaniensium
Bib	*Biblica*
BibInt	*Biblical Interpretation*
BJS	Brown Judaic Studies
BN	*Biblische Notizen*
BZAW	Beihefte zur Zeitschrift für die alttestamentliche Wissenschaft
CBQ	*Catholic Biblical Quarterly*
CQS	Companion to the Qumran Scrolls
CRINT	Compendia Rerum Iudaicarum ad Novum Testamentum
DCLS	Deuterocanonical and Cognate Literature Studies
DCLY	Deuterocanonical and Cognate Literature Yearbook
DJD	Discoveries in the Judaean Desert
DSD	*Dead Sea Discoveries*
DSSSE	*The Dead Sea Scrolls Study Edition*. Edited by Florentino García Martínez and Eibert J. C. Tigchelaar. 2 vols. Leiden: Brill, 1998.
EJL	Early Judaism and its Literature
FAT	Forschungen zum Alten Testament
FOTL	Forms of the Old Testament Literature
GBSOT	Guides to Biblical Scholarship Old Testament
HALOT	*The Hebrew and Aramaic Lexicon of the Old Testament*. Ludwig Koehler, Walter Baumgartner, and Johann J. Stamm. Translated and edited under the supervision of Mervyn E. J. Richardson. 4 vols. Leiden: Brill, 1994–1999.
HAT	Handbuch zum Alten Testament
HBM	Hebrew Bible Monographs
Hen	*Henoch*
HKAT	Handkommentar zum Alten Testament
HS	*Hebrew Studies*
HSS	Harvard Semitic Studies
HTR	*Harvard Theological Review*
HUCA	Hebrew Union College Annual

IBC	Interpretation: A Bible Commentary for Teaching and Preaching
ICC	International Critical Commentary
IEJ	Israel Exploration Journal
JAJ	Journal of Ancient Judaism
JAJSup	Journal of Ancient Judaism Supplements
JANER	Journal of Ancient Near Eastern Religions
JAOS	Journal of the American Oriental Society
JBL	Journal of Biblical Literature
JBS	Jerusalem Biblical Studies
JECS	Journal of Early Christian Studies
JJS	Journal of Jewish Studies
JNES	Journal of Near Eastern Studies
JNSL	Journal of Northwest Semitic Languages
JPS	Jewish Publication Society
JRA	Journal of Roman Archaeology
JRS	Journal of Roman Studies
JSJ	Journal for the Study of Judaism in the Persian, Hellenistic, and Roman Periods
JSJSup	Journal for the Study of Judaism in the Persian, Hellenistic, and Roman Periods Supplement Series
JSNTSup	Journal for the Study of the New Testament Supplement Series
JSOT	Journal for the Study of the Old Testament
JSOTSup	Journal for the Study of the Old Testament Supplement Series
JSP	Journal for the Study of the Pseudepigrapha
JSPSup	Journal for the Study of the Pseudepigrapha Supplement Series
JSQ	Jewish Studies Quarterly
JSS	Journal of Semitic Studies
JSSSup	Journal of Semitic Studies Supplement Series
JTS	Journal of Theological Studies
LCL	Loeb Classical Library
LHBOTS	Library of Hebrew Bible/Old Testament Studies
LNTS	The Library of New Testament Studies
LSJ	Henry George Liddell, Robert Scott, and Henry Stuart Jones. *A Greek-English Lexicon*. 9th ed. with revised supplement. Oxford: Clarendon, 1996.
LSTS	Library of Second Temple Studies
NETS	*A New English Translation of the Septuagint*. Edited by Albert Pietersma and Benjamin G. Wright. New York: Oxford University Press, 2007
NICNT	New International Commentary on the New Testament
NTL	New Testament Library
NTS	New Testament Studies
NTOA	Novum Testamentum et Orbis Antiquus
OBO	Orbis Biblicus et Orientalis
OBT	Overtures to Biblical Theology
OTS	Oudtestamentische Studiën
PFES	Publications of the Finnish Exegetical Society
PTSDSSP	The Princeton Theological Seminary Dead Sea Scrolls Project
RB	Revue biblique
RevQ	Revue de Qumrân

RevScRel	*Revue des sciences religieuses*
SBL	Society of Biblical Literature
SBLDS	Society of Biblical Literature Dissertation Series
SBLEJL	Society of Biblical Literature Early Judaism and Its Literature Series
SBLStBL	Society of Biblical Literature Studies in Biblical Literature
SPB	Studia Post-Biblica
STDJ	Studies on the Texts of the Desert of Judah
SUNT	Studien zur Umwelt des Neuen Testaments
SVTP	Studia in Veteris Testamenti Pseudepigraphica
TBT	*The Bible Today*
TDOT	*Theological Dictionary of the Old Testament.* Edited by G. Johannes Botterweck and Helmer Ringgren. Translated by John T. Willis et al. 8 vols. Grand Rapids: Eerdmans, 1974–2006.
ThWQ	*Theologisches Wörterbuch zu den Qumrantexten.* Edited by Heinz-Josef Fabry and Ulrich Dahmen. 3 vols. Stuttgart: Kohlhammer, 2010–2016.
TSAJ	Texte und Studien zum Antiken Judentum
TU	Texte und Untersuchungen
UTB	Uni-Taschenbücher
VT	*Vetus Testamentum*
VTSup	Vetus Testamentum Supplement
VWGTh	Veröffentlichungen der Wissenschaftlichen Gesellschaft für Theologie
WBC	Word Biblical Commentary
WUNT	Wissenschaftliche Untersuchungen zum Neuen Testament
ZAH	*Zeitschrift für Althebraistik*
ZAW	*Zeitschrift für die alttestamentliche Wissenschaft*
ZNW	*Zeitschrift für die neutestamentliche Wissenschaft und die Kunde der alteren Kirche*

Ariel Feldman and Timothy J. Sandoval
Introduction

The essays assembled in *Petitioners, Penitents, and Poets: On Prayer and Praying in Second Temple Judaism* are revisions and expansions of papers delivered at a conference by the same name held at Brite Divinity School at Texas Christian University on May 21–22, 2019. Fourteen scholars resident in the US Southwest and in different locales around the world were invited to join the scholarly conversation regarding the phenomenon of prayer as this can be discerned in and through different texts from Judaism's Second Temple period.[1] The "Second Temple period" can, of course, be delineated in rather rigid chronological terms, e.g., 538 BCE–70 CE. However, we prefer a "softer" approach and include in this volume several studies of texts—both Jewish and Christian—that are regularly dated after 70 CE, but which likely draw on pre-70 traditions. Although the papers from the conference, and subsequently the essays in this volume, primarily offer analyses of literary texts that represent prayers, or allude to the phenomenon of prayer and praying, such representations surely reflect in some reliable fashion "living practices of prayer in terms of forms, motifs, occasion, and posture."[2]

The conference and the volume have brought together scholars who work primarily on the Hebrew Bible, the Jewish Pseudepigrapha and Apocrypha, as well as the Dead Sea Scrolls and the New Testament, but whose scholarly endeavors have not been directed to, or at least not centrally oriented toward, questions of prayer in the Second Temple epoch. Subsequently, the essays that follow offer analyses of a range of texts—both poetry and prose—that allude to prayer and praying, or which actually present prayers, undertaken from each scholar's distinct research interests and concerns. The payoff for this approach is significant. What one discovers in the papers assembled here are illuminating studies of texts, long and short, from the Hebrew Bible, Early Judaism, and Christianity whose place in the larger picture of prayer in the Second Temple period might otherwise be blurred or overlooked. What the volume contributes to the flourishing study of prayer in the Second Temple period is thus a kind of "filling in" of any number of interstices in the edifice of scholarly work on prayer in this period. Filling the

---

[1] Two scholars invited to the Brite conference were not able to attend the gathering. However, we are pleased that their essays are included in this volume (Frolov and Zahn). We have unfortunately not been able to include the final essays of two other conference participants whose presentations significantly enhanced the gathering at Brite. These will be published elsewhere.
[2] Daniel Falk, "Hymns, Prayers, and Psalms," in *T&T Clark Encyclopedia of Second Temple Judaism*, ed. Daniel Gurtner and Loren T. Stuckenbruck (London: T&T Clark, 2019), 2:337–42 (337).

https://doi.org/10.1515/9783110624526-001

spaces between bricks with mortar is never as dramatic as the final construction itself. But without it, the next level of the building cannot be completed and the edifice will eventually collapse.

1. What is Prayer?

But what *is* prayer? And what did it look like during the Second Temple period? Such simple sounding questions conceal a complicated religious phenomenon and equally complex scholarly attempts to define the scope of what counts as prayer. Although several of the authors in the essays that follow offer their own brief working definitions of prayer and allude to previous scholarly work on prayer in the Second Temple epoch, for a volume like *Petitioners, Penitents, and Poets* some general, introductory observations are likewise in order.

Scholars of the Bible and Second Temple Judaism interested in prayer most often begin with simple and general descriptions of prayer. Samuel E. Balentine in his study of biblical prayer, for example, alludes to expansive definitions of prayer as "all communication addressed to God in the second person."[3] Likewise Daniel Falk speaks broadly of prayer in Second Temple Judaism as "an act of communication with the divine."[4] Yet, as Balentine and Falk (and most other scholars) recognize, such brief and broad definitions beg any number of questions about prayer—for example, about the literary shape or form of prayers one encounters in the texts, how individuals are represented as praying, who gets to speak in prayer, under what circumstances, with what ritual accouterments, in what sorts of liturgical contexts, and with what theological and ideological presuppositions. Hence, decades ago one leading voice in anthropological and sociological approaches to the study of texts in the biblical tradition, Bruce Malina, attempted to complexify our understandings of prayer. It is not merely "an act of communication with the divine." It is also an action that is regarded "as somehow supporting, maintaining, or controlling the order of existence of the one praying," and it is "performed with the purpose of getting results from or in the interaction of communication."[5] Others, such as Moshe Greenberg and Marc Zvi Brettler, also recognize that simple definitions of prayer as "address to God" ought to be nuanced, since prayer in the biblical tradition can also take the form of third-person speech *about* God and may

---

[3] Samuel E. Balentine, *Prayer in the Hebrew Bible: The Drama of Divine Human Dialogue* (Minneapolis: Augsburg Fortress, 1993), 30.
[4] Falk, "Hymns, Prayers, and Psalms," 337.
[5] Bruce Malina, "What is Prayer?" *TBT* 18 (1980): 214–20 (215).

not at all address God directly in the second person. As Greenberg puts it, though biblical prose prayer is regularly constituted as "speech to God," it "less often" can be speech "about God."[6] Judith H. Newman in her monograph on scripturalization of prayer acknowledges precisely this when she defines prayer as "address to God in the second person," which is not "conversational in nature," though it also "can include third-person description of God."[7]

Questions pertaining to the definition of prayer are of a significant concern also for the fast-growing scholarly work on the Dead Sea Scrolls. Multiple Scrolls, both sectarian and non-sectarian, yield prayers that would have been otherwise unknown.[8] In a seminal 1994 study Esther Chazon defined prayer (much like Falk) as "any form of human communication directed at God." This working definition led her to conclude that, besides prayers known from the books that came to be a part of the Hebrew Bible, the Qumran scrolls brought to light "well over two

---

[6] Marc Zvi Brettler, "Those Who Pray Together Stay Together: The Role of Late Psalms in Creating Identity," in *Functions of Psalms and Prayers in the Late Second Temple Period*, ed. Mika S. Pajunen and Jeremy Penner, BZAW 486 (Berlin: De Gruyter, 2017), 279–304; Moshe Greenberg, *Biblical Prose Prayer* (Berkeley: University of California Press, 1983), 7.

[7] Judith H. Newman, *Praying by the Book: The Scripturalization of Prayer in Second Temple Judaism* (Atlanta: Scholars Press, 1999), 7. Falk ("Hymns, Prayers, and Psalms," 337) and Balentine (*Prayer in the Hebrew Bible*, 31), of course, likewise recognize that although prayer regularly implies a direct address to God, this is not always so.

[8] For surveys of prayer and prayer-related texts in the Dead Sea Scrolls, see, amongst others, Esther G. Chazon, "Prayers from Qumran and Their Historical Implications," *DSD* 1 (1994): 265–84; Esther G. Chazon and Moshe J. Bernstein, "An Introduction to Prayer at Qumran," in *Prayer from Alexander to Constantine: A Critical Anthology*, ed. Mark Kiley (London: Routledge, 1997), 10–13; Esther G. Chazon, "Hymns and Prayers in the Dead Sea Scrolls," in *The Dead Sea Scrolls after Fifty Years: A Comprehensive Assessment*, ed. Peter W. Flint and James C. VanderKam (Leiden: Brill, 1998), 1:244–70; Esther G. Chazon, "Psalms, Hymns, and Prayers," in *Encyclopedia of the Dead Sea Scrolls*, ed. Lawrence Schiffman and James C. VanderKam (Oxford: Oxford University Press, 2000), 2:710–15; Eileen Schuller, "Prayer, Hymnic and Liturgical Texts from Qumran," in *The Community of the Renewed Covenant*, ed. Eugene Ulrich and James C. VanderKam, CJA 10 (Notre Dame: University of Notre Dame, 1993), 153–71; Eileen Schuller, "Prayer at Qumran," in *Prayer from Tobit to Qumran*, ed. Renate Egger-Wenzel and Jeremy Corley (Berlin: De Gruyter 2004), 411–28; Eileen Schuller, "Prayers and Psalms from the Pre-Maccabean Period," *DSD* 13 (2006): 306–18; Daniel Falk, "Prayers in the Qumran Texts," in *The Cambridge History of Judaism: Volume 3: The Early Roman Period*, ed. William Horbury, W.D. Davies, and John Sturdy (Cambridge: Cambridge University Press, 1999), 852–76; Daniel Falk, "The Contribution of the Qumran Scrolls to the Study of Ancient Jewish Liturgy," in *The Oxford Handbook of the Dead Sea Scrolls*, ed. Timothy H. Lim and John J. Collins (Oxford: Oxford University Press, 2010), 617–51; Daniel Falk, "Liturgical Texts," in *T&T Clark Companion to the Dead Sea Scrolls*, ed. George J. Brooke and Charlotte Hempel (London: T&T Clark, 2019), 423–34; Daniel Falk, "Hymns, Prayers, and Psalms," 2:337–42.

hundred prayers, hymns, and psalms."[9] A mere glance at the new texts included in her discussion, however, suggests that like others she too understands "communication directed at God" to be a much broader category than strictly a second-person address to the deity; her study includes blessings, psalms, and hymns that do not address God. Indeed, the question of whether the identification of early Jewish prayer in the Scrolls should include texts that contain religious poetry that does not directly address God is one not fully resolved.[10] On the one hand, more often than not, these texts provide no clues as to whether they might have been used liturgically. On the other hand, such a use remains a viable option.[11] Hence is the common scholarly practice to incorporate them in the surveys of prayer and liturgy from Qumran.

2. From Definition to Taxonomy

Yet even with the above sorts of definitions of prayer the scholarly imagination is left with much to query about and puzzle over when reckoning with the rich and diverse data on prayer and praying in Second Temple Judaism.

One can, for example, attempt to understand Second Temple prayer by focusing on the language of different speech acts usually regarded as prayer or through attempts to catalogue different types of "human to divine" efforts at communication. Falk, for instance, has identified, two primary "registers" of prayer: "prose and poetry." These registers, moreover, might roughly correspond to what can be reckoned theologically as the two primary modes of the discourse of prayer—request or petition on the one hand, and praise on the other.[12] In the Psalter, for instance, lament psalms (e.g., Psalm 13 and frequently), some of which are surely

---

9 Chazon, "Prayers from Qumran," 265–67. She counts more than three hundred prayers, if prayers and psalms known from the Hebrew Bible are included. One must bear in mind that this count was undertaken when the entire corpus of the Dead Sea Scrolls was still estimated at some 800 manuscript, in contrast to the current 900–1000 manuscripts from the Qumran caves alone. See Mladen Popović, "The Manuscript Collections: An Overview," *T&T Clark Companion*, 37–50 (38).

10 The challenge involved in this is nicely demonstrated by the recent *T&T Clark Companion to the Dead Sea Scrolls*, which includes one essay on the "Poetry and Hymns" (by Daniel Stökl Ben Ezra, pp. 413–22) and another on "Liturgical Texts" (by Daniel Falk, pp. 423–34).

11 Schuller concedes that it is not unlikely, yet quite difficult to prove from the texts themselves. See Eileen Schuller, "Some Reflections on the Function and Use of Poetical Texts among the Dead Sea Scrolls," in *Liturgical Perspectives: Prayer and Poetry in Light of the Dead Sea Scrolls*, ed. Esther G. Hazon, STDJ 48 (Leiden: Brill, 2003), 173–89.

12 Falk, "Hymns, Prayers, and Psalms," 337.

Second Temple compositions, constitute a discourse of petition—for relief from enemies, illness, or other distress. They stand at one end of a petition-praise pendulum. On the other hand, hymns of praise in the Psalms (e.g., Psalms 146–150) are primarily expressions of adoration and stand at the other end of the pendulum. Other types of psalms, and other sorts of prayer-texts in the Hebrew Bible and in Second Temple sources, might be said to occupy "in-between" (or hybrid) points on this pendulum.

To comprehend prayer in the Second Temple period one might also, and more specifically, consider the form or genre of prayer by focusing attention on the terminology that both scholars and the ancient texts themselves deploy to describe texts that somehow seem to constitute "prayers." However, as Falk explains, English words like psalm, hymn, song, prayer and so forth are used inconsistently by scholars. They also do not strictly correspond to the generic Hebrew terms (e.g., מזמור, שיר, תפלה) one encounters in the texts.[13] What's more, despite helpful attempts to parse or catalogue aspects of the Hebrew terminology—for example by Eileen Schuller—it appears that the ancient sources themselves betray no consistent use of the Hebrew terms for different sorts of prayers.[14] Indeed, some development and divergence in the forms, terminology, and understanding of prayer from the late sixth century BCE to the early second century CE is not only unsurprising, it was inevitable.

3. Prayer and Praying in the Dead Sea Scrolls

The challenge of identifying a proper nomenclature and taxonomy for the Second Temple Jewish prayers is particularly acute when it comes to the prayer-related materials that have emerged from the Caves of Qumran. One can hardly underestimate the impact of the Qumran corpus for endeavors to understand the phenomenon of prayer in this period. The Qumran texts make available to scholars a whole host of Second Temple "prayer texts" unknown prior to the discovery and publication of the Scrolls in the twentieth century. Of course, several of the major sectarian works that speak of prayer or present prayers as part of their literary composition, and a few (likely) liturgical prayer texts, such as Hodayot and Songs of the Sabbath Sacrifice, have long been widely available to scholarly scrutiny.

---

[13] Falk, "Hymns, Prayers, and Psalms," 337–38. On this terminology in the Psalter, cf. Frolov's essay in this volume.
[14] Eileen Schuller, "The Use of Biblical Terms as Designation for Non-Biblical Hymnic and Prayer Compositions," in *Biblical Perspectives*, ed. Michael E. Stone and Esther G. Chazon, STDJ 15 (Leiden: Brill, 1997), 125–44.

However, much other Qumran material relevant to the study of prayer has only in recent decades become available to a wide range of scholars.

These new materials present scholars with multiple challenges. First and foremost, what kind of terminology and rubrics should one use to describe these newly-discovered texts? Like Falk, Schuller aptly observes that, "A single composition might be designated a prayer in one English translation, a psalm or a hymn in another ... for there is no standard terminology nor set definitions for the most basic terms."[15] To be sure, several useful attempts at classifying these materials have been offered by Chazon and Falk. Both scholars experimented with different categories, some based on the perceived contents of the prayers, others on their current literary location.[16] A broadly agreed upon classification of the many new prayer-related texts in the Scrolls nonetheless remains a desideratum.

A quick glance at this volume will reveal that nearly a third of the studies included in it focus on the Scrolls' contribution to the study of Second Temple prayer (George Brooke, Ariel Feldman, Charlotte Hempel, Molly Zahn), whereas several others make use of Scrolls (Timothy Sandoval) or allude to them (Serge Frolov, John Levison, Carol Newsom, and Shelly Matthews). Hence before moving on to further reflections on recent scholarly work on Second Temple Jewish prayer and this volume's contribution to it, a brief survey of these new prayer-texts is appropriate. For such a bird's-eye overview of the relevant materials, we suggest a somewhat different taxonomy than those proposed by Chazon and Falk, one that reckons how the many new prayer and prayer-related texts that have been found among the Scrolls might be said to fall into three broad categories based on their current literary setting: (1) prayers embedded in literary works that are not prayer, (2) collections of prayers, and (3) self-standing prayers.[17]

---

15 Schuller, "Prayers and Psalms," 307–308.
16 Chazon, "Prayers from Qumran," 267–69, uses seven rubrics: liturgies for fixed prayer times; ceremonial liturgies; eschatological prayers; magic incantations; collections of psalms; Hodayot hymns; and prose prayers. Falk, "Prayers in the Qumran Texts," 852–76, suggests four broad groupings: prayers at fixed times; prayers for rituals; eschatological liturgies and blessings; miscellaneous prayers and religious poems (with multiple sub-categories). In his recent "Hymns, Prayers, and Psalms," 337–42, he offers the following rubrics: "petitionary prayer," "prayer of thanksgiving," "embedded prayers," and "pseudepigraphical prayers." See also the rubrics suggested by Schuller, "Prayers and Psalms," 314–16, though hers is not an attempt at classifying all the relevant materials.
17 We are well-aware that many fragmentary texts that now appear to be self-standing prayers could have belonged to larger compositions.

3.1 Prayers Embedded in Non-Prayer Texts

Among the Dead Sea Scrolls, the non-prayer compositions that contain embedded prayers are comprised of two major clusters of texts. The first cluster can be broadly described as *narrative texts*, written both in Hebrew and Aramaic, all non-sectarian.[18] Many of them belong to the so-called Rewritten Bible compositions. Of the new Aramaic texts to emerge from the Caves,[19] the Genesis Apocryphon yields prayers of the fallen Watchers, Abraham, and Melchizedek.[20] As to the Hebrew Scrolls, a text dubbed Narrative and Poetic Composition (2Q22, 4Q371–373, and 4Q373a), a retelling of Israel's past, contains a prayer by Joseph.[21] Several other Hebrew compositions reworking scriptural passages leave the identity of the prayers unknown.[22] The fragmentary 2Q21 1, perhaps rewriting the Abihu and Nadab episode, contains a non-biblical prayer, apparently, by Moses.[23] The so-called Apocryphon of Moses (1Q29, 4Q375–376, 4Q408), recasting biblical laws pertaining to the identification of the true prophet and permitted war, features a prayer praising God for establishing morning and evening as times to pray (4Q408 3+3a).[24]

---

[18] On prayers in Aramaic scrolls, all embedded in non-prayer texts, see Daniel A. Machiela, "Prayer in the Aramaic Dead Sea Scrolls: A Catalogue and Overview," in *Prayer and Poetry in the Dead Sea Scrolls and Related Literature*, ed. Jeremy Penner, Ken M. Penner, and Cecilia Wassen, STDJ 98 (Leiden: Brill, 2012), 273–93.

[19] For the relevant Qumran materials pertaining to prayers in 1 Enoch, Tobit, and Aramaic Levi Document, see Machiela, "Prayer in the Aramaic Dead Sea Scrolls," 282–83, 286-87. On possible prayers (anonymous in the current state of the fragments) in the Book of Giants, see Machiela, ibid., 283–84.

[20] 1QapGen 0:1–18; 19:7–8; 20:12–16. For other references to prayer in Genesis Apocryphon see Machiela, "Prayer in the Aramaic Dead Sea Scrolls," 276–82. For a recent discussion of 1QapGen, see Joseph McDonald, *Searching for Sarah in the Second Temple Era: Images in the Hebrew Bible, the Septuagint, the Genesis Apocryphon, and the Antiquities*, LHBOTS 693; Scriptural Traces 24 (London: T&T Clark, 2020).

[21] For Joseph's prayer, see 4Q372 1 16–31. Elisha Qimron suggests that other fragments contain prayers/praises of God by Moses. See his *The Dead Sea Scrolls: The Hebrew Writings: 3 Volumes, Between Bible and Mishnah* (Jerusalem: Yad Ben-Zvi, 2010–14), 2:77.

[22] While Jubilees contains several prayers, by Moses, Noah, and Abraham (Jub. 1:19–21; 10:3–6; 12:19–21; 22:6–9), none of the relevant passages are extant in Qumran Hebrew copies of Jubilees.

[23] Perhaps one could also mention here 4Q365, once classified as a Rewritten Bible work, but now commonly viewed as a scriptural manuscript. It features an otherwise unattested expanded version of Miriam's song addressing God (Exod 15:21; 4Q365 6a ii+6c 1–7).

[24] 4Q408 2//1Q29 3–4; 4Q408 3+3a. For a new edition and detailed discussion, see Liora Goldman, "4Q408: Prayers," in Ariel Feldman and Liora Goldman, *Scripture and Interpretation: Qumran Texts that Rework the Bible*, ed. Devorah Dimant, BZAW 449 (Berlin: De Gruyter, 2014), 323–50.

Anonymous prayers are also found in the texts rewriting Joshua, Samuel, and Kings.[25]

The second major cluster of non-prayer texts from Qumran with embedded prayers are the sectarian *rules*. Most of these are prayers prescribed for certain occasions. Thus, the ceremony for expulsion of a member of the community outlined in the Damascus Document includes a lengthy prayer.[26] Several texts outlining purification procedures, 4Q284, 4Q414, and 4Q512, feature prayers. 4Q502, often described as a marriage ritual, includes blessings referring to God in the third person.[27] The covenantal renewal ceremony in the Community Rule (1QS 1–2) incorporates a confession and blessings. While these too refer to the deity in the third person, it is clear that God is implored to make the said things happen. What, according to some, might be another version of the same ritual, 5Q13, includes an extensive prayer reviewing Israel's past.[28] Earlier scholarship also linked the blessings and curses found in 4QBerakhot (4Q286–290) to the covenant renewal ceremony. Of these five and possibly unrelated texts, the most obvious candidates for such a link are 4Q286 and 4Q287. The blessings found in these scrolls address God in the second person, while the presence of the "amen, amen" formula implies a liturgical use. Still, the connection between 4QBerakhot and a covenant renewal ceremony is

---

[25] For prayers in the rewritten Joshua scrolls, see 4Q378 6 ii 4–8; 13 i; 19 ii; 22 i; 4Q379 1; 5; 18. For prayers in rewritten Samuel and Kings, see 4Q160 4 i+5; 4Q382 15 5–8; 23; 30; 38; 49; 105; 110; 111; 115. Most of these are highly fragmentary. One exception is a prayer found both in 4Q160 2+6+10 and 4Q382 104 ii. The latter scroll, 4Q382 46, also preserves what appears to be a superscription of a prayer that has not survived, "]words of a prayer and a suppli[cation / Hezekiah king of[Judah." At the same time, the fragmentary manuscripts reworking Jeremiah and Ezekiel seem to yield no prayers at all. On these texts see further Ariel Feldman, *The Dead Sea Scrolls Rewriting Samuel and Kings: Texts and Commentary*, BZAW 469 (Berlin: De Gruyter, 2015); Devorah Dimant, *Qumran Cave 4.XXI: Parabiblical Texts, Part 4: Pseudo-Prophetic Texts*, DJD 30 (Oxford: Clarendon Press, 2001).
[26] 4Q266 11 8–14.
[27] On the interpretation of this text as a marriage ceremony, see recently, Aharon Shemesh, "Marriage and Marital Life in the Dead Sea Scrolls," in *The Dead Sea Scrolls and Contemporary Culture*, ed. Adolfo D. Roitman, Lawrence H. Schiffman, and Shani Tzoref, STDJ 93 (Leiden: Brill, 2011), 592–94. Joseph M. Baumgarten, "4Q502, Marriage or Golden Age Ritual," *JJS* 34 (1983): 125–35, suggested that the text represents a golden age celebration during the Festival of Booths (Sukkot). Michael Satlow, "4Q502 a New Year Festival?" *DSD* 5 (1998): 57–68, believes it represents a New Year ritual (and harvest season) during the month of Nisan, whereas Falk, "Liturgical Texts," 425, designates it as festival prayers.
[28] Menahem Kister, "5Q13 and the 'Avodah: A Historical Survey and its Significance," *DSD* 8 (2001): 136–48. On 5Q13 as another witness to the Covenant Ceremony, see Jutta Jokiranta and Hanna Vanonen, "Multiple Copies of Rule Texts or Multiple Rule Texts," in *Crossing Imaginary Boundaries: The Dead Sea Scrolls in the Context of Second Temple Judaism*, ed. Mika Pajunen and Hanna Tervanotko (Helsinki: The Finnish Exegetical Society, 2015), 11–60.

far from certain, and these texts may rather belong in our second category of collections of prayers (below).[29] Finally, mention should be made of the War Rules (or 1Q and 4Q War Texts) that prescribe prayers and hymns for various stages of the eschatological war.[30] A related composition, Sefer ha-Milhamah (4Q285; 11Q14), features an extensive blessing referring to God in the third person.[31]

3.2 Collections of Prayers

The second category of Qumran prayer texts includes works that can be described as collections of prayers. All of these compilations of prayers and religious poetry are in Hebrew; there is not a single one in Aramaic.[32] These texts can be divided into two sub-groups: collections of prayers that imply particular schedules of praying and those that do not.[33] Both sub-groups include texts of a sectarian provenance, as well as those coming from wider Jewish circles.

First, there are *daily* prayers. Three copies of Words of the Luminaries (4Q504–506) contain daily prayers for one week. The title suggests that these were offered at the time of the change of the luminaries. Introduced with a heading identifying each day of the week, these prayers, apparently of non-sectarian provenance, are communal petitions. Newman describes them as "an overview of Israel's corporate autobiography from the creation of Adam to the post-exilic era that serve as a confession for a continuing pattern of sin."[34] Unlike other days of the week, Sabbath prayer in this composition is a praise without any petition, reflecting the notion of this day being God's time of rest. Another cycle of daily

---

29 See Angela Kim Harkins, "Berakhot (4Q286–290)," in *T&T Clark Encyclopedia of Second Temple Judaism*, 1:133–34. Jutta Jokiranta, "Ritualization and the Power of Listing in 4QBerakhot[a] (4Q286)," in *Is There a Text in This Cave?* ed. Ariel Feldman, Maria E. Cioata, and Charlotte Hempel, STDJ 119 (Leiden: Brill, 2017), 438–58, highlights affinities between 4Q286, Songs of the Sabbath Sacrifice, and the later Jewish *merkavah* texts.
30 1QM 10:8–12:16//18:6–19:8 (//4Q492 1 1–8); 13:2–14:1 (//4Q495 2 1–4); 14:4–17 (//4Q491 8+9). On these prayers within the framework of scholarly attempts to elucidate the complex relationships between various War manuscripts, see most recently Rony Yishay, "Prayers in Eschatological War Literature from Qumran: 4Q491–4Q496, 1QM," *Meghillot* 5–6 (2007): 129–47 (Hebrew); eadem, "Column 19 of the War Scroll," *Meghillot* 8–9 (2010): 175–92 (Hebrew).
31 4Q285 8; 11Q14 1 ii.
32 As noted by Machiela, "Prayer in the Aramaic Dead Sea Scrolls," 292.
33 For a comprehensive survey of these texts, see Bilhah Nitzan, "The Liturgy at Qumran: Statutory Prayers," in *The Qumran Scrolls and Their World*, ed. Menahem Kister, Between Bible and Mishnah (Jerusalem: Yad Ben-Zvi, 2009), 1:225–60 (Hebrew).
34 Judith H. Newman, "Words of the Luminaries," in *T&T Clark Companion to the Dead Sea Scrolls*, 365–66 (365).

prayers is found in a single manuscript 4Q503. This text, apparently sectarian, features at least two prayers for each day, morning and evening (at the appearance of the sun and moon and the stars), and perhaps also nocturnal prayers, probably for a duration of a month.[35] Each prayer opens with a blessing of God and concludes with a blessing of the congregation. As with the Words of the Luminaries, it remains unknown whether these were intended for a particular time of the year or were to be repeated again and again.

Second, there is a liturgical compilation addressing *sabbath* days only—the Songs of the Sabbath Sacrifice, containing songs for thirteen consecutive Sabbaths (4Q400–407; 11Q17; Mas 1k).[36] None of these songs addresses God. Rather they are complex descriptions of various realia related to the heavenly temple and its angelic priesthood, with a particular emphasis on the angelic praise of God.[37] While the Maskil, a figure known from other sectarian texts, appears to be mentioned at the beginning of each song, it seems that they were not intended for him alone.[38] Some suggest that the Sabbath Sacrifice compositions served as a liturgical guide to *unio liturgica* between the praying community and the angels praising God.[39] Interestingly, however, the Songs never call for human praise. Noam Mizrahi thus suggests that the underlying notion of this work is that human language is unable to accomplish what angelic language does. Hence all that humans can do is "emulate angelic speech by describing the angels' liturgy and reciting it at the same time as they do, thus achieving a liturgical communion with them."[40] Newman conjectures that the Songs were likely supplemented by other prayer-like materials, e.g., thanksgivings, praises, or blessings.[41] Among other enigmas of this work are the contested issues of whether this liturgy was intended as a replacement of the Temple sacrifices and its provenance.

---

[35] See a detailed discussion by Jeremy Penner, *Patterns of Daily Prayer in Second Temple Period Judaism*, STDJ 104 (Leiden: Brill, 2013), 116–17, 190–95.
[36] For the Songs as liturgical compilation, see Judith H. Newman, "Songs of the Sabbath Sacrifice," in *T&T Clark Companion to the Dead Sea Scrolls*, 347–49 (347).
[37] Noam Mizrahi, "Songs of the Sabbath Sacrifice," in *T&T Clark Encyclopedia of Second Temple Judaism*, 1:503–506.
[38] Carol A. Newsom, "The Sage in the Literature of Qumran: The Functions of the *Maskil*," in *The Sage in Israel and the Ancient Near East*, ed. John Gammie and Leo G. Perdue (Winona Lake: Eisenbrauns, 1990), 373–82 (380–81).
[39] Falk, "Liturgical Texts," 425, speaks of them as "a script for a ritual of corporate mysticism." Newman, "Songs of the Sabbath Sacrifice," 348, describes them as "ecstatic" or "pneumatic," rather than as mystical.
[40] Noam Mizrahi, "The Cycle of Summons: A Hymn from the Seventh Song of the Sabbath Sacrifice (4Q403 1 i 31–40)," *DSD* (2015): 43–67 (65).
[41] Newman, "Songs of the Sabbath Sacrifice," 348.

Finally, among the Qumran prayer collections featuring a clearly specified praying routine are prayers for the *festivals* in 1Q34, 4Q507–509. The extant fragments of these scrolls preserve an explicit reference to only one festival, the Day of Atonement. These prayers appear to be non-sectarian.

The other sub-group within the category of collections of prayers comprises several compilations that do not reveal any temporal pattern of praying. Some of these bear clear sectarian marks. One such collection is Hodayot.[42] The many manuscripts associated with Hodayot (1QH^{a,b}; 4Q427–432), some of which vary significantly from the others, reveal an extended and complex process of literary growth. Several of these prayers, dubbed by scholars as Teacher Hymns (1QH^a 10–17), appear to relate distinctly personal experiences of the pray-er. Hence is the question as to whether they could have been used by an individual or in communal liturgy. Schuller suggests that some of the features of the 4Q copies of Hodayot strengthen the latter possibility.[43] Moreover, Carol Newsom proposes that these prayers, and Teacher Hymns in particular, might have served to solidify and maintain sectarian identity.[44] Taking another approach, Angela Kim Harkins argues that the intent of Hodayot is "to assist an ancient reader in re-enacting the emotions and phenomenal experiences of transformation described in these texts." However, for her, this sort of experience was reserved for select individuals, "the religious virtuoso."[45] Newman suggests an even stronger connection between these hymns and the Maskil, whom she perceives to be an ultimate petitioner on behalf of the community, a Moses-like figure, one who in his very person may hold the angel-like status described in the Self-Glorification Hymn embedded in several copies of Hodayot (4Q471b; 4Q427 7; 1QH^a 26).[46]

Another sectarian composition, 1QSb, features a collection of blessings commonly understood to be intended for eschatological times. These blessings, which were apparently also to be pronounced by the Maskil, refer to God in the third person. The list of those to be blessed include (in ascending rank?) all those who fear God, the sons of Zadok the priests, the prince of the congregation, and, appar-

---

[42] The description of Hodayot as a collection of prayer texts follows Angela Kim Harkins, "Hodayot (H)," *T&T Clark Companion to the Dead Sea Scrolls*, 314–17 (314). There are also several texts that have been described as Hodayot-like: 4Q433, 4Q433a, 4Q440, 4Q440a.
[43] Schuller, "Liturgical Perspectives," 179.
[44] Carol A. Newsom, *The Self as Symbolic Space: Constructing Identity and Community at Qumran*, STDJ 52 (Leiden: Brill, 2004) speaks of Hodayot as originating in an oral communal setting, "a fruit of an exercise of self-presentation" (276). These might have been used in a variety of ways (204), including accustoming members to the ways of the sect (276, 286, 349–50).
[45] Angela Kim Harkins, "Hodayot (H)," *T&T Clark Companion to the Dead Sea Scrolls*, 314–17 (316).
[46] Judith H. Newman, *Before the Bible: The Liturgical Body and the Formation of Scriptures in Early Judaism* (New York: Oxford University Press, 2018), 107–39.

ently, the High Priest.[47] Though composed for the end of days, these blessings might have been recited proleptically.[48] A further compilation or, rather, compilations (?) of prayer-like materials associated with the figure of the Maskil is found in 4Q510–511, two related, but apparently not identical texts.[49] These two scrolls seem to contain apotropaic songs or hymns to be uttered by the Maskil to scare away demons. In these text(s) God is referred to both in the third and the second person—the latter references are all in 4Q511.[50] The refrain "amen, amen" (4Q511 63–64 iv 3) suggests a communal response and so a use in a liturgical context.[51] Further apotropaic pronouncements and incantations are found in several other Dead Sea Scrolls.[52] Finally, one should also mention here a group of texts that some view as reflecting the worldview of a sectarian community, Barkhi Nafshi (4Q434–438), featuring a juxtaposition of a direct address to God and third-person references to the deity.[53]

Of the non-sectarian texts not concerned with temporal patterns of prayer, a collection of hymns/psalms referring to God in both second and third person is found in 4Q381. Some of these appear to be ascribed to biblical figures, though only one is explicit—a prayer attributed to King Manasseh.[54] Another scroll, 4Q448, features a prayer on behalf of the king Jonathan (apparently Alexander

---

[47] On the blessing of the unnamed individual who is often understood to be the High Priest, see Joseph Angel, *Otherworldly and Eschatological Priesthood in the Dead Sea Scrolls*, STDJ 86 (Leiden: Brill, 2010), 113.
[48] Angel, *Otherworldly*, 109–18.
[49] Joseph Angel, "The Material Reconstruction of 4QSongs of the Sage[B] (4Q511)," *RevQ* 27 (2015): 25–82, makes a case for these two being dependent on each other or a third text.
[50] 4Q511 8; 16; 28–30; 42; 52+54+55+57+59 iii; 63–64 ii–iv.
[51] Joseph Angel, "*Maskil*, Community, and Religious Experience in the Songs of the Sage (4Q510–511)," *DSD* 19 (2012): 1–27.
[52] With the texts commonly classified as incantations belong the Aramaic 4Q560 and the Hebrew 8Q5 and 11Q11. Among the previously unknown apotropaic prayers found among the Scrolls are Plea for Deliverance (11QPs[a] 19), 4Q444, 6Q18, and 1QH[a] 22:25. On these see further David Flusser, "Qumrân and Jewish 'Apotropaic' Prayers," *IEJ* 16 (1966): 194–205; Esther Eshel, "Apotropaic Prayers in the Second Temple Period," in *Liturgical Perspectives*, 69–88; Loren T. Stuckenbruck, "Pleas for Deliverance from the Demonic in Early Jewish Texts," in *Studies in Jewish Prayer*, ed. Robert Hayward and Brad Embry, JSSSup (Oxford: Oxford University Press, 2005), 55–73; Miryam T. Brand, *Evil Within and Without: The Source of Sin and Its Nature as Portrayed in Second Temple Literature*, JAJSup 9 (Göttingen: Vandenhoeck & Ruprecht, 2013), 198–217; Michael J. Morris, *Warding off Evil: Apotropaic Tradition in the Dead Sea Scrolls and Synoptic Gospels*, WUNT 2.451 (Tübingen: Mohr Siebeck, 2017), 51–147.
[53] On the classification of these texts as sectarian, see Qimron, *Hebrew Writings*, 2:36.
[54] For a recent re-edition of this scroll, see Mika S. Pajunen, *The Land to the Elect and Justice for All: Reading Psalms in the Dead Sea Scrolls in Light of 4Q381*, JAJSup (Göttingen: Vandenhoeck & Ruprecht, 2013).

Jannaeus) and a psalm known as Syriac Psalm 154. Finally, there are several scrolls containing both Masoretic and "non-canonical" psalms. Thus 11QPs^a (11Q5; cf. also 11Q6) features seven psalm-like compositions unknown from the Masoretic Psalter.[55] Of these, Plea for Deliverance (col. 19) and Syriac Psalm III (Ps 154; col. 24) are a direct address to God. Similarly, 4QPs^f (4Q88), yields, besides Masoretic psalms, such previously unknown texts as an Apostrophe to Judah (col. 10) that address God directly.

3.3 Self-Standing Prayers

Besides prayers embedded in non-prayer texts and collections of prayers, among the Qumran Scrolls are also self-standing prayers—at least they appear to be self-standing in their present state of preservation. These include two Hebrew prayers featuring extensive historical summaries, 4Q369 (//4Q499) and 4Q374, a prayer entitled 4Q501 Apocryphal Lamentations B, and an extended prayer found in 4Q393 (4QCommunal Confession).[56]

3.4 Practices and Customs Related to Prayer in Qumran Scrolls

This brief survey of the Qumran prayer-related materials would be incomplete without a mention of texts that illuminate various practices of prayer and customs related to praying. As noted above, Falk contends that literarily complex Second Temple sources likely reflect in some reliable fashion "living practices of prayer."[57] We have just seen repeated references to the timing of prayer in the Scrolls.[58] But

---

[55] The nature of this scroll is debated: some consider it to be an example of the pluriformity of Scripture, i.e., an edition of the book of Psalms, whereas others take it to be a liturgical scroll. For a recent discussion see Ulrich Dahmen, "Authoritative Scriptures: Writings and Related Texts," in *T&T Clark Companion to the Dead Sea Scrolls*, 273-79 (274-76).

[56] There are many more highly fragmentary Hebrew prayers among the Scrolls (following readings and classification in Qimron's *Hebrew Writings*): 1Q11+1Q30, 1Q25, 1Q36, 3Q6, 4Q291, 4Q292, 4Q293, 4Q433, 4Q440a, 4Q442? 4Q443, 4Q446, 4Q449, 4Q450, 4Q451, 4Q452, 4Q454, 4Q457b, 4Q468i, 4Q471c, 4Q481c, 4Q500, 4Q501, 4Q508, 11Q15, 11Q16. For an important prayer from from Naḥal Ḥever or Naḥal Ṣe'elim, XḤev/Se 6, see note 69 below.

[57] Falk, "Hymns, Prayers, and Psalms," 337.

[58] In addition to the foregoing discussion of collections of prayers, 1QM 14:12-14 (as also the Words of the Luminaries and 4Q408) seems to reflect a diurnal routine of prayers, whereas the calendar embedded in 1QH^a 20:7-14 and 1QS 9:26-10:17 appears to envision four divinely ordained (for Maskil?) daily prayers: at sunrise, midday, sunset, and midnight (on this see further

more than this, several Scrolls also speak of other customs associated with prayer. The sectarian 1QS 6:7–8 prescribes that small study groups gathering at night should "bless."[59] The same text mandates a grace before meals (1QS 6:4–6; 10:14–15; 1QSa 2:17–21), whereas the non-sectarian Jub. 2:21 and 4Q370 1 1–2 may imply a blessing after meals.[60] Texts that have emerged from the Scrolls, both old and new, also shed light on non-verbal elements of praying, such as washing prior to offering a prayer (4Q213a 1 7=ALD 2:5), posture (lifting one's face and eyes [4Q196 6 8=Tob 3:12; 4Q213a 1 3=ALD 3:1]), gesturing (stretching hands and fingers [4Q213a 1 9=ALD 3:2]; cf. also 4Q512 42–44 6), and an expression of emotions (sorrow and tears [1QapGen 20:12]).[61]

4. Studying Second Temple Prayer after Qumran

There can be no doubt that the sheer number of the new texts related to prayer and praying from Qumran was bound to change the trajectory of scholarly work on ancient Jewish prayer. Just as the study of the Scrolls revolutionized the story of the textual history of the Hebrew Bible, so the analysis of the Qumran material, if not effecting a full rewriting of the story of prayer in the Second Temple epoch, is certainly infusing new life into old debates and motivating scholars—young and senior alike—to explore the phenomenon/a afresh. The widespread accessibility of the Qumran material has, for example, enabled scholars to position early

---

Penner, *Patterns of Daily Prayer*, 137–64). These are to be followed by prayers on the first day of each season, the first day of each month, festivals, and sabbatical and Jubilee years (cf. also 1QM 14:13–14). The scroll 4Q409 lists special occasions, apparently festivals (including the Wood Festival), and requires one to praise and bless God on those days, while David's Compositions (11Q5 27) offers a list of occasions for which David composed psalms and songs linked to a 364-day calendar. Finally, a fragmentary 4Q334 appears to specify not only the times (day and night) for praises and songs, but also the number of such utterances to be pronounced. On the possibility that the latter text reflects an apotropaic ritual, see Penner, *Patterns of Daily Prayer*, 198–207.

59 For a helpful discussion of this text, see George J. Brooke, "Reading, Searching and Blessing: A Functional Approach to Scriptural Interpretation in the דחי," in *The Temple intext and Tradition: A Festschrift in Honor of Robert Hayward*, ed. R. Timothy McLay, LSTS 83 (London: T&T Clark, 2015), 140–56. Sandoval's essay in this volume also addresses the passage briefly.

60 4QDeut[j,n] contain selections from Deuteronomy that, according to Moshe Weinfeld, could possibly have been used for blessing after the meal. See Moshe Weinfeld, "Grace After Meals in Qumran," *JBL* 111 (1992): 427–40.

61 On the latter, see in more detail Ursula Schattner-Rieser, "Emotions and Expressions of Emotion as a Didactic Guide as to How to Pray: Berakhot in Aramaic Prayers of Qumran," in *Ancient Jewish Prayers and Emotions Associated with Jewish Prayer in and around the Second Temple Period*, ed. Stefan Reif and Renate Egger-Wenzel (Berlin: De Gruyter, 2015), 273–96.

Jewish prayer differently than has often been the case in the past. No longer need (ought?) "canonical" prayer—its genres, motifs, agents, ideologies, and so forth—be placed in the middle of the map of ancient Jewish prayer so that the Second Temple texts are explicitly or implicitly analyzed in terms of their relationship to categories established from the study of the (often) earlier biblical works whose social, ritual, ideological, and literary functions are distinct from subsequent texts. The discoveries in the Judean Desert have also invited a renewed and robust consideration of Early Jewish prayer texts as found in the (non-Qumran) Jewish Apocrypha and Pseudepigrapha—e.g., Ben Sira, Tobit, Judith, Maccabees and many more.[62] Appropriately, *Petitioners, Penitents, and Poets* includes a couple of essays that touch on this material (Matthias Henze and John Levison). The payoffs for this ongoing effort at highlighting the importance of the non-canonical Second Temple Jewish prayers are many.

4.1 The Emergence of Jewish Statutory Prayer

For instance, the new Qumran texts allow scholars to fill out in finer detail the historical development of Jewish prayer from the Bible through various Second Temple sources into Late Antiquity. Two views about this development have been prominent.[63] On the one hand, some scholars following and elaborating upon the work of especially Joseph Heinemann have argued for the plurality of early forms of Jewish prayer and the subsequent gradual evolution of fixed forms of Jewish prayer through the centuries. On this view, the fixed liturgical form of

---

[62] Among the many publications on the prayers embedded in these texts are James H. Charlesworth, "Jewish Hymns, Odes, and Prayers (Ca. 167 B.C.E.–135 C.E.)," in *Early Judaism and Its Modern Interpreters*, ed. Robert A. Kraft and George W. E. Nickelsburg (Philadelphia: Fortress, 1986), 411–436; David Flusser, "Psalms, Hymns and Prayers," in *Jewish Writings of the Second Temple Period: Apocrypha, Pseudepigrapha, Qumran, Sectarian Writings, Philo, Josephus*, ed. Michael E. Stone, SRINT 2.2 (Assen: Van Gorcum, 1984), 551–577; Rodney Alan Werline, *Penitential Prayer in Second Temple Judaism: The Development of a Religious Institution* (Atlanta: Scholars Press, 1998); Newman, *Praying By the Book*; Markus McDowell, *Prayers of Jewish Women: Studies of Patterns of Prayer in the Second Temple Period* (Tübingen: Mohr Siebeck, 2006); Pieter van der Horst and Judith H. Newman, *Early Jewish Prayers in Greek*, Commentaries on Early Jewish Literature (Berlin: De Gruyter, 2008); Michael D. Matlock, *Discovering the Traditions of Prose Prayers in Early Jewish Literature*, LSTS 81 (London: T&T Clark, 2012), as well as studies collected in Egger-Wenzel and Corley, *Prayer from Tobit to Qumran*; Reif and Egger-Wenzel, *Ancient Jewish Prayers and Emotions*; Pajunen and Penner, *Functions of Psalms and Prayers*.
[63] Different scholars recount this story more or less fully with varying emphases. See, for example, Stefan C. Reif, "The Place of Prayer," in *Ancient Jewish Prayers and Emotions*, 1–17; Penner, *Patterns of Daily Prayer*, 3–24; Newman, *Praying by the Book*, 231–40.

Jewish prayer has its origins in the Second Temple period, with measured innovation introduced throughout Late Antiquity, after which forms of prayer were more fully frozen in the Middle Ages.[64] As Penner says, Heinemann "ends up arguing— or perhaps we should say, affirming, rabbinic opinion—that the origins of the basic forms of fixed daily prayer began 'hundreds of years before the destruction of the Second Temple....'"[65]

On the other hand, other scholars, largely following and elaborating the work of Solomon Zeitlin and (more recently) Ezra Fleischer, have contended that not many liturgical or fixed forms of prayer existed in the Second Temple period, with perhaps the exception of the practices, here and there, of marginal pious groups such as the Dead Sea Scrolls community. Instead, the stable liturgical prayers of Judaism were more foundationally established later, perhaps as the innovation of the community at Yavneh after the destruction of 70 CE.[66] As Reif has contended, for Fleischer "there was no obligatory prayer whatsoever in the Second Temple period, primarily because of respect for the Temple service, but a total revolution took place in the second Christian century when Rabban Gamaliel and his Court created the wholly innovative idea of the daily '*Amidah*."[67]

The prayers that have emerged from the Dead Sea Scrolls may not be decisive, but, as many before us have suggested, they do seem to support Heinemann's views over Fleischer's, especially since the Scrolls contain what appears to be non-sectarian fixed prayers.[68] Further support for this view seems to emerge from the many studies exploring the affinities between the language and modes of prayer as found in the Scrolls and later Jewish liturgy.[69]

---

[64] Joseph Heinemann, *Prayer in the Talmud: Forms and Patterns*, trans. Richard Sarason (Berlin: De Gruyter, 1977); cf. Penner, *Patterns of Daily Prayer*, 10–11.

[65] Penner, *Patterns of Daily Prayer*, 11; Heinemann, *Prayer*, 13.

[66] Solomon Zeitlin, "The Tefillah, the Shemonah Esreh: An Historical Study of the First Canonization of the Hebrew Liturgy," *JQR* 54 (1963–64): 228–38; Ezra Fleischer, "On the Beginnings of Obligatory Jewish Prayer," *Tarbiẓ* 59 (1990): 297–344 (Hebrew); cf. Penner, *Patterns of Daily Prayer*, 19–24.

[67] Reif, "The Place of Prayer," 9.

[68] See, for instance, Chazon's publications cited above.

[69] See, among others, David Flusser's early studies edited by Serge Ruzer in *Judaism of the Second Temple Period: Qumran and Apocalypticism* (Jerusalem: Yad Ben-Zvi, 2002), esp. 54–118 (Hebrew); Esther G. Chazon, "A Liturgical Document from Qumran and Its Implications: 'Words of the Luminaries' (4QDibHam)" (Ph.D. diss., Hebrew University, 1991; Hebrew); Bilha Nitzan, *Qumran Prayer and Religious Poetry*, STDJ 12 (Leiden: Brill, 1994); Moshe Weinfeld, *Early Jewish Liturgy: From Psalms to the Prayers in Qumran and Rabbinic Literature* (Jerusalem: Magnes Press, 2004; Hebrew); Falk's studies cited above and the many articles by Menahem Kister. On the limited nature of these affinities see Menahem Kister, "Liturgical Formulae in the Light of Fragments from the Judaean Desert," *Tarbiẓ* 77 (2008): 331–55 (333–34; Hebrew). In this study he suggests

4.2 Penitence, Petition, and Praise

Of course, in recent decades the study of prayer in the Second Temple period has not been confined to the sorts of questions and answers, imminent and presupposed, in the two sides of the debate usually identified in the history of the study of Jewish liturgy. Scholars, for example, have more and more recognized and underscored the abundant (re)presentation of penitential prayer in Second Temple sources. From Ezra's words in Ezra 9 or Daniel's utterances in Daniel 9 to certain prayers found in Pseudepigraphical and Apocryphal works, penitential prayer infuses the sources.[70] The Dead Sea Scrolls, too, point to the prevalence and importance of communal penitential prayer in this period, which may reflect a shift in the Second Temple period from an emphasis on lament to a focus on confession of sin or guilt.[71] For Falk such a shift may have "originated in communal fasts (Zech 7:1–4; 8:18–22) as a response to exile [citing Boda], and under the influence of the Deuteronomic prescription to 'turn and seek' (Deut 4, 30) and the emphasis in Leviticus (Lev 5, 16, 26) on confession of guilt [citing Werline]."[72] For her part, Newsom has associated the prominent expressions of penitential prayer in the literary texts of the Second Temple with an increased fascination in this epoch with the emergence of a particular kind of moral subject—the "repenting sinner."[73] In the present volume, the essays by Matthias Henze, John Levison, and Jonathan Kaplan, each to an extent, reflect the central phenomenon of penitential prayer (and pray-ers) in Second Temple period texts and traditions.

By contrast, petitionary prayers are not as prevalent as other sorts of prayers at Qumran, at least not in the sectarian texts.[74] In fact, it has been argued that sec-

---

that some of the most remarkable parallels to rabbinic liturgy are found in a rather late scroll (~100 CE) from Naḥal Ḥever or Naḥal Ṣe'elim, XḤev/Se 6.
70 Werline, *Penitential Prayer in Second Temple Judaism*; Mark Boda, Daniel K. Falk, and Rodney Werline, *Seeking the Favor of God: Volume 1: The Origins of Penitential Prayer in Second Temple Judaism* (Atlanta: SBL, 2006); *Seeking the Favor of God: Volume 2: The Development of Penitential Prayer in Second Temple Judaism* (Atlanta: SBL, 2007); *Seeking the Favor of God: Volume 3: The Impact of Penitential Prayer beyond Second Temple Judaism* (Atlanta: SBL, 2008).
71 This observation seems to apply to Hebrew prayers in the Dead Sea Scrolls. For the absence of prayers of communal confession and repentance in the extant Aramaic texts from Qumran, see Machiela, "Prayer in the Aramaic Dead Sea Scrolls," 291.
72 Falk, "Hymns, Prayers, and Psalms," 338; cf. Mark J. Boda, "Form Criticism in Transition: Penitential Prayer and Lament, *Sitz im Leben* and Form," in *Seeking the Favor of God: Volume 1*, 181–92; Werline, *Penitential Prayer*, 11–64.
73 Carol A. Newsom, *The Book of Job: A Contest of Moral Imaginations* (Oxford: Oxford University Press, 2003), 213.
74 Falk, "Hymns, Prayers and Psalms," 339.

tarian prayer in particular avoids petition, foregrounding praise instead.[75] Taking this observation one step further, Mika Pajunen suggests that much like penitential prayer, praise becomes a dominant feature of Second Temple prayer.[76]

4.3 Prayer and Method

To be sure, understanding the phenomenon of prayer in the Second Temple period requires more than a set of definitions, generic study of works, terminological clarity, rigorous classification, or discerning traces of possible real, historical practices of prayer in and through our textual sources. As Ingunn Aadland has reminded us, prayer can be "expressed or performed through the body as fasting, weeping, prostrating, and praise." It is "words and acts that are directed toward the deity in order to communicate with the deity" that count as prayer.[77] In other words, as the above taxonomy of prayer texts at Qumran has already intimated, prayer can, and often is, ritualized—that is, performed in regular ways within a regular schedule of worship. Such ritualization can also constitute part of a liturgy—when a ritual of prayer is the practice of a community. Indeed, more and more scholars have turned directly or indirectly to anthropology—and ritual studies in particular—to refine questions and modes of analysis of texts that speak of, or represent, prayers and praying. Instead of a focus on the historical development of liturgy or of liturgical prayer (themselves obviously ritual acts), the turn to ritual studies has entailed a move away from purely text centered analysis. Ritual studies applied to questions of prayer proves to be more concerned with how the words, gestures, and objects associated with prayer function together to create meaning precisely as these words are spoken, the gestures performed, and the objects manipulated in more or less fixed ways in particular contexts.

Thus, in several studies on Qumran liturgy, Falk includes analyses of objects that might have been used liturgically, such as small scriptural scrolls and the many Qumran tefillin (phylacteries) containing passages from Exodus and Deu-

---

75 Eileen Schuller "Petitionary Prayer and the Religion of Qumran," in *Religion in the Dead Sea Scrolls*, ed. John J. Collins and Robert Kugler (Grand Rapids: Eerdmans, 2000), 29–45. Newman, *Before Bible*, 125–26, notes, while dealing with Hodayot, that there might be a tendency to limit petitioning to the Maskil alone.
76 Mika S. Pajunen, "The Praise of God and His Name as the Core of the Second Temple Liturgy," *ZAW* 127 (2015): 475–88.
77 Ingunn Aadland, "Prayer and Remembrance in Sapiential Work (4Q185)," in *Functions of Psalms and Prayers*, 122–33 (122).

teronomy.[78] Furthermore, like Chazon before him, he considers incantations, such as those found in the Hebrew 11Q11 and Aramaic 4Q560, that address (or, better, adjure) demons, rather than God.[79] Along the same lines as Falk, Newman in a book on liturgy and scripture criticizes anachronistic approaches to liturgy in Second Temple times, suggesting that it should encompass "the whole gamut of worship in and around the study of sacred texts, the acts of eating and fasting, and of course, benedictions, prayers and amulets."[80] In *Petitioners, Penitents, and Poets*, the essays by George Brooke, Charlotte Hempel, Ariel Feldman, and Shelly Matthews, all address the apotropaic functions of prayer; they thus reflect—even if indirectly—the methodological tendencies and concerns of a turn to ritual studies in the study of Second Temple prayer, as does John Levison's attention to weeping, posture, and manipulation of dirt (or dung) in the prayers presented in Greek Life of Adam and Eve (GLAE).

Besides a turn to analyzing prayer within a broader context of ritual and liturgical studies, other approaches to the study of prayer in the Second Temple epoch have continued apace. On the one hand, newer trends and innovative, interdisciplinary methods, questions, and concerns have been brought to bear on Jewish prayers and praying in the Second Temple period. Carol Newsom and Jutta Jokiranta, for example, have each looked to the cognitive sciences for insights when considering prayer and praying in Second Temple sources.[81] In her essay in this volume, Newsom continues to draw on this scholarly discourse to analyze especially Psalm 73. On the other hand, the categories of analysis and observations about biblical depictions of prayer—whether the form critical approach to the Psalms or the recognition of Deuteronomic theological motifs in many prayers elsewhere in Hebrew Bible—continue to be cultivated and remain influential in studies of prayer in Second Temple works.[82] In this volume the contributions by Jonathan Kaplan, Serge Frolov, and to an extent Carol Newsom constitute such refinements in studies applied to "prayer texts" in the Bible.

---

78 See, especially, Daniel K. Falk, "Material Aspects of Prayer Manuscripts at Qumran," in *Literature or Liturgy*, ed. Clemens Leonhard and Hermut Löhr (Tübingen: Mohr Siebeck, 2014), 33–87.
79 Falk, "Material Aspects," 71–75; Chazon, "Hymns and Prayers in the Dead Sea Scrolls," 263–64.
80 Newman, *Before the Bible*, 8, citing Stefan Reif, "Prayer in Early Judaism," *Prayer from Tobit to Qumran*, 439–64 (442).
81 Carol A. Newsom, "Toward a Genealogy of the Introspective Self in Second Temple Judaism," in *Functions of Psalms and Prayers*, 63–79; Jutta Jokiranta, "Towards a Cognitive Theory of Blessing: The Dead Sea Scrolls as Test Case," in *Functions of Psalms and Prayers*, 27–47.
82 For biblical prayer see, most prominently perhaps, Greenberg, *Biblical Prose Prayer*, and Balentine, *Prayer in the Hebrew Bible*.

Other essays in *Petitioners, Penitents, and Poets* employ still further methodological and hermeneutical approaches, well-known among biblical scholars, in order to understand Second Temple texts that speak of prayer and praying. Matthias Henze, Ariel Feldman, and Charlotte Hempel, for instance, each deploy the traditional tools of historical and textual criticism in their respective studies of prayer in 2 Baruch, on miniature inscriptions of Jewish amulets, and in the final hymn embedded in multiple copies of the Community Rule. By contrast, Levison offers what can well be described as "close reading" of prayer passages in GLAE while Kaplan turns to understandings of pastiche drawn from literary studies in his rereading of Jonah's psalm uttered from the belly of the great fish. Timothy Sandoval's approach to Prov 30:1–4 similarly presumes broader discussions of literary theory—in this case regarding intertextuality—both inside and outside of biblical studies. Both George Brooke and Molly Zahn, while not as concerned as Sandoval with intertextuality, are nonetheless very interested in exploring historical, literary, and ideological relations among especially Qumran texts. Shelly Matthews, for her part, studies a Lukan allusion to prayer with a robust feminist-gender critical lens, and Warren Carter turns to both sociology and empire studies in his consideration of a passage from Matthew's Gospel about prayer and praying.

The twelve studies assembled in this volume add to the already rich and complex tapestry of the recent post-Qumran scholarship on Second Tempe Jewish prayer. It is to a brief overview of these essays that we turn now.

5. The Contributions

Although above we have at different moments alluded to how various essays in *Petitioners, Penitents, and Poets* intersect with larger trends in the study of prayer and praying in Second Temple period, a few more words about each contribution are in order.

The volume begins with four articles that focus on biblical texts that arguably emerge in the Second Temple period. **Jonathan Kaplan**'s essay "Pastiche, Hyperbole, and the Composition of Jonah's Prayer" opens the volume by taking up the old question of the origin of Jonah's prayer (Jonah 2:3–10). Like others before him, Kaplan observes multiple features of this psalm that make it incongruous with the rest of the book. However, unlike his predecessors, Kaplan suggests that these features should not be taken as indications that this prayer is a transplant from elsewhere, since the evidence for this seems to be rather inconclusive. He argues that the "simultaneously integral and disjunctive character" of Jonah's prayer could be plausibly viewed as a part of "the satirical and parodic character" of this book. To support his thesis, he highlights the pastiche character of the prayer. It appears to echo several passages found elsewhere in the Hebrew Bible, yet without interpretatively engaging them. He proposes that this artistic use of a pastiche technique fits rather well the parodic aspect of the book—newly repentant Jonah offers a prayer of thanksgiving, instead of a plea for deliverance, and this out-of-place prayer is no more than a recycling of sources he knows. Kaplan suggests that this, along with the prayer's hyperbolic diction, indicates that Jonah 2:3–10 was composed by the author of Jonah who wished to "heighten the satire in the work."

In "Psalms: *Sitz im Leben* vs. *Sitz in der Literatur*," **Serge Frolov** questions the commonplace scholarly assumption that psalms find their *Sitz im Leben* in the cult, noting that the vast majority of the evidence for the use of psalms in the context of temple worship comes from late, post-exilic and Second Temple texts. Building on the studies of Rolf Knierem and Marvin Sweeney, Frolov intimates that the cult is not the *Sitz im Leben* of psalms and instead seeks to examine the *Sitz in der Literatur*—the literary setting—of these works. In light of the often enigmatic superscriptions of psalms, which hardly unequivocally point to the oral (and thus likely cultic) nature of psalms, Frolov contends that such compositions are best regarded as texts composed for their literary context in the Psalter. In particular, given the tendency of many psalms to wrestle with issues of the suffering of the just and innocent, Frolov believes the writers of psalms are participating in an ongoing conversation in ancient Israel regarding questions of theodicy—issues that continue to be significant for contemporary readers of the Psalter.

Following Frolov's forays into the Psalms, **Carol A. Newsom** draws on the work of neuroscientists, psychologists, and philosophers on metacognition to explore a phenomenon that she calls "retrospective introspection" in select psalms from the Second Temple period, especially Psalm 73. In "'If I had said...' (Ps 73:15): Retrospective Introspection in Didactic Psalmody of the Second Temple Period," Newsom explains how Psalm 73 combines elements of thanksgiving psalms and the didacticism of sapiential works, which together supply the conceptual resources for the practice of retrospective introspection. In Psalm 73 the psalmist recounts the crisis of "inner spiritual conflict," namely "the cognitive dissonance" produced by his acknowledgement of the well-known sapiential *topos* of the prosperity of the wicked and the suffering of the pious. Importantly, however, the resolution of this state of affairs comes not in the form of the "restoration of well-being to the speaker," as in traditional thanksgiving psalms. Rather it emerges through "the resolution of his experience of cognitive dissonance." Key for Newsom in all this is the psalmist's ability to articulate and appraise his past thoughts and earlier "psychological conflict" through a consideration of "hypothetical subsequent states of affairs"— which is introduced by the psalmist's words, "If I had said..." in v. 15. For Newsom, the sort of "self-reflective prayer" modeled by Psalm 73 is evidence of the emergence and significance of the "cultivation of introspective practices of the self" in Second Temple Judaism.

If Newsom highlighted sapiential elements in the Psalm texts she analyzed, the next essay in the volume shifts attention a bit further away from the Psalter to focus it more fully in the wisdom tradition. In "Agur's Words to God in Proverbs 30 and Prayerful Study in the Second Temple Period," **Timothy J. Sandoval** accepts a version of a very common emendation to Prov 30:1b in order to understand Agur's words in this chapter as constituting one of the very few allusions to prayer in the wisdom book. Subsequently, by identifying a series of intertextual links with (other) Second Temple texts concerned with moral knowledge and prayer, he claims that Agur's weariness is a function of his prayerful efforts at attaining a kind of divinely revealed, likely eschatological wisdom (a "knowledge of holy ones," as Prov 30:3b puts it), which is not unlike the prayerful study and acquisition of knowledge alluded to in 4QInstruction and in 1QS 6.

While Sandoval is keen to compare certain Qumran texts with what he perceives as happening in and behind Prov 30:1–4, the next cluster of essays in *Petitioners, Penitents, and Poets* turn to the Dead Sea Scrolls more fully. **George J. Brooke**'s essay focuses on prayer in the Scrolls, but it begins in 21st century England with a prayer for the newly born Prince Louis of Cambridge. Noting that the somewhat oddly constructed prayer for the prince was surely written by a Christian priest, Brooke wonders "what self-understanding of priesthood the prayer conveys." It is precisely this question that Brooke poses to Second Temple prayer texts, especially representations of prayer in the Qumran material. Taking a cue from Michael E. Stone, Brooke contends that there were two conceptions of evil in the Second Temple period, which required distinct responses. The evil of human sin demanded penitence and atonement; external malevolent forces constituted another source of sin and required the protection of apotropaic prayers and rites. Brooke is, of course, careful to insist and demonstrate that no strict dichotomy of priestly roles and groups can be maintained. Nonetheless, he persuasively suggests that priests in the Aaronic tradition (or sympathetic to it) were likely most concerned with the evil of sin and appropriately affecting atonement for it; other priestly traditions, like those associated with several of the ancestors (e.g., Enoch, Noah, Levi), were perhaps more concerned not only with esoteric lore and teaching, but with protection from malevolent forces of evil external to humans.

In her paper, "The Absence of Prayer in the Temple Scroll," **Molly M. Zahn** explores the somewhat puzzling omission of prayer and praying from the longest of Qumran scrolls, 11QTemple[a]. Noting the ubiquity of prayer in Second Temple Jewish literature, she considers several possible scenarios that may explain its absence from 11QTempleª. First, she wonders whether the genre of this text, a legal/halakhic work that emulates the Pentateuch in featuring very few prayers, can offer a clue. However, as she observes, other halakhic texts from Qumran include prayers, while an attempt to produce "Torah" did not prevent the authors of 11QTempleª from introducing several major (but non-prayer) innovations into the rewritten text, such as the plan for the utopian temple and the extended Law of the King. She next turns to the ideological underpinnings of this scroll and asks whether its emphasis on an unmediated revelation and therefore lack of interest in human role models, such as Moses, makes it different from other contemporary texts in which exemplary protagonists often pray. She also explores the Temple Scroll's lack of engagement with themes of exile and restoration, topics which often invite or allow for introduction of penitential prayer and/or confession in Early Jewish literature. Finally, Zahn focuses on the Temple Scroll's particular "temple-focused priestly ideology" and suggests that "its authors did not see prayer as a primary element in maintaining or restoring the covenant relationships between God and Israel." Instead of adopting any one of these scenarios as sufficient to explain the absence of prayer in 11QTempleª, Zahn suggests that all the factors she sketches might have had a role in shaping a text that lacks interest in prayer and praying.

"On Amulets, Apotropaic Prayers, and Phylacteries: The Contribution of Three New Texts from the Judean Desert" by **Ariel Feldman** reviews the three recently deciphered miniature texts from the Judean Desert, 4Q147–148 from Qumran and Mur5 from Wadi Murabbaʻat. Though these three were initially classified as tefillin and mezuzah, their newly-deciphered contents have nothing in common with either mezuzot or tefillin as known from the findings in the Judean Desert and rabbinic sources. With the two of the three possibly containing a language of prayer, the article suggests that these are amulets. A close comparison of the three texts with Jewish written amulets from Late Antiquity (as known from archaeological findings and rabbinic writings) suggests several affinities, as well as significant differences. Noting in particular the absence of an adjuration from the three new texts, Feldman highlights several linguistic parallels between the best-preserved 4Q147 and Second Temple apotropaic prayers. Finally, he suggests that if these are indeed apotropaic objects, amulets, they may illuminate the well-known reference to "phylacteries" in Matt 23:5.

Like Brooke, Zahn, and Feldman, **Charlotte Hempel** in "The Apotropaic Function of the Final Hymn in the Community Rules," is concerned primarily with a form of prayer and its function in the texts preserved by the Qumran community. Hempel's focus is specifically on the final hymn attested in several manuscripts of the Community Rule; and she offers a full and erudite, synoptic translation of the hymn based on all the available textual evidence. She notes how a cluster of Qumran prayer, and especially apotropaic, texts published in the last two decades or so have helped to expand our understanding of the ways "malevolent forces were feared and contained" in Early Judaism. As Hempel argues, for the Qumranites obedience to "a core of rules of conduct" helped to ensure the wellbeing of community members in the face of such threats. Yet expressions of praise and blessing—"a liturgical framework" like that which one encounters in the final hymn—likely functioned apotropaically too. Such texts thus likewise served to protect community members "from the menacing malevolence that loomed large in the lives and minds of ancient Jews."

After a number of essays that focus on questions of prayer at Qumran and in the texts from the Judean Desert, **Matthias Henze** in "Prayer in 2 Baruch" offers a careful analysis of Baruch's diverse modes of communication with the divine in the Syriac Apocalypse of Baruch (2 Baruch). Although the text, an historical apocalypse, is a late response to the destruction of the Jerusalem temple in 70 CE, as Henze observes, "in form and content 2 Baruch is very much part of the literature of the second temple period." He notes that the structure of 2 Baruch is not easy to discern, but very often a seven-fold compositional organization has been ascribed to the work, which is based on the widely accepted seven-fold structure of the more widely studied 4 Ezra. Henze, by contrast, seeks to understand the compositional format of 2 Baruch on its own terms, which importantly includes significant passages that report Baruch's communication with God. Via the genre of the dialogue, the scribe can argue with the divine and press God for answers to difficult questions regarding the post-70 fate and future of the people. Through more traditional forms of prayer (e. g., lament, petition, and praise), Baruch as a Moses-like representative of the people asks for interpretations of his visions and comes to terms with the temple's demise. Baruch's dialogues with God and the other forms of prayer he utters thus contribute to the broader rhetorical purpose of 2 Baruch, *viz* to advocate for a Torah centered form of Judaism in the wake of the national disaster of 70 CE.

Like Henze's essay, **John R. Levison**'s contribution to *Petitioners, Penitents, and Poets* remains focused on the Jewish Pseudepigrapha, but this time the Greek Life of Adam and Eve (GLAE) is front and center. Although likely not reaching its final form until the fourth century CE, GLAE's origins may go back to the first century; it thus probably makes use of pre-70 CE traditions, including, likely, prayer traditions. Levison's close reading of this work reveals how GLAE portrays "Adam as a forgiven sinner who endures the pain of existence, faces mortality with uncertainty, but ultimately receives mercy after death. Prayer in GLAE is embedded in this tortured journey toward hope." Levison, however, is most interested in "The Prayers of Eve in the Greek Life of Adam and Eve," which is the title of his essay. Although Eve is a prominent character in GLAE, when it comes to communication with the deity her words and actions are not always prominent, especially as compared to those of Adam. As a pray-er Eve is a "shadow figure," though her words to God do figure prominently in what Levison identifies as the fourth section of GLAE (esp. GLAE 31). The climax of Eve's prayer in this section of the work is her confession of responsibility for the origin of sin: "And all sin because of me has come about in the creation."

The two final essays in *Petitioners, Penitents, and Poets* focus on early Christian texts that like 2 Baruch and GLAE were also likely composed in the wake of the Temple's destruction in 70 CE. An essay entitled "I have prayed for you … strengthen your brothers" (Luke 22:32): Jesus's Proleptic Prayer for Peter and Other Gendered Tropes in Luke's War on Satan" by **Shelly Matthews** takes a closer look at the Lukan reference to Jesus's prayer on Peter's behalf, which could broadly speaking be classified as an apotropaic prayer. Noting the uniqueness of this intercessory prayer for protection of others against Satan's violent claims, Matthews sets out to explore its function within the immediate context of the passion narrative. She highlights Luke's consistent framing of the encounter with demonic forces as a battle, requiring "virile male subjects," a military combat, which will ultimately result in victory over the devil, a notion "embodying Roman ideals of masculinity." If Falk has insisted that prayers in literary texts might function in one way as isolated "prayers" but also serve other literary purposes in the compositions in which they are embedded, Matthews essay reveals how the gender dynamics in Jesus's prayer for Peter not only is a prayer for the disciple's future restoration; it contributes to Luke's larger ideological construction of the early Christian movement in masculinist terms.

Finally, **Warren Carter** in an essay entitled "Praying the Lord's Prayer in (Some Sort of) *Tameion* (Matt 6:6)" seeks to shed light on the Matthean use of the expression often rendered into English as "your room." With Lyn Osiek, he takes as his point of departure an association of *tameion* with Roman *cubiculum*, suggested already in Jerome's translation. Next, he explores in some detail the various uses of *cubiculum* in ancient Roman elite houses, where they served as much needed spaces for various private activities, including, as noted by Osiek, reception of intimate friends. Unlike Osiek who reads *tameion* as a place where a believer could encounter "the most precious guest," God himself, Carter suggests that nothing in Matt 6:6 and its immediate context mandates such a "restricted, individualized, spiritualized" interpretation. On the contrary, Carter asserts the passage may have in mind one's praying in the company of other followers of Jesus. Carter thus subsequently explores what might have taken place when two or three believers met in a *tameion/cubiculum* to pray. He is particularly interested in asking what might have served as a *tameion/cubiculum* for the Gospel's non-elite hearers, who lived in far more modest housing than the elite, or on the streets without any literal access to *cubicula*. Subsequently, Carter utilizes two theoretical frameworks, James Scott's "Hidden Transcripts" and Social Identity theory, to imagine what kind of effects such small gatherings in some sort of a *tameion* might have had on Jesus following pray-ers, focusing on the dignity-bestowing and identity-securing features of such occasions.

Conclusion

What should be clear from this brief introduction to a necessarily limited, even if wide ranging, collection of essays on prayer in Second Temple Jewish texts is that the topic is a remarkably complex one. The volume offers no definitive statement on the phenomenon of Second Temple prayer. Most of the essays are in fact studies of prayer and praying as these are textually represented in literary works from the Hebrew Bible (Psalms, Proverbs, Jonah), the New Testament (Luke, Matthew), or from the Jewish Pseudepigrapha (Greek Life of Adam and Eve, 2 Baruch) and the Qumran library (Community Rule, Temple Scroll). These essays, thus, contribute to the study of Second Temple prayer not only by filling in some of the small gaps or interstices in this enormous ongoing scholarly project. By thematizing passages, questions, and representations of prayer, praying, and pray-ers in a range of Second Temple works, the articles also further scholarly understandings of the primary texts themselves. As such, the contributions to *Petitioners, Penitents, and Poets* enhance our comprehension of what Falk has called "the larger patterns of Jewish piety" in the Second Temple period, "including conceptions of God, socio-religious identity, religious dispositions and priorities, and personal, communal and national concerns."[83]

---

[83] Falk, "Hymns, Prayers, and Psalms," 377.

Jonathan Kaplan
Pastiche, Hyperbole, and the Composition of Jonah's Prayer

1. Introduction

During the Second Temple period, textual evidence emerges in ancient Judah for a plethora of forms of prayer. One example of this diversity is the eight verse "Psalm of Jonah" (Jonah 2:3–10 [vv. 2–9]), which plays a central role in this eponymous postexilic prophetic book.[1] Jonah is a short book. That eight of its forty-eight verses consist of this prayer is an important factor for understanding the book as a whole and for appreciating one way in which prayer is employed in ancient Judean literature. Scholarly discussion heretofore on the role of this psalm in the book of Jonah has primarily engaged two related questions: (1) how the psalm comes to be a part of the book, and (2) what the nature of the psalm's composition history means for the book's interpretation. In this essay, I offer another contribution to these areas of discussion, and, I hope, present plausible solutions to some of the more persistent interpretive challenges related to the Jonah psalm and its role in the work. In the first section, I will examine earlier proposals for the origins of the Jonah psalm before turning, in the second section, to apply the literary-critical categories of pastiche and hyperbole to the analysis of the Jonah psalm. I will argue that the Jonah psalm is most likely a product of the creative genius of the author of Jonah who composed the psalm as an evocative pastiche of quotes from earlier Israelite literature. I further contend that the tone of this pastiche is intentionally hyperbolic and thus further reinforces the book of Jonah's overall satirical and parodic character.

---

[1] On the post-exilic dating of Jonah, see for instance James Nogalski, *Redactional Processes in the Book of the Twelve*, BZAW 218 (Berlin: De Grutyer, 1993), 255, 270–73.

Note: I would like to thank the participants in the "Petitioners, Penitents, and Poets" conference for their interaction with my work. In particular, I benefited greatly from the suggestions of and questions posed by George Brooke, Charlotte Hempel, Joseph McDonald, and Carol Newsom. Brian R. Doak, Karen Grumberg, and Suzie Park read and provided very helpful comments on revised versions of this essay. I would also like to thank John Huehnergard and Na'ama Pat-El for their consultation on several matters of historical Hebrew grammar. All remaining deficiencies in this essay are my own.

2. The Origins of Jonah's Prayer

The most commonly agreed upon feature of the psalm in Jonah 2 is its form: it is a stereo-typical example of an individual thanksgiving psalm.[2] The psalm begins with recounting Yhwh's deliverance of the speaker and concludes with a vow for the speaker to make an offering to Yhwh in thanksgiving.

³I called from my distress to Yhwh, and he answered me.
    From the belly of Sheol, I pleaded. You headed my voice.
⁴You cast me into the depths, into the heart of the sea, while a current hems me in.
    All your breakers and waves crash over me.
⁵As for me, I said, "I am driven from your view.
    May I yet again look upon your holy sanctuary."
⁶Waters engulfed me to my neck.
    The deep hems me in.
        Reeds cling to my head.
⁷To the base of the mountains, I descended.
    The earth, its bars about me, forever.
And you raised me up from the pit alive, O Yhwh, my God.
⁸Even when my spirit is exhausted, I remembered Yhwh.
    And my prayer reached you, to your holy sanctuary.
⁹Those who rely upon empty folly abandon their bounty.
¹⁰As for me, with a voice of thanksgiving, I shall offer you sacrifices.
    That which I have vowed, I shall pay. Deliverance belongs to Yhwh.

Despite widespread agreement on the formal features of this psalm as a psalm of thanksgiving, there are diverse opinions regarding its origins. These opinions range from viewing it as a preexistent psalm incorporated into Jonah either by the writer of Jonah or by a later redactor to understanding the psalm as a product of the author of Jonah. In this section, I will evaluate each of these approaches to the origins of the Jonah psalm. I will argue that the author intentionally crafted this psalm so that it is lexically distinct from the rest of Jonah while positioning it as integral to the whole work.

---

2 E.g., Frank M. Cross, "Studies in the Structure of Hebrew Verse: The Prosody of the Psalm of Jonah," in *The Quest for the Kingdom of God: Studies in Honor of George E. Mendenhall*, ed. Herbert B. Huffmon, Frank A. Spina, and Alberto R. Whitney Green (Winona Lake: Eisenbrauns, 1983), 159–67 (159). For a classic discussion of the features of the individual thanksgiving psalm, including the Jonah psalm, see Sigmund Mowinckel, *The Psalms in Israel's Worship*, trans. Dafydd R. Ap-Thomas (New York: Abingdon Press, 1967), 2:31–43.

Though the book of Jonah is generally understood as a postexilic pseudepigraphic prophetic story, the psalm itself shares features with other Israelite and Near Eastern texts that have been dated much earlier. Frank Moore Cross, for instance, highlights "rich parallels in Babylonian hymns and Ugaritic mythology" to the psalm.³ Additionally, he points out two features in vv. 3–7 that are found elsewhere in pre-exilic classical poetry and reflect "an oral-formulaic style": (1) a near absence of prose particles; and (2) the presence of the *yaqtul* preterite, without a prefixed *vav*, in vv. 4 and 6.⁴ Cross further notes what he understands to be signs of redactional activity in the psalm, with vv. 3–7 being distinct from vv. 8–10. In his analysis, vv. 8–10 were likely added to the psalm at a later date.⁵ While these features are not conclusive in determining the date of the psalm (and Cross himself makes no judgment about its dating), George Landes has pointed to the presence of the *yaqtul* preterite in the psalm as evidence for a pre-exilic date for the psalm's composition.⁶ These features are, however, limited and, in and of

---

3 Cross, "Prosody of the Psalm of Jonah," 160.
4 Cross ("Prosody of the Psalm of Jonah," 161) cites three instances in the psalm of the *yaqtul* preterite, without a prefixed *vav*: (1) יְסֹבְבֻנִי in v. 4; (2) יְסֹבְבֻנִי in v. 6; and (3) a reconstruction of תַּשְׁלִיכֵנִי for וַתַּשְׁלִיכֵנִי in v. 4 based on the absence of the conjunction καὶ before the word in OG. Notably, καὶ is present in the reconstruction of Emanuel Tov of this verse in the Greek Minor Prophets Scroll found at Naḥal Ḥever (8ḤevXIIgr). See Emanuel Tov with the collaboration of Robert A. Kraft and a contribution by Peter J. Parsons, *The Greek Minor Prophets Scroll from Naḥal Ḥever (8ḤevXIIgr) (The Seiyal Collection I)*, DJD 8 (Oxford: Clarendon Press, 1990), 29, 84. Notably, Dominique Barthélemy (*Les devanciers d'Aquila*, VTSup 10 [Leiden: Brill, 1963]) understands 8ḤevXIIgr as evincing the later Kaige-Theodotion recension/revision of LXX. The reconstruction of καὶ in 48ḤevXIIgr by Tov et al. is based on space considerations in the manuscript and on the presence of a prefixed *vav* in MT. According to Tov (*Textual Criticism of the Hebrew Bible*, 3d ed. [Minneapolis, MN: Fortress, 2012], 142–43), Kaige-Theodotion is generally regarded as a correction of LXX to align with MT. Additionally, the *vav* in וַתַּשְׁלִיכֵנִי is extant in 4QXII^g (4Q82), the oldest surviving Hebrew manuscript of Jonah, which is dated paleographically to the Herodian period. See Eugene Ulrich, et al., *Qumran Cave 4: X: The Prophets*, DJD 15 (Oxford: Clarendon Press, 1997), 310–11. The presence of the *vav* at this point in 4QXII^g and the reconstruction of καὶ in 8ḤevXIIgr, which is based on the prevailing understanding of the relationship of Kaige-Theodotion and MT, draws into question Cross's reconstruction of תַּשְׁלִיכֵנִי without a prefixed *vav* in 2:4.
5 Cross, "Prosody of the Psalm of Jonah," 167.
6 George M. Landes, "The Kerygma of the Book of Jonah: The Contextual Interpretation of the Jonah Psalm," *Int* 21 (1967): 3–31 (8). On the *yaqtul* preterite and its relevance for the history of the Hebrew verbal system, see Anson F. Rainey, "The Ancient Hebrew Prefix Conjugation in the Light of Amarnah Canaanite," *HS* 27 (1986): 4–19; Edward L. Greenstein, "On the Prefixed Preterite in Biblical Hebrew," *HS* 29 (1988): 7–17; John Huehnergard, "The Early Hebrew Prefix-Conjugations," *HS* 29 (1988): 19–23; Ziony Zevit, "Talking Funny in Biblical Henglish and Solving a Problem of the Yaqtûl Past Tense," *HS* 29 (1988): 25–33; Anson F. Rainey, "Further Remarks on the Hebrew Verbal System," *HS* 29 (1988): 35–42; and T. David Andersen, "The Evolution of the

themselves inconclusive for establishing a pre-exilic dating for the psalm. Notably, though יְסֹבְבֵנִי does appear twice in the psalm in vv. 4–6, it is the only instance of a *yaqtul* preterite in surviving Hebrew manuscripts of Jonah. It is equally plausible that whoever composed this psalm simply employed this archaic verbal form based on exemplars in existing ancient Israelite poetry.[7] This point receives additional support from the high frequency of quotations and allusions to early psalmic material throughout the psalm in Jonah 2, a point to which I will return in greater detail in what follows.

A number of other features make the psalm seemingly incongruous with the prose narrative of the book. These features further enhance the impression that the psalm predates the book of Jonah.[8] Perhaps the most notable disconnection between the psalm and the surrounding narrative is, as Phyllis Trible notes, that the reader arrives at the start of the psalm expecting it to be a psalm of lament uttered in the midst of distress, while Jonah is trapped in the belly of a big fish, only for the poem to be a psalm of thanksgiving.[9] Some other narrative incongruities are (1) the peril described in the song is drowning rather than being eaten by a big fish; and (2) the psalm makes no reference to the events described in chapter one.[10] In addition to these narrative incongruities, the lexicon of the psalm is different from that of the rest of the book. For instance, chapter one describes the sailors "hurl[ing]" Jonah into the sea (ויטלהו; v. 15). In the psalm, Jonah depicts God as "casting" him into the depth of the heart of the sea (ותשליכני; v. 4).[11] This distinc-

---

Hebrew Verbal System," *ZAH* 13 (2000): 1–66 (51–52). Note also the cohortative forms in Jonah 2:10, which are, generally, found in pre-exilic texts. On this point, see Jan Joosten, *The Verbal System of Biblical Hebrew: A New Synthesis Elaborated on the Basis of Classical Prose*, JBS 10 (Jerusalem: Simor, 2012), 404–6.

7 Though most of the instances of the *yaqtul* preterite appear in ancient Israelite poetry dating to before or during the early Israelite monarchy, there is one instance of the *yaqtul* preterite appearing in a text dating after the beginning of the sixth century BCE: יבחרו in Jer 52:7. Note, however, that most scholars amend the text of this word, based on Jer 39:4, to ויבחרו. On this point, see the notes in BHS ad loc. and William L. Holladay, *Jeremiah 2: A Commentary on the Book of the Prophet Jeremiah, Chapters 26–52*, Hermeneia (Minneapolis: Fortress, 1989), 436. On the presence of archaisms in Biblical Hebrew poetry, see Joosten, *Verbal System of Biblical Hebrew*, 413.

8 As Landes ("Kerygma of the Book of Jonah," 3n1) notes, these incongruities have drawn the attention of critical analysts of the book since at least the late eighteenth century.

9 Phyllis Trible, *Rhetorical Criticism: Context, Method, and the Book of Jonah*, GBSOT (Minneapolis: Fortress, 1994), 222.

10 James S. Ackerman ("Satire and Symbolism in the Song of Jonah," in *Traditions in Transformation: Turning Points in Biblical Faith*, ed. Baruch Halpern and Jon D. Levenson [Winona Lake: Eisenbrauns, 1981], 213–46 [213–14]) has delineated a total of eight such incongruities, which he admits is not an exhaustive list.

11 As noted in Ackerman, "Satire and Symbolism," 214.

tion extends beyond simple word choice; the psalm itself depicts Jonah's plight with language that evokes the rhetoric of the Northwest Semitic Combat Myth, while chapter one seems to have great affinities with the types of divinely-initiated adversity faced in heroic literature of both the ancient Mediterranean and ancient Near East.[12] These numerous points of disconnection have led scholars to posit diverse origins for the psalm and for the process by which it becomes integrated into the work as a whole.

Perhaps the most provocative thesis regarding the relationship of the psalm in Jonah 2 to the work as a whole has been advanced independently by Hugh S. Pyper and Alastair G. Hunter in a series of complementary articles.[13] In short, Pyper and Hunter both view the psalm as having literary precedence to the work as a whole. Pyper points to the earliest historical-critical studies on Jonah by M.J.G.A. Müller, who was the first to maintain "the independence and pre-existence of the psalm."[14] Pyper, himself, argues that there are four instances in which the metaphors of the psalm are literalized in the prose narrative and indicate a direction of development from the psalm to the prose: (1) from סוּף ("seaweed") in 2:6 to קִיקָיוֹן in 4:6–7; (2) בֶּטֶן שְׁאוֹל ("belly of Sheol") in 2:3 to (גָדוֹל) דָּג ("[great or big] fish") in 2:1, 11; (3) Jonah's vow to sacrifice at the end of the psalm (2:10) to the sailors' actual sacrifices in 1:16; and (4) the abandonment by the sailors and the Ninevites of their worship of others gods for devotion to Yhwh in chapters one (v. 16) and three (vv. 5–8) as a literalization of Jonah's declaration of similar singular devotion in 2:8.[15] In his 2001 article, Hunter argues similarly that the Jonah psalm is literalized in the prose section. In a later article in 2007, he

---

[12] On divinely-initiated adversity faced in heroic literature, see the sources discussed in Jack M. Sasson, *Jonah: A New Translation with Introduction, Commentary, and Interpretations*, AB 24B (New York: Doubleday, 1990), 90–92; on the evocation in Jonah 2 of rhetoric from the Northwest Semitic Combat Myth found also in other biblical texts, see Cross, "Prosody of the Psalm of Jonah," 165–66; and Alastair G. Hunter, "Jonah from the Whale: Exodus Motifs in Jonah 2," in *The Elusive Prophet: The Prophet as Historical Person, Literary Character, and Anonymous Artist*, ed. Johannes C. de Moor, OTS 45 (Leiden: Brill, 2001), 142–58.

[13] Hunter, "Jonah from the Whale"; idem, "Inside outside Psalm 55: How Jonah Grew out of a Psalmist's Conceit," in *Psalms and Prayers: Papers Read at the Joint Meeting of the Society of Old Testament Study and Het Oud Testamentisch Werkgezelschap in Nederland en België, Apeldoorn August 2006*, ed. Bob Becking and Eric Peels, OTS 55 (Leiden: Brill, 2007), 129–39; Hugh S. Pyper, "Swallowed by a Song: Jonah and the Jonah-Psalm through the Looking-Glass," in *Reflection and Refraction: Studies in Biblical Historiography in Honor of A. Graeme Auld*, ed. Robert Rezetko, Timothy H. Lim, and W. Brian Aucker, VTSup 113 (Leiden: Brill, 2006), 337–58.

[14] Pyper, "Swallowed by Song," 342. See M.J.G.A Müller, "Jona, eine moralische Erzählung," *Memorabilien* 6 (1794): 142–88.

[15] Pyper, "Swallowed by Song," 343–49. On the challenges in identifying קִיקָיוֹן, see Bernard P. Robinson, "Jonah's Qiqayon Plant," *ZAW* 97 (1985): 390–403.

further develops this argument by positing a more complex literary process in "which Psalm 55 sparked a literary response in the form of Jonah, which was in turn taken up by a later contributor to Kings."[16]

While both Pyper and Hunter point to the ways in which Jonah's prayer is knitted into the literary fabric of the book as a whole, neither scholar's work addresses longstanding research on the relationship of poetry to the larger narrative context in which a given poem is embedded. For instance, as James S. Ackerman and Jonathan Magonet note independently, there are other clear instances in "the Hebrew Bible in which prayer material has been secondarily incorporated into prose narrative" (see, for instance, 1 Sam 2:1–10; 2 Kgs 20:11–12; and Isa 38:7–39:1).[17] More importantly, neither Pyper nor Hunter cite Baruch Halpern's important study on the relationship of the Song of Deborah in Judges 5 to the narrative in the preceding chapter or employ the important methodological contribution that he makes.[18] Halpern not only argues for the priority of Judges 5 to Judges 4 but also establishes important methodological criteria for evaluating the relationship and priority of a poetic text to a prose text, criteria that might be helpful in analyzing the relationship of Jonah's prayer to the surrounding narrative. Halpern notes importantly, "there must be substantive points of difference, preferably several, such that one text only could be derived from the other. In practice, this means that the author of the derivative version must have interpreted the source in a manner with which the modern analyst takes issue."[19] In the case of Pyper and Hunter, while they note points of connectivity and difference between Jonah's prayer and the rest of the work, their analyses do not foreclose the possibility that the psalm was necessarily composed so as to have points of connectivity with the rest of the work and, as such, heighten the satirical quality of Jonah as a whole.

Hunter and Pyper are not alone in their perspective that Jonah's prayer was a preexisting composition utilized by the author of Jonah. Other scholars, however, do not agree with the position that the poem was the seed out of which the prose

---

16 Hunter, "Inside outside Psalm 55," 138. Jonah son of Amittai is a prophetic figure mentioned in 2 Kgs 14:25.
17 Ackerman, "Satire and Symbolism," 213; Jonathan Magonet, *Form and Meaning: Studies in the Literary Techniques in the Book of Jonah*, BBET 2 (Frankfurt: Peter Lang, 1976), 39.
18 Baruch Halpern, *The First Historians: The Hebrew Bible and History* (San Francisco: Harper & Row, 1988), 76–103. As Halperin notes (100n1), this chapter builds on material presented earlier in his essay "Doctrine by Misadventure," in Richard E. Friedman, ed., *The Poet and the Historian: Essays in Literary and Historical Biblical Criticism*, HSS 26 (Chico, CA: Scholars, 1983), 41–73; and idem, "The Resourceful Israelite Historian: The Song of Deborah and Israelite Historiography," HTR 76 (1983): 379–401.
19 Halpern, *First Historians*, 77.

narrative emerged. For instance, Halpern and Richard Elliot Friedman contend, "the author selected this particular psalm both because of its water imagery—which was available in other poems as well—and because of its specific vocabulary (note 2:8 ht'tp and 4:8 wyt'lp, both unusual), which he also shaped his prose to accommodate."[20] Uriel Simon notes that the psalm can either be viewed as a freestanding psalm or as something embedded in its narrative context.[21] Trible, on the grounds of rhetorical analysis, views the psalm as an entirely independent poem whose insertion into the work "disrupts the symmetry [of the narrative portions of the work], prolongs a focus on Jonah, delays the movement of the plot, exploits irony, and introduces perspectives at variance with the narrative."[22] Hans Walter Wolff views the prayer as a redactional addition designed to enhance a positive portrayal of Jonah.[23] James D. Nogalski interprets the prayer as "a preexisting poem composed independently and inserted here by a later editor to provide the content of Jonah's prayer."[24] Of course, the structural and rhetorical analysis of Jonah could proceed in an entirely different direction. Jonathan Magonet, for his part, contended in 1976 that the poem was integral to the structure of Jonah.[25] Claude Lichtert also argues that the poem cannot be separated from the narrative sections of the book but rather is at the heart of Jonah's narrative.[26] I have also maintained that the poem is integral to the structure of the work.[27] In my analysis, Jonah situates two chapters (2 and 3) that affirm the default model of moral agency in ancient Israelite literature, as has been elaborated by Carol A. Newsom, within two chapters (1 and 4) that question the limits of this model.[28] Ultimately, there seems to be an endless variation of scholarly responses to the questions of (1) whether the poem preexisted the prose or was composed by the

---

[20] Baruch Halpern and Richard Elliott Friedman, "Composition and Paronomasia in the Book of Jonah," *Hebrew Annual Review* 4 (1980): 79–92 (80n2).
[21] Uriel Simon, *Jonah: The Traditional Hebrew Text with the New JPS Translation and Commentary*, trans. Lenn J. Schramm (Philadelphia: Jewish Publication Society, 1999), 17.
[22] Trible, *Rhetorical Criticism*, 173.
[23] Hans Walter Wolff, *Obadiah and Jonah: A Commentary*, trans. Margaret Kohl, Continental Commentary (Minneapolis: Augsburg, 1977), 128–31.
[24] James D. Nogalski, *The Book of the Twelve: Hosea-Jonah* (Macon: Smyth & Helwys, 2011), 427; see also idem., *Redactional Processes*, 252–55, 265–69. As Nogalski notes, Julius A. Bewer (*A Critical and Exegetical Commentary on Jonah*, ICC [New York: Scribner's, 1912], 23) argued similarly.
[25] Magonet, *Form and Meaning*, 44.
[26] Claude Lichtert, "La prière de Jonas (Jon 2, 3-10) comme élément narrative," in *Analyse narrative et Bible: deuxième colloque international d'analyse narrative des textes de la Bible*, ed. Camille Focant and André Wénin, BETL 191 (Leuven: Peeters, 2005), 407–14.
[27] Jonathan Kaplan, "Jonah and Moral Agency," *JSOT* 43 (2019): 146–62.
[28] See Kaplan, "Jonah and Moral Agency," 147, 155; Carol A. Newsom, "Models of the Moral Self: Hebrew Bible and Second Temple Judaism," *JBL* 131 (2012): 5–25.

author or was inserted by an editor and (2) its relevance for understanding the book of Jonah as a whole.

These responses to the origins of the Jonah psalm seem to multiply because Jonah resists compositional analysis in a conclusive way. Other than the seeming lexical and ideological disjunctions between the prose sections of the work and the psalm, Jonah lacks clear signs of compositional seams such as a narrative doublet or a resumptive repetition (*Wiederaufnahme*), key criteria in compositional analysis of biblical material.[29] Thus, arguing for the insertion of the psalm into the work is a position built on the limited internal evidence of lexical dissimilarity. Notably, the textual evidence from antiquity exhibits no clear signs of recensional activity. The Minor Prophets Scroll from Naḥal Ḥever, for instance, attests to the inclusion of Jonah's prayer in the work in antiquity.[30] Given the challenges to excavating the compositional history of Jonah, I think the safest position is to approach the psalm as being either the product of an editorial insertion at a very early stage of the work's development, or, what I consider to be more plausible, that the prayer was composed by the author as an integral part of the work. Viewed from this perspective, the author of the book of Jonah intentionally crafted this psalm in such a way so that it was both marked as distinct from the rest of the work and as integral to understanding the meaning of Jonah. This simultaneously integral and disjunctive character to the poetry enables readers to make diverse and plausible arguments for its originality to or original independence from the rest of the work. In the following discussion, I will advance the argument that this feature of the psalm was an intentional compositional feature on the part of the author. From this perspective, the poem was generated by the author of Jonah with the aim of heightening the perception of its simultaneous integrity to and disjunction from the rest of the work. I contend that this binary of compositional integrity and disjunction is central to reinforcing the satirical and parodic character of Jonah.

---

29 See the discussion in Joel S. Baden, *The Composition of the Pentateuch: Renewing the Documentary Hypothesis*, AYBRL (New Haven: Yale University Press, 2012), 16–20. On supplementation as a compositional feature of biblical narratives, see the essays in Saul M. Olyan and Jacob L. Wright, eds., *Supplementation and the Study of the Hebrew Bible*, BJS 361 (Providence: Brown University, 2018). See also, Jan C. Gertz et al., eds., *The Formation of the Pentateuch: Bridging the Academic Cultures of Europe, Israel, and North America*, FAT 111 (Tübingen: Mohr Siebeck, 2016).
30 See DJD 8:29, 84.

3. The Prayer of Jonah, Pastiche, and Hyperbole

Two features of Jonah's prayer support my contention that the author of Jonah composed the psalm intentionally in order to mark it both as integral to the work and as bearing signs of lexical and ideological disjunction: (1) the pastiche character of its assemblage of phrases and (2) the hyperbolic character of its diction. The Jonah psalm's pastiche character and its hyperbolic diction reinforce, I contend, the book's overall satirical and parodic character. First, charting literary parallels between Jonah's prayer and various prayers in the book of Psalms and other parts of ancient Israelite literature remains a central focus of Jonah scholarship. Jack M. Sasson, for instance, cites five "illustrative" passages for comparison in his discussion of just verse three.[31] In an earlier study, Magonet identifies sixteen "quotations from the psalter" in the Jonah psalm.[32] Other scholars have likewise charted numerous other parallels.[33] While one may quibble with particular identifications of a given parallel or "quotation," it is fairly clear that the author of Jonah employed highly formulaic and evocative language in composing the psalm. Indeed, when one looks at the psalter itself, one can see a similar recycling of language. How much of that is an intentional reuse of language or a factor of stylistic convention is a matter open to interpretation. For instance, when the eighth verse of Ps 145:8 reads חנון ורחום יי ארך אפים וגדל חסד, "Yhwh is gracious and merciful, slow to anger and abounding in steadfast love," is the author making an intertextual allusion to Exod 34:6–7 and the thirteen-fold attributes of Israel's god or is the psalmist simply importing a phrase in order to fill out the acrostic structure of the psalm? In other words, is this phrase interpretively meaningful or did the psalmist just need a stock phrase that began with the letter *khet*?[34]

In the case of Jonah, we are left in many instances with a similar degree of ambiguity. For example, one of the most clearly apparent "quotations" in the Jonah psalm is the word-for-word citation of Ps 42:8b in Jonah 2:4, as has been noted by Magonet: כל משבריך וגליך עלי עברו "all your breakers and waves crash over

---

31 Sasson, *Jonah*, 168–69.
32 Magonet, *Form and Meaning*, 44–49. Magonet (129 n. 28) also points to the list of such quotations in numerous commentaries. See also Otto Kaiser, "Wirklichkeit, Möglichkeit und Vorurteil. Ein Beitrag zum Verständnis des Buches Jona," *EvT* 33 (1973): 91–103 (97n22).
33 E.g., Bewer, *Jonah*, 44–48.
34 On the quotation of Exod 34:6–7 in Ps 145:8, see Nathan C. Lane, "Yhwh's Gracious and Compassionate Reign: Exodus 34.6–7," in *Imagination, Ideology and Inspiration: Echoes of Brueggemann in a New Generation*, ed. Jonathan Kaplan and Robert Williamson, Jr., HBM 72 (Sheffield: Sheffield Phoenix Press, 2015), 69–82; and idem, *The Compassionate, but Punishing God: A Canonical Analysis of Exodus 34:6–7* (Eugene: Wipf & Stock, 2010), 132–39. On the structure and meaning of Ps 145, see Reuven Kimelman, "Psalm 145: Theme, Structure, and Impact," *JBL* 113 (1994): 37–58.

me."³⁵ Magonet does not elaborate on the significance of this quotation. Psalm 42, often interpreted as contiguous with Psalm 43, is an individual psalm of lament.³⁶ In this larger context, Ps 42:8b gives expression to the speaker's present experience of distress. Because the psalm of Jonah is a thanksgiving psalm, the use of this verse fragment from Ps 42 in Jonah does not activate the broader context of the psalm. Rather, Jonah 2:4 describes Jonah's apparent past experience of distress. In this way, the Jonah psalm merely echoes the language of Ps 42 at best and should not be construed as an allusion to the whole psalm or even a quotation that evokes the context of the psalm.³⁷

The same can be said for nearly all of the other echoes of language in the Jonah psalm. For instance, Magonet highlights the adaptation of a quote from Ps 31:23 in Jonah 2:5a. The verse from Jonah reads: ואני אמרתי נגרשתי מנגד עיניך אך אוסיף להביט אל היכל קדשך ("As for me, I said, "I am driven from your view. May I yet again look upon your holy sanctuary"). The verse from Ps 31 reads: ואני אמרתי בחפזי נגרזתי מנגד עיניך אכן שמעת קול תחנוני בשועי אליך ("As for me, I said in my haste, 'I am cut off from before your sight.' Nevertheless, you have heard the sound of my supplications when I cried out to you."). As Magonet has noted, Jonah adapts the language of the verse from Ps 31 in notable ways.³⁸ First, the version of the phrase in Jonah deletes the adverbial phrase בחפזי "in my haste." Second, the author of the Jonah psalm changes the main verb of the first half of the verse from נגרשתי, "I was cast off," to נגרזתי, "I was cut off."³⁹ Third, the continuation of the first half of the verse is different in Jonah (אך אוסיף ...) than in Ps 31 (אכן שמעת ...). Magonet sees these transformations as intentional, highlighting the transformation in Jonah from "all his selfishness and absurdity" into a person who experiences some degree of change and reorientation toward "God's command and teaching."⁴⁰ While Magonet is correct that the second half of the verse

---

35 Magonet, *Form and Meaning*, 44.
36 See, for instance Mitchell Dahood, S.J., *Psalms I: 1–50*, AB 16 (New York: Doubleday, 1966), 255, 261; Peter C. Craige, *Psalms 1–50*, WBC 19 (Waco: Word Books, 1983), 322–29.
37 On the methodological challenges of detecting literary allusions and echoes as well as judging their interpretive import, see Benjamin D. Sommer, *A Prophet Reads Scripture: Allusion in Isaiah 40–66* (Stanford: Stanford University Press, 1998); Ziva Ben-Porat, "The Poetics of Literary Allusion," *PTL* 1 (1976): 105–28; and Jonathan Kaplan, "The Song of Songs from the Bible to the Mishnah," *HUCA* 81 (2010/2013): 43–66. See also the recent collection of essays on citation and allusion in the Hebrew Bible: Ziony Zevit, ed., *Subtle Citation, Allusion, and Translation the Hebrew Bible* (Bristol: Equinox, 2017).
38 Magonet, *Form and Meaning*, 45.
39 Though, admittedly, the words are phonologically similar. On this point, see Wolff, *Obadiah and Jonah*, 135.
40 Magonet, *Form and Meaning*, 53.

from Ps 31 is changed in the Jonah psalm, it is not altogether clear that the author of the Jonah psalm is evoking the greater narrative context of Ps 31 through his quotation of this excerpt. At best, as in the first example from Ps 42, the writer of the Jonah psalm just seems to be echoing the language from Ps 31 rather than engaging in an interpretation of this quote that specifically evokes its original setting.

The lack of interpretive import for the purported quotations from the psalter gives Jonah's prayer the character of a pastiche. Classically, pastiche is an artistic technique in which a work of art consciously "imitates the style, gestures, or forms of an older work."[41] Because pastiche involves the combination of earlier material with the minimal contribution of new elements, the term has often been used pejoratively to characterize a work of pastiche as being unoriginal and derivative.[42] Pastiche has been notably reanimated in postmodern theory because of postmodernism's interest in pastiche's inherent and persistent focus on "referentiality."[43] Recently, in Biblical Studies and allied fields, pastiche has also begun to be employed as a productive category for analyzing the ways in which later texts evoke the language of earlier texts. For instance, in a recent monograph, Michelle Fletcher engages the book of Revelation through the critical horizon of pastiche. Notably, she describes the literary practices of "imitation and combination," so characteristic of pastiche, "as worthy practices" and offers four case studies in which she examines the ways in which Revelation imitates and recombines earlier literature.[44] Like Fletcher, I value the use of pastiche as an analytical category for examining ancient literature. This critical stance is essential as ancient literature consistently assumes a reverential and referential posture toward earlier texts and expresses its originality not through the generation of new forms or language but through the creative citation, echo, and recombination of earlier phrases and forms.

George Brooke has also used pastiche, building on the work of Gérard Genette, to characterize the use of material from the Psalms in the Hodayot as "a kind of imaginatively creative and playful imitation through anthologization."[45] Gen-

---

[41] Claire Bowen, "Pastiche," in *The Princeton Encyclopedia of Poetry and Poetics*, ed. Roland Green et. al., 4th ed. (Princeton: Princeton University Press, 2012), 1005.

[42] Bowen, "Pastiche," 1005; Michelle Fletcher, *Reading Revelation as Pastiche: Imitating the Past*, LNTS 571 (London: Bloomsbury T&T Clark, 2017), 49; and Richard Dyer, *Pastiche* (New York: Routledge, 2007), 7.

[43] For a helpful treatment of pastiche in postmodern literary theory, see Fletcher, *Reading Revelation as Pastiche*, 48-61.

[44] Fletcher, *Reading Revelation as Pastiche*, 2.

[45] George J. Brooke, "Hypertextuality and the 'Parabiblical' Dead Sea Scrolls," in *Reading the Dead Sea Scrolls: Essays in Method*, EJL 39 (Atlanta: Society of Biblical Literature, 2013), 67–84 (79). This essay was originally published in *In the Second Degree: Paratextual Literature in Ancient*

ette himself characterized pastiche as "conscious and (nearly) lucid imitation" and thus placed emphasis in defining the category on the author's intention rather than on the reader's capacity to discern whether a given work is consciously imitating an earlier work.[46] Genette's emphasis on the authorial intentionality of pastiche is an important consideration for my suggestion that the pastiche character of the Jonah psalm is an intentional compositional strategy on the part of the author. As a pastiche, the Jonah psalm consists of individual phrases that have been lifted from their original contexts and then reshaped and reformulated in the new context of Jonah's prayer. The originality of the Jonah psalm is found not in its innovative language (of which there is little innovation) but rather in the artistry of its composition and how it combines fragments of earlier works.

Appreciating Jonah's prayer as a pastiche helps to account for the seeming disjunction between the prayer and its narrative context. This pastiche of phrases reinforces the insight that prayer is not often a high literary art that has clear linguistic and narrative cohesion with a person's circumstances. People pray regularly in markedly different registers from the circumstances that precede and follow the intoning of a prayer and often in highly formulaic language that betrays a similar lack of originality or easy continuity with their immediate situation.[47] Why should we expect anything else from the character of Jonah? The difference in language and register, let alone the pastiche character of his prayer, gives the impression that Jonah is putting on piety and stringing together evocative citations from Israel's prayer book because that is what one should do when you are in the rather absurd situation of being stuck in the belly of a big fish, recently rescued from drowning in the mythic watery depths.

Near Eastern and Ancient Mediterranean Culture and Its Reflection in Medieval Literature, ed. Philip S. Alexander, Armin Lange, and Renate J. Pillinger (Leiden: Brill, 2010), 43–64. I would like to thank Professor Brooke for pointing me to this essay. On allusions to scriptural material in the Hodayot, see also Julie A. Hughes, *Scriptural Allusions and Exegesis in the Hodayot*, STDJ 59 (Leiden: Brill, 2006).

46 Gérard Genette, *Palimpsests: Literature in the Second Degree*, trans. Channa Newman and Claude Doubinsky (Lincoln: University of Nebraska Press, 1997), 45. On this emphasis in Genette's work, see Simon Kemp, "Pastiche, Structuralism and Authorial Intention," *Journal of Romance Studies* 12 (2012): 93–105 (98).

47 Perhaps one extreme example of this phenomenon occurs in the movie *Meet the Parents* (2000). In one scene, Jack Byrnes (Robert De Niro) invites his prospective son-in-law, Greg Focker (Ben Stiller), to say grace before dinner. After an awkward silence and an attempt by Greg's fiancée, Pam (Teri Polo), to get Greg out of saying grace because he is Jewish, Greg offers up a prayer in a booming voice that combines a series of stereo-typical platitudes ("You are thoughtful, Kind. Gentle. And … accommodating. God.") with a quote from the song "Day by Day" from the 1971 Stephen Schwartz and John-Michael Tebelak musical *Godspell*. I would like to thank Joseph McDonald for reminding me of this scene.

As a pastiche, Jonah's prayer "imitates the style, gestures" and "forms of" the "older" model of the psalms.[48] The highly formulaic character of the psalm and its evocative and referential character may have helped to engender the perception that the psalm predates the prose sections of the work. Some phrases in the psalm may indeed predate the work insofar as the recycling of earlier poetic forms entails the reuse and repurposing of earlier material. For instance, Ps 42:8 is possibly a pre-exilic text and certainly predates the book of Jonah. Similarly, the use of the *yaqtul*-preterite in verses 4 and 6 may have been in imitation of the use of similar forms found in ancient Israelite poetry, such as in Exodus 15. While these observations about what features in the Jonah psalm engender the perception that it predates Jonah may be speculative, they should not distract from my central observation about the pastiche character of Jonah's prayer.

As a compositional technique, pastiche has noted affinities with parody. Genette recognized this point and devoted substantial energy to differentiating pastiche from parody.[49] He distinguishes the two techniques both on the basis of function, or the degree to which a text is satirical, and on the basis of whether a text is transformative of its source material (parody and travesty) or merely imitative of it (caricature and pastiche).[50] In his essay on Jonah's prayer as a satire, Ackerman evoked parody in his analysis, though he does not explain his use of the description.[51] While Ackerman does not employ pastiche in his analysis of the composition of the prayer, his use of both satire and, secondarily, parody highlights the overlap between these three compositional techniques. Parody, however, may be distinguished from pastiche in terms of function as Genette suggested. As Linda Hutcheon and Michael Woodland note, "Though both are forms of acknowledged borrowing ... pastiche does not aim at ironic inversion leading to difference."[52] In other words, whereas parody marks its difference from or opposition to its source material, pastiche does not share this aim. In the case of the Jonah psalm, its pastiche of psalmic phrases evokes their language without opposing the aims of the prayer's source material. Nevertheless, that the Jonah

---

[48] Bowen, "Pastiche," 1005.
[49] In fact, critical reflection on the nature of parody is central to Genette's *Palimpsests*. See also the discussion in Dyer, *Pastiche*, 40–48.
[50] Genette, *Palimpsests*, 24–25.
[51] Ackerman, "Satire and Symbolism," 227. I have also described the opening scene of Jonah as a parody of the prophetic call narrative. See Kaplan, "Jonah and Moral Agency," 152.
[52] Linda Hutcheon and Michael Woodland, "Parody," in *The Princeton Encyclopedia of Poetry and Poetics*, 1001–3 (1002). On parody and "ironic inversion," see Linda Hutcheon, *A Theory of Parody: The Teachings of Twentieth-Century Art Forms* (Urbana: University of Illinois Press, 2000), 6.

psalm is a pastiche should not dissuade one from appreciating its parodic elements as well as those throughout the book. The inversion, the parodic element, is at the level of Jonah's character rather than in the pastiche of quotes that make up the psalm. On the level of the narrative, the pastiche of his psalm is an entirely earnest effort by Jonah as he seeks to marshal his sources in prayer. Viewed from this perspective, Jonah should be understood as intoning this psalm as the pious act of a newly repentant devotee of Yhwh. The uttering of this pastiche of quotes, however, parodies what a pious individual should be doing at this moment; it is seemingly the wrong pastiche: a psalm of thanksgiving rather than a prayer for deliverance. And in the next verse of the chapter (2:11), the big fish who swallowed Jonah vomits him out on dry land, perhaps as a critical response, at Yhwh's command, to Jonah's inappropriate prayer.[53]

In addition to pastiche, the other feature of the Jonah psalm, which I believe supports my contention that the author of Jonah composed this psalm intentionally in order to mark it as both integral to the work and also bearing signs of lexical and ideological disjunction from it, is the hyperbolic character of its diction. As Sasson notes, the differing register of Jonah's prayer, with its distinct vocabulary, verbal tense, and setting, can be accounted for as "organic to the distinctive dictions obtaining in poetry and prose." For Sasson, biblical poetry, indeed any poetry, has a certain "hyperbolic flavor."[54] Hyperbole, as "a figure of speech," is "marked by flagrant exaggeration."[55] Once we assume that poetry will be hyperbolic, and therefore pushing the bounds of truth past credibility, then we should not, in Sasson's analysis, be taken off guard by Jonah expressing fear over the threat of drowning in flood water rather than over being digested by the big fish.[56] For Sasson, this point is reinforced by the fact that drowning is a common theme in numerous psalms (e. g., Pss 18:4; 42:8; and 69:1).[57] Similarly, Jonah's vow to

---

53 I would like to thank Carol Newsom for this observation.
54 See Sasson, *Jonah*, 202. Note that Carolyn J. Sharp (*Irony and Meaning in the Hebrew Bible* [Bloomington: Indiana University Press, 2009], 180) also describes Jonah 2 as hyperbolic but does not elaborate on her use of this descriptor.
55 Kevin McFadden, "Hyperbole," in *The Princeton Encyclopedia of Poetry and Poetics*, 648.
56 As the late first century CE rhetorician Quintilian (H. E. Butler, trans., *The Institutio Oratoria of Quintilian*, 4 vols. [New York: Putman's Sons, 1922], 3.345) notes concerning the import of hyperbole, "when the magnitude of the facts passes all words, and in such circumstances our language will be more effective if it goes beyond the truth than if it falls short of it." In this regard, Quintilian understands the use of hyperbole to be virtuous when the subject itself is out of the ordinary. This disjunction between the rhetorical characterization of something and the thing itself is, for Quintilian, the means through which hyperbole articulates truth about the object of description.
57 Sasson, *Jonah*, 202. Ronald S. Hendel ("Myth and Mimesis in the Psalm of Jonah," in *Psalms In/On Jerusalem*, ed. Ilana Pardes and Ophir Münz-Manor, Perspectives on Jewish Texts and Con-

offer sacrifices in vv. 8–10 should not be understood as an inappropriate prayer in place of petitioning God to set him on firm ground but rather a prolepsis that extends narratively beyond Jonah's current circumstances. Indeed, the expectation of worshiping Israel's god in a temple location is an old trope of prayers of thanksgiving that is found as early as the Song of the Sea in Exodus 15, interestingly a prayer intoned after Israel's deliverance through the chaotic waters of ים סוּף (see v. 17). When viewed together with the pastiche character of this poetry, its hyperbolic tone reinforces my observation that Jonah's prayer was composed by the author of Jonah for precisely the aim of using pastiche and hyperbole to heighten the satire and the parody in the work as a whole.

4. Conclusions

The hyperbolic character of Jonah's prayer coheres with the satirical and parodic nature of the book of Jonah as a whole. Other satirical elements in Jonah include Jonah's forsaking of his prophetic call in Jonah 1:1, the pious devotion to Yhwh of the newly repentant non-Israelite sailors in chapter one, Jonah's consumption by a "big fish" in chapter two, the wild success of his prophetic message in chapter three, and the unresolved dialogue about the limits of Yhwh's mercy between Jonah and Yhwh in chapter four. As Ackerman notes, "Only satire … permits such a blend of wild improbabilities with ironic incongruities."[58] Locating a grandiose, hyperbolic, and contextually inappropriate pastiche of quotes in Jonah's mouth is but another example of the satirical and parodic elements in Jonah. Viewed in this light, the psalm should be understood as integral to the work and likely the intentional product of the author of Jonah rather than an insertion of the author or a later editor of the book. In doing so, the author employed the literary techniques of pastiche and hyperbole in order to nod to Israel's psalmic tradition while also intensifying the satirical and parodic character of the book of Jonah as a whole.

In addition to deepening our understanding of this psalm and its role in Jonah, my analysis also highlights another example of the use of pastiche as a compositional technique in prayer literature from the Second Temple period. As with Brooke's examination of the Hodayot using this same category, my interpretation of the Jonah psalm suggests a productive direction for further scholarship on the diversity of prayer literature from this period and its reuse and transforma-

---

texts 9 [Berlin: De Gruyter, 2019], 1–10, [5]) has also similarly noted the hyperbolic character of the language in the psalm in Jonah 2.
58 Ackerman, "Satire and Symbolism," 227.

tion of earlier prayer traditions. Notably, the Hodayot and Jonah highlight the markedly different ways in which the same literary technique can be employed in the Second Temple period in the production of prayer texts. Whereas the Hodayot employ pastiche as a literary technique in the composition of liturgical texts, the writer of the Jonah employs pastiche precisely to parody piety. This difference highlights the importance of attending in our analysis not only to the literary features of particular prayer texts from this period but also the unique ways in which the same compositional technique can be employed in diverse texts to achieve very different ends.

Serge Frolov
Psalms: *Sitz im Leben* vs. *Sitz in der Literatur*

1. Introduction

Classical form criticism rested on two conceptual pillars: *Gattung* (genre) and *Sitz im Leben* (positioning in life). Its founder, Hermann Gunkel, believed that origins of biblical texts could be traced in a way distinct from classic literary criticism's concern with discovering well-defined sources, exemplified by the Documentary Hypothesis for the formation of the Pentateuch. Instead, Gunkel sought to classify relatively small (or, at least, more or less self-contained) units by their literary form and link this form to the social-institutional setting to which it was organically related.[1]

These concerns made psalms an ideal form-critical playground. They are generically distinctive, if also diverse, and for the most part short and self-contained (something signaled by the presence of numerous superscriptions). Gunkel devoted two monographs and a commentary to the Psalter, and his close follower Sigmund Mowinckel is mostly known for his monumental study of the book.[2] For both it was self-evident that the social and institutional matrix of the Psalter was that of ancient Israelite temple liturgy. However, the two differed substantially as to how exactly the supposed *Sitz im Leben* of the psalms relates to their various *Gattungen*. Gunkel saw them as imitations of cultic compositions, whereas Mowinckel maintained that they are transcripts of actual liturgical speech acts. The vast majority of biblical scholars continue to regard the cult as the *Sitz im Leben* of most psalms.

---

[1] Gunkel did not leave a consistent account of his method; coming closest is Hermann Gunkel, "Die Grundprobleme der israelitischen Literaturgeschichte," in Hermann Gunkel, *Reden und Aufsätze* (Göttingen: Vandenhoeck & Ruprecht, 1913), 29–38. For good summaries and demonstrations, see Klaus Koch, *Was ist Formgeschichte? Methoden der Bibelexegese*, 5th ed. (Neukirchen-Vluyn: Neukirchener Verlag, 1989); Marvin A. Sweeney, "Form Criticism," in *To Each Its Own Meaning: An Introduction to Biblical Criticisms and Their Application*, ed. Steven L. McKenzie and Stephen R. Haynes (Louisville: Westminster John Knox, 1999), 58–89.

[2] Hermann Gunkel, *Ausgewählte Psalmen* (Göttingen: Vandenhoeck & Ruprecht, 1904); idem, *Die Psalmen übersetzt und erklärt*, HKAT 2/2 (Göttingen: Vandenhoeck & Ruprecht, 1926); Hermann Gunkel and Joachim Begrich, *Einleitung in die Psalmen. Die Gattungen der religiösen Lyrik Israels*, HKAT 2/2 Supp (Göttingen: Vandenhoeck & Ruprecht, 1933); Sigmund Mowinckel, *Psalmenstudien*, 2 vols. (Amsterdam: P. Schippers, 1961).

Yet, today this convention may no longer align with the evolving form-critical methodology, especially as represented by the theoretical contributions of Rolf Knierim and Marvin Sweeney. Among other things, Sweeney has built upon Knierim's ideas to argue that in addition to the text's *Sitz im Leben* a form-critical investigation should deal with its *Sitz in der Literatur*—literary setting.³ In Sweeney's words, "literary setting ... plays a key role, especially since the basis for reconstruction of the social setting of a text must lie in the literature itself, which in turn functions in a literary context that has some bearing on how that literature is shaped and understood."⁴

The new understanding has, in turn, undermined the unspoken assumption that every biblical text has its *Sitz im Leben* and raised the possibility that the only milieu of at least some of them is the Bible itself—or, to be more precise, the Israelite/Jewish literature of the Second Temple known to us primarily from the Hebrew Bible. Here, I will demonstrate that this is the case with the Psalter, some of whose texts were likely adopted for public liturgy during the Second Temple period and whose language, concepts, and imagery came to be foundational for still later Second Temple Jewish articulations of prayer.

2. Psalms in the Temple: External Evidence

Let me begin by noting the obvious: while providing detailed instructions with regard to the layout, engineering design, decoration, and transportation of the sanctuary, the sacrificial procedures, the responsibilities and privileges of the priests and the Levites, as well as their ritual purity and garments, the Torah has little use for any ritual acts of verbal nature. No prayers, hymns, or incantations are prescribed for public or even private performance, either generally or for specific occasions. The only clear exceptions are the brief recitation of the Exodus story that Deut 26:5–9 stipulates in conjunction with the offering of the first fruits and the declaration that all proper procedures were followed with regard to the tithe (Deut 26:13–15). However, these pronouncements, clearly prosaic in nature, bear little generic semblance to any of the canonical psalms. A few psalms overlap with Deut 26:5–9 as far as content is concerned (e.g., Psalm 105), but in terms of literary form it seems to stand closer to the non-liturgical "four sons" com-

---

3 Sweeney, "Form Criticism," 79–82; cf. Rolf Knierim, "Old Testament Form Criticism Reconsidered," *Int* 27 (1973): 445–49, 463–66. The term *Sitz in der Literatur* was apparently introduced by Wolfgang Richter, *Exegese als Literaturwissenschaft: Entwurf einen alttestamentlichen Literaturtheorie und Methodologie* (Göttingen: Vandenhoeck & Ruprecht, 1971).
4 Sweeney, "Form Criticism," 79.

mandments of Exod 12:27; 13:8, 14–15 and, especially, Deut 6:21–25, as well as to the equally non-liturgical historical resumes in Josh 24:2–13 and 1 Sam 12:8. Moreover, in both Deut 26:5–9 and 26:13–15 the utterance is required of the layperson rather than the cultic professional, and both occasions are peripheral to the temple service dominated by animal sacrifices. Yehezkel Kaufman and Israel Knohl were consequently right on the mark when they described the cult envisioned by the Torah as, respectively, "the kingdom of silence" and "the sanctuary of silence."[5]

Neither does the Torah or the Enneateuch (Genesis-Kings) as a whole mention actual performance in a cultic setting of anything even remotely resembling the psalms. The prayers of David and Solomon are quoted at length (respectively, 2 Sam 7:18–29 and 1 Kgs 8:23–53), but both are in prose and, as far as content is concerned, obviously tailored for a specific occasion (respectively, the dynastic promise to David and Solomon's dedication of the temple). Gary Rendsburg maintains that "during the dedication of the Temple as described in 1 Kgs 8, the author places in the mouth of Solomon a speech that refers repeatedly to the Temple as a place of prayer ..."[6] However, a closer look at the text reveals that the only prayer *in* the temple mentioned in it is Solomon's dedicatory pronouncement. Otherwise, the king talks about Israel praying *towards* (אל) the temple or in its direction (דרך), not just from outside the compound or the city of Jerusalem but also from a foreign land (vv. 28–29, 38–39, 41–43, 44–45, 48–49), i.e., from exile or diaspora (or both).

A similar pattern is traceable in prophetic literature. On the one hand, references to a vocal aspect of the temple service are scant to non-existent. Rendsburg, in arguing that such an aspect was present already in the pre-exilic period, turns to Isa 38:20, Jer 33:11, and Amos 5:23 for support.[7] However, the first of these fragments only mentions music, not singing or chanting, and while the performance is associated with the temple, it is not explicitly the locus: "Yhwh is to help me, and *my melodies* (נגנותי) shall we *play* (ננגן) all the days of our lives *concerning* (על) the house of Yhwh." The second does quote what is perhaps the most famous refrain of the Psalter: "Give thanks to Yhwh, for good is Yhwh, for his faithfulness is forever" (cf. Pss 100:5; 106:1; 107:1; 118:1, 29; 136:1; in Psalms 118 and 136, the

---

[5] Yehezkel Kaufman, *The Religion of Israel: From Its Beginnings to the Babylonian Exile*, trans. Moshe Greenberg (Chicago: University of Chicago Press, 1960), 303; Israel Knohl, *The Sanctuary of Silence: The Priestly Torah and the Holiness Code* (Minneapolis: Fortress, 1995).

[6] Gary A. Rendsburg, "The Psalms as Hymns in the Temple of Jerusalem," in *Jesus and Temple: Textual and Archaeological Explorations*, ed. James H. Charlesworth (Minneapolis: Fortress, 2014): 95–122 (97).

[7] Rendsburg, "Psalms," 98–100.

last clause of the formula also serves as a refrain)—which is why for Rendsburg it is "a most illuminating text."[8] Yet, it is not clear that the formula is pronounced in the temple: "The voice of gladness and the voice of joy, the voice of the groom, and the voice of the bride, the voice of those saying, 'Give thanks to Yhwh of hosts, for good is Yhwh, for his faithfulness is forever,' bringing the [offering of?] thanksgiving to the house of Yhwh." It is possible to read the verse as placing the psalmodic line in conjunction with the thanksgiving sacrifice ("The voice of those saying, 'Give thanks to Yhwh etc.' *while* bringing the thanksgiving"); but it is just as plausible that the two actions are related only insofar as both express gratitude to the deity ("The voice of those saying, 'Give thanks to Yhwh, etc.' [and the voice of those] bringing the thanksgiving").

This leaves us with Amos who does seem to place singing in the context of temple service:

> I hate, I revile your festivals (חגיכם), and I would not savor your assemblies; rather, even if you brought your burnt offerings (עלות) and your meal offerings to me I would not want it, and I would have no regard for the peace offering (שלם) of your fatlings. Remove from me the noise of *your songs* (שריך) and the tunes of your harps! (5:22–23)

For our purposes, the key term here is "song" (שיר) because it often appears in the superscriptions of individual psalms. It is difficult to deny that the deity is quoted here as speaking about a poetic text, likely a hymn (given the implication that the addressees expect it to be as pleasing to Yhwh as various sacrifices), performed at a shrine to musical accompaniment. Still, it would be premature to conclude that the author of Amos saw such performance as a normative cultic practice. The prophet speaks at Bethel (7:10–13), a paradigmatically illicit shrine, if there has ever been one, especially due to the presence of the notorious golden calf (1 Kgs 12:25–13:6; cf. Exodus 32), and the only one that is specifically named among the numerous altars destroyed during Josiah's purge of the cult (2 Kgs 23:15–20). It is possible then that by mentioning songs at Bethel the book was trying to bolster the perception of the sanctuary's illegitimacy. Notably, in the golden calf episode, a festival (חג), during which the people bring burnt offerings (עלת) and peace offerings (שלמים), is also accompanied by singing (Exod 32:5–6, 18), although admittedly the root denoting it is ענה rather than שיר.

It is only when we come to Writings, more specifically, to the Chronicles-Ezra-Nehemiah multiplex, that a drastic change takes place.[9] A mere six chapters into

---

8 Rendsburg, "Psalms," 99.
9 Other books included in Writings cannot be expected to provide much information on the subject at hand due to their genre and implied setting.

the narrative part of Chronicles, David appoints Levites to perform verbal acts accompanied by music at the sanctuary housing the ark of the covenant (1 Chr 16:4–6). Placed at their head is Asaph (v. 5), featured in the superscriptions of Psalms 50, 73–83. Even further, the king dictates to Asaph and others a hymn (1 Chr 16:8–36) that, as pointed out by Rendsburg, is a pastiche of excerpts from Psalms 96, 105, and 106, with the addition of the "give thanks to Yhwh, for he is good, for his faithfulness is forever" discussed above.[10] More singers and musicians are appointed to the sanctuary in 1 Chr 16:41–42, and Yhwh's eternal faithfulness is mentioned again (v. 41). In 1 Chronicles 25, David selects singers and musicians for the future temple, starting with the sons of Asaph, although the account rather unexpectedly lists "prophesying to the accompaniment of harps, lutes, and cymbals" first among their tasks (v. 1; cf. vv. 2, 3); "thanking and praising Yhwh" comes almost as an afterthought (v. 3). When Solomon completes the temple, "the trumpeters and singers like one, in a single voice praise and give thanks to Yhwh ... because he is good, because his faithfulness is forever" (2 Chr 5:13; the formula also rings out, with variations, in 2 Chr 7:3; 20:21). In 2 Chr 6:41–42, Solomon's prosaic dedicatory prayer largely identical to that in 1 Kgs 8 is augmented by a poetic piece strongly resembling Ps 132:8–10. In Ezra 3:10–11, the "sons of Asaph" with cymbals praise Yhwh with a variation on the ubiquitous "for he is good, for his faithfulness is forever" when the foundation of the restored temple is laid. Both Ezra and Nehemiah repeatedly mention temple singers (משררים; e.g., Ezra 2:65; 10:24; Neh 10:29; 11:22–23; 12:47) as contemporaries of their title characters; overall, the term is both common in Chronicles-Ezra-Nehemiah (more than 30 occurrences) and unique to it.

What are we to make of this picture? Obviously, when it comes to psalms being a part of public worship, different biblical corpora have drastically different ideas. The Enneateuch, including its normative parts, does not seem to know anything about such a practice; and neither does prophetic literature, with Amos 5:23 being the only potential exception. Chronicles-Ezra-Nehemiah, by contrast, views singing of compositions that are identical or similar to parts of the Psalter as a routine and uncontroversial aspect of the temple ritual. The contrast cannot be interpreted in terms of implicit intra-communal debate. If the author(s) of the Enneateuch and the prophetic books were opposed to singing in the temple, they would have undoubtedly made it known, probably in more than one way; instead, this possibility simply does not seem to occur to them (again, Amos 5:23 may be the only exception). Consequently, the practice in question must postdate the completion of the Enneateuch and (most of the) prophetic books but predate

---

10 Rendsburg, "Psalms," 104–105.

Chronicles-Ezra-Nehemiah. If psalms originated after this shift, chances are that the temple is their *Sitz im Leben*, but this cannot be the case if they existed earlier (although they could still be secondarily repurposed once vocality became an accepted component of the cult—much like many of them are used in synagogues and churches today).

This conclusion may seem to lead nowhere because the dating of biblical texts, especially in relation to each other, is a fraught and controversial exercise, with few certainties to anchor the reasoning. The *terminus a quo* for Chronicles is, obviously, 539 BCE, because the concluding catchline (2 Chr 36:22–23) presupposes Cyrus's takeover of Babylon, and Ezra and Nehemiah cannot be earlier than the second half of the fifth century, but there is hardly any consensus on the exact date and even on the order in which the three books came into being.[11] Things are even murkier on the opposite side of the equation. Classical source criticism as represented by Karl Heinrich Graf and Julius Wellhausen placed the "priestly" source of the Pentateuch (which could be expected to affirm or prohibit performance of psalms in the temple, had the idea occurred to the author) in the late sixth or fifth century BCE, meaning that it could be contemporaneous with, or slightly postdate, not only Chronicles, but also Ezra and Nehemiah.[12] At least one relatively recent study has shifted the date of P to the pre-exilic period, but this re-dating has yet to gain broad acceptance.[13] Martin Noth believed that what he saw as a more or less integral Deuteronomistic composition (Deuteronomy through Kings), whose account of the dedication of Solomon's temple so drastically differs from that of Chronicles with regard to singing, was mostly completed soon after the latest event it mentions—the exaltation of King Jehoiachin in 561 BCE.[14] The present writer has offered additional arguments in favor of this dating and even suggested that it may be expanded to the entire Enneateuch,[15] but other scholars have argued for later provenance or maintained that an early version of the corpus came into being in the late seventh or even late eighth

---

11 For a good survey of widely divergent opinions on the matter, see Gary N. Knoppers, *1 Chronicles 1–9: A New Translation with Introduction and Commentary*, AB 12 (New York: Doubleday, 2004), 101–17.

12 Karl Heinrich Graf, *Die Geschichtlichen Bücher des Alten Testaments: Zwei historisch-kritische Untersuchungen* (Leipzig: T. O. Weigel, 1866); Julius Wellhausen, *Die Composition des Hexateuchs und der historischen Bücher des Alten Testaments*, 4th ed. (Berlin: De Gruyter, 1963).

13 Richard Elliott Friedman, *Who Wrote the Bible?* (New York: Summit Books, 1987), 161–216.

14 Martin Noth, *Überlieferungsgeschichtliche Studien: Die sammelnden und bearbeitenden Geschichtswerke im Alten Testament*, 2nd ed. (Tübingen: Max Niemeyer, 1957), 1–110.

15 Serge Frolov, "Evil-Merodach and the Deuteronomist: The Sociohistorical Setting of Dtr in the Light of 2 Kgs 25,27–30," *Bib* 88 (2007): 174–90; idem, *Judges*, FOTL 6b (Grand Rapids: Eerdmans, 2013), 337–41.

century BCE.¹⁶ With the prophets, difficulties are even greater. Their implied setting is for the most part pre-exilic to early exilic (only Haggai and Zechariah are clearly said to have been active around 520 BCE, and there are no obvious chronological markers in Joel, Obadiah, and Malachi), but this does not mean that the *books* ascribed to them cannot be later, indeed, much later.¹⁷

Much worse, even if we could date the Enneateuch, prophetic literature, and Chronicles-Ezra-Nehemiah with any degree of certainty, that still would not do us much good without at least tentatively positioning the Psalter vis-à-vis these dates. Unfortunately, that is next to impossible because the content of psalms is for the most part timeless and thus provides precious few clues to their sociohistorical background. Psalm 137 is clearly post-exilic, in that it speaks about Babylonian exile (597–539 BCE) in the past tense, and a few others, in particular Psalms 122, 126, and 147, seem to reference the return from exile. Two psalms—74 and 79—respond to the destruction of Jerusalem, and especially the temple of Yhwh, in 586 BCE (see especially Pss 74:3–8; 79:1), and a few—e.g., Psalms 78 and 80—to the fall of the Northern Kingdom in 721 BCE. However, even in all these cases *termini ad quem* are not available. As far as language is concerned, several psalms—in particular, Psalms 18 (= 2 Samuel 22) and 68—as well as wholly or partially psalmodic pieces elsewhere, such as the Song of the Sea in Exod 15:1–18 and the song of Deborah in Judges 5 have been repeatedly touted as exemplars of Archaic (or Early) Biblical Hebrew (ABH/EBH).¹⁸ However, recent studies have raised serious questions about the possibility of dating texts based on their language as well as about the very existence of a distinctive ABH.¹⁹

---

16 Pre-exilic redactions: Frank Moore Cross, *The Institutio Oratoria of Quintilian* (Cambridge: Harvard University Press, 1973), 274–89; Richard D. Nelson, *The Double Redaction of the Deuteronomistic History*, JSOTSup 18 (Sheffield: JSOT, 1990); Iain W. Provan, *Hezekiah and the Books of Kings: A Contribution to the Debate about the Composition of the Deuteronomistic History*, BZAW 172 (Berlin: De Gruyter, 1988). Post-exilic provenance: Raymond F. Person, *The Deuteronomic School: History, Social Setting, and Literature*, SBLStBL 2 (Atlanta: Society of Biblical Literature, 2002).
17 To cite just one example, Edgar W. Conrad, *Reading Isaiah*, OBT (Minneapolis: Fortress, 1991), has argued that the entire Book of Isaiah—not just chapters 40–66—is of post-exilic origin, even though it features a prophet who supposedly lived in the eighth century.
18 See especially Paul Korchin, "Glimpsing Archaic Biblical Hebrew through Thetical Grammar," *HS* 58 (2017): 49–79. Cf. Frank Moore Cross and David Noel Freedman, *Studies in Ancient Yahwistic Poetry*, The Biblical Resource Series (Grand Rapids: Eerdmans; Livonia: Dove, 1975), 82–106; Tania Notarius, *The Verb in Archaic Biblical Hebrew Poetry: A Discursive, Typological, and Historical Investigation of the Tense System*, Studies in Semitic Languages and Linguistics 68 (Leiden: Brill, 2013).
19 E.g., Ian Young, Robert Rezetko, and Martin Ehrensvärd, *Linguistic Dating of Biblical Texts* (London: Equinox, 2008), esp. 1:312–40; Ian Young, "Starting at the Beginning with Archaic Biblical Hebrew," *HS* 58 (2017): 99–118.

All that notwithstanding, a set of entirely straightforward observations offers a simple way out of the impasse. Both the Enneateuch and prophetic books contain several texts that would be perfectly at home in the Psalter, including one that actually is there. Defining psalmody as second- or third-person poetic discourse that is predominantly or exclusively about God, these would include the Song of the Sea, the Song of Moses in Deut 32:1–43, Hannah's prayer in 1 Sam 2:1–10, David's "last words" in 2 Sam 23:1–7, and, most importantly, his song in 2 Sam 22:2–51 that doubles, with a few minor variations, as Psalm 18.[20] Significantly, their setting is not cultic.[21] The contrast is especially striking when it comes to David: he prays at the sanctuary in a non-psalmodic way, while both psalmodic discourses of his are not associated with the sanctuary in any way.

Prophetic books likewise contain several substantial psalmodic pieces. The most characteristic among them is, of course, the "prayer" in Habakkuk 3. It displays several formal elements that are typical for the Psalter but do not occur in the psalmodic texts of the Enneateuch, even in 2 Samuel 22 (= Psalm 18). These include: a superscription following the "genre + ל + implied author + על + term of uncertain meaning" template (v. 1); the interjection סלה (vv. 3, 9, 13); and the reference to somebody or something called מנצח (unusually placed at the end of the composition).[22] Also of note are Jonah's prayer in Jonah 2:3–10 and Hezekiah's prayer in Isa 38:10–20, which, like that of Habakkuk, begins with a superscription identifying the implied author, the genre (albeit one never mentioned in the Psalter—מכתב, "letter"), and, typically for the Psalter, the circumstances that generated the discourse. Thematically, these texts complement their Enneateuchal counter-

---

20 Deborah's song in Judges 5 displays psalmodic exordium (vv. 2–3) and doxological frame (vv. 4–5, 31a), as well as similar elements in the body of the discourse (vv. 9–13), but most of it does not fit with regard to content. Several scholars have recognized generic hybridity of this composition (Barry Webb, *The Book of Judges: An Integrated Reading*, JSOTSup 46 [Sheffield: Sheffield Academic Press, 1987], 139, has described it as "part ballad, part hymn"), usually explaining it in diachronic terms (e.g. Christoph Levin, "Das Alter des Deboralieds," in idem, *Fortschreibungen: Gesammelte Studien zum Alten Testament*, BZAW 316 [Berlin: De Gruyter, 2003], 124–41; Charles L. Echols, *"Tell Me, O Muse": The Song of Deborah [Judges 5] in the Light of Heroic Poetry*, LHB/OTS 487 [New York: T&T Clark, 2008]). For the same reason, I exclude Jacob's blessing in Gen 49:2–27; Moses's blessing in Deut 33:2–29 and Balaam's pronouncements in Num 23–24 do not fit in terms of both content and form (repeated quotation formulae).
21 Admittedly, Hannah prays after dedicating her son Samuel to the temple of Shiloh. However, the prayer is almost entirely unrelated to its immediate context (even the reference to the barren woman giving birth to seven in v. 5 does not quite match the background story), and its concluding words ("he [sc. Yhwh] will give strength to his king and raise the horn of his anointed one") are ill-suited to it but make perfect sense within the framework of the book as a whole.
22 Here, שגינות; cf. Ps 7:1. On this and related terms occurring in superscriptions of individual psalms, see below.

parts: while the latter are predominantly hymnic, combining praise and thanksgiving (with a massive admixture of historical retrospective in Deuteronomy 32), the former are heavy on complaint and supplication. Even more importantly, not one of the psalmodic discourses in the prophetic books is set at the temple or shrine of any kind, even though both Hezekiah and Jonah mention "the house of Yhwh" (Isa 38:20, see above; Jonah 2:8) and the latter also promises to make sacrifices (v. 10).

The sparse but persistent presence of psalmody in the corpora that display no to very little awareness of vocality in liturgy, even as a possibility, can be plausibly understood in only one way: psalms originated when there was no cultic setting for them, *ergo* they did not originate in such a setting.[23] In the next section of the essay, I will demonstrate that psalms proper suggest likewise.

3. Psalms in the Temple: Internal Evidence

The thesis of Gunkel, Mowinckel, and others that temple service was the *Sitz im Leben* of psalms presupposes that they were intended, at least in the beginning, for oral performance. However, both formal and conceptual elements and features commonly found in the Psalter militate against this presupposition.[24]

---

[23] I set aside the possibility that psalmodic texts may be later additions to narratives and prophecies. On generic grounds, going down this path would be a fine exemplar of *petitio principii*: a generically distinctive fragment can be legitimately excised from its place in the Bible as we know it only if it has already been established that the genre did not exist at the time when the larger composition came into being. As to linguistic evidence, it is usually seen as indicating that such texts are much older than their received context (especially when it comes to the Enneateuch—see, for example, Cross and Freedman, *Studies*, 1–81; Korchin, "Glimpsing Archaic Biblical Hebrew," on Genesis 49, Exodus 15, Numbers 23–24, Deuteronomy 32, 33, Judges 5, and 2 Samuel 22). That would, of course, further bolster my case but, as pointed out above (see nn. 18 and 19), recent studies have cast a pall of doubt over the assumption that biblical texts can be dated based on their language.

[24] In this section of the article, I will mostly reference the MT Psalter, noting only those differences between it and other ancient witnesses that may affect the arguments developed here. While overall there is no reason to privilege one text-form attested in the Second Temple period over others, the MT best serves my purposes because other witnesses are beset by uncertainties. In the case of the LXX, lack of confidence is inherent in its status as a translation. When there are divergences between Greek and Hebrew, is it due to different *Vorlagen*, conscious or unconscious alterations by the translator, or his mighty struggle with an unintelligible original? One well-known example is the Septuagint's consistent rendition of למנצח in the superscriptions of many psalms as εἰς τὸ τέλος. Is it evidence of לנצח in the *Vorlage*, a desperate attempt to make at least some sense of obscure Hebrew, or an eschatologically motivated substitution? While such ques-

3.1 Superscriptions

Most individual psalms – 116 out of 150 in the MT and almost all in the LXX—open with superscriptions that range in length from a word or two to a couple of lines. With regard to this feature, the scholarly community seems, almost Orwell-style, to hold two mutually exclusive convictions at the same time. On the one hand, most of the evidence cited in favor of the psalms' liturgical provenance comes from their superscriptions. On the other, "the headings of the psalms are broadly considered later additions, separate from the composition of the psalms themselves, and added at different times over the course of the psalms' transmission and translation"—in which case they tell nothing about the *Sitz im Leben* of the texts that they usher in.[25] Rather than discussing the relative merits of the two conflicting propositions (something that most publications neglect to do),[26] I will argue here that, given the content of the superscriptions, the assumption of their being integral to the psalms weakens, rather than bolsters, the case for the psalms' cultic setting.

A superscription could hardly be sung or chanted aloud together with the rest of the psalm, and it is difficult to conceive of any other way in which it could be

---

tions can be answered in a more or less satisfactory fashion with regard to some specific formulations, raising them here would take us too far afield. As to the Dead Sea Scrolls, those of them that contain psalms are much shorter than the MT or LXX Psalters; even by far the longest and best-preserved psalms manuscript from Qumran—11QPs[a] a.k.a. 11Q5—contains just 49 or 50 compositions, including 39 that also appear in the Masoretic Psalter. That is not nearly enough for a meaningful juxtaposition with canonical psalters, especially since the random circumstances of these manuscripts' preservation and discovery make it impossible to determine how representative they are. Are we dealing here with (pieces of) alternative psalters (thus, e.g., Peter W. Flint, *The Dead Sea Psalms Scrolls and the Book of Psalms*, STDJ 17 [Leiden: Brill, 1997], esp. 202–27; Eugene Ulrich, *The Dead Sea Scrolls and the Origins of the Bible*, Studies in the Dead Sea Scrolls and Related Literature 2 [Grand Rapids: Eerdmans, 1999], 115–17; Gerald Henry Wilson, *The Editing of the Hebrew Psalter*, SBLDS 76 [Chico: Scholars Press, 1985], 64–92) or with derivative collections, such as *florilegia* and liturgical compilations (thus, e.g., Menahem Haran, "11QPs[a] and the Canonical Book of Psalms," in *Minḥah le-Naḥum: Biblical and Other Studies Presented to Nahum M. Sarna in Honour of His 70th Birthday*, ed. Marc Brettler and Michael Fishbane, JSOTSup 154 [Sheffield: JSOT Press, 1993], 193–201; according to Timothy H. Lim, "Authoritative Scriptures and the Dead Sea Scrolls," in *The Oxford Handbook of the Dead Sea Scrolls*, ed. John J. Collins and Timothy H. Lim [Oxford: Oxford University Press, 2010], 311, "The question remains open"; similarly, Eva Jain and Annette Steudel, "Les manuscrits psalmiques de la mer Morte et la reception du psautier à Qumran," *RevScRel* 77 [2003]: 532–36).

25 Eva Mroczek, *The Literary Imagination in Jewish Antiquity* (Oxford: Oxford University Press, 2016), 58; similarly, Flint, *Dead Sea Psalms Scrolls*, 117.
26 Notably, Flint does not cite any authors supporting this supposed consensus and Mroczek refers to an obscure 1961 monograph.

preserved, transmitted, or exchanged orally. It could only exist in a written form, and since a superscription without a text to follow would be nonsensical, this means that, even if psalms originated as an oral component of the temple service, they must have been put into writing from the outset or at the very least while still in their original *Sitz im Leben*. Of course, a text's existence in a written form does not preclude its oral performance. Today, it is common for synagogues and churches to provide worshippers with prayer books or at least printouts of some sort to make it easier for them to follow the service and participate in it. However, in antiquity, when it took much longer and required much greater resources to put a text to writing—not to mention that such media as tablets or scrolls were much less wieldy than printed and bound volumes—it is highly unlikely that nearly enough copies could be produced for the lay people who participated in the temple ceremonies. It is much more probable that no more than one or two existed at any given time, with even the professional singers repeatedly mentioned in Chronicles-Ezra-Nehemiah having severely limited access to the written text.

This conclusion may seem eminently compatible with an element that is present in the superscriptions of fifty-five psalms (36.7% of the total according to the Masoretic canon and 47.4% of those with superscriptions), as well as, uniquely, in the postscript of Habakkuk's prayer (Hab 3:19). This element is the word מנצח. With the meaning "to oversee, to supervise" reliably established for the verbal root נצח in general (Ezra 3:8–9; 1 Chr 23:4) and the verbal noun מנצח in particular (2 Chr 2:1, 17; 34:12, 13), English Bibles routinely translate the latter in Psalms along the lines of "choirmaster" or "leader."[27] Could the written copies of the psalms be intended for a single person (or perhaps a select group) directing the performance, as reference materials (sheet music of sorts) where lyrics are supplemented by stage or musical directions?

That is possible, but what are we to do with the large majority of psalms—ninety-five out of one hundred and fifty—whose superscriptions do not read למנצח? If they were not intended for the "leader," we are back to square one with regard to the purpose of writing them down. Even if the actual total of performers never came close to the round two hundred and eighty-eight (24x12), number that David set according to 1 Chr 25:7, it is still doubtful there could be enough copies around to be of any use for the group as a whole. And if all the psalms were written down for the use by the מנצח, why make this explicit in only some of them? Indeed, why mention it at all?

---

27 E.g., KJV, NKJV, RSV, CEV, and JPS. Note, however, the grave doubts expressed by Hans-Joachim Kraus, *Psalms 1–59: A Commentary*, trans. Hilton C. Oswald (Minneapolis: Augsburg, 1988), 29–30.

Another major problem is that it is not clear how the superscriptions could facilitate the performance. Moreover, at least two elements routinely found in them could hardly function in this way. One of them, by far the most common one, is a personal name with the preposition ל, which suggests the implied author or perhaps the dedicatee. Seventy-four compositions (almost half of the Psalter) are associated in this way with David, twelve with Asaph, eleven with the sons of Korah (one of them, Psalm 88, also with Heman the Ezrahite), two with Solomon, and one each with Ethan the Ezrahite and Moses—for the grand total of a hundred and one (more than two-thirds of the book by count). To a *reader*, these notations offer intriguing interpretive possibilities by relating the psalms to the Enneateuchal narratives and/or the underlying traditions (in the cases of David, Solomon, Moses, and Ethan—on the latter, see 1 Kgs 5:11) or building the ancient equivalent of hyperlinks between them (in the cases of Asaph, the sons of Korah, and perhaps David as well). Antiquarian interest, often posited by diachronically minded modern scholars, is also a possibility: a name could help trace the psalm's origin to a specific collection.[28] But what would a *performer* do with that particular piece of information?

An additional element of this kind is a reference to a specific event of the past, always associated with King David and for the most part recounted in the book of Samuel. Thus Ps 3:1: "David's מזמור, when he was on the run from his son Absalom" (cf. 2 Sam 15–17). Likewise, in Ps 57:1: "David's מכתם, when he escaped from Saul in a cave" (cf. 1 Sam 22:1). Comments of this type can be instrumental in shaping the audience's perception of the text that follows. Even the minor variations in the way the psalms report these events may be thought-provoking. Thus, when Ps 34:1 calls the Philistine king Abimelech rather than Achish (cf. 1 Samuel 27–29), it may remind us about David setting up the priest Achimelech right before defecting to Philistia, about the Philistine king Abimelech in Genesis 20, 26, or about Gideon's son Abimelech who becomes a king in Judges 9. But what would a performer care that Ps 60:1b–2 differs from both 2 Samuel 8 and 1 Chronicles 18 as to which king David fought alongside that of Zobah and who exactly defeated the Edomites?

The contrast between the oral and written settings of some psalms is thrown into particularly sharp relief by the unique opening line of Psalm 102: "Prayer of an afflicted one, when he is exhausted and pours out his complaint before Yhwh." The line seems to suggest an individual lament, and it indeed sounds like one initially (vv. 2–12), but the speaker's actual plea is for the restoration of Zion

---

28 See, e.g., Peter C. Craigie, *Psalms 1–50*, WBC 19 (Waco: Word, 1983), 28–29; James Luther Mays, *Psalms*, IBC (Louisville: John Knox, 1994), 12–14.

(vv. 13–18). The superscription thus invites the reader to reflect on the complex interplay between the destinies of a single person and those of the community as well as to consider the possibility that other individual laments in the Psalter (especially those associated with David) may in fact be those of personified Israel (or a king standing for it). Yet, in an oral setting, such as temple service, these layers of meaning would be lost for the audience and useless for the performers.

Two elements common in the superscriptions of the psalms may look more like the equivalents of *allegro ma non troppo* and *andante cantabile* in modern musical scores because both appear in very short nominal clauses (usually between one and three words). One of them is represented by nouns in the nominative case, with the personal names discussed above often serving as qualifiers. The second includes mostly what looks like nouns or strings of nouns preceded by אל, על, -ב, or -ל, but the apparently vetitive אל־תשחת can be included as well. In modern scholarship, the former element is often construed as dealing with the type of performance and the second as designating the instruments or the manner of playing them and/or singing.²⁹ Both construals are questionable at the very least.

With regard to the first group, the problem is insufficient variation and lack of consistency. Out of ninety-nine psalms that contain this element, in fifty-seven (58%) it is represented by the word מזמור. Even worse, the next most common term from the same group, שיר (thirty-two occurrences), is its synonym (both mean "song" or "tune"). In essence, we deal here with lexical distinction without real difference; for all practical purposes, precisely half of the psalms overall and more than three-quarters of those marked this way are blandly described as "songs" or "tunes"—or, in fourteen cases, "tune songs" or "song tunes" (מזמור שיר or שיר מזמור). Such a description would not only be of no use to performers but also could confuse them by implying that the rest of the psalms somehow do not qualify as "songs" or "tunes."

The next most common term in the same group, משכיל (thirteen occurrences), is derived from the root שכל whose semantic field covers the notions of learning, smartness, and prudence (as an adjective, משכיל means "discerning, enlightened"—see, above all, Pss 14:2; 41:2; 53:3). It would appear then that it describes the speaker's intent—much like the terms תהלה, "praise," in Ps 145:1, תפלה, "prayer," in Pss 17:1; 86:1; 90:1; 102:1, as well as perhaps עדות, "testimony," in 60:1; 80:1, and in line with the remarks ללמד, "to teach" (Ps 60:1), and להזכיר, "to

---

29 E.g., Artur Weiser, *The Psalms: A Commentary*, OTL (Philadelphia: Westminster, 1962), 22; Kraus, *Psalms 1–59*, 26–32; Nancy DeClaissé-Walford, Rolf A. Jacobson, and Beth Laneel Tanner, *The Book of Psalms*, NICOT (Grand Rapids: Eerdmans, 2014), 12–13.

remind" (Ps 70:1)—rather than providing stage directions of any kind.³⁰ The meaning of מכתם, occurring six times, and שגיון of Ps 7:1, unique in the Psalter but also apparently occurring as שגינות in the superscription of Habakkuk's prayer (Hab 3:1), is more difficult to ascertain. However, the former may have to do with the noun כתם, "choice gold," or the verb נכתם, apparently meaning "to be dirty" in Jer 2:22, and the latter with the root שגה, "to err"—all having nothing to do with music but possibly related to the psalms' content.

With the second group (mostly nouns with prepositions), the issues are an even greater lack of consistency combined with an excessive variation and a sheer unintelligibility. First, this element is present in just thirty-one psalms (20% of the total), raising the question why the notation was needed at all if the performers could do just fine without it in the vast majority of the cases. Second, these thirty-one superscriptions contain among them up to thirteen distinctive terms, with only one of them—נגינה—appearing seven times and nine occurring just once or twice. If there were at least thirteen different ways to perform psalms, we could reasonably expect this aspect to be specified in much more than just a handful of them. Just like with the comments of the מזמור type, this places a question mark over the supposition that what we deal with here is musical notation of any kind.

In this respect, it may be worth its while to consider the semantics of the terms that constitute the group in question.

נגינה–"instrumental music" (mostly in pl.)
יום שבת–"Sabbath day"
שושן/ששנים/שושנים–"lily/lilies"
ששנים עדות/שושן עדות (?)–"lily/lilies of testimony"³¹
מחלת–possibly, "illness"³²
אילת השחר–"deer of the dawn"
מות–"death"³³
יונת אלם רחקים–"dove of silence of the distant ones"

---

30 Since both occurrences of עדות in the superscriptions of psalms follow שושן or ששנים it is possible that we deal here with construct state—"lily/lilies of testimony"—as distinct from plain "lilies" in Pss 45:1; 69:1. In such case, the whole construction belongs to the group of terms with prepositions.
31 See n. 30 above.
32 The lexeme מחלה, "sickness," is attested in Exod 15:26; 23:25; 1 Kgs 8:37; Prov 18:14; 2 Chr 6:28; 21:15, but in such case the word would be in construct state with no suitable *nomen rectum* in sight. A more remote possibility is that this is the proper name מחלה mentioned in Gen 28:9; 2 Chr 11:18.
33 On the relationship between על־עלמות in Ps 46:1 and על־מות in Ps 9:1; 48:15, see below.

אל־תשחת–"do not slaughter"
שמינית–"eighth, of eight" (fem.)
גתית–"of Gath, of a winepress" (fem.)
נחילות–unknown
ידותון–unknown

With a single exception to be discussed below, none of these seems to have anything to do with music, singing, or, for that matter, performance of any kind.[34] In particular, not a single one is identifiable, even tentatively, as a musical instrument; actually—and this is a highly instructive fact—while the Hebrew Bible, including the Psalter, knows about a dozen of such instruments (see, for example, the lists of four in 1 Sam 10:5 and five in 2 Sam 6:5), superscriptions of the psalms never mention them. Conversely, only two of the terms listed here, עלמות and שמינית, appear outside the Psalter, both in 1 Chronicles 15 (vv. 20 and 21 respectively). Both occurrences demonstrate beyond reasonable doubt that to the Chronicler these were not musical instruments. When referring to the musicians playing the highly familiar harps and lyres, both verses use the preposition ־ב, which is standard for such occasions (e. g., Judg 11:34; 2 Sam 6:5; 2 Chr 15:14). By contrast, both עלמות and שמינית are introduced—as they are in the Psalter—by ־על, suggesting something of a different kind; indeed, if these were instruments, why would the former be associated with harps and the former with lyres?

On top of all that, it is highly probable that עלמות, appearing only in Ps 46:1, is a product of dittography, with the preposition preceding the *makkeph* in על־מות inadvertently repeated after it.[35] This, among other things, may be another indication that, as argued in the previous section, psalms predate Chronicles-Ezra-Nehemiah. It would appear that the Chronicler was familiar with technical minutiae of the Psalter and considered it sufficiently authoritative to believe that sprinkling these minutiae upon the account of David's reign might be helpful as far as verisimilitude is concerned; but his understanding of these minutiae left much to be desired. A similar pattern may be operative in the transmogrification

---

34 Richard J. Clifford, "Psalms of the Temple," in *The Oxford Handbook of the Psalms*, ed. William P. Brown (Oxford: Oxford University Press, 2014): 326–37 (331), states, "Psalm superscriptions contain tantalizing allusions to liturgy ... but it is impossible to draw solid conclusions from them." If there is no way to be sure, how do we know the superscriptions are about music at all?

35 It is possible, of course, that על־עלמות is the correct sequence that suffered haplography. However, since על־מות appears twice in the Psalter (9:1; 48:15) and על־עלמות only once, this appears much less likely. An even stronger consideration is that while על־מות at least marginally fits the context in Ps 9:1 (see below) and Ps 48:15 ("he will direct us unto death"; LXX 47:15 εἰς τοὺς αἰῶνας). Replacing it with על־עלמות would render both sequences nonsensical.

of ידותון into a personal name. In the superscriptions of the psalms, all obvious anthroponyms (Moses, David, Solomon, and Ethan the Ezrahite) are introduced by the preposition -ל; in the case of ידותון, it is employed only in Ps 39:1 while in the other two cases (Pss 62:1; 77:1), the preposition is על, which makes it likely that the lexeme belongs to the group of terms discussed here. Yet, in Chronicles-Ezra-Nehemiah, Jedutun becomes a lyre player and heads a clan of Levitical musicians (e. g., 1 Chr 25:3, 6; 2 Chr 5:12; Neh 11:17).

Many modern English Bibles tacitly speculate that the terms under discussion denote tunes; thus, NRSV translates על־ששנים in Ps 45:1 as "according to Lilies." However, if that were true, psalms with identical designations in the headings would be metrically identical or at least similar. This is not the case, as can be shown, for example, by comparing the prosodies of Psalms 8 and 81, both of which are marked with על־הגתית in the superscriptions:[36]

Ps 8:2: הוה אֲדֹנֵינוּ מָה־אַדִּיר שִׁמְךָ בְּכָל־הָאָרֶץ אֲשֶׁר תְּנָה הוֹדְךָ עַל־הַשָּׁמָיִם
--/--/---/-/-/--/--/-/---/-
Ps 81:2: הַרְנִינוּ לֵאלֹהִים עוּזֵּנוּ הָרִיעוּ לֵאלֹהֵי יַעֲקֹב
-/---/-/--/---/--/

Neither does the Chronicler seem to regard שמינית and עלמות as tunes or musical styles. In 1 Chr 15:20–21, they are prescribed to different groups of Levites. Reserving each melody for a different team of singers does not seem to make much sense.

Even נגינה, the only term in this group clearly associated with a performance of any kind, is the kind of exception that confirms the rule. If psalms were indeed sung in the temple, it is highly unlikely that it was done with instrumental accompaniment in less than 5% of the cases. On the contrary, in Chronicles-Ezra-Nehemiah instrumental music seems more prominent in the liturgical setting than singing: "And David told the princes of the Levites to place their brethren, the singers, who *play musical instruments, harps, lyres, and cymbals*, to raise the voice of joy" (1 Chr 15:16); "All these under the direction of their father were engaged in *singing* in the house of Yhwh *on cymbals, harps, and lyres* ..." (1 Chr 25:6); "And they placed the priests in their garments, *with trumpets*, and the Levites, the children of Asaph, *with cymbals*, to praise Yhwh ... And they *sang* in praise and thanksgiving to Yhwh, for he is good, for his faithfulness to Israel is forever ..." (Ezra 3:10–11).

At the same time, at least three of the terms listed above are interpretable as summarizing the content of the psalms rather than prescribing how to perform

---

36 The diagrams below run left to right.

them. It would make sense for certain psalms to be described as "concerning death" (and more specifically, "concerning the death of a son" or "concerning the death of Laban/Laben," depending on how לבן in Ps 9:1 is read; the LXX reads "concerning the secrets of the son"), for others to be associated with illness, and for yet others to petition the deity to refrain from destruction. Granted, these headings are not always borne out by the texts that come under them: thus, while one of the psalms introduced by אל־תשחת is indeed dominated by pleas for help (Psalm 57), three others are much heavier on the impending devastation of the unworthy (Psalms 58, 59, and 75). And, of course, it is anybody's guess what on God's green Earth are "lilies of testimony," "dove of silence of the distant ones," or "deer of the dawn." Nor do we have the slightest idea—or have much hope of ever figuring out—who מנצח is, why the labels שיר and מזמור are attached, in different combinations, to most psalms but not all of them, and why the seemingly meaningless refrain סלה appears in some psalms but not in others. That, however, does not in and of itself bring the liturgical *Sitz im Leben* in through the back door. If the superscriptions in the Psalter were meant for a *reader*, lack of consistency, variation without differentiation (for aesthetic—dare we say poetic—purposes?), and vagueness to the point of unintelligibility (to stir emotion by generating a sense of mystery and awe?) are of no account. No one finds it confusing that Tchaikovsky's *Romeo and Juliet* is sometimes called a "symphonic poem" and sometimes a "fantasy overture" (the composer preferred the latter). But while playing *Romeo and Juliet* by memory may not be the best idea, it would still beat using scores where woodwind parts are not harmonized with the strings. By the same token, a *performer* would be better off having no directions whatsoever than trying to follow what we have in Psalms.

In the overall context of the Psalter, even what looks like an unmistakable direction for the performers—ליום שבת in 92:1—is in fact highly confusing as such. Does it mean that out of the dozens of psalms only this one can, or should, be sung on the seventh day of the week? Are any designated for other specific days, or even for business days in general?[37] Why are no psalms earmarked for annual festivals with their distinctive temple rituals? Given these uncertainties, it appears likely that just like the remarks discussed above, ליום שבת has to do with the psalm's content ("concerning the Sabbath day" rather than "for the Sabbath day") and therefore is intended for a reader.

---

37 Rendsburg, "Psalms," 109–10, stresses that the Septuagint also identifies psalms for the first, second, fourth, and sixth days. However, with two days still missing and the psalms in question not consecutive in any manuscript tradition (Psalm 24 for day 1, Psalm 93 for day 6, Psalm 94 for day 5, etc.), it appears clear that these designations (supported in part by m. Tamid 7:5) are of an interpretive nature.

3.2 Psalms Proper

The very concept of religious service presupposes directionality: actions, such as sacrifices or prayers, are messages sent, individually or collectively, by the worshippers with "Attention: God" (or "gods") on the envelope. With this elementary but often overlooked point in mind, it is difficult to place many, perhaps most, of the psalms in the milieu of ancient Israelite liturgy. As acknowledged by Adele Berlin and Marc Zvi Brettler, "several [psalms] do not address God at all, and can only with great difficulty be classified as prayers."[38] Instead, time and again the Psalter sounds like a sermon:

> Come, children, listen to me:
> I will teach you to fear Yhwh.
> Who is the man that desires life,
> Loves seeing the good for days on end?
> Keep your tongues from evil,
> And your lips from speaking lies.
> Turn away from evil and do good;
> Seek peace and pursue it.

This is Ps 34:12–14; but it might just as well be Proverbs—or, for that matter, one of the Latter Prophets.[39] Similarly Ps 37:1–3:

> Do not compete with evildoers,
> Do not be jealous about those engaged in injustice,
> For like foliage will they quickly wilt,
> And like green grass will they wither.
> Rely on Yhwh and do good;
> Live in the land and keep faith.

The vector of such discourses clearly points from one human to another, for example, from a catechist to a catechumen. Such may even be the case when the deity is technically the addressee (Ps 15:1–2):

> O Yhwh, who will live in your tents,
> Who will reside on the mountain of your holiness?
> Those who walk in innocence, and work for justice,
> And speak truth in their hearts!

---

[38] Adele Berlin and Marc Zvi Brettler, "Psalms," in *The Jewish Study Bible*, ed. Adele Berlin and Marc Zvi Brettler (Oxford: Oxford University Press, 2004), 1283.
[39] In fact, Ps 111:10aα ("The beginning of wisdom is the fear of Yhwh") is very similar to Prov 1:7a.

That, in turn, raises the possibility that even when the speaker of the psalms complains, calls for help, gives thanks, or praises the deity rather than explicitly offering instruction, it is done for educational rather than properly liturgical purposes. Perhaps nothing demonstrates this better than Psalm 119 where an extraordinarily verbose address to Yhwh rests upon the foundation of impersonal maxims (vv. 1–7):

> Happy are those whose way is pure,
> Who walk according to Yhwh's instruction.
> Happy are those who keep his testimonies,
> Who wholeheartedly seek him
> And do not commit iniquity
> But walk down his path.
> You have commanded that your orders be strictly kept;
> My plea is that my path be established towards keeping your laws—
> Then I will not be ashamed when regarding your commandments.
> I will thank you from the bottom of my heart when studying the judgments
> of your righteousness, etc.

Pivotal in this respect is the home key of sorts set by the book's opening compositions, Psalms 1 and 2, both of which are addressed to fellow humans, not to Yhwh. Working in tandem, they launch arguably the most pervasive theme of the entire book: the juxtaposition of the wicked (Psalm 1)/the nations (Psalm 2) and the righteous (Psalm 1)/Israel (Psalm 2). This dichotomy can be traced, sometimes strongly and sometimes in trace amounts, in more than two-thirds of individual psalms by count (3–7, 9–12, 14–22, 24–28, 31–37, 39, 40, 42–50, 52–56, 58–60, 62, 64, 66, 68, 69, 71, 73–77, 79, 81– 84, 89–92, 94, 96, 97, 101, 102, 104–110, 112, 115, 118–120, 123, 125, 128, 129, 135–137, 139–141, 144–147, and 149). When the Psalter begs the deity for help or expresses confidence in its support, it is usually against evildoers and/or the Gentiles, who are explicitly or implicitly described as the enemies not only of the speaker but also of Yhwh. When the deity is praised, it is usually for keeping the same malefactors in check. Unsurprisingly, the only major variation on the theme is the recognition that Israel can also break bad— and that they have already paid dearly for that (e.g., Psalms 106 and 107). Of course, any liturgical text is to a certain degree aimed at the worshippers rather than the deity, and it would not be unusual to find in liturgy a degree of faith affirmation, including in contradistinction to other religions (the opening lines of the traditional Jewish hymn *Aleinu* being one example). However, the sheer volume and pervasiveness of the didactic streak in the Psalter makes one wonder whether it was generally intended for an equivalent of a Sunday service or Sunday school.

Tellingly, didactics in the Psalter regularly cross over into the polemical territory. In several cases, the speaker quotes his opponents as saying, "Where is their God?" (Ps 115:2), "There is no God" (Pss 10:4; 14:1), or "There is no salvation for him in God" (Ps 3:3). Such quotations may be a very efficient didactic tool, but in a cultic setting they would border on blasphemy, regardless of the refutation and scorn that follow.

A much greater blasphemy may lurk in the Psalter repeatedly quoting the deity. To be sure, other parts of the Hebrew Bible do that time and again, but there is a major difference between citing Yhwh's words in writing and giving them voice. There is no indication of the biblical narrators being speakers rather than writers, and although the prophets are presented as the former, they liberally use introductory formulae to make sure the audience understands that they are quoting Yhwh rather than speaking for him.[40] In the Psalter, the divine voice cuts in on several occasion without any introduction (e.g., Pss 46:11; 50:5, 7–15, 16–23; 75:3–5, 11; 81:7–15; 82:1–7; 89:4–5; 91:14–16; 95:8–11; 132:14–18). Those singing these lines would be essentially playing Yhwh's part; it is hard to imagine anyone agreeing to do that among those who believed that the very name of the deity is to be handled with extreme care (Exod 20:7; Deut 5:11)—to say nothing of the objects and spaces associated with Yhwh (e.g., Exod 28:34–35; 2 Sam 6:6–7).

Similarly, the Levitical singers mentioned in Chronicles-Ezra-Nehemiah would probably be less than enthusiastic about the psalms playing down the importance of sacrifice (e.g., Pss 40:7; 50:8–13; 51:18–19). Analogous pronouncements can also be found elsewhere in the Hebrew Bible (e.g., Isa 1:11–12; Amos 5:21–22; Prov 21:3), and they are best understood not as rejecting sacrifice altogether but rather as arguing that offerings, no matter how rich, do not compensate for unethical behavior.[41] Still, with sacrifice being the temple's *raison d'être* —and the main source of livelihood for its personnel—it would be the least appropriate place for musings on the subject. Indeed, it would be discouraging, if not outright offensive, to the worshippers who brought the offering—more likely than not at substantial personal expense—for the Levites to sing during the act that the deity does not really need or want it.

Finally, it is important to mention that at least seven psalms—25, 34, 37, 111, 112, 119, and 145—are acrostics. Even a highly educated person cannot be reasonably expected to discern an alphabetic arrangement aurally, and especially to appreciate the extremely sophisticated techniques of Psalms 34 and 119.[42] For the

---

40 On such formulae, see in particular Samuel A. Meier, *Speaking of Speaking: Marking Direct Discourse in the Hebrew Bible*, VTSup 46 (Leiden: Brill, 1992).
41 See, for example, Marvin Sweeney, *Isaiah 1–39 with an Introduction to Prophetic Literature*, FOTL 16 (Grand Rapids: Eerdmans, 1996), 80–81 on Isa 1:11–12.
42 Victor Avigdor Hurowitz, "Additional Elements of Alphabetical Thinking in Psalm XXXIV," *VT* 52 (2002): 326–33, finds in Psalm 34 a highly intricate web of six interwoven alphabetizing sequences.

vast illiterate and semi-literate majority of the ancient Israelite population, it was a patent impossibility. The compositions in question were designed for reading, not for a performance.

In sum, there is not a single unambiguous indication of a liturgical setting in either the psalms proper or their superscriptions. At the same time, multiple elements and aspects are poorly compatible with such a setting. Temple service should, accordingly, be discounted as the Psalter's *Sitz im Leben*—which, again, does not preclude secondary adoption, and adaptation, of some psalms, in whole or in part, for this service.[43] Given the generic uniqueness of the psalms, that leaves us with only one option—that they were composed for their present literary setting (broadly conceived), in other words, that their *Sitz in der Literatur* is their *Sitz im Leben*.[44]

4. Psalms in the Bible

In all canons, the Tanak/Old Testament is opened—and, in terms of length, dominated—by the long narrative sequence that begins with creation of the world in Genesis 1 and ends with King Jehoiachin's release from prison in 2 Kings 25. It traces the history of the relationship between the deity known as Yhwh and humankind, almost exclusively focusing (from Genesis 12 onward) on the people of Israel, starting with its ancestors. The central point of the retrospective is that in order to prosper, and especially to have a land of its own, Israel needs to stick to its covenant with Yhwh by observing the deity's commandments. The binary choice between observance as a source of blessing and non-observance as a source of curse is operative in the very composition of the Enneateuch. The sections where almost all commandments are concentrated—Exodus 20 through Deuteronomy—occupy the structural center of the corpus. The preceding narrative builds towards the promulgation of commandments and everything that follows demonstrates the positive consequences of Israel following them (Josh 1:1–

---

43 It is within the realm of the possible that some of the psalms—those of purely doxological or thanksgiving nature, not arranged as acrostics, never quoting the deity or disparaging sacrifice, etc.—were indeed created for liturgical purposes. However, not a single psalm definitely hails from this setting.

44 Erhard S. Gerstenberger, "Non-Temple Psalms: The Cultic Setting Revisited," in *The Oxford Handbook of the Psalms*, 338–49, links psalms to the synagogue rather than the temple. The obvious problem with this *Sitz im Leben* is that synagogues are not attested archeologically or in written sources until the third century BCE. Consequently, they most likely postdate not only the Enneateuch and the Latter Prophets with their psalmodic pieces, but also Chronicles and therefore the introduction of psalms into temple service.

Judg 1:26) and the dire outcome of its failing to do so, up to and including the loss of the land (Judg 1:27–2 Kgs 25:30).[45]

The Enneateuchal narrator is entirely anonymous and therefore cannot be identified with either Yhwh or Israel; the corpus thus presents itself as a voice of an impartial third party.[46] For the most part, both paraenetic and condemnatory discourses are put in the mouths of characters, such as Yhwh, Moses, Joshua, or Samuel. Only in Kings does the mask of evenhandedness slip, with the narrator predictably revealing himself as the deity's partisan (especially 2 Kgs 17:7–23). However, Yhwh's own take on what is reported in the Enneateuch is limited to the Latter Prophets.

Rounding off the debate is Israel's response, found only in the Writings section of the Masoretic canon.[47] It can be heard in the furious complaints of Job and more subdued—and despondent—moans of Lamentations. It can be heard in the skepticism of Ecclesiastes and the Song of Songs' rejoinder to the prophetic metaphor of Israel as a cheating wife.[48] But this voice would be much less resounding without the Psalter, with its sheer heft (almost 20,000 words according to the traditional Jewish count—close to a quarter of Writings and the third longest book of the Hebrew Bible), rich generic variety, and broad range of thought and emotion.

On its face, the Psalter is one of the least contrarian books in Writings. Unlike Job, it does not directly challenge the deity or show it acting in an unheard-of and potentially scandalous manner. Unlike Ecclesiastes, the book does not start by rejecting the most basic premises behind the rest of the Hebrew Bible (1:2–18). Unlike the Song of Songs, it does not have the potential of placing the story of the relationship between Yhwh and Israel told by the Enneateuch and metaphorized in conjugal terms by the prophets on its head by telling the woman's side of a rocky romance. Unlike the Book of Ruth, it does not seek to demonstrate that ignoring Enneateuchal commandments, even as basic as prohibition of mixed marriages, may sometimes be a good idea. Unlike the Book of Esther, it does not suggest that Israel may be able to survive without divine help. Neither do the psalms present alternatives to other corpora along the lines of the Chronicler's rewriting of the Enneateuchal story or Proverbs' advertisement of (God-fearing) wisdom as a substitute for, or at least supplement to, the Torah of Moses.

---

45 See Serge Frolov, "Structure, Genre, and Rhetoric of the Enneateuch," *Vestnik SPbSU. Philosophy and Conflict Studies* 33 (2017): 354–63.

46 I am indebted to Kelsey Spinnato for this incisive observation.

47 In Christian Old Testaments, God has the final word, which makes sense given the centrality of spontaneous divine action in the New Testament.

48 See Frolov, "The Comeback of Comebacks: David, Bathsheba, and the Prophets in the Song of Songs," in *On Prophets, Warriors, and Kings: Former Prophets through the Eyes of Their Interpreters*, ed. George J. Brooke and Ariel Feldman, BZAW 470 (Berlin: De Gruyter, 2016): 41–64.

Psalmists share the conventional description, going back to Genesis 1, of Yhwh as the creator god who brought order to chaos. As pointed out above, their entire didactics builds upon the conventional premise of Leviticus 26 and Deuteronomy 28 that the righteous should prosper and the wicked should suffer, with observance of the Enneateuchal commandments making all the difference between the two groups. They do not deny the conventional wisdom, conveyed by the Enneateuch and affirmed by prophets, that Israel enjoys a special relationship with Yhwh, from which the people have benefited in the past, suffering only on account of their transgressions, and still benefit in the present. And they enthusiastically agree that all this makes Yhwh worthy of effusive and boisterous praise.

The Psalter is thus making a herculean rhetorical effort to affirm the theological premises that underlie the preceding biblical corpora. But while doing so it also implicitly but persistently acknowledges that in many, perhaps most, cases these premises run in the face of the empirical reality.

Within the framework set by the Enneateuch and upheld by the prophets, it may seem entirely normal for an individual who perceives himself as righteous to request help from Yhwh, especially against the evildoers who are the deity's enemies as well. Yet, by voicing such a request the Psalter presupposes a situation in which wicked infidels have the upper hand over Yhwh's faithful. Indeed, with close to a half of psalms containing at least a hint of such a situation and many dominated by it the book creates the impression—without saying it in so many words—that it is common for things not to be the way they should according to Leviticus 26 and Deuteronomy 28.[49] Moreover, the discrepancy between the theological constructs and the empirical reality is repeatedly described as chronic (note especially the famous "how long?!" in Pss 6:4; 13:2–3; 62:4; 74:10; 80:5; 82:2; 90:13; 94:3)—so chronic, in fact, that it even permits the opponents of the speaker and Yhwh to question and mock the former's faith in the latter (e.g., Pss 3:3; 10:4; 14:1; 115:2). Worst of all, the speaker's fidelity to the deity may be the very source of his suffering (Pss 44:23; 69:8–13).

The Psalter's responses to the discrepancy also fall within conventional parameters: the speaker acknowledges that what he gets may be just desserts, because he is not sufficiently observant (e.g., Pss 7:4–6; 19:13–14; 25:7; 32:5; 38:19; and the entire Psalms 51, 78, and 79), expresses confidence that Yhwh's help is eventually forthcoming (most of the "lament" psalms), and even seems to suggest that the

---

49 DeClaissé-Walford, Jacobson, and Tanner, *Psalms*, 27, count sixty-six psalms of lament in the MT Psalter, and Sweeney, *Reading the Bible after the Shoah: Engaging Holocaust Theology* (Minneapolis: Fortress, 2008), 172–73, counts sixty-two. However, if passing complaints are included the total will exceed seventy. In any case, this thematic grouping is by far the largest in the Psalter.

deity should be praised no matter what (e.g., Psalms 9, 13, 16, 26, 57, and especially 66). But that is of no consequence, especially since even the boldest challenges to the facile righteous-wicked, blessing-curse dichotomies of the Enneateuch and the prophets also ultimately slide into this track: Job grovels when the deity dazzles him with an inventory of its supreme powers (42:2–6), Ecclesiastes acknowledges that there will be judgment (11:9) and calls upon the reader to "remember the Creator" (12:1), and the woman in the Song of Songs never removes her affections from the man. What matters is that the Psalter shows how such challenges grow out of their very object—the idea of a single deity, omnipotent and benevolent, that punishes vice and rewards virtue.

The Psalter thus sits very snugly in its literary environments, including those of Writings and of the Hebrew Bible canon in general. Firmly rooted in the conventions of the Enneateuch and the Latter Prophets, it also provides a springboard for the audacious nonconformity of Job, Ecclesiastes, and the Song of Songs. In sum, it functions as a theological nexus of sorts between Writings and the rest of the canon.

This is not to say that the Psalter as we know it came into being as an integral composition designed from the outset to be read *in toto* alongside the Enneateuch and the prophets on the one hand and the balance of Writings on the other. It is quite possible that individual psalms were created one by one or in small batches (perhaps represented by some Dead Sea manuscripts) and were only eventually brought together in larger collections that ultimately found their way into various canons. At the very least, there is ample evidence that the order of the psalms and especially the distribution of the text between individual psalms remained fluid not only in antiquity but also throughout the Middle Ages and even into the early modern period.[50] What I do claim, however, is that the psalms emerged as a part of an ongoing conversation on theodicy initiated by the Enneateuch and the prophets, taking a new turn in such books as Job, Ecclesiastes, and the Songs of Songs, and ultimately leading to the attempts of Daniel, intertestamental literature, some Qumran texts, the New Testament, and subsequent Jewish, Christian, and Muslim theological oeuvre to resolve the issue by shifting the final reckoning beyond normal human experience. This conversation was particularly relevant for the post-exilic Israelite/Jewish community that had to grapple with both the catastrophe of the exile in its recent past and the fact that despite trying hard to be observant, it remained economically weak and politically dependent while polytheistic empires flourished.

---

50 As convincingly demonstrated by William Yarchin, "Were the Psalms Collections at Qumran True Psalters?" *JBL* 134 (2015): 775–89.

5. Conclusion

The investigation undertaken in the present article demonstrates that form criticism—and Hebrew Bible scholarship overall—stands to benefit from abandoning the quest for the *Sitz im Leben* of the biblical texts and focusing instead on their *Sitz in der Literatur*. In the case of the Psalter, the former path leads nowhere while the latter produces meaningful results.

First, Gunkel's assumption that literary forms always emerge elsewhere before finding their way into the Bible turns out to be incorrect. This has important ramifications in terms of *Religionsgeschichte*. Rather than being a record of the temple liturgy, the Psalter presents itself as its launching pad. When musical performance was introduced into worship sometime after the exile, most likely during the Persian period, some of the pre-existing psalms (judging by the few quotations in Chronicles-Ezra-Nehemiah and subsequent literature as well as by Jewish and Christian liturgies, mostly if not exclusively of doxological and thanksgiving kind) came in handy as lyrics, in full or in excerpts.[51] Life imitates art, not the other way round.

Second, in terms of *Sitz in der Literatur* rather than *Sitz im Leben*, the Psalter becomes a window not on the verbal aspect of the temple liturgy but rather on the struggle with the problem of theodicy that the ancient Israelite/Jewish community had to endure. This greatly increases exegetical gain. How exactly Yhwh was worshipped more than two millennia ago is today a matter of antiquarian interest at best. Theodicy, by contrast, remains acutely, even painfully relevant for monotheistic communities, especially after the Holocaust and other genocides of the twentieth and twenty-first centuries, and it is not likely to go away any time soon.

Finally, it appears that, when applied to rather large literary units, such as corpora, form criticism necessarily incorporates a canonical dimension. Since in its Knierim-Sweeney formulation it already presents itself as "greater literary criticism," the present paper further confirms that, as I have suggested elsewhere, form criticism "may even be coterminous with text-oriented biblical criticism as a whole."[52]

---

51 And then Chronicles retrojected it upon Davidic times.
52 Serge Frolov, "Is Form Criticism Compatible with Diachronic Exegesis? Rethinking Genesis 1– 2 after Knierim and Sweeney," in *Partners with God: Theological and Critical Readings of the Bible in Honor of Marvin A. Sweeney*, ed. Shelley L. Birdsong and Serge Frolov, Claremont Studies in Hebrew Bible and Septuagint 2 (Claremont: Claremont Press, 2017), 26.

Carol A. Newsom
"If I had said ..." (Ps 73:15): Retrospective Introspection in Didactic Psalmody of the Second Temple Period

The phenomenon I have termed retrospective introspection is a virtually universal trait among hominins, absent only in very young children, some autistic persons, and those with particular kinds of brain injuries.[1] Neuroscientists, psychologists, and philosophers often refer to this and related phenomena with a set of terms that include metacognition (the ability to think about one's thought), episodic memory (the ability to recall significant events from one's past experience together with relevant details and feelings at the time), and autonoetic consciousness or the projectable self (the ability to envision oneself in the past, present, and future or in counterfactual contexts). This capacity for metacognition is thought to have evolved early in the history of the human species, and although it is frequently associated with language and the phenomenon of inner speech, it is likely that some non-linguistic primates and even other higher mammals and some birds may possess elements of metacognition, including episodic memory and autonoetic consciousness.[2] The evolutionary advantages of this capacity, especially for social animals, are evident. Most scientists who investigate this phenomenon, however, do so without reference to the cultural and historical variations that may influence how this capacity develops and functions in individuals and in society. It is clear, however, that even though this phenomenon is a basic characteristic of being human, not all cultures ask its members to *pay particular attention to* or to *cultivate* the capacity in the same way or to the same ends. Thus, there is a history and a cultural variegation in the phenomena associated

---

[1] Beate Sodian et al., "Metacognition in Infants and Young Children," in *Foundations of Metacognition*, ed. Michael J. Beran et al. (New York: Oxford University Press, 2012), 119–33; Katherine Nelson, "Emerging Levels of Consciousness in Early Human Development," in *The Missing Link in Cognition: Origins of Self-Reflective Consciousness*, ed. Herbert S. Terrace and Janet Metcalfe (New York: Oxford University Press, 2015), 116–41. Both volumes contain numerous articles on related topics.
[2] Bennett L. Schwartz, "Do Nonhuman Primates Have Episodic Memory?" in Metcalf and Nelson, *The Missing Link*, 225–41; Justin J. Couchman et al., "Evidence for Animal Metaminds," in Michael J. Beran et al., *Foundations of Metacognition*, 21–35.

https://doi.org/10.1515/9783110624526-004

with metacognition. The fact that cultures can be distinguished by the degree of second order "talk about" present and past thoughts and feelings and their significance is important in its own right. But more is at stake than just the presence or absence of a certain kind of cultural discourse. Although comparative research is still limited, it appears that cultural practices can have an effect on the forms of metacognition, on individual proficiency, and on the social uses of this capacity.³ If a culture has names for sub-individual motives (e.g., the *yēṣer hā-raʿ* or the spirits of truth and deception)—if a culture has practices, such as prayers or meditations that draw attention to interior states (thoughts, emotions, the operation of interior agencies)—if a culture lifts up models of individuals who engage in such practices (e.g., authoritative figures who describe the contents of their interior experience), then the populace as a whole is more likely to attend to the emotions, impulses, and thoughts that are part of the interior life.⁴ Thus the development of a richer vocabulary for interiority, the creation of practices, and the highlighting of role models likely do represent real changes in the nature of self-experience. While considerable attention has been directed toward the development of such vocabularies, models, and practices in late antique culture, particularly in Christian traditions, one already sees a distinct interest in the cultivation of introspective practices in Second Temple Judaism.⁵

---

3 See the essays collected in Joëlle Proust and Martin Fortier, *Metacognitive Diversity: An Interdisciplinary Approach* (New York: Oxford University Press, 2018). The essays by Rolf Reber and Ara Norenzayan, "Shared Fluency Theory of Social Cohesiveness: How the Metacognitive Feeling of Processing Fluency Contributes to Group Processes," 47–67; Tanya M. Luhrmann, "Prayer as a Metacognitive Activity," 297–318; and Uffe Schjødt and Jeppe Sinding Jensen, "Depletion and Deprivation: Social Functional Pathways to a Shared Metacognition," 319–342, are particularly relevant to the role of metacognition in religious dimensions of culture.
4 One way of accounting for the development, spread, and effects of beliefs and commitments is shared fluency theory. As Rolf Reber and Ara Norenzayan describe it, "shared exposure promotes shared beliefs; shared beliefs increase interpersonal fluency; behavioral coordination independently increases interpersonal fluency; interpersonal fluency in turn increases mutual liking; mutual liking feeds back to behavioral coordination; shared exposure increases shared object fluency; shared object fluency, in turn, increases liking of the objects that interacting individuals or members of a group are exposed to; mutual liking and shared liking (together constituting social cohesiveness) increase the likelihood that interacting individuals or group members will expose themselves again to the same object" ("Shared Fluency Theory," 48–49). Something like this process took place, in my opinion, in establishing new forms of prayer and psalmody in the early Second Temple period.
5 The literature is vast. Recent collections and studies include Anna Marmodoro and Sophie Cartwright, eds., *A History of Mind and Body in Late Antiquity* (Cambridge: Cambridge University Press, 2018); Joel Kalvesmaki and Robin Darling Young, *Evagrius and His Legacy* (Notre Dame: Notre Dame University Press, 2015); Jörg Rüpke and Greg Woolf, eds., *Religious Dimensions of the*

Ancient Israelite literature (i.e., pre-exilic literature) already reflected a basic sense of human interiority and had a vocabulary for a number of interior phenomena, as Christian Frevel, among others, has argued.[6] But pre-exilic Israelite culture does not seem to have been particularly invested in developing models of, or practices for the cultivation of interiority or introspection.[7] This interest is clearly attested, however, in various strands of Second Temple literature.[8] Psalm 73 is an example of a type of cultural model for piety that features introspection prominently as one of its practices.[9] Specifically, it models retrospective introspection, that is, the recall, examination, and evaluation of past states of mind.

Self in the Second Century CE, Studien und Texte zu Antike und Christentum 76 (Tübingen: Mohr Siebeck, 2013); David Brakke, Michael L. Satlow, and Steven Weitzman, eds., *Religion and the Self in Antiquity* (Bloomington: Indiana University Press, 2005); Philip Carey, *Augustine's Invention of the Inner Self: The Legacy of a Christian Platonist* (Oxford: Oxford University Press, 2000).

6 Christian Frevel, "Von der Selbstbeobachtung zu inneren Tiefen: Überlegungen zur Konstitution von Individualität im Alten Testament," in *Individualität und Selbstreflexion in den Literaturen des Alten Testaments*, ed. Andreas Wagner and Jürgen van Oorschot, VWGTh 48 (Leipzig: Evangelische Verlagsanstalt, 2017), 13–44.

7 The psalms of the individual, especially lament psalms, have a highly developed repertoire of images and forms for directing attention to and expressing emotional states, as well as for shaping identities and empowering agency. They do not, however, often feature recursive or self-reflective introspection. See, e.g., Marianne Grohmann, "Individualität und Selbstreflexion in den Klageliedern," 259–278; Susanne Gillmayr-Bucher, "Selbstwahrnehmung und Selbsreflexion in Krisensituationen," 279–296; and Anna Zernecke, "Vom 'Sich Unterbringen' in den Psalmen," 297–311 in Wagner and van Oorschot, *Individualität und Selbstreflexion*. Also see Amy C. Cottrill, *Language, Power, and Identity in the Lament Psalms of the Individual*, LHBOTS 493 (New York: T&T Clark, 2008).

8 I have explored some of the texts that reflect this interest in "Toward a Genealogy of the Introspective Self in Second Temple Judaism," in *Functions of Psalms and Prayers in the Late Second Temple Period*, ed. Mika S. Pajunen and Jeremy Penner, BZAW 486 (Berlin: De Gruyter, 2017), 63–79; "Sin Consciousness, Self-Alienation, and the Origins of the Introspective Self" in *Rhetoric and Hermeneutics*, FAT 130 (Tübingen: Mohr Siebeck, 2019), 225–37; and in "When the Problem is Not What You Have Done but Who You Are: The Changing Focus of Atonement in Second Temple Prayer and Poetry," in *Atonement: Jewish and Christian*, ed. Max Botner, Justin Duff, and Simon Dürr (Grand Rapids: Eerdmans, 2020), 67–88.

9 A growing consensus of scholars locates Psalm 73 in the Persian period. See Klaus Seybold, *Die Psalmen* HAT I/15 (Tübingen: J.C.B. Mohr [Paul Siebeck], 1996), 282; Frank-Lothar Hossfeld and Erich Zenger, *Psalms 2: A Commentary on Psalms 51–100*, trans. Linda M. Maloney. Hermeneia (Minneapolis: Fortress Press, 2005), 400–401; John Goldingay, *Psalms, Volume 2: Psalms 42–89* (Grand Rapids: Baker Academic, 2007), 400.

1. The Confluence of Thanksgiving Psalmody and Sapiential Instruction

The distinctive representation of interior experience one encounters in Psalm 73 appears to develop at the confluence of two forms of discourse: one is the tradition of thanksgiving psalmody and the other is sapiential instruction. Commentaries and studies of Psalm 73 almost always note the presence of both of these elements.[10] The basic structure of praise of God that frames a recollection of past distress, now resolved through God's intervention, locates the composition in relation to the tradition of the thanksgiving of the individual. But the content of the past distress in Psalm 73—namely, the scandal of the well-being of the wicked and the distress of the righteous—identify the theme as one that is frequent in wisdom compositions (e.g., Job 15; 18; 20; 21; Psalms 1; 37; 49). Each discourse—thanksgiving and didactic literature—also offers certain resources for the creation of the first-person singular persona who speaks in the text of Psalm 73 and who takes an introspective turn.[11]

The tradition of first-person singular prayer is a natural environment for the cultivation of introspective practices. Complaint and thanksgiving psalms are speech forms that model attention to and expression of a stylized repertoire of emotional states, often vividly described. But, as David Lambert has argued, modern readers tend to overestimate the extent and self-reflexive nature of emotions expressed in the psalms.

> Today, when we read prayer texts from the Bible, many of us imagine an individual conscience expressing its purest thoughts and innermost feelings ... That the Psalms give no explicit indication of their original contexts abets the multiplication of such readings and their penitential applications. When considering narrative material, however, a more materialist view of prayer, one that is bound up in a robust sense of the afflicted's self-interest, emerges with ample clarity.[12]

---

10 See the summary discussion in Clinton J. McCann, Jr., "Psalm 73: An Interpretation Emphasizing Rhetorical and Canonical Criticism" (Ph.D. diss., Duke University, 1985), 90–101. In the older literature comparisons to the psalms of lament or confidence were also noted.

11 The recognition of the significance of the first-person persona and its distinctive relation to the community is reflected in the suggestions that the psalm be understood by means of the genre of "testimony" (Marvin E. Tate, *Psalms 51–100*, WBC 20 [Dallas: Word Books, 1990], 231) or "confessional address" (James L. Mays, *Psalms* [Louisville: John Knox, 1994], 240).

12 David Lambert, *How Repentance Became Biblical: Judaism, Christianity, and the Interpretation of Scripture* (New York: Oxford University Press, 2016), 36. Although Lambert's focus is specifically on penitential dispositions, his analysis applies to the relation of psalms to psychological states more broadly.

I am more inclined than Lambert is to posit a correlation between such expressions and actual inner feelings—not simply because prior feelings oftentimes do generate the expressions in lament and thanksgiving, but also because the expression itself encourages the relevant feelings and dispositions. Indeed, in a recent essay anthropologist Tanya Luhrmann makes a strong case for the metacognitive function of prayer in focusing and re-directing both emotions and beliefs of the one who prays, even as the prayer attempts to influence the dispositions and actions of the deity to whom one prays.[13] Whatever is the case about the emotional state of the pray-er in ancient Israelite culture, however, it does seem to be the case that the emphasis in lament psalms is on the efficacy of expression to secure the desired result rather than on the examination of the emotions themselves. Similarly, thanksgivings serve as testimony to God's power and goodness. The emotions and thoughts of the psalmist are not the primary focus of attention. Nevertheless, because lament and thanksgiving psalmody are genres that feature self-presentation, they may contribute to forms of speech that *do* self-consciously examine the internal state of the speaker.

The contribution of the didactic tradition to self-presentation is a bit less obvious, but it deserves to be examined. Wisdom instructions, such as one finds in Proverbs 1-9 and in shorter sections later in the book, typically do not feature first-person singular style, in which the teacher draws on his own experience. There are a few instances in Proverbs. In Prov 4:3 the teacher recalls his past, saying, "Once I was a son to my father, the tender darling to my mother. He instructed me and said to me…," using his own receptivity to ground his admonition in vv. 10–11, "My son, heed and take in my words … I instruct you in the way of wisdom," etc. And in Proverbs 30 Agur begins his wisdom discourse with a self-evaluation, "I am brutish—less than a man; I lack common sense." The use of personal experience to ground an argument occurs at least three times in Eliphaz's speeches in the book of Job. In Job 4:12–21 Eliphaz vividly recounts his eerie dream as a teaching. And in two other contexts he frames his teaching in relation to prior experience: "As I have seen" (4:8), and "I will hold forth; listen to me; What I have seen, I will declare" (15:17). The most bravura example of self-foregrounding in the book of Job, however, is Elihu's self-introduction in Job 32, where we learn perhaps more than we wanted to know about how he is feeling, his perspectives on his colleagues, the reasons for his decision to speak, and so

---

13 Although Luhrman's primary fieldwork is with Christian evangelicals who have a particularly developed introspective set of prayer practices, she makes her arguments in terms of a variety of cross-cultural prayer traditions. She finds that the cognitive restructuring that is one of the effects of prayer is similar in many respects to cognitive behavioral therapy in psychology (Luhrmann, "Prayer as Metacognition, 303).

forth. Although the dialogical form of the book of Job may be partly responsible for the appeals to personal experience, Qohelet develops the use of first-person self-presentation as an element of sapiential instruction to a remarkable degree.[14] A few examples of a first-person didactic persona occur in Psalms, notably the wisdom introduction to Ps 78:1–3. And, as in Eliphaz's speeches, there are occasional appeals to first-person experience, for example, Ps 37:25 ("I have been young and am now old, but I have never seen a righteous person abandoned …"; cf. v. 35). In most of the didactic psalms, however, even though the teaching voice is distinctive, there is no developed use of first-person testimony and no self-reflexive turn that makes the speaker's experiences the subject of critical examination.

Where one does find evidence of a particularly important development is in texts from the sapiential tradition that reflect on efficacious prayer. Consider, for example, the way in which Zophar advises Job to pray in Job 11. He begins by describing a preparatory action, "directing the mind" (*kûn lēb*). It is not clear precisely what that novel phrase refers to in this context, but at the very least it is an explicit instruction to perform a metacognitive action. Job is explicitly instructed to pay attention to his thoughts and to exercise intentional control in focusing them in some way.[15] In later rabbinic texts the expression refers to the practice of an hour spent in "directing the mind to God" before standing to pray (*ykwnw 't lbm lmrwm*, m. Berakot 5:1). The practice involves developing such concentration that even the greeting of a king or the presence a snake on one's foot would not dislodge the person's focused attention.[16] In Job 11:13 the instruction to direct the mind is paralleled by the direction to "spread your hands toward him," which

---

14 See Eric S. Christianson, *A Time to Tell: Narrative Strategies in Ecclesiastes*, JSOTSup 280 (Sheffield: Sheffield Academic Press, 1998), 173–215; Susan Niditch, *The Responsive Self: Personal Religion in Biblical Literature of the Neo-Babylonian and Persian Periods* (New Haven: Yale University Press, 2015), 40–46. I take both Elihu and Qohelet to be somewhat later in the chronology of the development of the didactic first-person persona than the psalms I consider in this essay, though it is not possible to discuss the chronological issues in detail here.
15 "The central act of praying is paying attention to inner experience—to thoughts, images and the awareness of one's body—and treating those sensations as important in themselves rather than as distractions from the real business of living. That is what makes it a metacognitive activity: a cognitive action (broadly conceived) that takes the cognition of the actor as its focus," Luhrman, "Prayer as Metacognition," 299–300.
16 Luhrmann refers to this phenomenon as "absorption" and observes that "absorption is perhaps the most important metacognitive feature of prayer, because absorption is the practice through which the inner object of attention comes to feel more real" ("Prayer as Metacognition," 309–311). She also notes that though persons vary in their ability to experience absorption, it is to a certain extent a skill in which a person can become more proficient.

similarly suggests God-directed attention.[17] The following verse advises that "if there is iniquity in your hands, make it far from you, and do not let injustice reside in your tent" (11:14). This advice suggests a kind of interior inventory and separation from wrongful aspects of one's values, thoughts, and actions. David Clines notes that the spatial imagery of distancing oneself from sin is a distinctively sapiential conceptual model (cf. Ps 1:1; Prov 1:10–15; 4:14, 24; 5:8; 30:8).[18] The similar imagery in Eliphaz's advice on preparation for prayer in 22:21–27 suggests that this model contributed to the development of a sapiential style of prayer practice.

2. Psalm 32

Psalm 32 is a didactic psalm that shares the perspectives of Zophar and Eliphaz's advice. It advocates and models the appropriate mode of confession of sin and embodies a form of reflective self-assessment. The composition is often grouped with the thanksgiving psalms, and so, like Psalm 73, appears to represent an experimental hybridization of psalmic and sapiential discourse on the topic of prayer.[19] Its wisdom framing is evident from the *ʾašrê* introduction ("Happy is the one whose transgression is forgiven, whose sin is covered over …," v. 1) and in the concluding admonitions in vv. 8 and 9–10.[20] But the psalm's focus is, like

---

[17] For the later rabbinic debate about the relative significance of focused intention (*kavannah*) and physical posture in prayer see Uri Ehrlich, *The Nonverbal Language of Prayer*, trans. Dena Ordan (Tübingen: Mohr Siebeck, 2004), 248–53. In Job 11:13, however, the two appear to be coordinated aspects of the same act of preparation.
[18] David J. A. Clines, *Job 1–20*, WBC 17 (Dallas: Word Books, 1989), 268.
[19] Most recently, Simon Chi-Chung, *Wisdom Intoned: A Reappraisal of the Genre 'Wisdom Psalms,'* LHBOTS 613 (London: T&T Clark, 2015), 138. Its mixed nature is also noted by Bernd Willmes, *Freude über die Vergebung der Sünden: Synchrone und diachrone Analyse von Psalm 32*, Fuldaer Hochschulschriften 28 (Frankfurt am Main: Verlag Josef Knecht, 1996), 28. My understanding of this psalm is significantly indebted to the unpublished study of Evan E. Bassett, "A Story of Transformation: Psalm 32 as a Window into the Life of the Thanksgiving Genre," May, 2018). Basset argues that "this psalm represents an intentional use of the thanksgiving genre toward a particular purpose" (8), that is, "an *explicit* instructional task" (10), "based *directly* on the experience just described by the psalmist" (11).
[20] Many treat v. 8 as YHWH's instruction to the psalmist, with the wisdom admonition by the psalmist to a broader audience occurring in vv. 9–11. So Bassett, "Story of Transformation," 6; John Goldingay, *Psalms, Volume 1: Psalms 1–41* (Grand Rapids: Baker Academic, 2006), 458–59; Hans-Joachim Kraus, *Psalms 1–59: A Continental Commentary*, trans. Hilton C. Oswald (Minneapolis: Fortress Press, 1993), 368–9; Peter Craigie, *Psalms 1–50*, WBC 19 (Waco: Word Books, 1983), 267.

Zophar's advice, on the value of self-examination and the confession of sin. The core of the psalm is developed in vv. 3–5 in an act of retrospection. "As long as I said nothing, my limbs wasted away ..." (v. 3, NJPS). The turning point comes when "I acknowledged my sin to you; I did not cover up my guilt" (v. 5 aα). This moment in the past is even dramatized with the citation of speech, "I said, 'I will confess my transgressions to the Lord'." That resolution is apparently effective, for "You forgave the guilt of my sin" (v. 5b). Although thanksgiving psalms typically include an address to the congregation instructing them to praise (e.g., Pss 22:24; 31:24), based generally on the narrative of transformation that the psalmist has recited, here the instruction is explicitly connected to the testimony with a concluding "therefore" (*'al kēn*; v. 6).[21] Moreover, the instruction—both that from God to the psalmist ("Let me instruct you and show you the way by which you should walk," v. 8) and from the psalmist to the community ("Do not be like a horse or a mule that has no sense," v. 9)—has to do with the audience's moral conduct and perception. Thus, the emphasis in the psalm has shifted from focus on God's actions (though these are important) to the actions of the speaker as moral exemplar and model. This shift is also indicated in the way in which the past crisis is framed. The physical distress is explicitly related to an internal struggle between a reluctance to confess sin and the efficacy of confession. Although the introspective potential of the situation is not highly elaborated, the locus of the problem is an internal conflict and its resolution, framed as an instructive model for the audience.

3. Psalm 73

Psalm 73 shares with Psalm 32 a combination of thanksgiving and didactic elements. The didactic framing of the psalm is indicated by the use of a proverbial saying to open the composition ("Truly God is good to Israel, those whose heart is pure").[22] The affinities to the thanksgiving tradition are present in the focus on a recollected time of distress and its resolution that forms the body of the psalm. This account is quite lengthy, running from v. 2 to v. 20. As in Psalm 32 the crisis and resolution that it recalls is one of inner spiritual conflict. In this case it is the cognitive dissonance of the prosperity of the wicked, while the pious speaker experiences suffering. The resolution comes, not as the restoration of well-being

---

21 Bassett, "Story of Transformation," 5.
22 An attractive emendation involves re-dividing and repointing the first colon as follows: *'ak ṭôb layyāšār 'ēl*, so that the verse reads "Truly El is good to the upright, God to those whose heart is pure." No manuscript evidence supports the emendation, however.

to the speaker, as one might expect in a traditional thanksgiving psalm, but rather as the resolution of his experience of cognitive dissonance. Thus, like Psalm 32, Psalm 73 serves as a model of piety to be emulated. But going beyond Psalm 32, Psalm 73 develops the potentialities of the retrospective examination of inner spiritual conflict in a performance that is a *tour de force* of introspection.

Verse 2, the beginning of the self-narrative, is presented as a retrospective judgment by the psalmist on his own previous views and mental states. "As for me, my feet had almost stumbled,[23] my footsteps had nearly slipped."[24] What he now judges to be wrong was the fact that he envied the arrogant and the wicked (v. 3). Then, for twelve entire verses the speaker depicts the mistaken perspectives that he previously held. Although textual difficulties obscure some details, the passage makes use of tropes familiar from other accounts of the prosperity of the wicked, such as one finds in Job 21. The final two verses of this section are cast as first-person speech and appear to depict the psalmist's own inner reflections at that previous time: "Truly, it is for nothing that I have kept my heart pure and washed my hands in innocence, as I am afflicted every day, and each morning brings me punishment" (vv. 13–14). Since these are *no longer*, according to v. 2, the views that the speaker holds, it might seem surprising that they are given such elaborate representation. Rhetorically, the vivid presentation of the prosperity of the wicked and the emotional frustration of the speaker do two things. It recreates the mental state for the speaker himself and so draws him back into the past experience. But it also serves to draw the audience into a similar mindset. Indeed, the words are a kind of spiritual enticement for those who are perhaps subject to similar doubts about the order of reality. The imagery is varied and vivid. The ease, well-being, and even physical sleekness of the wicked is contrasted with the painful work (*'āmāl*, v. 5) of ordinary humans. The wicked's moral arrogance is as ostentatiously displayed as fine clothes and gaudy jewelry (v. 6). And their utter contempt for God, even as they grow wealthier (vv. 11–12), especially as contrasted with the pious psalmist's own experience of pain and hardship that feels like a divine rebuke, makes the speaker's moral despair compelling (vv. 13–14).

Since the psalmist has already characterized these views as representing moral peril (v. 2), one must ask what is gained by exposing the audience to a vivid recreation of such dangerous perspectives. The rhetorical strategy makes sense if

---

[23] Following the Qere, *nĕṭāyû*. The verb *nṭh* indicates stretching or twisting, and translators variously interpret the idiom as indicating stumbling or straying. Within the metaphorical field of walking along a path as representing morally appropriate conduct, stumbling or straying indicates a morally problematic situation.

[24] Following the Qere, *šuppĕkû*. The "pouring out" of footsteps also appears to be an idiom of stumbling or slipping.

the psalm functions as something like a spiritual exercise, both creating and resolving a moral challenge by means of emotional engagement with the scenario.[25] Thus the critical part of the account is how the improper thoughts were dispelled or resolved. This part of the narrative begins in v. 15, a verse that presents one of the most psychologically and rhetorically complex moments in the psalm. The counterfactual introduction ("if I had said …") removes the speaker—and his audience—from full immersion in the past and re-situates them as critical observers of a past state of mind. From this perspective the psalmist recalls the internal struggle he had at that time in the past concerning whether or not to voice his complaints and doubts, a struggle that he represents as inner speech. What he considered saying to himself, ʾim ʾāmartî ʾăsappĕrāh kĕmô ("If I had said, 'I will say these things …'") is sometimes interpreted as referring to talking in the manner of the wicked (v. 11),[26] but it is better understood as a debate about whether to voice his own troubling thoughts.[27] In either case these were never public statements but only internal thoughts. Thus, the speaker is constructing a past state of mind. It is unclear grammatically whether the judgment "I would have betrayed the circle of your disciples" (v. 15b) is a judgment that he made at the time or only now makes about what would have been the impact of his potential words. Since the problematic words were not in fact spoken, it is likely that that "I would have betrayed the circle of your disciples" renders his past counter-thoughts against his initial impulse. Thus, the psalmist depicts a very complex psychological state: a state of cognitive dissonance that seeks expression, and a counter inhibiting thought that is based not on a clear mental resolution of the dissonance but a judgment of the social or ethical effect of speaking subversive words. I can think

---

25 Luhrmann, "Prayer as Metacognition," 313, refers to this process of framing and reframing an emotionally charged experience as one that "flips the script." She compares the work of prayer both to the ancient work of tragic drama in constructing a dynamic of catharsis and to the contemporary work of psychological therapy that posits that "the patient who does not have intense feelings during therapy will not change their emotional patterns." Thus, the luring of the hearer into the same moral danger as the speaker is part of the therapeutic work of the psalm, an "imaginative immersion" that works to discharge the danger by framing a narrative in which the danger is overcome.
26 E.g., Hans-Joachim Kraus, *Psalms 60–150: A Commentary*, trans. Hilton C. Oswald (Minneapolis: Augsburg, 1989), 83, suggests "I will talk like them," emending kĕmô to kāhem; see also Seybold, *Die Psalmen*, 281.
27 So, e.g., Goldingay, *Psalms, Volume 2*, 408; also NJPS, NRSV. The preposition kĕmô appears to lack an object. It is often suggested that hēnnāh has been omitted by haplography with the following hinnēh, or that the lines should be re-divided, and hinnēh repointed as hēnnāh. McCann, "Psalm 73," 36, following a suggestion of Dahood, takes kĕmô adverbially, "thus." The referent could be either to the inner speech of vv. 13–14 or to the entire set of thoughts summarized in vv. 3–14.

of no other such extensive representation in the Hebrew Bible of past thoughts, including the depiction of the inner processing of psychological conflict by means of the evaluation of hypothetical subsequent states of affairs. That is a highly sophisticated modeling of mental activity.

Although the speaker indicates that he did not utter these words because they would have been deleterious to the community, he has, in fact, just uttered them in vv. 3–14. They are not deleterious now, however, because the speaker has presented them as views he once held but no longer does. And if the audience has been drawn into experiencing these thoughts also, then they, too, must be ready to judge and relinquish them. But to this point the audience has not been told *how* the psalmist came to change his mind. In raising this subject, the speaker first recalls a failed attempt, again presented as a recollection of a past psychological state. "But when I considered how to understand this, it seemed a wearisome task in my eyes" (v. 16). Although the sentence is somewhat elliptical, the expression ʿāmāl ("painful toil," "wearisome task") suggests that the speaker refers obliquely to the difficult mental process of arguing with oneself, of dividing the mind so that one is aware of one set of thoughts and beliefs and then sets up a heuristic alternate self who thinks and believes differently and can argue against one's presenting thoughts.[28]

The decisive event in the radical change in cognition, however, comes "when I entered the sanctuary of God and I reflected on their fate" (v. 17).[29] The speaker does not elaborate on why this change in place effects a change in thought. Numerous scholars have attempted to fill in the gap with suggestions that, as McCann observes, "range from the possible to the ridiculous."[30] But perhaps it was, in fact, nothing more than the change of location, as the text seems to sug-

---

28 Self-talk is one of the important forms of cognitive control of emotions. See Kevin N. Ochsner and James J. Gross, "Cognitive Emotion Regulation," *Current Directions in Psychological Science* 17 (2008): 153–58; Todd F. Heatherton, "Neuroscience of Self and Self-Regulation," *Annual Review of Psychology* 62 (2011): 363–90. Apparently, referring to oneself in the third person (i.e., by name), rather than using "I," makes self-talk even more effective in self-regulation with less effort. See Jason S. Moser et al., "Third-Person Self-Talk Facilitates Emotion Regulation without Engaging Cognitive Control: Converging Evidence from ERP and fMRI," *Scientific Reports* 7 (2017): 1–9; DOI:10.1038/s41598-017-04047-3. Little if any research appears to have been done on cross-cultural differences in practices of self-talk.
29 The text has *miqdĕšê-'ēl* ("the sanctuaries of God"), which plausibly refers to the various components of the temple (see Lev 21:23; Jer 51:51; Ezek 21:7; Ps 68:36). Although most commentators assume that a physical entry into the sanctuary is intended, Hossfeld and Zenger, *Psalms 2*, 231–32, suggest that the experience of God's presence is referred to metaphorically "as a sanctuary" for the speaker. There is no compelling reason for such a metaphorical interpretation, however.
30 McCann, "Psalm 73," 212.

gest. The power and persuasiveness of thoughts and beliefs are often conditioned upon various environmental and social-contextual cues. When the speaker was in an ordinary environment—especially in public places where the wealth, good fortune, arrogance, and violence of the impious were prominently on display—then the idea that their lawlessness is rewarded rather than punished seemed more persuasive. In the sanctuary, where the symbolic reminders of the divine would be present in physical and sensorial immediacy, the thoughts that are congruent with the ideals of divine justice would simply be easier to think. The set of beliefs specifically associated with the sanctuary and those who are permitted to enter (e.g., Pss 15; 27:4–6; 36:8–13; 63:3; 118:19–20), along with the the social support of other worshipers (e.g., 42:5–6), would reaffirm the belief in God's justice.[31] The ʿāmāl of resolving the cognitive dissonance (v. 16) itself dissolves. Consequently, the psalmist envisions how the wicked actually exist in a state of false consciousness on account of the "flattery" and "deception" that characterizes their social environment, as a result of which they come to sudden ruin (vv. 18–20). In this observation about the distorted perception of the wicked, the psalm again implicitly points to the socially constructed basis for perception and conviction, though the wicked have no means of assessing and correcting the inadequacy of their perspectives.

The author concludes the exploration of his cognitive experiences with one final contrast. Translators and commentators, however, are divided as to whether vv. 21–24 are better understood as part of the speaker's retrospective reflection, general statements and future affirmations, or, as most suggest, reflections that begin with the past but continue to describe present reality and future expectation.[32] The grammatical forms are not unambiguously dispositive. In my opinion the devastatingly negative critique that the psalmist gives of his own cognitive capacities in vv. 21–22 are best understood as part of his self-critical retrospective. Woodenly translated, the verses say, "My mind was soured; my kidneys were pierced through" (yitḥammēṣ lĕbābî; wĕkilyôtay ʾeštônān). It is not entirely clear what form of impairment this represents, but that it is a cognitive/emotional disorder is clear, for he continues: "I was a brute, without knowledge; I was an animal toward you" (waʾănî-baʿar wĕlōʾ ʾēdāʿ; bĕhēmôt hāyîtî ʿimmāk).[33] Here the analogy is clear. The speaker considers himself sub-human in his lack of under-

---

31 Othmar Keel, *Schöne, Schwierige Welt: Leben mit Klagen und Loben*, Bibelwoche 54 (Berlin: Evang. Haupt-Bibelges, 1991), 41.
32 See e.g., Seybold, *Die Psalmen*, 284; Tate, *Psalms 51–100*, 227; Hossfeld and Zenger, *Psalms 2*, 222; Goldingay, *Psalms, Volume 2*, 399. The translation of the NJPS, however, frames all of the statements as referring to the recollected past.
33 See the discussion of McCann, "Psalm 73," 42.

standing (cf. Prov 30:2–3). Thus, his experience in arriving at a new understanding appears to be less a kind of disciplinary correction than a transformation. If one takes v. 23 as also referring to the conditions of the past, then the speaker acknowledges a second, at-the-time unrecognized agency that was guiding him in the right direction. "Yet I was always with you, you held my right hand; you guided me by your counsel, and afterward you received me in honor" (vv. 23–24). Much debate surrounds the interpretation of 24b (wĕ'aḥar kābôd teqqāḥēnî). The imagery of holding by the right hand and receiving an honor recalls the presentation scenes of the worshiper before his or her god in Mesopotamian iconography.[34] The motif is also found in Israelite royal presentation topoi, as in Ps 110:1 and Isa 45:1, though in Ps 73:24a the divine assistance is not military but cognitive: "you guided me by your counsel." Since vv. 23–24 immediately follow the psalmist's description of his sub-human state of understanding and confused emotion (vv. 21–22), these verses appear to describe why the speaker did not utter his despairing words (v. 15), and why, in the midst of his mental struggle, he went to the temple and experienced relief (vv. 16–17, 18–20). If so, then these words represent another quite sophisticated representation of a complex mental state. Essentially, the speaker is saying that he is *now* aware of a past divine assistance that was at the time unknown and unknowable but that was in fact operative in directing him. The speaker recognizes that he was not the sole agent in his own mind and actions, although he now recognizes and acknowledges the process of shared agency and cognition that brought him to his present insight into reality.[35]

---

34 See, e.g., Othmar Keel, *The Symbolism of the Biblical World: Ancient Near Eastern Iconography and the Book of Psalms*, trans. Timothy J. Hallett (New York: Seabury Press, 1978), 199, fig. 272. I disagree with Keel's assumption that the psalm refers to a post-mortem reception of the psalmist. The reference to being received in honor or glory may simply be an idealized way of referring to the sense of being in God's presence in the temple, drawn from the common ancient Near Eastern iconography.

35 The conception of shared agency is quite common in biblical narrative. The example most similar to the experience reported by the psalmist is that in the narrative about Abimelech in Gen 20:3–6. Acting on Abraham's representation that Sarah is his sister, Abimelech takes Sarah for himself. But he does not have sex with her. When God threatens Abimelech in a dream for his actions and Abimelech protests, God discloses that "I knew that you did this with a blameless heart, and so I kept you from sinning against Me. That was why I did not let you touch her" (trans. NJPS). Prior to the dream, if one had asked Abimelech why he had not slept with Sarah, he would presumably have given some reason or other. But he would not have known the actual cause of his decision, which he now understands to have been the force of divine intention acting imperceptibly on his own. A similar model is operative in Joseph's assessment that although his brothers acted with the intention of doing him harm, their actions were actually orchestrated by God's intention to bring about a more comprehensive good result, keeping the whole household of Jacob alive (Gen 50:20). In neither case is human intentionality and will negated. But humans do

Thus the past change in the speaker's perception is not something that can be attributed to his own capacities. His own "mind and body fail" (v. 26a), and it is God who is the "rock of my mind and my portion forever" (v. 26b). This recognition ensures that the cognitive shift is not an unstable one that is subject to further fluctuation.

4. Conclusion

Since the corpus of first-person singular psalm texts from the early Second Temple period is relatively small, it is difficult to say whether or not Psalm 73 was part of a significantly widespread practice of self-reflective prayer. I have attempted to show, by reference to Zophar and Eliphaz's advice concerning prayer in the book of Job, and by comparison with Psalm 32, that sapiential approaches to prayer did encourage this type of attentiveness to one's cognitive, emotional, and moral experience. Prayers such as Psalm 51 and Syriac Psalm 155 (11QPs^a 24) also provide evidence for a kind of introspection in which the speaker experiences a form of self-alienation in which the problematic aspect of the self can only be remedied by means of God's agency. The Hodayot, too, with their model of retrospective judgment of past cognitive incapacity, viewed from a post-transformation state, may represent another development of this trajectory. In other non-prayer genres, such as the Two Spirits Teaching from the Serek ha-Yahad and the Testaments of the Twelve Patriarchs, the elaboration of speculation about spirits that influence dispositions and behavior and that must be monitored contributes to a concern for developing practices of introspective self-control.[36] When the various strands of evidence are considered together, they make a compelling case for the significance of Second Temple Judaism in the history of the cultivation of introspective practices of the self. Psalms 32 and 73, with their remarkable representation of critical retrospection, are an important contribution to this development.

---

not always have conscious access to the factors influencing their intentions. I discuss these and other cases of shared agency more extensively in a forthcoming study.

36 I examine these topics more fully in the essays referred to in n8. See also Carol A. Newsom, "Deriving Negative Anthropology Through Exegetical Activity: The Hodayot as Case Study," in *Is there a Text in This Cave? Studies in the Textuality of the Dead Sea Scrolls in Honor of George J. Brooke*, ed. Ariel Feldman, Maria Cioată, and Charlotte Hempel, STDJ 119 (Leiden: Brill, 2017), 258–74.

Timothy J. Sandoval
Agur's Words to God in Proverbs 30 and Prayerful Study in the Second Temple Period

1. Introduction

Daniel Falk has broadly defined prayer in Second Temple Jewish texts as "an act of communication with the divine." Bruce Malina suggests that prayer in the biblical tradition ought to be reckoned as discourse directed toward a being who is also regarded "as somehow supporting, maintaining, or controlling the order of existence of the one praying and [is] performed with the purpose of getting results from or in the interaction of communication."[1]

On the terms laid out by Falk and Malina, there is not much in the book of Proverbs that is regularly identified as prayer. Only Prov 15:8 and 29 deploy the term תפלה ("prayer") and it is only in Prov 30:1–14, that collection of sayings associated with a certain Agur and often regarded as a late (perhaps even Hellenistic) appendix to the central collections of the book, that one finds human words directed to the deity.[2] Prov 30:7–9 begins with the words, "Two things I ask of you," and hence is regularly thought to constitute a brief petition to the divine. However, a very common emendation to the second half of Prov 30:1, if admitted, permits one to hear Agur's initial words in the chapter (vv. 1–3) as an effort at "communication with the divine" as well.

After describing this common emendation to Prov 30:1b, a version of which I accept, I will point to a feature of the "prayer" in the emended line that is rarely fully explained—namely Agur's self-proclaimed weariness. I will contend that Agur's fatigue can be well elucidated by reference to a cluster of passages from biblical and Second Temple compositions that stand in intertextual relation with

---

[1] Daniel K. Falk, "Hymns, Prayers, and Psalms," in *T&T Clark Encyclopedia of Second Temple Judaism*, ed. Daniel Gurtner and Loren T. Stuckenbruck (London: T&T Clark, 2019), 2:337–42; Bruce Malina, "What is Prayer?" *TBT* 18 (1980): 214–220 (215). Cf. Jeremy Penner, *Patterns of Daily Prayer in Second Temple Period Judaism*, STDJ 104 (Leiden: Brill, 2012), 1–33.

[2] Proverbs 30 is itself a composite text. The initial section of the chapter—the "words of Agur"—may extend to v. 14 since Prov 30:1–14 is an ancient collection, as testified by the Greek, which places these lines after (an expanded) Prov 24:22. Some modern scholars, however, reckon vv. 10–14 to be literarily distinct from earlier lines and hence consider the chapter's first pericope to end at v. 9. Prov 30:15–33 are almost always regarded as a collection distinct from the chapter's initial fourteen verses.

Prov 30:1–4. These intertexts subsequently can be said to support indirectly the common emendation of Prov 30:1b.

Prominent among the intertexts I highlight is the traditional wisdom discourse of most of the rest of Proverbs, texts in Numbers 22–24 that recount the prophecies of the seer Balaam, certain passages from the early Enoch tradition, several verses in Isaiah 40, and key lines from 4QInstruction. These intertextual connections reveal first how the final redaction of Proverbs 30 promotes the ongoing worth of traditional wisdom epistemology and ethics in generating this-worldly human well-being in the face of challenges to this moral epistemology from other Second Temple discourses that privilege the acquisition of esoteric, heavenly or inspired wisdom necessary for right religious-moral conduct in the present eschatological moment, or for post-mortem salvation.[3] The relationship of Agur's discourse with further key passages in 4QInstruction and 1QS 6, which describe how human actors, through intensive effort and study, strive to acquire divinely inspired, esoteric knowledge, also points to ways Agur's words of weariness can be well understood in terms of the ideologies and practices of prayer in certain Second Temple communities. Subsequently, one might suggest these texts from the Qumran library describe a complex practice of "prayerful study" in Second Temple times and surmise that Agur's weariness in Prov 30:1b derives from his participation in just such a practice.

2. Prayer in Prov 30:1b

MT of Prov 30:1 reads:

דברי אגור בן־יקה המשא נאם הגבר לאיתיאל לאיתיאל ואכל

A straightforward translation of the line, according to the Masoretic division of consonants and pointing, is:

> The words of Agur, son of Yakeh, the oracle, the utterance of the man, for Ithiel, for Ithiel and Ukhal.

---

[3] The dialogue of Second Temple discourses of knowledge in Proverbs 30 does not end with Agur's words, or what I regard as an initial response to his claims in Prov 30:4 (see below). Prov 30:5–14 continues the conversation as it evokes both the ethics of traditional wisdom and a rhetoric of Second Temple Deuteronomistic and Psalmic Torah piety. See, for example, Bernd U. Schipper, "When Wisdom is Not Enough! The Discourse on Wisdom and Torah and the Composition of the Book of Proverbs," in *Wisdom and Torah: The Reception of "Torah" in the Wisdom Literature of the Second Temple Period*, ed. Bernd U. Schipper and D. Andrew Teeter (Leiden: Brill, 2013), 55–79.

2.1 The Central Problem[4]

The names Agur and Yakeh are obscure and some scholars wish to emend המשא ("the oracle") to המשאי ("the Massaite") or ממשא ("from Massa") in order to understand the term as a reference to "the north Arabian tribe mentioned in Gen 25:14 and 1 Chron 1:30."[5] However, the main difficulty in the line is how to understand Prov 30:1b, which appears to mention the names of Agur's addressees—Ithiel and Ukhal.[6] The problem is that the name Ithiel, preceded by the preposition *lamed*, is both awkwardly repeated and relatively unknown (appearing only in Neh 11:7), while Ukhal is not at all attested as a proper name in HB.[7]

Charles C. Torrey long ago noted that "since the late 19th century" the most common scholarly tack to address the difficulties of Prov 30:1b has been to re-divide and re-point the repeated לאיתיאל.[8] Instead of MT's text one can read, for example,

לאיתי אל לאיתי אל ואכל

In this scenario, the repeated לאיתיאל of MT becomes a twice written *qal* perf. 1cs of ל־א־ה, "to grow weary" (*lā'îtî*), followed by the vocative "O God." The final ואכל (*we'ūkāl*)—can be understood as a defectively written *qal* 1cs imperfect verb from י־כ־ל—"to be able, have power, prevail"; or it can be repointed as *wā'ēkel*, the 1cs *qal* *waw*-consecutive of כ־ל־ה—"to be completed, finished, exhausted."[9] The emended line can subsequently be rendered something like, "I am weary, O god, I am weary, O god, but I will prevail" or "... I am weary ... and am exhausted." Torrey's observation from over half a century ago regarding the prominence of such a solution to the line's problems still stands. An identical or similar emendation of

---

4 The arguments and language of some of the following sections of this essay follow Timothy J. Sandoval, "Texts and Intertexts: A Proposal for understanding Proverbs 30:1b," *JSOT*, forthcoming.
5 Roger N. Whybray, *Proverbs* (Grand Rapids: Eerdmans, 1994), 407. Cf. משא in Prov 31:1, which is also sometimes regarded as a proper noun.
6 The כי in v. 2 of MT is also difficult since it "presumes an earlier sentence, not only a title compounded of nouns." Michael V. Fox, *Proverbs 10–31: A New Translation with Introduction and Commentary* (New Haven: Yale University Press, 2009), 853.
7 Ukhal is also not yet attested in other Second Temple or late antique sources, at least judging by its absence in Tal Ilan's *Lexicon of Jewish Names: Parts 1–4* (Tübingen: Mohr Siebeck, 2002, 2008, 2011, 2012).
8 Charles C. Torrey, "Proverbs, Chapter 30," *JBL* 73 (1954): 93–96 (94).
9 A significant objection to understanding ואכל as a defective writing of the *qal* 1cs imperfect of י־כ־ל is the fact that imperfect verbal forms of this root are essentially always attested *plene* in BH; such a form would thus be unexpected, even "aberrant." Cf. Fox, *Proverbs 10-31*, 854.

Prov 30:1 is adopted, for example, by the Lutherbibel, NRSV, NIV, and major commentators (e.g., Plöger, Fox).[10]

Given that LXX—the most important of the ancient versions—provides little text critical help with Prov 30:1b, some version of the usual emendation of the verse probably should be adopted.[11] Of course, if one accepts the common emendation, problems with the line remain. For instance, the undetermined vocative אל is somewhat strange. It is not the "true form" of the vocative, as Torrey put it.[12] However, although the vocative "should always have the article, in fact that article is often omitted, especially in poetry or lofty prose" (e.g., Num 12:13; Ps 10:11; 83:2).[13]

More problematic for any reading of Prov 30:1 that accepts the common emendation of the line is the fact that like the twice-stated "for Ithiel" in MT's vocalization, the phrase "I am weary, O God" in the emended text is repeated verbatim. Torrey, in fact, declared the presence of the duplicated phrases with their inauthentic vocatives to be "intolerable," while Fox, who himself argues *for* the common emendation that Torrey rails against, concedes that "perhaps the second *l'yty'l* should be omitted, as in LXX and Syr."[14] But the repetition of לאיתיאל is *lectio difficilior* and should not be so easily eliminated.

Otto Plöger, for one, addresses this concern regarding repetition in the common emendation of Prov 30:1b, even when the consonants לאיתיאל are re-divided. He emends MT's initial לאיתאל (the proper noun with *lamed*, "for Ithiel") to לאה את־האל (*lō'ê 'et-hā'el*) rendering, "der sich um Gott abmühte." Like many others, however, he reads the second לאיתיאל as לאיתי אל—"Ich habe mich abgemüht um Gott"; or with a determined vocative—לאיתי האל—"Ich habe mich abgemüht o Gott." For Plöger, MT's ואכל should likewise not be understood as a proper name, "doch wird es eine Verbform im impf. cons. sein: וָאֻכַל (»damit ich es fassen könnte«)."[15]

---

10 Otto Plöger, *Sprüche Salomos (Proverbia)* (Neukirchen-Vluyn: Neukirchener Verlag, 1984), 351, 354; Fox, *Proverbs 10-31*, 850.
11 LXX Prov 30:1 reads: Τοὺς ἐμοὺς λόγους, υἱέ, φοβήθητι καὶ δεξάμενος αὐτοὺς μετανόει· τάδε λέγει ὁ ἀνὴρ τοῖς πιστεύουσιν θεῷ, καὶ παύομαι ("My son, fear my words, and repent when you receive them; this is what the man says to those who believe in God: Now I stop"; NETS). As Fox (*Proverbs 10-31*, 1060) says, LXX has taken significant "liberties" with its *Vorlage* at this point.
12 Torrey, "Proverbs," 94.
13 Paul Joüon and Takamitsu Muraoka, *A Grammar of Biblical Hebrew*, 2nd ed. (Rome: Biblical Institute Press; 2006), 476. Cf. Paul Franklyn, "The Sayings of Agur in Proverbs 30: Piety or Scepticism?" *ZAW* 95 (1983): 238–52 (243).
14 Fox, *Proverbs 10-31*, 854.
15 Plöger, *Sprüche*, 351, 354, 358. Cf. Eva Strömberg Krantz, "'A Man Not Supported by God': On Some Crucial Words in Proverbs XXX 1" *VT* 46 (1996): 548–53, who reads *nĕ'ūm haggeber lō' 'ittô*

Taking a cue from an old, though in some ways problematic, suggestion by Torrey, my own reckoning with the problems of Prov 30:1b suggests that the corrupt MT of Prov 30:1b reflects a mistranslated Aramaic original. This reconstructed text, like Plöger's proposal, avoids undue repetition of terms in Agur's utterance: לאית אלה לאיתיני אלה ואוכל ("I am weary, O God; I am not divine but I will prevail").[16] Agur's assertion here that he is no divine figure is, as we shall see, important; it resonates with similar ontological claims in the key intertexts for Prov 30:1–4 that I will identify below.

Yet if one adopts the common emendation to Prov 30:1b—or some version of it—one still needs to explain well Agur's fatigue. Such explanations, unfortunately, are not usually forthcoming.[17] For Plöger it seems Agur's fatigue is simply a result of the fact that "Gott zu begreifen, ihn zu fassen," was simply "Ein zu hoch angesetztes Ziel." Tremper V. Longman, for his part, merely contends that the generally negative connotation of being tired in the emended v. 1 "fits in well with the rather depressing continuance of the speech." Similarly, Roger N. Whybray only supposes that of all the proposed emendations for v. 1 "perhaps that which best fits the context" is the one that highlights Agur's weariness. Richard J. Clifford also passes quickly to the following verses and (like others) contends that what Agur has grown tired of is trying to attain "heavenly wisdom" (cf. v. 3b).[18]

3. Proverbs 30:2–3

Although Clifford (like others) is right to suspect that the key to understanding the cause and nature of Agur's weariness in an emended Prov 30:1b has to do with

---

'ēl lā'îtî ēl wā'ēkel ("The word of a man not supported by God: 'I am weary, O God, and exhausted'").

16 See Torrey, "Proverbs," 93–96. For a critique of Torrey's view and fuller arguments for my proposal, see Sandoval, "Texts and Intertexts."
17 Fox's suggestions (*Proverbs 10-31*, 853) regarding Agur's weariness are some of the fullest, but move in an interpretive direction different from most others. He connects the rhetoric of weariness in Prov 30:1 both to the speaker in v. 7 who asks for two things "before I die" and to David's last testament in 2 Samuel 23, which uses some of the same rhetoric as Prov 30:1. For Fox, Agur's weariness and exhaustion is due to the fact that he is near death (cf. Franklyn, "Sayings," 241). However, unlike Fox, I discern a clear shift in voices in the passage starting at v. 4 (see below). Subsequently, the connections between Agur's words of weariness in v. 1 with the voice in v. 7 is not compelling to me.
18 Plöger, *Sprüche*, 358; Tremper V. Longman, III, *Proverbs* (Grand Rapids: Baker, 2006), 520; Whybray, *Proverbs*, 408; Richard J. Clifford, *Proverbs: A Commentary* (Louisville: Westminster John Knox, 1999), 261.

Agur's claim regarding heavenly wisdom or דעת קדשים in v. 3b (discussed below), Clifford does not describe this wisdom much and says little about why pursuing it exhausts Agur.[19] However, Agur's relationship to דעת קדשים is itself related to his failed efforts, or refusal, in Prov 30:2b and 3a to attain human understanding and wisdom (ולא־בינת אדם לי ולא־למדתי חכמה). Two ambiguities of v. 3 can helpfully be treated prior to addressing Agur's other statements about human wisdom.

The first ambiguity of Prov 30:3 is syntactical. The line reads:

ולא־למדתי חכמה ודעת קדשים אדע

Because v. 3a has Agur claim he has not learned traditional human *hokmah* (cf. hokmah v. 2), many commentators assume the לא of v. 3a does double duty in v. 3b, and regard the *waw* of ודעת as conjunctive.[20] The verse might thus be rendered: "And I have not learned wisdom, nor have I דעת קדשים" (NRSV). However, as Fox and others recognize, "Since the negative [in v. 3b] is not explicit, the clause could also be read as affirmative, hence adversative" to the preceding. Although Agur has no human wisdom, he confidently proclaims, "'but I *do* have'" דעת קדשים.[21]

A second ambiguity in the line has do with what, precisely, דעת קדשים might refer to in a wisdom composition like Proverbs 30.[22] Like most others, Fox understands the phrase to refer to "knowledge of the Holy One, that is God."[23] He rejects the notion that דעת קדשים is the esoteric, cosmological, and eschatologically-oriented knowledge that heavenly beings possess and to which certain humans have access, that other Second Temple texts know of. However, קדשים as an independent locution for the divine is not clearly attested in HB.[24] By contrast, attesta-

---

19 Clifford, *Proverbs*, 261.
20 The LXX of 30:3a, θεὸς δεδίδαχέν με σοφίαν, possibly points to a Hebrew text where an original ואל ("and God/El") at the beginning of v. 3 was read as the negative adverb ולא.
21 Fox, *Proverbs 10-31*, 855 (italics original).
22 Fox (*Proverbs 10-31*, 855), has helpfully sketched the most likely possibilities:
1. דעת קדשים is "knowledge of holy matters ... sacred mysteries of some sort";
2. דעת קדשים is "knowledge such as is possessed by the holy ones, that is, the angels";
3. דעת קדשים is "knowledge of the Holy One, that is God."
Fox believes option three is the "most probable."
23 Fox, *Proverbs 10-31*, 855.
24 In Prov 9:10 דעת קדשים may refer either to sacred matters, or in a more mythological sense, to "holy ones" who serve in the divine's heavenly court. However, since the phrase parallels "fear of the Lord," it possibly refers to knowledge of God. In MT Hos 12:1b (11:12b) קדושים is paralleled to ויהודה עד רד עם־אל ועם־קדושים נאמן—אל ("but Judah still walks with God, and is faithful to the Holy One"; NRSV). However, LXX Hos 11:12 (12:1) renders ועם קדשים as καὶ λαὸς ἅγιος; NETS subsequently renders the Greek half-verse (νῦν ἔγνω αὐτοὺς ὁ θεός, καὶ λαὸς ἅγιος κεκλήσεται θεοῦ) as "now God has come to know them, and the holy people shall be called God's." Robert B. Coote

tions of קדשים referring to heavenly beings are well established in both biblical (e. g., Deut 33:3; Zech 14:5; Ps 89:6 [5], 8 [7]; Job 5:1; Dan 8:24) and Second Temple sources (e. g.,1 Enoch; 4QInstruction, see below).[25] What's more, as we shall see shortly, the rhetoric of the broader passage and its relation to a number of other Second Temple discourses of knowledge also warrant understanding Agur's דעת קדשים precisely as esoteric, heavenly, eschatologically-oriented wisdom—a form of knowledge that Agur contrasts with human traditional wisdom like that which the first twenty-nine chapters of Proverbs offers.[26]

With these exegetical observations about Prov 30:3 in place, one can turn next to an understanding and rendering of Prov 30:2a. The full sense of this line, however, is somewhat difficult to discern since its meaning depends not only on the language of the superscription in v. 1a, but also on attending to an important intertextual allusion that these words and Agur's own discourse evoke.

4. Balaam in Numbers, Agur in Proverbs

If Agur in fact possesses heavenly, eschatological knowledge one might wonder why in v. 2a he states he is more בער than human? Surely knowing דעת קדשים would elevate his moral-epistemological status above that of a "brute" (or a "dolt"; cf. the play of בער, "dolt," and בעיר, "beast"). To resolve this conundrum, one must fully 'hear' in Agur's words the first key intertext for the opening lines of Proverbs 30, which essentially all commentators to an extent recognize: namely, the

---

"Hosea XII," *VT* 21 (1971): 389–402, acknowledges the broader mythological rhetoric of the line and translates, "And Judah again knows El, And with the Holy Ones he invokes El."

25 This is so even if puzzling out across texts and history the exact status and role of the heavenly figures who can transmit this knowledge to humans is a remarkably complex undertaking. See George W.E. Nickelsburg's excurses on watchers, holy ones, and angels in *1 Enoch 1* (Minneapolis: Fortress, 2001), 140–41; 208–10, and the discussions of John J. Collins, *Daniel* (Minneapolis: Fortress, 1993), 313–17, and Carol Newsom, *Songs of the Sabbath Sacrifice: A Critical Commentary* (Atlanta: Scholars Press, 1985), 23–38.

26 4Q402 4 6 offers a possible, albeit fragmentary, attestation of the phrase דעת קדשים outside of Prov 30:3. It reads, according to Newsom's transcription, [-- מכ]לכלי מחשב[תו] ודעת קדו[שי קדושים --]. Given the repetition of the phrase קדושים in the Songs of the Sabbath Sacrifice, Newsom's reconstruction of קדושי קדושים is likely correct, though קדושים does appear alone at least once in the work at 4Q400 1 i 17. Songs of the Sabbath Sacrifice repeatedly characterizes angelic beings as possessors of knowledge (e. g., אלי דעת) and appears to acknowledge that these beings pass this knowledge on to humans (e. g., 4Q401 14 ii 7—השמיעו נסתרות). A few lines after mentioning "knowledge of the [most] holy ones," 4Q402 4 11 (restored from MasShirShabb i 1) likewise speaks of נסתרות ("A[l]l these things He has done wondrous[ly] *together with those things which are eternally hidden* ..."). Newsom, *Songs*, 154, 156.

Balaam cycle of tales in Numbers, and Num 24:3 and 15 in particular. By tending to this intertext with Proverbs 30, it is possible to perceive the double-voiced nature of Agur's discourse, which for the tradents of Proverbs 30 ultimately helps to undermine any claims to esoteric wisdom that might challenge the primacy of the traditional wisdom of the rest of the book.

The intertextual relationship between the opening lines of Proverbs 30 and the Numbers passages is to a certain extent obvious. Both traditions, for example, share the precise terminology of נאם הגבר (Prov 30:1; Num 24:3, 15; cf. 2 Sam 23:1) and both traditions play on the consonants ב-ע-ר. Balaam is son of $b^{e\,}\bar{o}r$ (Num 24:3, 15); Agur, is "more a dolt/beast (ba'ar) than human" (Prov 30:2a).

However, less obvious intertextual connections between the initial lines of Proverbs 30 and the Balaam tales can also be discerned. First, both the Balaam cycle and Prov 30:1 cast their principal human characters as prophetic figures. Balaam is one who communicates with the divine (Num 22:9–12) and acts and speaks as the deity instructs him (Num 22:20, 38; 23:3, 16, 26; 24:1–3). Similarly, the tradition that introduces Agur's words also clearly casts him as one who speaks like a prophet. Prov 30:1a not only describes Agur's words as נאם הגבר ("the utterance the man"), just as Numbers describes Balaam's discourse. The Proverbs verse also introduces Agur's utterance as "the oracle" (המשא), a term that like נאם belongs firmly to a discourse of divinely revealed prophetic speech.[27] Although the word משא is not directly deployed in the Balaam texts, both Num 23:7 and 18 introduce Balaam's words with the phrase וישא משלו ("then Balaam uttered his oracle"; NRSV). Given the other clear intertextual relations between Proverbs 30 and the Balaam stories, this expression's use of the root (נשא) to introduce Balaam's prophetic voice was likely sufficient evidence for the tradents of Proverbs to regard Agur's words as a משא. Yet because what Balaam utters is itself called a משל, the expression also likely warranted the decision by the redactors of Proverbs to append Agur's words to the *Mishle Shlomo*. Just as "the utterance of the man" (נאם הגבר) Balaam, which "he lifted up" could be called a משל, so "the utterance of the man" (נאם הגבר) Agur was surely also reckoned by the later wisdom tradents not only as a משא, but as a kind of משל—even if it was not explicitly named such in Proverbs 30; it was thus rightly appended to a משלי scroll.[28]

---

27 Seventeen of the twenty occurrences of "oracle" (משא) are in prophetic contexts; נאם is exceedingly common in prophetic works.
28 Elsewhere in HB משל can refer not merely to short proverbial utterances (like those in Proverbs 10–29), but to a range of figurative discourses, or rhetoric in need of interpretation, including certain prophetic speech, such as Ezekiel's allegories in Ezek 17:2 and 24:3. Cf. Otto Eissfeldt, *Der Maschal im Alten Testament* (Giessen: Töpelmann, 1913); A. R. Johnson, "מָשָׁל," in *Wisdom in Israel and in the Ancient Near East*, ed. Martin Noth and D. Winton Thomas (Leiden: Brill, 1955), 162–69;

The intertextual relation between Agur in Prov 30 and Balaam in Numbers 22–24 is also evidenced by the fact that the knowledge both Balaam and Agur possess can be associated with heavenly beings. In Numbers the angel of the Lord (מלאך יהוה; Num 22:23–35), famously brought to Balaam's attention via an uncooperative talking ass, communicates to the seer what he ought to speak to Balak. In Prov 30:3b Agur similarly claims to possess angelic wisdom (see above), though in Proverbs the heavenly beings Agur knows of are called קדשים instead of מלאך/מלאכי יהוה.

When one acknowledges all these intertextual identifications of Agur in Proverbs with Balaam of Numbers, it is possible to discern the double-voiced nature of Agur's words, which creates an irony that ultimately places Agur, and his claim to angelic knowledge, in a negative light. First, despite Agur's subsequent claim to possess angelic knowledge, his words "I am more dolt/beast than human," which seem to denigrate his moral-intellectual status, can now be heard on more than one level. Although Agur's utterance literally or straightforwardly suggests he is a dolt, with the Balaam intertexts in mind it can also be playfully heard as this character's own grander claim—though not necessarily that of the tradents of Proverbs—that he is more akin to that ancient custodian of divinely revealed knowledge, the son of Beor, than he is like other humans: בער אנכי מאיש [כ]י—"I am more [like the son of] Beor (בער) than a [normal] person."

The irony of this double-voiced discourse emerges not only via a reader's recognition of the Balaam intertexts, but especially through the recollection that throughout most of the rest of Proverbs the wisdom necessary for human flourishing is not revealed heavenly knowledge but that which is preserved and transmitted by human teachers and communities. By attending to such traditional teaching, Proverbs insists that the book's addressees can attain a robust practical wisdom by which to discern the good, reject evil, and thereby hopefully flourish. This is so even if some humans will fail to greater and lesser extents in this endeavor and be labeled foolish, wicked, or even a בער (12:1). Because Agur does not learn traditional wisdom (30: 2, 3a) and instead in Prov 30:3b claims to possess—like Balaam son of בער—revealed, heavenly knowledge, the tradents of traditional human wisdom responsible for the integration of Agur's discourse of esoteric knowledge into Proverbs 30 have the weary seer himself proclaim—in critical-ironic fashion—that he is indeed בער (a dolt/beast). On the terms of the sages' long-established moral discourse in Proverbs, one like Agur who does not attain,

---

Timothy Polk, "Paradigms, Parables, and *Měšālîm*: On Reading the *Māšāl* in Scripture," *CBQ* 45 (1983): 564–83.

or refuses, traditional human understanding (ולא־בינת אדם לי; 30:2b) and wisdom (ולא־למדתי חכמה; 30:3a) could be no other.²⁹

5. Angelic Wisdom in Proverbs 30 and 4QInstruction

We are thus left in the opening three lines of Proverbs 30 with:
a. An Agur who claims he is weary and exhausted; or who is weary but is confident he will nonetheless prevail; and
b. An (ironically construed) Agur who is unable to attain, or who more likely rejects, human understanding and traditional *hokmah* in favor of esoteric, eschatological wisdom—"knowledge of holy ones."

Features of Agur's rhetoric thus evoke the moral-epistemological discourse of another Second Temple wisdom work, namely, 4QInstruction. Like Agur and other Second Temple texts, 4QInstruction too deploys a rhetoric of esoteric, angelic wisdom. Importantly, however, this Qumran text also speaks of human weariness in the context of the pursuit of such knowledge.

In the symbolic universe of 4QInstruction, the text's "understanding" addressee, the מבין, in contrast to a "spirit of flesh," belongs to a community whose "spirit" and work is somehow aligned with that of angelic beings. For example, 4Q417 1 i 16–17 intimates not only that the מבין belongs to a "spiritual people" (עם רוח) but that "according to the likeness of the holy ones He [God] fashioned him [the spiritual people]" (כתבנית קדושים יצרו).³⁰ The community imagined by

---

29 Of course, not all readers will hear, or be open to hearing, the sort of irony in Agur's words that I just described. Instead, they will insist on the text's straightforward meaning as the only possible one. This is a perennial problem for the interpretation of irony and other double-voiced discourses: some hear it and others do not. Although regularly arguments for interpreting utterances as instances of irony are based on textual (and intertextual and contextual) features of a work like those I offer, it remains a fact that competent readers can and do come to different conclusions about the ironic nature of certain utterances. What is in any case clear is that unless we hear both the straightforward meaning of an utterance *and* the unspoken, playful, ironic meaning of that utterance, "we are not interpreting the utterance *as ironic* at all." For all these matters, see Linda Hutcheon, *Irony's Edge: The Theory and Politics of Irony* (London: Routledge, 1994); the quotation is from p. 67 (italics original).
30 Matthew J. Goff, *4QInstruction* (Atlanta: SBL Press, 2013), 139, 164; cf. John J. Collins, "In the Likeness of the Holy Ones: The Creation of Humankind in a Wisdom Text from Qumran," in *The*

4QInstruction, because of its relation to the angels, may thus have access to esoteric, heavenly knowledge like heavenly beings do.

One important passage from 4QInstruction that likewise suggests this may be the case, and which constitutes an apt intertext with the words of Agur in Prov 30:1–3, is the fragmentary 4Q418 55 8–11.[31]

]הלוא יד[עתם אם לוא שמעתמה כיא מלאכי קודש לו בשמים
] [אמת וירדפו אחר כול שורשי בינה וישקדו על] [
] לפי[דעתם יכבדו איש מרעהו ולפי שכלו ירבה הדרו
] [הכאנוש הם כי יעצל ובן אדם כי ידמה

Do you not know? Have you not heard, that the holy angels to him in heaven [ ]
[ ] truth and they chase after all the roots of understanding. And they keep watch over [ ]
[accor]ding to their knowledge they are gloriful, one more than the other. And according to his insight his splendor is great.
Are they like man? For he is lazy. And (like) humankind? For he comes to a standstill.

Two points about these lines are significant for understanding Agur's words. First, the angelic beings—the holy angels (מלאכי קודש)—are associated with key terms of moral epistemology—truth (אמת), understanding (בינה), knowledge (דעת), and insight (שכל), a rhetoric that Agur likewise in part deploys. However, recall, in Prov 30:2–3a Agur disclaims possession of *human* understanding (ולא־בינת אדם לי) and wisdom (ולא־למדתי חכמה). The angels in 4QInstruction, unlike humans (אנוש; בן אדם), seek after the *roots* of understanding (וירדפו אחר כול שורשי בינה).[32] Second, the angelic, heavenly beings of 4Q418 55 (cf. perhaps 4Q418 164 2)—elsewhere in 4QInstruction called קדושים (4Q417 1 i 17; 4Q418 81+81a 1, 11–12; cf. 4–5), "sons of heaven" (4Q416 2, 2a–c 4; 4Q418 69 ii 13; see below), and perhaps "spirits of holiness" (4Q418 76 3; cf. 4Q403 1 i 44 and רוחי צבא in 1QH[a] 5:25)—are ontologically distinct from humans, even if the "spiritual people" of the work are imagined as standing in close relation to the angels.

Provo International Conference on the Dead Sea Scrolls, ed. Donald W. Parry and Eugene Ulrich (Leiden: Brill, 1999): 609–18.
31 Subsequent texts and translations of 4Q418 55 and 69 ii follow Arjen Bakker, "Sages and Sayings: Continuous Study and Transformation in *Musar le-Mevin* and *Serek ha-Yaḥad*," in *Tracing Sapiential Traditions in Ancient Judaism*, ed. Hindy Najman et. al. (Leiden: Brill 2016), 106–18.
32 As Goff (*4QInstruction*, 219) recognizes, "The key question [of line 10] is whether those who are glorified are the elect or angels." Like Goff I assume line 10 is "an assertion that the angels are being rewarded for their devotion to the pursuit of knowledge." Bakker's translation above is ambiguous; he does not explicitly address the issue when discussing the passage in "Sages," 110–12.

Because of this ontological distinction between humans and angels, the angelic beings in 4Q418 55 also appear to be, in part, characterologically distinct from humans. As the rhetorical questions at the end of the pericope make clear, the angels are active and diligent; they pursue understanding and apparently keep watch over forms of knowledge, advancing in status in relation to their possession of the same. By contrast, humans are characterized as lazy (עצל) or inactive (דמה) presumably in respect to their own epistemological efforts. This rhetoric of laziness and inaction, of course, is not precisely a discourse of weariness like that which Agur utters in Prov 30:1. Yet in a certain sense it can be said to belong to the same conceptual field. If one grows weary in an activity and thus no longer desires or is able to engage in it, this subsequent inactivity could be characterized as laziness, if there were an underlying belief that the activity, or enduring in it, was not, or should not be regarded as, burdensome.

The second text from the *Musar le-Mevin* that elucidates Agur's words is 4Q418 69 ii + 60 10–14.

ואתם בחירי אמת ורדפי [דעת]משח[רי בינה ו]שוקד[ים] על כול דעה
איכה תאמרו יגענו בבינה ושקדנו לרדוף דעת
[ ] בכול מ[ ] ולא עיף בכול שני עולם
הלוא באמת ישעשע לעד ודעה[לנצח] תשרתנו
וב[ני] שמים אשר חיים עולם נחלתם האמור יאמרו יגענו בפעלות אמת ויעפ[נו]
בכול קצים
הלוא באור עולם יתהלכו [כ]בוד ורוב הדר אתם

> And you, chosen ones of truth, and those who chase [knowledge,] those who diligently se[ek understanding and] those who keep watch over all knowledge.
> How can you say, "we weary ourselves in understanding and we keep watch to chase knowledge"?
> [ ] in all [ ] and He does not grow tired in all years of eternity.
> Does He not delight in truth forever and (does not) knowledge [eternally] serve him?
> And the sons of heaven, whose lot is eternal life, do they really say, 'we grow weary in deeds of truth and we grow tired throughout all ages'?
> Do they not walk in eternal light? Glory and great splendor is with them.

As with the 4Q418 55 text, several points about these lines from fragment 69 ii are relevant for understanding Agur's words. First, in these verses, it is not the angels alone who are said to pursue knowledge and understanding and to watch over the same. Humans, the addressees of the text—the "chosen ones of truth"—do so as well. However, this pursuit of esoteric knowledge is said to be tiring, and the humans in the lines, again via rhetorical questioning, are chided for articulating their fatigue—"How can you say, we weary ourselves in understanding ...?" Finally, the text once more articulates a clear ontological distinction between humans and heavenly beings. On the one hand, the deity itself, unlike humans, does not grow weary. On the other hand, the angelic beings, the sons of heaven, likewise do not tire in their "deeds of truth."

The fatigue humans experience in their quest for knowledge in the above 4Q418 fragments is related to their mortality. Unlike humans, however, angelic beings in 4QInstruciton enjoy eternal life. "Do they not walk in eternal light?" line 14 above asks rhetorically, articulating a view common in Second Temple Judaism. As Arjen Bakker explains, in 4QInstruction, "Human beings may strive to gather knowledge, but they have their limitations: they become faint, they grow tired and eventually they die...." "Nevertheless," Bakker continues, "the sage is expected to continually expand his wisdom" probably by studying Torah and "other forms of knowledge" such as the *raz nihyeh*.[33] Through such study the addressee of 4QInstruction has, as Matthew J. Goff avers, "the potential to attain a blessed afterlife." As Goff explains, if in 4Q417 2 i 10–12, "mourning is a cipher for the present existence of the *mebin,* 'eternal joy' in that passage is reasonably understood as a reference to the eternal life he can obtain after death."[34] The ontological distance between the angels and the human "insider" community of 4QInstruction is thus reckoned as one that will be eschatologically adjusted. One might say that in 4QInstruction, despite the human addressee's weariness in striving after esoteric knowledge, with such knowledge he will in the end, much like Agur, prevail.

Of course, the terminology of weariness in the lines from 4Q418 is not לאה, as is the case in the suitably emended Prov 30:1b; it is עיף and יגע.[35] Yet all three terms belong to the same semantic field and can be rendered by the same or related Greek terms in LXX.[36] What's more, at times the Aramaic Targums render יגע precisely with a form of ל-א-י. This is the case, for instance, in Targum Jonathan

---

33 The enigmatic *raz nihyeh* ("mystery of existence"; "mystery that is to come") is the "means by which the addressee [of 4QInstruction] obtains wisdom. It is supernatural revelation disclosed to him, upon which he is to reflect and contemplate." Goff, *4QInstruction*, 15.
34 Goff, *4QInstruction*, 17–18.
35 According to the transcription of Pancratius C. Beentjes (*The Book of Ben Sira in Hebrew* [Atlanta: SBL, 2006], 77), Ben Sira 43:30 (MS B 13r:15) intriguingly reads: [--] הרימו קול בכל תוכלו כי [ ]חת לא כי תלאו ואל כח החליפו מרוממיו עוד יש. In the immediate context of 43:30 MS B refers to an angelic being (מלאך in 43:26; cf. קדושי אל in 42:17) while according to Newsom, מרוממים ("those who exalt") in Songs of the Sabbath Sacrifice, is an occasional epithet for angelic beings (e. g., 4Q405 14-15 i 3; Newsom, *Songs*, 28, 280). Although here one must leave aside a number of critical questions about how best to understand Sira 43:30 (including the fact that the transcription is at points uncertain), it may obliquely evoke a tradition regarding praise/prayer, angelic beings, and weariness (לאה).
36 See Helmer Ringgren, "לָאָה," *TDOT* 7:396; Gerhard F. Hasel, "יעף," *TDOT* 6:152; "יָגַע," *TDOT* 5:388.

on at least three occasions with respect to Isaiah 40 alone, including Isa 40:28, a verse 4Q418 clearly invokes.³⁷ In the Isaiah text, the prophet also distinguishes humans, and their potential to gain knowledge, sharply from the heavenly "Creator of the ends of the earth," who

לא ייעף ולא ייגע אין חקר לתבונתו

does not faint or grow weary; his understanding is unsearchable.³⁸

6. Proverbs 30:4 and Isaiah 40

Isaiah 40, however, is not merely an important intertext for 4Q418 69. As is often pointed out, Prov 30:1–4, especially v. 4 and Isa 40:12–14 (cf. Job 38) also share significant terminology and important rhetorical features.

מי־מדד בשעלו מים ושמים בזרת תכן וכל בשלש עפר הארץ ושקל בפלס הרים וגבעות במאזנים מי־תכן את־רוח יהוה ואיש עצתו יודיענו את מי נועץ ויבינהו וילמדהו בארח משפט וילמדהו דעת ודרך תבונות יודיענו

Who has measured the waters in the hollow of his hand and marked off the heavens with a span, enclosed the dust of the earth in a measure, and weighed the mountains in scales and the hills in a balance? ¹³ Who has directed the spirit of the LORD, or as his counselor has instructed him? ¹⁴ Whom did he consult for his enlightenment, and who taught him the path of justice? Who taught him knowledge, and showed him the way of understanding? (NRSV)

מי עלה־שמים וירד מי אסף־רוח בחפניו מי צרר־מים בשמלה מי הקים כל־אפסי־ארץ מה־שמו ומה־שם־בנו כי תדע

Who has ascended to heaven and come down? Who has gathered the wind in the hollow of the hand? Who has wrapped up the waters in a garment? Who has established all the ends of the earth? What is the person's name? And what is the name of the person's child? Surely you know! (NRSV)

First, the rhetoric of knowledge (e. g., forms of בין, ידע) and teaching (forms of למד), deployed in Isa 40:12–14 to express divine wisdom, resonates with Agur's words in Prov 30:2–3. There, recall, Agur eschews human understanding and the learning of traditional wisdom, opting instead for knowledge of holy ones. Both the Isaiah passage and Prov 30:4 also obviously make use of the interrogative pro-

---

37 Isa 40:28, 30, 31. Targum Jonathan in its final form is, of course, a text significantly later than 4QInstruction. However, scholars debate whether and which traditions it preserves may be traced back to the Second Temple period. See Robert Hayward, "Targum Pseudo-Jonathan and Anti-Islamic Polemic," *JSS* 34 (1989): 77–93 (77).
38 The Targum reads: לָא בַעֲמָל וְלָא בְלִיאוּ לֵית סוֹף לְסוּכְלְתָנוּתֵיהּ.

noun מי, besides the already mentioned forms derived from ידע. However, they also both deploy the lexemes שמים (heavens), רוח (wind), מים (waters), and ארץ (earth). Similarly, the two passages each make use of an image of holding natural phenomenon in one's hands —wind (in Proverbs) and water (in Isaiah).

The evocation by Prov 30:4 of Isaiah's discourse of divine incomparability and the unsearchable nature of the divine's wisdom underscores the Proverbs passage's insistence that the sort of heavenly knowledge Agur claims to hold is, in fact, unattainable. As Fox explains, the intended response to the series of rhetorical questions in Prov 30:4 may logically be either "someone," "God," or "no one." For Fox, "no one" is "the intended response" since he believes the verse represents the continuation of Agur's "self-humbling" acknowledgment in vv. 2 and 3 that he does not possess human wisdom, the worth of which—according to Fox—Agur ultimately subordinates to knowledge of God's words in v. 5.

However, the precise relation of Prov 30:4 to the verses that precede and follow it is debated. There is no need to rehearse all the possible relations that scholars have hypothesized; suffice it to say Prov 30:4 is not always reckoned as an extension of Agur's words, but as the beginning of another voice's critical reply to them.[39] Indeed, if one regards v. 4 as introducing a new textual voice and understands Prov 30:3b as a positive, adversative statement in relation to the first half of that verse—that is, if v. 3b does not represent Agur's epistemic humility but a positive claim to possess esoteric knowledge—a very different rhetorical picture for the relationship of v. 3b with v. 4 emerges than that which Fox (and others) imagines. No longer does v. 4 constitute a continuation of Agur's words that essentially call into question the value of traditional human wisdom; it rather represents a rhetorical strategy to question the worth of *esoteric* wisdom! By evoking Isaiah's majestic words concerning the incomparability of the divine, and this God's wisdom, the new voice in Prov 30:4 essentially scoffs at the sorts of claims to esoteric, heavenly knowledge that Agur and his ilk make.

The new voice of Prov 30:4—likely that of traditional wisdom—thus inquires as to who the person is that might have the necessary access to cosmic and eschatological realities that would warrant Agur's claim to possess "knowledge of holy ones." "Who is the human who has gone up to heaven and come down?", this critical voice asks, concluding sarcastically with a play on Agur's earlier claim to such knowledge (ודעת קדשים אדע) with the words, כי תדע—"Because you know" (cf. Job 38:21).

---

39 "There is no agreement among the commentators whether the speaker" in Prov 30:4 "is the same as in vv. 2–3...." Whybray, *Proverbs*, 408.

Although Fox understands the broader rhetorical logic of Prov 30:4 differently than I, his verdict that the obvious answer to the line's questions is "no one" should still be adopted. No one has made the necessary journey and hence no one has access to the celestial realities that might constitute or enable the sort of heavenly "knowledge of holy ones" Agur pretends to.

7. Proverbs 30 and Early Enoch Traditions

Fox, however, also notes that representatives of the "later parts of the Enoch traditions," such as 1 Enoch 72–82, might have responded to the rhetorical questions in Prov 30:4 by insisting that "Enoch went up to the heavens and came back down."[40] Although Fox ultimately refuses to admit a connection between Enoch and Agur, there are good reasons to acknowledge an intertextual relation between the early Enochic material and the initial lines of Proverbs 30.

First, the evocation in Prov 30:4 of Enoch may be intimated not only by the rhetoric of ascending and descending, as Fox sensed. It is also signaled by a curious rhetorical construction. As Whybray has pointed out, the effort to identify someone by inquiring of their son's name does not otherwise seem to be attested in HB. He writes: "There are no other examples of such a request for identification in the Old Testament," adding that it is more usual for the Bible to have someone inquire about a person's father.[41] Although Whybray may well be correct about all this, the turn of phrase, שם בנו, which Prov 30:4 deploys in its rhetorical questioning, appears six times in the Bible simply to identify someone's son. Intriguingly, the first of these attestations is in Gen 4:17.

וידע קין את־אשתו ותהר ותלד את־חנוך ויהי בנה עיר ויקרא שם העיר כשם בנו חנוך

> Cain knew his wife, and she conceived and bore Enoch; and he built a city, and named it Enoch after his son Enoch. (NRSV)

The ambiguous syntax of the Hebrew of this line indicates either that Cain names a city he built after his son Enoch (so NRSV), or as Claus Westermann supposed, that Enoch (the most immediate antecedent of ויהי in the second half of the line and possibly the explicit subject delayed until the end of the line) names the city *he* built after *his* son. In either case, the terms שם בנו are closely connected to the name Enoch. On Westermann's understanding, however, the name of Enoch's

---

40 Fox, *Proverbs 10-31*, 857.
41 Whybray, *Proverbs*, 410.

"son" (שם בנו) in the line may have been implicitly assumed to be Methuselah—though the relationship of the Cain traditions of Gen 4:17 to the genealogies of Enoch and Methuselah in Gen 5:18–27 is complex and debated.[42]

What is just as noteworthy as Gen 4:17's relation to Prov 30:4, however, is the fact that in 1 Enoch both the Book of the Luminaries (those chapters Fox alluded to) and the Book of the Watchers associate Enoch's esoteric knowledge with his heavenly, angelic guides. These texts also note clearly that the scribe transmitted this knowledge to others. For example, 1 Enoch 81, a text in the Book of the Luminaries, but which according to Nickelsburg probably originally belonged to the Book of the Watchers, indicates that Enoch passed on his heavenly, angelic wisdom—what one might call his דעת קדשים—to his descendants; and the text specifically names his *son* Methuselah as a primary recipient.[43] After Enoch learns cosmological-eschatological knowledge from the heavenly tablets that an angel shows him (1 En. 81:1–2), he says,

> ... seven holy ones brought me and set me on the earth in front of
> the door of my house and said to me, "Make known everything to
> Methuselah your son ... (1 En. 81:5; cf. 82:1–4)[44]

If one conceivable answer to the question of Prov 30:4 about who it is that has ascended to the heavens and come back down is Enoch, as Fox intuited but resisted, the best response to the peculiar question about the name of such a person's *son* is Methuselah!

The nature and extent of the intertextual links between Agur's words in Proverbs 30 and the biblical and Second Temple texts already noted might be detailed further, and other intertexts might be identified.[45] Yet enough has been

---

42 Whybray, *Proverbs*, 408–409; Claus Westermann, *Genesis 1-11* (Minneapolis: Augsburg, 1984), 326–28.
43 Nickelsburg, *1 Enoch 1*, 334–38.
44 Nickelsburg, *1 Enoch 1*, 338.
45 For example, a trace of the rhetoric of שם בנו (Prov 30:4; Gen 4:17) also appears in the Balaam texts. Although the Bible regularly refers to Balaam as בלעם בן בעור (e. g., Num 22:5 and elsewhere), in the introduction to the seer's oracles themselves he is called בלעם בנו בער (Num 24:3, 15; cf. בלק ... בנו צפר in Num 23:18). The latter, curious construction is likely "an anticipatory genitive" and can be rendered as "Beor's own son" or literally "his son, (namely), of Beor." See Baruch A. Levine, *Numbers 21–36: A New Translation with Introduction and Commentary*, AB (New York: Doubleday, 2000), 181. Also, Num 24:3–4 and 15–16, especially the phrase וישא משלו ויאמר ("and he took up his discourse and said") is echoed in 1 En. 1:2–3. This Enoch text also deploys images of esoteric, angelic knowledge that resonate both with Balaam's visions and with Agur's "knowledge of holy ones." It reads: "And he took up his discourse and said: Enoch, a righteous man whose eyes were opened by God, who had the vision of the Holy One and of heaven, which he

said to conclude that together a cluster of key intertexts evoked by Prov 30:1–4—the Balaam cycle of material in Numbers, 4QInstruction, Isaiah 40, and the early Enoch material—function to articulate traditional wisdom's rejoinder to competing discourses of knowledge in the late Second Temple epoch. For the redactors of Proverbs 30 any attempt to subordinate traditional human *hokmah*, like that which is found in the rest of the book of Proverbs, to esoteric, sometimes eschatologically-oriented knowledge—whether that of Balaam, Enoch, the *raz nihyeh*, Agur, or someone/something else—was ultimately misguided.

8. Ontological Distinction

However, it remains to explain why Agur in a suitably emended Prov 30:1b claims to be so weary. To discern plausible reasons for Agur's fatigue, it is necessary to highlight one aspect of 4QInstruction, Isaiah 40, and the early Enoch material that is *not* obviously represented in the corrupted text of Prov 30:1, or in Agur's further words in vv. 2–3, though it is evident in v. 4. This is the implicit or explicit insistence on the ontological difference between humans and divine beings. This difference is, however, evident in my proposed Aramaic *Vorlage* for Prov 30:1b noted above.[46] Aramaic Agur simply articulates this ontological distinction from his own first-person perspective—לאית אלה לאיתיני אלה ואוכל ("I am weary, O God; I am not divine but I will prevail"). The assertion of such a difference between the divine and humans also appears in a portion of the Balaam traditions of Numbers not yet mentioned. In Num 23:19 Balaam reminds Balak that "God is not a person" nor "the child of a human"—לא איש אל ... ובן אדם.

The assertion of the human-divine ontological distinction, however, is most intriguing in 4QInstruction. In this composition, as we saw, the pursuit of esoteric wisdom is what provokes the fatigue that that text attributes to humans while God and angels do not grow weary in their tasks. Put otherwise, it is humans' humanness that makes their study of esoteric knowledge such a hard row to hoe.

If the fatigue that 4QInstruction attributes to humans in their pursuit of knowledge or wisdom is due to their ontological status as humans and not heavenly, angelic figures, a further passage in the *Musar le-Mevin* helps clarify why exactly, for 4QInstruction at least, the pursuit of esoteric, eschatological knowl-

---

showed me. From the words of the watchers and holy ones I heard everything; And as I heard everything from them, I also understood what I saw." Nickelsburg, *1 Enoch 1*, 132, 137.
46 Cf. Sandoval, "Texts and Intertexts."

edge is so wearying for people: it is, or ought to be, a constant undertaking. In 4Q417 1 i 6 (cf. 4Q418 43–45 4) the text commands its addressee:

יומם ולילה הגה ברז נהיה ודורש תמיד

Day and night meditate on the *raz nihyeh* [the mystery of existence] and study continuously.

Although 4QInstruction is not universally regarded as a work of the Qumran community, its rhetoric and conceptual world are closely aligned with the discourse of indisputably sectarian works, especially Hodayot. The enigmatic expression *raz nihyeh*, which 4QInstruction deploys on a number of occasions, is also attested once in the Community Rule (1QS) and twice in the Book of Mysteries (1Q27, 4Q299–301). As Carol A. Newsom explains, this mystery of existence, or the mystery that is to be, seems to encompass "knowledge concerning the structures of the natural world, the course of human history, and the hidden principles that guide them."[47] The meditation on and continuous study in (-ב) the *raz nihyeh* in the *Musar le-Mevin* also resonates profoundly with the sorts of sectarian practices of which 1QS 6:6–8 speaks.

ואל ימש במקום אשר יהיו שם העשרה איש דורש בתורה יומם ולילה תמיד על יפות איש לרעהו
והרבים ישקודו ביחד את שלישית כול לילות השנה לקרוא בספר ולדרוש משפט ולברך ביחד

And in the place in which the Ten assemble there should not be missing a man to interpret the law day and night, always, one relieving another. And the Many shall be on watch together for a third of each night of the year in order to read the book, explain the regulation, and bless together.[48]

As Bakker explains, members of the *Yaḥad* seem to ensure that constant study occurs "by taking turns: if the one studying becomes exhausted he has to be replaced by a fellow."[49]

The nature of the interpretive knowledge the *Yaḥad* produces in this context is not explicitly stated, but it is likely halakhic in a broad sense and may not be constituted by, or depend for its emergence on, the same sort of cosmological-eschatological mysteries that are probably to be associated with (study of/in) the *raz nihyeh*. The community's efforts, nonetheless, likely do produce a kind esoteric knowledge—insight directed to, and comprehended by, a small group of Qumranite insiders. As Lawrence H. Schiffman has contended, "The legal materi-

---

47 Carol A. Newsom, "Models of the Moral Self: Hebrew Bible and Second Temple Judaism," *JBL* 131 (2012): 5–25 (23n43). Cf. Goff, *4QInstruction*, 14–17.
48 Text and translation are from Florentino García Martínez and Eibert J.C. Tigchelaar, *The Dead Sea Scrolls Study Edition* (Leiden: Brill, 2000), 1:82–83 (henceforth: *DSSSE*).
49 Bakker, "Sages," 109.

als of the sect are to a great extent derived from biblical interpretation, an activity that took place at regular study sessions as part of sectarian life."⁵⁰ Given the significance of both revelatory knowledge and eschatological concerns in other Qumran texts, the halakhic insight alluded to in 1QS 6 might reasonably be imagined as a kind of divinely inspired knowledge that emerges in light of the Yaḥad's eschatological beliefs and interests. On the one hand, as Schiffman explains, the Qumran "sect divided the law into two categories—the *nigleh*, 'revealed,' and the *nistar*, 'hidden.' The revealed laws were known to all Israel … but the hidden laws were known only to the sect and were revealed solely through sectarian exegesis."⁵¹ On the other hand, for Schiffman the Qumran community— at least the author of the Rule of the Congregation—"looked to the End of Days" not only "for the restoration of Israel's ancient glories…," but also for "a level of sanctity and purity" that "would be attained when all Israel observed perfectly the law of Torah."⁵²

Although not explicitly stated, in the emended text of Prov 30:1b, the weariness Agur complains of—or *prays* to God about—as he seeks דעת קדשים makes good sense when it is understood against the background of the sort of continuous study and pursuit of esoteric, divinely-inspired wisdom or halakhic knowledge alluded to in 4Q417 1 i and 1QS 6:6–8.

9. Prayerful Study and Agur's Weariness

Yet if Agur's suitably emended words directed to the divine in Prov 30:1b—"I am weary, O God …"—count as prayer on the broad definition Falk and others adopt; and if the fatigue Agur prayerfully laments can be accounted for as a result of his all too human pursuit of esoteric, heavenly knowledge in the context of a community that day and night seeks such wisdom, still more might be said about how Agur's efforts might be imagined to fit within a broader landscape of Second Temple discourses and ideologies of prayer.

In *Before the Bible: The Liturgical Body and the Formation of Scriptures in Early Judaism*, Judith Newman has criticized anachronistic approaches to liturgy in Second Temple times, pointing out the tendency to analyze Second Temple texts and practices in view of the "later classical Jewish and Christian conceptions of liturgy that center on worship according to fixed liturgical texts that have come to

---

50 Lawrence H. Schiffman, *Reclaiming the Dead Sea Scrolls: Their True Meaning for Judaism and Christianity* (New York: Doubleday, 1994), 247.
51 Schiffman, *Reclaiming*, 247, 339.
52 Schiffman, *Reclaiming*, 339.

replace the sacrificial system."⁵³ She, however, believes that our understandings of ancient liturgy should encompass "the whole gamut of worship in and around the study of sacred texts, the acts of eating and fasting, and of course, benedictions, prayers and amulets."⁵⁴ I do not wish to claim that the rhetoric of either 4Q417 1 i 6 and 1 QS 6:7 might be regarded as simply pointing to liturgical practices so understood. However, it does intimate that certain Second Temple groups not only undertook day and night study in pursuit of esoteric, often eschatological knowledge, but that this quest for revealed insight included elements that might well be reckoned as prayer, and that the entire enterprise constituted, if not a liturgy, a complex practice of constant *prayerful study*—"an act of communication with the divine."

9.1 Nocturnal Prayer in the Second Temple Period

In a wide ranging study on prayer in the Second Temple epoch, Jeremy Penner has noted that prior to the widespread introduction of artificial lights, human nocturnal rhythms were quite distinct from what they are for many people in the modern world; and this afforded people opportunities for religious expression at night.⁵⁵ Following the work of A. Roger Ekirch, Penner, for example, points to studies on the anthropology of sleep that indicate people in epochs without significant artificial light might well engage in a first sleep, subsequently be awake for a time, and then retire for a second sleep.⁵⁶ The periods of wakefulness during the night provided the occasion not only for attending to bodily functions and social intercourse, but also for the performance of certain religious practices.⁵⁷

Pre-modern nocturnal religious practices, however, were not solely a function of the sleep rhythms of humans without electric light. They also were predicated on other sorts of presuppositions about the supernatural realm, sleep, and the nighttime hours. For instance, throughout the ancient Near East, nocturnal reli-

---

53 Judith H. Newman, *Before the Bible: The Liturgical Body and the Formation of Scriptures in Early Judaism* (New York: Oxford University Press, 2018), 8.
54 Newman, *Before Bible*, 8, citing Stefan Reif, "Prayer in Early Judaism," in *Prayer from Tobit to Qumran*, ed. Renate Egger-Wenzel and Jeremy Corley (Berlin: De Gruyter, 2004), 439–64 (442).
55 Penner, *Patterns*, 167.
56 A. Roger Ekirch, *At Day's Close, Night in Times Past* (New York: Norton & Company, 2005), esp. 300–323, and "Sleep We Have Lost: Pre-industrialized Slumber in the British Isles," *The American Historical Review* 1006 (2001): 343–86.
57 See, for example, the evidence for nocturnal worship in rabbinic and other sources Penner alludes to in *Patterns*, 165–68, esp. notes 1–5.

gious practices were associated with the celestial bodies that were identified with particular deities. This ancient view of the cosmos, together with the fact that these celestial bodies were visible only at night, meant nighttime was an obvious period when humans might worship and otherwise strive to communicate with the celestial deities. As Penner explains, these sorts of perceptions of the cosmos "provided the underlying impetus for nocturnal religious activities, particularly rituals and prayers addressed to these celestial gods." This was true in ancient Israel and Judah as well, as certain biblical texts that condemn the practice of astral worship make clear (e. g., Jer 10:22; 1 Kgs 23:13; etc.). In later Second Temple Judaism, of course, divine status was more fully denied the celestial bodies.[58] Nonetheless they continued to be associated with heavenly figures, but now lesser beings—angels—figures who could be "incorporated into a monotheistic framework," as a text like 1QH^a 9:2–15 makes clear.[59] Instead of celestial bodies being identified as various deities to be worshiped, they are identified with angels whose own worship of the one God a human community, like the Qumranites, might in some fashion seek to emulate. As Penner notes, although, nocturnal prayer in pre-modern epochs does not necessarily signal a special piety, it may in fact be more common in communities that engage in significant ritual practices, as did the Qumran sect.[60]

Nighttime in the ancient Near East was also believed to be a period when malevolent supernatural beings were especially active and to whose aggressions humans during the liminal state of sleep—not conscious, but not dead—were particularly vulnerable. The fact that humans were "most susceptible to attacks from demonic spirits at night time" seems to have "spurred the development of prayers for protection and their recitation at night."[61] "If the forces of darkness were equated to any extent with night time continued vigilance would have been required."[62]

For Penner, the "mythically conceived cosmos, both in the configuration of the deities as celestial beings, and in the deities' ability to affect the human world, made its way into the prayer traditions of the Second Temple period, particularly in the recitation and timing of apotropaic and incantational prayers to ward off affliction and demonic spirits."[63] Yet, as Penner further contends, for Second Tem-

---

[58] Penner, *Patterns*, 175.
[59] Penner (*Patterns*, 176–77) also refers to the Book of the Watchers, other apocalyptic texts, as well as 1 En. 82:9–20; 1Q20 7:2; 4Q511 2 i 8; 4Q503 7–9 3–4; 4Q408 3+3a 5–11; 4Q502 27 3; 4Q88 10:5–6 as evidence for the "association between astronomical phenomena and angels."
[60] Penner, *Patterns*, 165.
[61] Penner, *Patterns*, 180.
[62] Penner, *Patterns*, 189.
[63] Penner, *Patterns*, 177.

ple Jewish communities who understood themselves as participating in the praise of God by the angels, equally demanding of vigilance as the need constantly to protect oneself from harm would have been the obligation to worship God throughout the nighttime hours, perpetually, as do the celestial-angelic beings.

That at least some Second Temple Jews understood their ritual expressions of devotion to God to be a participation in the celestial worship of the angels is a fact long recognized, especially from texts from the Dead Sea Scrolls (e.g., Songs of the Sabbath Sacrifice).[64] Certain Second Temple communities, however, appear also to have understood their regular nocturnal worship in particular to be a means of participating in the perpetual angelic praise of the divine. In relation to a likely, but not certainly, sectarian text like 4Q503, Penner, for instance, notes:
1. Angels were associated with luminaries.
2. Humans and angels praise God in concert.
3. The timing of praise is indicated by astronomical phenomena in the heavens.[65]

These features of 4Q503 suggest to Penner that the timing of worship in the Qumran community was not fixed merely to moments in the "morning and evening, sunrise and sunset," as is often thought. Rather the thrice repeated phrase בכול מועדי לילה—"in all appointed times of the night"—in 4Q503 (33 i+34 21; 40 ii–41 3; 51–55 10) suggests that for the Qumranites "there [was] *more than one* appointed time of the night" (italics original). For Penner, "prayer during the 'evening'/ 'night' was not coordinated according to the cycle of the sun, but rather the moon and the stars."[66] Since the angels are associated with the luminaries, the human community 4Q503 imagines would coordinate their prayerful worship with the movement of these celestial bodies or angels.

If there is evidence for regular nocturnal practices of prayer in the Second Temple epoch associated with angelic worship of the divine, to what extent might 1QS 6:7–8 and 4Q417 1 i—those passages that speak clearly of human efforts to

---

64 Falk calls the Songs of the Sabbath Sacrifice "a script for a ritual of corporate mysticism." See, "Liturgical Texts," in *T&T Clark Companion to the Dead Sea Scrolls*, ed. George J. Brooke and Charlotte Hempel (London: T&T Clark, 2019), 423–34. Noam Mizrahi believes this work regards human language as unable to accomplish what angelic language does. Hence humans can only "emulate angelic speech by describing the angels' liturgy and reciting it at the same time as they do, thus achieving a liturgical communion with them." Noam Mizrahi, "The Cycle of Summons: A Hymn from the Seventh Song of the Sabbath Sacrifice (4Q403 1 i 31–40)," *DSD* (2015): 43–67 (65).
65 Penner, *Patterns*, 191.
66 Penner, *Patterns*, 191. Penner cites as further evidence for his view 1QH[a] 20:9 and the phrase שלישית כול לילות השנה in 1QS 6:7.

attain esoteric knowledge, and which illumine Agur's fatigue in Proverbs 30—also evidence similar practices of day and night prayer?

9.2 Constant Prayer in 1QS 6

In 1QS 6:7–8 the "many" are exhorted to be on watch throughout the night in order to read (קרא) in the scroll (presumably of Torah, at least), to seek or study regulations (דרש משפט), and to bless (ברך) together. How, or to what extent, do these activities—individually or together—count as prayer or communication with the divine?

As George J. Brooke has noted in his study of the trilogy of key terms in 1QS 6, in the sectarian Dead Sea Scrolls קרא "seems to involve" not mere recitation of a memorized text, but "comprehension and even some kind of active engagement with the text as it was performed."[67] By contrast, the meaning of דרש in the Qumran literature is more contested. The controversy concerns whether the root should be primarily understood in its biblical sense of "to search" or in its later sense of "to study."[68] In the Bible דרש can also be employed in an oracular sense to speak of human communication with other worldly beings—spirits and gods— by which people attain particular knowledge. For instance, Isa 8:19–20a, which interestingly also employs the root הגה that appears in 4Q417 1 i 6 (as well as in other key expressions from sectarian texts; e.g., ספר הגו), says:

> וכי־יאמרו אליכם דרשו אל־האבות ואל־הידענים המצפצפים והמהגים הלוא־עם אל־אלהיו ידרש בעד החיים אל המתים לתורה ולגעודה
>
> Now if people say to you, "Consult (דרש) the ghosts and the familiar spirits that chirp and mutter; should not a people consult their gods, the dead on behalf of the living, for teaching and for instruction?" (NRSV)

This sort of biblical usage of דרש suggests to Brooke that in the Second Temple period "the verb could also have just such [oracular] things as its object."[69] Indeed, as Brooke further notes, Johann Maier believes the root דרש develops in part into a technical term for "requesting an oracle and being told what such an oracle might contain."[70] For Brooke himself, however, the meaning of דרש in

---

67 Brooke, "Reading," 145.
68 Brooke, "Reading," 147.
69 Brooke, "Reading," 149.
70 Brooke, "Reading," 148; Johann Maier, "Early Jewish Biblical Interpretation in the Qumran Literature," in *Hebrew Bible/Old Testament: The History of Its Interpretation: Vol 1: From the Begin-*

1QS 6:7 has less to do with learning the content of an oracle and most fundamentally entails "investigative searching of the scriptures."[71] It "implies some kind of instruction in the form of exegetical activity and has such investigative activity as its referent." Indeed, the object of the verb in 1QS 6 is "the rule or regulation (משפט), scriptural or otherwise."[72]

Neither of the terms קרא or דרש necessarily suggest that the day and night activity of the *Yaḥad* noted in 1QS 6:7–8 constitutes "prayer."[73] However, the last activity noted in 1QS 6:8, "to bless," more obviously intimates that part of the constant activity of the community was a form of prayer, or that the entire work of reading and interpreting authoritative texts—*and* acts of blessing—can be well regarded as a complex practice of prayer—communication with the divine.

As Jutta Jokiranta has noted, "the Hebrew root *brk* (ברך) ... denotes two different yet related actions: it is used for both praising God and for mediating God's favor to humans."[74] This means that at least some actions described by this root would surely count as prayer. As Jokiranta says: humans can bless other humans; God might bless "humans and things," and humans ("and/or angels and natural objects") might bless God. In the latter case, blessing is a form of "praise."[75] In 1QS all three senses of ברך are evident. In 1QS 1:18–19, for instance, 1) humans obviously bless God:

> ובעוברם בברית יהיו הכוהנים והלויים מברכים את אל ישועות ואת כול מעשי אמתו

> When they enter the covenant, the priests and the levites shall bless the God of victories and all the works of his faithfulness.[76]

And in 1QS 2:1–4 it is clear that 2) humans bless other humans by 3) invoking the blessing of the divine on these humans:

---

nings to the Middle Ages (Until 1300), ed. Magne Sæbø (Göttingen: Vandenhoeck & Ruprecht, 1996), 108–129 (113–15).
71 Brooke, "Reading," 148.
72 Brooke, "Reading," 150.
73 However, as Brooke ("Reading," 150) concedes, the oracular consulting (דרש) of spirits and gods (as in Isaiah 8) can be regarded as communication with the divine, as might also the expression מדרש התורה in 1QS 8:15, a line that subsequently speaks of revealed teaching.
74 Jutta Jokiranta, "Towards a Cognitive Theory of Blessing: The Dead Sea Scrolls as a Test Case," in *Functions of Psalms and Prayers in the Late Second Temple Period*, ed. Mika S. Pajunen and Jeremy Penner (Berlin: de Gruyter, 2017), 27–47 (27).
75 Jokiranta, "Cognitive Theory," 29.
76 Text and Translation are from Martínez and Tigchelaar, *DSSSE* 1:70–71.

והכוהנים מברכים את כול אנשי גורל אל ההולכים תמים בכול דרכיו ואומרים יברככה בכול
טוב וישמורכה מכול רע. ויאר לבכה בשכל חיים ויחונכה בדעת עולמים וישא פני חסדיו לכה לשלום עולמים

> And the priests will bless all the men of God's lot who walk unblemished in all his paths and they shall say: "May he bless you with everything good, and may he protect you from everything bad. May he illuminate your heart with the discernment of life and grace you with eternal knowledge. May he lift upon you the countenance of his favour for eternal peace."[77]

In his study of 1QS 6:7–8 Brooke calls attention both to the distinct nature of the three activities the lines mention, but also notes the relationship between the three—reading, studying, and blessing. He concludes that blessing in the community "included a wide range of thanksgivings and prayers that had an intertwined double function." First, drawing on the work of Bilhah Nitzan, he contends that blessings functioned "to interpret and reinterpret earlier scriptural materials to extend the repertoire of prayer."[78] Second, blessings served to "endorse the kinds of right interpretation that had been the subject of the earlier searching of the study of both the law and the Prophets and some other authoritative texts."[79] Subsequently, "The production and performance of bouquets of blessings can be understood as an inspired activity."[80]

Jokiranta's study of blessing offers a creative path by which to complement Brooke's insights and conclusions. Jokiranta makes clear that although earlier scholarship might acknowledge that the ancients regarded the words of curses and blessing to be efficacious in essentially magical terms, later studies moved away from this view. Instead, such utterances came to be understood in terms of speech-act theory and so "have been increasingly understood as prayers and petitions, rather than spells or invocations."[81] Jokiranta, however, notes that the rejection of magic in such a view is problematic; it is "based on an outdated dichotomy between magic and religion" where the former is unduly disparaged. Instead, she suggests that "in a ritual setting, the human mind is directed toward searching for magical agency and seeing ordinary actions as producing unordinary effects."[82] Subsequently, "blessing God can be understood as creating a 'channel' to the sacred domain that enables a change in the cosmic world and its order."[83] An

---

77 Text and Translation are from Martínez and Tigchelaar, *DSSSE* 1:70–73.
78 Brooke, "Reading," 152, 154; Bilhah Nitzan, *Qumran Prayer and Religious Poetry* (Leiden: Brill, 1994), esp. 145–71.
79 Brooke, "Reading," 153.
80 Brooke, "Reading," 154.
81 Jokiranta, "Cognitive Theory," 32.
82 Jokiranta, "Cognitive Theory," 45.
83 Jokiranta, "Cognitive Theory," 36.

important piece of evidence for Jokiranta is a passage from the Damascus Document (4Q266 11:7–14), which speaks of "expelling a member by blessing/praising God."[84]

> In rebellion, he will be expelled from the presence of the Many. And the priest who governs [ov]er the Many will speak to him; he will begin to speak, [sa]ying: "Blessed are you, who art everything, in your hands is everything, you do everything, you have founded the [na]tions according to their families, and according to their languages, and according to their tribes, and you have led them astray in a trackless wilderness. You chose our fathers and gave their descendants your truthful regulations and your holy precepts so that man could carry them out and live. And you established frontiers for us, and you curse those who cross them. And we are the people of your ransom and the flock of your pasture. You curse those who cross them but us you have raised up." And the one who has been expelled will leave...."[85]

To some modern readers blessing the divine in the process of expelling a person from one's community may appear odd. Part of the rhetorical function of the blessing here, however, is fairly obvious; it transfers responsibility for the excommunication from human decision makers to God, who has established the community's rules and regulations. However, as Jokiranta says, this sort of ritualized act of blessing or praising "could have been perceived as action through which one gained the things for which one praised God"—in this case the excommunication of the one who has transgressed the *Yaḥad*'s symbolic, divinely ordained, boundaries.[86]

It is possible that the term ברך in 1QS 6:8 carries traces of these sorts of ancient understandings of the magical or causal efficacy of blessing. If so, the broader religious-magical and ritual beliefs that may inform and infuse the complex activity to which the famous trilogy of verbs in the line point, come into view. Not only does blessing in 1QS 6:8 "endorse" the community's inspired interpretation, as Brooke aptly contends. It may also indicate that the "praise-blessings" of the community's day and night activities were regarded as requisite to the production of its inspired interpretations; or, to adopt Jokiranta words, they may have been "perceived as action through which one gained the things for which one praised God." Indeed, in 1QS itself, a version of the Aaronic blessing alludes to the sort of inspired exegetical knowledge that came from reading, studying, and blessing. The expanded Aaronic blessing of 1QS 2:2–4 (cited above), says in line 3, "May He enlighten your mind with wisdom for living, be gracious to you with the knowledge of eternal things,"—words that according to

---

84 Jokiranta, "Cognitive Theory," 47.
85 Translation is from Martínez and Tigchelaar, *DSSSE* 1:596–97.
86 Jokiranta, "Cognitive Theory," 47.

Bilhah Nitzan concern right interpretation of the "Law according to its Zadokite-priestly halakhah."[87]

Of course, the blessing in 1 QS 2:2–4 is not a human blessing or praise of God, the sort of prayer-utterance Jokiranta suggests "enables a change in the cosmic world and its order."[88] It is a human utterance to mediate divine favor or blessing to other humans. However, as Brooke contends, versions of the Aaronic blessing would hardly have been the only sort of blessings uttered "when the community came to bless together as the third aspect of their threefold task of reading, searching, and blessing." He astutely contends that the "time of blessing might well have been a suitable opportunity for the rehearsal of one or more of the Hodayot."[89] Hodayot, of course, not only contain explicit blessings of the divine beginning with the words ברוך אתה, they also deploy expressions of thanksgiving like that of 1QH 15:26. This line explicitly gives thanks to God for providing the speaker with revelatory knowledge. "I give [you] thanks, [Lord] because you have taught me your truth, you have made me know your wonderful mysteries...."[90]

It is, of course, vital to discern the distinct nuances of each activity mentioned in the piling up of key verbs—קרא, דרש, and ברך—in 1QS 6:7–8. However, in light of the possible "magical" function of blessing God in the community's three-fold work of 1QS 6:7–8, it is also important to underscore how the line's phraseology might function together as something like a conceptual hendiadys and thereby understand the *Yaḥad*'s efforts at reading, interpreting, and blessing as a kind of single, though complex, occupation—a practice of "prayerful study." Such prayerful study constitutes a form of communication with the divine not only because human words of blessings are directed to the deity, but because the community receives esoteric knowledge—whether halakhic, cosmological, eschatological, or something else—through the practice. Such an understanding of 1QS 6:7–8, whereby blessing is viewed as a magical ritual facilitating reception of esoteric insight also fits with Malina's broad definition of prayer as communication with the divine: it is "performed with the purpose of getting results from or in the interaction of communication."[91] If so, in the opening lines of Proverbs 30 it may not have been a simple human pursuit of דעת קדשים that wearies Agur so, but

---

87 "Bilhah Nitzan, "The Benedictions form Qumran for the Annual Covenantal Ceremony," *The Dead Sea Scrolls Fifty Years after their Discovery*, ed. Lawrence H. Schiffman, Emanuel Tov, and James C. VanderKam (Jerusalem: Israel Exploration Society and the Shrine of the Book, 2000), 265; cited by Brooke, "Reading," 152.
88 Jokiranta, "Cognitive Theory," 36.
89 Brooke, "Reading," 153.
90 Translation is from Martínez and Tigchelaar, *DSSSE*, 1:179.
91 Malina, "What is Prayer?" 215, noted at the outset of this essay.

instead his participation in a community's complex practice that produces such knowledge—a practice of day and night prayerful study.

9.3 Constant Prayer in 4QInstruction

If the day and night activity of the *Yaḥad* in 1QS 5:6–7 sheds some possible light on the sort of prayerful, knowledge-seeking activities that might explain Agur's expression of weariness in Prov 30:1b, the day and night activity of which 4QInstruction speaks adds to this picture. Rather than קרא, דרש, and ברך, the text of 4Q417 1 i 6 deploys only the verbs הגה and דרש to speak of what should be the addressee's constant engagement with the רז נהיה. Above we briefly considered the debated meanings and connotations of דרש in texts of the Second Temple epoch in relation to 1QS 6:7. Arriving at the meaning and resonances of the second lexeme 4QInstruction uses to speak of the addressee's relation to the *raz nihyeh*—הגה—constitutes just as an elusive task as understanding דרש.

In HB הגה means to meditate, moan, or murmur. Lions can הגה over prey (Isa 31:4); one can mutter (הגה) wickedness (Isa 59:3); and so forth. And, of course, one can also murmur, or meditate on (הגה), (the content of) texts, as Josh 1:8 and Ps 1:2 make clear. Importantly, in these biblical passages, the meditation on divine *Torah* is one that is said to be undertaken day and night, just as the activities in 1QS 6 and 4Q417 are. As others have also noted, the Qumran community apparently took these scriptural models of study quite seriously, with 1QS 6:6 echoing Josh 1:8 in particular. In the Bible, however, the root הגה can also be deployed to speak of prayer, to express a form of communication with the divine, as in Isa 38:14 and various psalms.

Isa 38:9–20 contains what appears to be Hezekiah's thanksgiving psalm, which he uttered "after he had been sick and had recovered from his sickness" (v. 9).[92] In v. 14 the king claims that because of the affliction he has experienced "from day until night" (v. 12, 13), he has clamored, moaned, and grown weary of looking upward for deliverance.

כסוס עגור כן אצפצף אהגה כיונה דלו עיני למרום אדני עשקה־לי ערבני

Like a swallow or a crane I clamor, I moan (הגה) like a dove. My eyes are weary with looking upward. O Lord, I am oppressed; be my security! (NRSV)

---

92 The "superscription" to the thanksgiving psalm, however, calls Hezekiah's discourse a מכתב (a "writing").

Hezekiah's vocalization of his distress in these lines is no simple expression of his suffering; it is part of his plea for rescue directed heavenward to God. His fatigue is caused not merely by his persistent suffering; it is also a function of his petition for deliverance.

In the lament of Psalm 35, the psalmist's murmuring is likewise a form of prayer, a blessing uttered constantly (or at least for an extended period of time) —namely, "all day long." Upon his vindication from his opponents, the speaker promises in the last line of the psalm (v. 28),

ולשוני תהגה צדקך כל־היום תהלתך

Then my tongue shall tell (הגה) of your righteousness and of your praise all day long. (NRSV)

The lament of Psalm 71 concludes similarly in v. 24:

גם־לשוני כל־היום תהגה צדקתך

all day long my tongue will talk (הגה) of your righteous help. (NRSV)

Psalm 63 is a further important text in which הגה is deployed to speak of an utterance of prayer, or communication directed to the deity. In this psalm, which is explicitly attributed to David "when he was in the Wilderness of Judah," (63:1 [0]), the speaker alludes in v. 7 [6] to his acts of remembering and murmuring to the deity, not "all day long," but (likely) throughout the night.

אם־זכרתיך על־יצועי באשמרות אהגה־בך

when I think of you on my bed, and meditate (הגה) on you in the watches of the night. (NRSV)

Although in Ps 77:12–13 [11–12] there is no mention of a time frame for the speaker's meditative praise, we similarly read:

אזכור[93] מעללי־יה כי־אזכרה מקדם פלאך והגיתי בכל־פעלך ובעלילותיך אשיחה

I will call to mind the deeds of the LORD; I will remember your wonders of old. I will meditate (הגה) on all your work, and muse on your mighty deeds. (NRSV)

Likewise, Ps 143:5 says:

זכרתי ימים מקדם הגיתי בכל־פעלך במעשה ידיך אשוחח

I remember the days of old, I think about (הגה) all your deeds, I meditate on the works of your hands. (NRSV)

---

93 Reading the *Qere*; *Ketiv* = אזכיר.

Although in all the above Psalms one might imagine the speaker's articulation (הגה) of God's justice, praise, wonders, and deeds as speech directed to other humans, the likely cultic use of many psalms supports the suggestion that they be reckoned as prayers of praise directed to the deity.[94] As many scholars insist, a definition of prayer need not be limited to second person address to the deity; it can include third person discourse as well, especially when such speech is uttered in a liturgical context.[95] Hezekiah's utterance (הגה) in Isa 38 is, of course, explicitly directed to God (v. 14).

The meditating or murmuring (הגה) undertaken in the above passages by some human voice, then, is most naturally regarded as a form of praise directed to the deity. God's wonderous works call forth meditative and recollective adoration. This is significant since in 4QInstruction the addressee is exhorted to meditate (הגה) on the *raz nihyeh*, the enigmatic concept that encompasses "knowledge concerning the structures of the natural world, the course of human history, and the hidden principles that guide them."[96] All of these matters fall under the dominion of the deity and were regarded by at least some Second Temple Jews as the praise evoking, marvelous works of his hands, as Psalm 143 puts it.

To meditate or murmur on the *raz nihyeh* in 4QInstruction is surely thus not merely an intellectual exercise, a simple quest for esoteric, eschatological knowledge. The rhetoric of הגה in the work surely also bears traces of its usages in some Psalms as part of a practice of praise of the deity for God's great and mysterious works in designing the cosmos and directing human history—things now more fully revealed to the one who in fact studies (דרש) and prayerfully meditates (הגה) on/in the *raz nihyeh*.

Like the reading, studying, and blessing of 1QS 6, to meditate and investigate in/on the *raz nihyeh* can thus be reckoned as a complex practice of prayerful study; in Falk's broad definition of prayer in the Second Temple period, with which this essay began, it is a form of communication with the divine. The prayerful meditation and study on the *raz nihyeh*, however, is also undertaken, as Malina might say, with the expectation that it will result in something—in this case new insight. As 4QInstruction states, if one prayerfully studies and meditates on the *raz nihyeh* (and/or cognate concepts), "then you will know"—ואז תדע—"truth and evil, and wisdom [and folly] (4Q417 1 i 6); or "the difference between [goo]d [and [evil...] (4Q417 1 i 8); or "the glory of [...]" *something* (417 1 i 13; cf. 4Q418 43, 44, 45 i 4, 9).

---

94 For a critique of the view that many psalms should be associated with the cult, see Frolov's contribution to this volume.
95 See the "Introduction" to this volume.
96 Newsom, "Models," 23n43.

10. Conclusions

Certain communities of Second Temple Jews, such as the Qumranites, might have "sought wholly to become angelic-like by cultivating those qualities innate to angelic life, which included such attributes as sleeplessness, watching, perpetual praise, and illumination."[97] The practice of constant—day and night—prayerful study alluded to in 4Q417 1 i 6 and 1QS 6:7–8 are articulations of the sorts of religious practices that constituted the *imitatio angeli*. The effort and vigilance required of humans to align themselves with the angelic beings in this way would have been significant. Indeed, 1QS 6:7 indirectly acknowledges the fatigue it might produce when it insists that during the day and night study of *Torah* one community member should relieve another. This sort of Second Temple practice of perpetual prayerful study, and the effort required to participate in it, may well form the conceptual background of Agur's pursuit of דעת קדשים—"angelic knowledge"—in Proverbs 30, provoking his prayerful complaint, "I am weary, O God."

---

97 Penner, *Patterns*, 192.

George J. Brooke
Patterns of Priesthood and Patterns of Prayer in the Dead Sea Scrolls

1. Introduction

On the 23rd of April 2018, St George's Day, Prince Louis of Cambridge was born in London, England. Shortly afterwards the Church of England webpage carried "A Prayer for the New Royal Baby" to mark the occasion. It runs as follows:

> Heavenly Father, we give thanks for the birth of a new son to The Duke and Duchess of Cambridge; surround him with your blessing that he may know your love, be protected from evil, and know your goodness all his days. May God give wisdom, patience and faith to his parents; and, by their example, reveal the love and truth that are in Jesus Christ. Amen.

The prayer is interesting for several reasons. It is strangely constructed in two sentences, the first of which is addressed directly to God the Father, presumably in the second person; the second speaks of God in the third person. Such a shift in person is not unknown in some biblical prayers and psalms, but the change is very awkward in such a short text, almost as if the author of the prayer had not properly proof-read the text. The first sentence is of two parts: the opening clause is a thanksgiving, a *hodayah*, and the second is a petition for divine blessing which seems to understand blessing as chiefly apotropaic; it is a request for a force-field to protect Louis from evil, to provide a safe zone in which divine love and goodness might be made known to him. The second sentence is petitionary with its didactic focus on right thought, right practice, and right attitude; if such things are voiced to God, then those listening will grasp what they need to learn and do. The repetitions of "know" in the set of petitions and of "love" in the two parts might be thought of as two forms of inclusion, but in the light of the other awkward phrasing are more likely included without much thought to the pattern of the prayer. Who wrote that prayer, with what intention in mind, and for whose use? It was probably composed by a Christian priest; we may wonder what self-understanding of priesthood the prayer conveys.

In 2016 I published a paper entitled "Patterns of Priesthood, Priestliness and Priestly Functions in Some Second Temple Period Texts."[1] It sought to move

---

[1] George J. Brooke, "Patterns of Priesthood, Priestliness and Priestly Functions in Some Second Temple Period Texts," *Judaïsme Ancien – Ancient Judaism* 4 (2016): 1–21.

beyond talking yet again about the problems of understanding the Sons of Aaron and the Sons of Zadok in the scrolls found in the caves at and near Qumran.[2] The paper was inspired very much by Michael Stone's *Ancient Judaism: New Visions and Views* in one section of which he rehearses and develops the idea that in the Second Temple period there were at least two competing views of evil, the one a matter of human disobedience, the other an external force to be controlled in whatever way possible.[3] The prayer for the new royal baby seems to reflect the persistence of such Second Temple views: its first sentence perceives evil as an external force requiring protection; its second sentence implies that without wisdom, patience, and faith, William and Catherine, the Duke and Duchess of Cambridge, will be liable to common human failings which will need forgiveness.[4]

"Patterns of Priesthood" suggested that priesthood in Second Temple times was a complex affair, but that at least two significant priestly ideologies were articulated. On the one hand, there was the dominant continuation of the Aaronic priesthood, whose antecedents were traced back by some to Adam himself with Eden understood as either the Temple or as the holy of holies; the key role of that Aaronic priesthood was ultimately through an elaborate sacrificial system to enable atonement for sins.[5] On the other hand, there were patterns of priesthood linked with various figures from Enoch to Noah to Levi and beyond whose role was to be learned in books and to transmit priestly lore from one generation to another so as to facilitate, amongst other things, the divine protection of the people and to enable the practice of various healing powers. This paper is a move away from thinking of prayer solely in terms of literary genre, towards also thinking about how prayer can reflect particular ideological positions as those can be embedded in priestly practice and ritual functions.

---

[2] Amongst notable recent discussions of priesthood in the community compositions, see Charlotte Hempel, "Do the Scrolls Suggest Rivalry between the Sons of Aaron and the Sons of Zadok and If So Was It Mutual?" *RevQ* 93 (2009): 135–54; Heinz-Josef Fabry, "Priests at Qumran—A Reassessment," in *The Dead Sea Scrolls: Texts and Contexts*, ed. Charlotte Hempel, STDJ 90 (Leiden: Brill, 2010), 243–62.
[3] Michael E. Stone, *Ancient Judaism: New Visions and Views* (Cambridge: Cambridge University Press, 2011).
[4] Both views, forgiveness for the evil of human failings and protection from external evil, are also present in a nutshell in the Lord's Prayer: "Forgive us our debts, as we also have forgiven our debtors. And do not bring us to the time of trial, but rescue us from the evil one" (Matt 6:12–13; cf. Luke 11:4).
[5] It is widely recognized that in Leviticus the sacrificial system is described as a matter of both effective priestly performance and non-priestly participation rather than being presented theoretically with theological explanations as to how sacrifice works.

2. Priestly Practices and Prayer

It is certainly overly precise to distinguish neatly on ideological grounds between those priests with a sacrificial role and those with a more bookish job description. The depiction of Noah in the book of Jubilees speaks tellingly against such precise demarcation and division of roles. There Noah has at least four aspects to his paradigmatic priesthood, each of which is likewise discernible, explicitly or implicitly, in the prayer on behalf of Prince Louis. Firstly, there is recollection of Noah's sacrificial offerings (Jub. 6:1–3; 7:1–6). To mark disembarkation from the ark a whole burnt offering atoning for the land is made that inaugurates the Feast of Weeks. In addition, to celebrate the success of his vines Noah holds a feast on the first day of the first month when he makes a whole burnt offering "in order that he might thereby seek atonement for himself and his sons" (Jub. 7:3). Secondly, there are the practices of blessing and cursing, namely the blessing of Shem and the cursing of Canaan, both of which are tied in the book of Jubilees to power politics concerning the land (Jub. 7:7–19). Thirdly, there is specific priestly instruction about the requirements to avoid fornication, blood pollution, and injustice (Jub. 7:20–33)—all of which characterize a righteousness that stems from Enoch's commands to Methuselah, which Methuselah passed on to Lamech (Jub. 7:37–38). And fourthly, there are concerns with healing and with coping with evil forces which were probably formulated in apotropaic prayers against the demons (Jub. 10:1–6): "and Noah wrote everything in a book just as we taught him according to every kind of healing. And the evil spirits were restrained from following the sons of Noah" (Jub. 10:13–14).[6]

The same need to avoid an overly precise distinction between priests concerned with sacrifice and those concerned with written tradition can be found in the Aramaic Testament of Qahat. On the one hand, Qahat transmits the lore he had from his father Levi to his son Amram, lore that is preserved in "my books" (4Q542 2:12). But on the other hand, in the Testament of Qahat the additional mentions of Abraham, Isaac, and Jacob might be understood as further indications not just of the even longer pedigree of priestly lore but also of the sacrificial content of that lore. As Stone has noted, "in *Jub* 21:10, Abraham concludes a catalogue of detailed sacrificial *halachot* that he has given Isaac by saying, 'Because thus I have found written in the books of my forefathers and in the words of Enoch and in the words of Noah.' *Jubilees* introduces Enoch into the teaching's genealogy and mentions Noah, which evokes *ALD*."[7] Thus, although Jubilees seems to iden-

---

6 For more detail on Noah and books see Michael E. Stone, "The Book(s) Attributed to Noah," *DSD* 13 (2006): 4–23.
7 Stone, *Ancient Judaism: New Visions and Views*, 40.

tify the contents of Noah's books especially with healing and the control of demons, by the time of Abraham, according to Jubilees, written priestly lore is also associated with sacrifice. There do indeed seem to be two broad priestly concerns, even if the ways in which they are expressed in prayer are very varied and even if the institution of the priesthood cannot simply be divided into two specialist functions.

3. Prayer, Ideology, and Evil in the Dead Sea Scrolls

After the general release of all the unpublished Cave 4 and Cave 11 compositions in the early 1990s, there were expressions of surprise at the large quantity of written prayer texts. In the two decades that followed, most of the debate about prayer and liturgy in the Dead Sea Scrolls corpus focused on the definition and classification of the texts by attention to their literary character, especially their genres and sub-genres as usually defined by content; such discussions have been helpful in describing the variety of the material now available.[8] A solid summary of where the discussion had reached after two decades was provided by Daniel Falk in his survey contribution to *The Oxford Handbook of the Dead Sea Scrolls*.[9] Falk's essay also tried to offer a program for future research on prayer and liturgy. He explicitly encouraged the nuanced study of issues of ideology and theology as reflected in prayer texts, distinguishing three matters: (1) that there can be a difference between the ideologies lying behind and motivating prayer from those that are communicated in prayers themselves; (2) that what is expressed in any prayer as originally composed should often be distinguished from its subsequent uses; and (3) that the surface meaning of prayer language should be distinguished from its rhetorical and ritual functions.[10] Quite how far scholars have picked up on his agenda can be seen from his own more recent survey in the *T&T Clark Companion*

---

[8] Chief amongst such approaches have been Esther G. Chazon, "Psalms, Hymns, and Prayers," in *Encyclopedia of the Dead Sea Scrolls*, ed. Lawrence H. Schiffman and James C. VanderKam (New York: Oxford University Press, 2000), 2:710–15; and Eileen M. Schuller, "Prayer at Qumran," in *Prayer from Tobit to Qumran: Inaugural Conference of the ISDCL at Salzburg, Austria, 5–9 July 2003*, ed. Renate Egger-Wenzel and Jeremy Corley, DCLY (Berlin: De Gruyter, 2004), 411–28.

[9] Daniel K. Falk, "The Contribution of the Qumran Scrolls to the Study of Ancient Liturgy," in *The Oxford Handbook of the Dead Sea Scrolls*, ed. Timothy H. Lim and John J. Collins (Oxford: Oxford University Press, 2010), 617–51.

[10] Falk, "The Contribution of the Qumran Scrolls to the Study of Ancient Liturgy," 639–42.

to the Dead Sea Scrolls.[11] At least in that essay, his own perspective has shifted more explicitly away from generic analysis towards consideration of the various functions of texts, and his article is organized with the six ritual categories proposed by Catherine Bell very much in mind.[12]

As mentioned above, this essay is an example of trying to come to terms with some ideological aspects of prayer.[13] At the center of the discussion are the two views of the origin of evil as outlined by Stone. In some ways what can be said has been anticipated by Carol Newsom with fine insight and in language that is rich in methodological self-awareness: she has paid attention to the function of prayer in the formation of the self through the way in which it configures reality. Falk has summed up her approach: "the experienced tension expressed in many of the sectarian prayers between a sense of nothingness and exaltation — what she [Newsom] calls the masochistic sublime — allows the speaker to explore 'the terrifying paradox of his being — a part of sinful humanity and yet one of the redeemed elect'."[14] For me the "masochistic sublime" is present in the tension between the two views of the origin of evil. On the one hand, evil is a result of human sin; subsequently the community member is in need of available systems of atonement. On the other hand, that member is persistently threatened by malevolent forces outside of himself; as elect, however, he is constantly protected by the presence of angels in the midst of the community. Such protection is depicted, for example, in 4Q174 1 i 3–7:

> "The temple of] YHWH your hands will establish. YHWH shall reign for ever and ever." This (refers to) the house into which shall not enter [... for] ever either an Ammonite, or a Moabite, or a bastard, or a foreigner, or a proselyte, never, because his holy ones are there. "Y[HW]H [shall reign for] ever." He will appear over it forever; foreigners shall not again lay it waste as they laid waste, in the past, the tem[ple of I]srael on account of their sins. And he commanded to build for himself a temple of man {*mqdš 'dm*}, to offer him in it, before him, the works of thanksgiving.[15]

---

11 Daniel K. Falk, "Liturgical Texts," in *T&T Clark Companion to the Dead Sea Scrolls*, ed. George J. Brooke and Charlotte Hempel (London: T&T Clark, 2019), 423–34.

12 Catherine M. Bell, *Ritual: Perspectives and Dimensions* (New York: Oxford University Press, 1997), 93–117.

13 Because of the concern with ideology I am overlooking other significant aspects of prayer such as consideration of the location of its practice. On the role of "wilderness" as the place of human–divine relationship, see Hindy Najman and Nicole Hilton, "Revelation," in *T&T Clark Companion to the Dead Sea Scrolls*, 487–88.

14 Falk, "The Contribution of the Qumran Scrolls to the Study of Ancient Liturgy," 642, referring to Carol A. Newsom, *The Self as Symbolic Space: Constructing Identity and Community at Qumran*, STDJ 52 (Leiden: Brill, 2004).

15 All the English translations of Scrolls are cited from Florentino García Martínez and Eibert J. C. Tigchelaar, *The Dead Sea Scrolls Study Edition* (Leiden: Brill, 2000). Cf. also, e.g., the apotropaic role of Raphael in the exorcism narrative of Tobit.

Some modern readers might be anxious about how such a spiritual tension might compromise a sense of predestination through its concern for human weakness, though to my mind Philip Alexander has addressed the theological problems in such tension rather neatly by appealing to his own experience and insisting on a pragmatic approach to daily existence for the elect.[16]

It seems to me that this two-part framework for appreciating prayer and spiritual practice, as part of the means for atonement of sin and as the guarantee of protection from external evil, based on the bifold explanation of the origins of evil (within or outside of humans), should additionally be held against a larger overarching category of reference—that of thanksgiving together with the blessing of God.

4. Thanksgiving and Dependence

In the volume produced in honor of Eileen Schuller I set out to consider some of the theological significance of prayer and worship in the Scrolls. The principal point of my contribution was to draw attention to the way that several prayer and liturgical texts found in the Qumran caves variously express a sense of utter dependence upon God.[17] That sense of dependence, in part an outworking of a very negative view of the human condition, is best expressed in terms of thanksgiving, but it is also present in several compositions including those associated with the so-called "calendrical rites."[18]

It is no surprise that scholars have not been able to identify a liturgical or ritual moment for such thanksgivings as are present in various exemplary forms

---

[16] Philip S. Alexander, "Predestination and Free Will in the Theology of the Dead Sea Scrolls," in *Divine and Human Agency in Paul and His Cultural Environment*, ed. John M. G. Barclay and Simon J. Gathercole, LNTS 335 (London: T&T Clark, 2006), 27–49. As Alexander says in relation to predestination in Calvinist theology, however "strong the arguments may be for determinism, we all—even those of us who may theoretically subscribe to it—normally interact with each other in everyday life on the assumption that we are free agents" (Alexander, "Predestination and Free Will," 48–49).

[17] George J. Brooke, "Aspects of the Theological Significance of Prayer and Worship in the Qumran Scrolls," in *Prayer and Poetry in the Dead Sea Scrolls and Related Literature: Essays in Honor of Eileen Schuller on the Occasion of her 65th Birthday*, ed. Jeremy Penner, Kenneth M. Penner, and Cecilia Wassén, STDJ 98 (Leiden: Brill, 2012), 35–54.

[18] See Carol A. Newsom, "Deriving Negative Anthropology through Exegetical Activity: The Hodayot as a Case Study," in *Is There a Text in This Cave? Studies in the Textuality of the Dead Sea Scrolls in Honour of George J. Brooke*, ed. Ariel Feldman, Maria Cioată, and Charlotte Hempel, STDJ 119 (Leiden: Brill, 2017), 258–74.

in the Hodayot manuscripts.[19] That is not simply a factor of their first-person singular formulation, but also because of a fundamental way that the content of the Hodayot presents this sense of dependence which is suitable for all occasions and most commonly assumed by them.[20] The sense of dependence also has two corollaries relevant to the concerns of this study. First, for those who need an altar to facilitate atonement, there is a huge risk in taking oneself away from the wider community's cultic spaces, even though that risk can be compensated in some measure by paying attention to God himself. Second, a heightened sense of powerlessness and social marginalization, together with a mindset that considers that the end-times have begun, places both the community and the individual in need of divine protection. The Hodayot are thus both a reflection of the problems that prayer needs to address and a significant part of the answer to those problems.[21]

The Scrolls found in the caves at and near Qumran thus seem to give modern readers access to understandings of priesthood and prayer that reflect a complex set of ideologies which are changing as the movement responsible for variously collecting the Scrolls together moves from one generation to another, and from one set of political circumstances to another. Against a backdrop of thanksgiving and the blessing of God, and within a framework of two basic explanations for the problem of evil—human sin and external malevolent forces—together with the corresponding worldviews that they envisage, there are two systems of cultic rites and accompanying prayer that enable the maintenance and occasional repairing of the community status quo, namely the sacrificial and the apotropaic. But alongside those two systems of cultic rites and prayers, there are other types of prayer, which overlap with them and complement them in various ways; most especially there are blessings and curses. Some of those rites and prayers might be deemed to require specialist composers and compilers, or specialist performers, such as priests and Levites.

---

19 Thus, the Hodayot are commonly classified separately from other types of prayer in the Qumran collection: see, e. g., Esther G. Chazon and Moshe J. Bernstein, "An Introduction to Prayer at Qumran," in *Prayer from Alexander to Constantine: A Critical Anthology*, ed. Mark Kiley (London: Routledge, 1997), 11: "6. *Hodayot hymns*: individual thanksgiving hymns, often opening with the formula, 'I thank you, Lord', characterize the Hodayot collections from Caves 1 and 4."
20 Falk, "Liturgical Texts," 429–30, sees the Hodayot from an anthropological perspective as among texts to do with rites of exchange and communion.
21 And thus, it is no surprise that Newsom, *The Self as Symbolic Space*, has a whole chapter (chapter 5) devoted to the place of the Hodayot in identity construction.

5. Atonement and Protection, Blessings and Curses

The issue of prayer that is an attempt to deal with evil arising from human wrongdoing raises the question for the Scrolls concerning where the themes of penitence expressing the need for atonement and forgiveness of sins are to be found. Two texts are commonly cited as indicating such a concern. First, in the Damascus Document it seems that the community's origins are understood as lying in acts of penitence: "And they realised their iniquity and they knew that they were guilty {men}" (CD 1:8–9). And, though much debated, it is most probable that the repeated phrase, שבי ישראל, is best understood as "the penitents of Israel."[22] Second, in the Cave 1 version of the Rule of the Community the so-called covenant ceremony is described in language reminiscent of Lev 16:21: "And the Levites shall recite the iniquities of the children of Israel, all their blameworthy offences" (1QS 1:22–23). The text continues: "[And al]l those who enter the covenant shall confess after them and they shall say: 'We have acted sinfully, we have transgressed, we have sinned, we have committed evil, we and our fathers before us ...'" (1QS 1:24–25). Despite Falk and others rightly insisting on important differences between the covenant ceremony and the thorough-going rituals with penitential prayers in texts such as Nehemiah 9, enough language of confession and penitence is retained in the presentation as a whole in the Rule of the Community to merit considering the ceremony as a ritual that is both transformative as well as confirmatory.[23] The place of atonement and the means for facilitating it are engaged with in several other places as has been discussed by others.[24]

It is important to note that one of the rites of penance in 1QS 1 occurs in the context of what configures entry into the covenant of the community. Many have traditionally considered the ceremony described to reflect an actual moment of covenant renewal, probably taking place at Shavuot, Pentecost, when new members might be admitted to the *Yaḥad*. That might have taken place at Qumran or,

---

22 On this and the place of penitential prayer in the community compositions, see especially Rodney A. Werline, *Penitential Prayer in Second Temple Judaism: The Development of a Religious Institution*, SBLEJL 13 (Atlanta: Scholars Press, 1998), 126–57.
23 Falk, "The Scrolls and the Study of Ancient Jewish Liturgy," 619.
24 See, e.g., Paul Garnet, "Atonement: Qumran and the New Testament," in *The Bible and the Dead Sea Scrolls: The Princeton Symposium on the Dead Sea Scrolls*, ed. James H. Charlesworth (Waco: Baylor University Press, 2006), 3:357–80; Eyal Regev, "Atonement and Sectarianism in Qumran: Defining a Sectarian Worldview in Moral and Halakhic Systems," in *Sectarianism in Early Judaism: Sociological Advances*, ed. David J. Chalcraft (London: Equinox, 2007), 180–204.

at its first enactments, more likely elsewhere, given that the form and likely date of the text quite possibly precedes the actual occupation of the Qumran site by some members of the sectarian movement. The so-called covenant renewal ceremony has at its heart the priests reciting the just deeds of God and the Levites reciting the iniquities of Israel, which creates the moment of penance, as just mentioned. Penitence is then followed by blessing and cursing.

First, there is the blessing of "all the men of God's lot who walk unblemished in all his paths." The blessing takes the form of an expanded Aaronic benediction as is found in Numbers 6: "May he bless you with everything good, and may he protect you from everything bad. May he illuminate your heart with the discernment of life and grace you with eternal knowledge. May he lift upon you the countenance of his favour for eternal peace" (1QS 2:1–4). This blessing is followed, second, by the Levities' cursing of all the men of the lot of Belial, some of whose elements are the inverse of the priestly blessing:

> Accursed are you for all your wicked, blameworthy deeds. May God hand you over to terror by the hand of all those carrying out acts of vengeance. May he bring upon you destruction by the hand of all those who accomplish retributions. Accursed are you, without mercy, according to the darkness of your deeds, and sentenced to the gloom of everlasting fire. May God not be merciful when you entreat him. May he not forgive by purifying your iniquities. May he lift the countenance of his anger to avenge himself on you, and may there be no peace for you by the mouth of those who intercede (1QS 2:5–9).

The blessing and the curse are followed by what seems to be a closing statement: "And all those who enter the covenant shall say, after those who pronounce blessings and those who pronounce curses: 'Amen, Amen'" (1QS 2:10). However, the text continues with a further set of five curses uttered jointly by the priests and the Levites; the group of five begins with a single '*rwr* formula and ends with an inclusio inasmuch as the final element of curse is to be assigned with the accursed for ever (*btwk 'rwr 'wlmym*).[25] One element in the list of curses is for the accursed to be cut off from the midst of all the sons of light; it thus seems that the significant purpose of the cursing is to purge evildoers from the community, to protect it from the idolatry which comes with any arrogant and idolatrous claim, such as "I will have peace, in spite of my walking in the stubbornness of my heart" (1QS 2:13–14). Once penitence has occurred and atonement delivered, the blessings and curses have an apotropaic function.

---

25 On the character and function of blessings and curses see, notably, the comments by Bilhah Nitzan, *Qumran Prayer and Religious Poetry*, trans. Jonathan Chapman, STDJ 12 (Leiden: Brill, 1994), 119–71; eadem, "Blessings and Curses," in *Encyclopedia of the Dead Sea Scrolls*, ed. Lawrence Schiffman and James C. VanderKam (Oxford: Oxford University Press, 2000), 1:95–100.

6. Apotropaic Utterances

The recognition that blessings and curses have an apotropaic character belongs to Falk's 2019 study in which he has offered a catalogue of compositions designed to protect the movement and its members in the movement's various communities.[26] This development in cataloguing the materials is significant because the association of the apotropaic with the problematic categories of miracle and magic has led modern readers of ancient Jewish texts towards being inclined to see such texts as few and far between, as features of a wrong-headed minority in the community.[27] Quite how such texts fit if the description of their setting is shifted from utterances of the wrong-headed to one concerning the esoteric and the secret has yet to be determined.[28] Whatever the case, Falk has suggested that apotropaic prayer texts and rituals of similar effect are more widespread in the Scrolls than might at first be supposed. He has suggested that there are five sub-categories of such texts.

In Falk's categorization of apotropaic prayer in the Scrolls, pride of place goes to prayers and poems designed to fend off demons.[29] Alongside the most explicit texts, such as the Apocryphal Psalms (11Q11) with its formulae for protection from the demonic, and the so-called Exorcism (4Q560), there are hymns, such as those in the Songs of the Sage (4Q510–4Q511), to frighten demons and protect the community, as well as Incantation texts (4Q444) and hymns (6Q18).[30] Falk has noted that some of these ritual texts are for use by an expert (4Q560; 8Q5). Though the identity of such an expert is not clear, it seems likely that such practitioners would be in need of the kinds of texts for healing and other purposes that might well be present in those books associated with the priestly tasks of several of the ances-

---

26 Falk, "Liturgical Texts," 426–27.
27 See the discussion of some of the issues in George J. Brooke, "Deuteronomy 18.9–14 in the Qumran Scrolls," in *Magic in the Biblical World: From the Rod of Aaron to the Ring of Solomon*, ed. Todd Klutz, JSNTSup 245 (London: T&T Clark, 2003), 66–84.
28 See the discussion by Michael E. Stone, *Secret Groups in Ancient Judaism* (Oxford: Oxford University Press, 2018), 55–77, who argues that in the groups associated with the Dead Sea Scrolls there were hierarchies of knowledge.
29 A more detailed and more extensive list of apotropaic texts in the Scrolls is found in Michael J. Morris, *Warding off Evil: Apotropaic Tradition in the Dead Sea Scrolls and Synoptic Gospels*, WUNT 2/451 (Tübingen: Mohr Siebeck, 2017), 81–143.
30 This subcategory might be extended to include love incantations (and possibly their accompanying potions). Was Canticles excerpted in 4QCant^a and 4QCant^b to form such incantations? Was the story of Tobias and Sarah of interest because of the way Raphael chased away Asmodeus and his lustful eyes? See, e.g., Ida Fröhlich, "'Because He Loves Her …': The Figure of the Demon in the Book of Tobit," *The Arabist: Budapest Studies in Arabic* 37 (2016): 25–35.

tors from Enoch and Noah onwards, especially as those are mentioned in certain Aramaic compositions.³¹ Furthermore, Levi instructs his sons to teach their sons "reading (ספר) and instruction and wisdom" (4Q213 1 i 9).³² Special scribal skills would be needed for the production of phylacteries (tefillin) which have been found in considerable numbers and can be considered to belong in this sub-category: on the basis of the work of Yehudah Cohn, Falk has described them as probably functioning "as long-life amulets."³³ There are also possibly other amulets in the collections from the Qumran caves.³⁴

In second place Falk has included all those texts which reflect rites for the removal of impurities of any kind. Most obvious are the Ritual of Purification compositions (4Q284; 4Q414; 4Q512), which deal with both ad hoc and regular occasions of defilement, but also to be included are compositions referring to other irregularities, such as concern with the calendar (4Q512 33+35 [IV] 1–3; 4Q284 1 3–6) and meal practice (4Q512 7–9 3; 4Q414 7 8).

Thirdly, Falk has gathered together texts that deal with threats to or breeches of boundaries.³⁵ Most commonly these involve curses of various kinds and are certainly apotropaic when supernatural beings are named (4Q286–4Q290). Some of the prayers of the War Texts also belong in this group; they are particularly

---

31 E.g., "the writing of the book of Noah concerning the blood" (ALD 10:10); "Book of the words of Noah" (1QapGen 5:29).

32 Henryk Drawnel renders *spr* as "scribal craft" (ALD 88 l. 17): Henryk Drawnel, *An Aramaic Wisdom Text from Qumran: A New Interpretation of the Levi Document*, JSJSup 86 (Leiden: Brill, 2004), 158.

33 Yehudah B. Cohn, *Tangled up in Text: Tefillin and the Ancient World*, BJS 351 (Providence: Brown Judaic Studies, 2008), esp. 55–102. Little is known of how scribes trained for the production of or actually produced Tefillin; perhaps the Nash Papyrus with its excerpted scriptural texts is a manuscript from which Tefillin might have been produced. Is 4Q341 a scribal exercise for the writing of amulets? In favour of such a possibility, see George J. Brooke, "4Q341: An Exercise for Spelling and for Spells?" in *Writing and Ancient Near Eastern Society: Papers in Honour of Alan R. Millard*, ed. Piotr Bienowski, Christopher B. Mee, and Elizabeth A. Slater, LHBOTS 426 (London: T&T Clark, 2005), 271–82; against reading too much into the fragment, see Joan E. Taylor, "4Q341: A Writing Exercise Remembered," in *Is There a Text in This Cave?*, 133–51.

34 See Ariel Feldman and Faina Feldman, "4Q147: An Amulet?" *DSD* 26 (2019): 1–29; Ariel Feldman and Faina Feldman, "4Q148 (4QPhylactère U): Another Amulet from Qumran?" *JSJ* 50 (2019): 197–222. Mezuzot might be considered to have a similar protective function. There are some in the Qumran collection (4Q149–4Q155); see also Ariel and Faina Feldman, "Is Mur 5 a Mezuzah?" *RevQ* 31 (2019): 291–98.

35 Falk is concerned at this point with how some texts are about the maintenance of some boundaries, but prayer might also be about the overcoming of other boundaries, notably those between the human and the divine.

powerful items of performative speech, variously upgraded in the different forms of the composition.[36]

Falk's fourth sub-category "includes rites to address error and disruption in the social order. Numerous texts attest formal and public procedures for reproof and discipline (e.g., CD 9:16–10:3; 1QS 5:23–6:1) involving an overseer who records the reproof."[37] Some aspects of those three categories seem to have transformative as well as protective elements, though the spiritual maintenance of the movement and its sub-groups, as Falk has suggested, is probably to the fore.

The suitability of Falk's fifth and last subcategory is more debatable: Falk has allocated to it rites for atoning for sin and penitential prayers. Such might be deemed to be indicating rituals for the alleviation of affliction, but as this study has indicated they probably belong elsewhere because of what they imply about the ideology around the problem of evil. Prayers and rituals that seek to manage evil caused by human wrongdoing and sin would seem to be concerned principally with the transformation and restoration of the individual, community, or land, rather than with the issue of straightforward protection, the control of external evil. Whilst it could be that the role of blessings and curses within any such rite would seal the transformation or restoration in a protective manner, such would seem to indicate that blessings and curses occupy something of a shared space between atonement and protection.

If there is such a shared space between atonement and protection, containing a broad field of blessings and curses which can serve multiple functions, then the question can be asked concerning what ideology or theology might lie behind or enable the conjoining of those two perspectives of atonement and protection.[38] Commonly associated with the so-called covenant renewal ceremony as described in 1QS 1–2, is the communal ritual text 4QBerakhot (4Q286–4Q287). Although the extant manuscript copies of 4QBerakhot do not "contain a single mention of the Law, the covenant, Israel, the nation, or any figures connectable with it, such as Abraham or Moses,"[39] and so should be juxtaposed with the rite discernible in the

---

36 See, e.g., the comments on the performative speech in M by George J. Brooke, "Text, Timing and Terror: Thematic Thoughts on the *War Scroll* in Conversation with the Writings of Martin G. Abegg, Jr.," in *The War Scroll, Violence, War and Peace in the Dead Sea Scrolls and Related Literature: Essays in Honor of Martin G. Abegg, Jr. on the Occasion of His 65th Birthday*, ed. Kipp Davis et al., STDJ 115 (Leiden: Brill, 2016), 49–66. It should also be recalled, however, that phrases concerning atonement from Leviticus 16 seem to lie behind 1QM 2:4–6.
37 Falk, "Liturgical Texts," 427.
38 As is implied in the wide-ranging comprehensive philological analysis of James K. Aitken, *The Semantics of Blessing and Cursing in Ancient Hebrew*, ANESSup 23 (Leuven: Peeters, 2007).
39 On how the perception of creation is a possible bridge between the two ideologies, see Mika S. Pajunen, "Creation as the Liturgical Nexus of the Blessings and Curses in 4QBerakhot," in

Rule of the Community (1QS 1–2) with caution, in a recent study Mika Pajunen has suggested that the background of the ritual is a theology of creation reflected in the use and reuse of certain elements of Gen 1:1–2:3 in 4QBerakhot combined with the obligation of the praising of God's name. Such is also the case, most especially in Jub. 2:21 in relation to how the Sabbath acts as a sign to indicate God's purpose in the creation of humanity: "And thus he created a sign by which they might keep the sabbath with us on the seventh day, to eat and drink and bless the one who created all things." Blessing is a two-way phenomenon: from God to humanity, and especially the elect, it provides peace and protection; from humanity to God it is the right response to having been created; from God to humanity it confirms restoration and serves as a force-field for keeping those inside secure and at peace; from humanity to God it reflects the *terra firma* of thanksgiving that is reflected in the acknowledgement that all is dependent on God.

7. Conclusions

Much more could be said about "patterns of prayer" in Second Temple Judaism; and indeed much has been said by others. However, in paying attention to something of the ideological background of the various types of prayer in Second Temple texts, the point of this paper is to highlight the ways in which such prayers might have been performed and processed by a range of practitioners. The two discourses about evil—whether the evil of sin that requires atonement, or the evil of external spiritual forces that requires apotropaic response—create patterns of prayer in which there are differing sets of interests. The suggestion of this essay is that the priests who see themselves in line with Aaronide concerns, not necessarily just the Sons of Aaron, would be likely to be ideologically aligned with atoning practices as a spiritual priority. Such practices may or may not have involved animal sacrifice at the Qumran site itself or elsewhere; Jodi Magness has recently tipped the discussion on that point back in the direction of seeing the distinctive animal bone deposits as evidence of sacrifice having taken place.[40] But, whatever the case with actual sacrifice, the language of atonement with reference to both people and land remains. Other priestly practitioners could be more concerned to engage in prayer with a view to establishing the divine protection of the indivi-

---

Ancient Readers and their Scriptures: Engaging the Hebrew Bible in Early Judaism and Christianity, ed. Garrick Allen and John A. Dunne, AJEC 107 (Leiden: Brill, 2018), 27–39 (30).

[40] Jodi Magness, "Were Sacrifices Offered at Qumran? The Animal Bone Deposits Reconsidered," *JAJ* 7 (2016): 5–34. Other articles in the same issue are studies variously in support of or against Magness's view.

dual and the community. Such priests seem familiar in particular with how priesthood is portrayed in Aramaic sources that survive in the caves. They are in control of specialist, even esoteric, priestly lore, written in books.

Behind the two approaches lie compositions like the Hodayot. Commonly associated in some way with how other texts remember the Teacher of Righteousness, the priestly perspective of the Hodayot is such that its compositions could be deployed and developed in relation to both perspectives on evil, either encouraging divine mercy and forgiveness for sin or expressing hope for divine protection from external evil. In Commentary on Psalms A (4Q171) the Teacher is identified as a priest, and also the interpretation of Ps 45:2, "And my tongue is the pen of a skilled scribe," links the text to the Teacher who apparently does something before God "with the reply of the tongue" (4Q171 4:26–27). With his exegetical prowess based in the way God has made known to him "all the mysteries of the words of his servants, the prophets" (1QpHab 7:5), the Teacher has a didactic role too. From the way that the memory of the Teacher is constructed he can be seen to lie behind both priestly approaches, the atoning and the apotropaic.

In the foreground of the two understandings and approaches to evil are the blessings and curses, which likewise represent aspects of both ideologies. In some ways blessings and curses are endorsements of the stability of individual and community life as that is maintained through regular attention to prayer and purification. In other ways blessings and curses are the performative speech acts that create the protective shield around those inside and keep out the wicked, both human and supernatural forces of pollution and destruction. Let it be remembered that in the Cave 1 version of the Rule of the Community the covenant ceremony mentions both blessings and curses which are performed by unspecified priests and Levites. The priests are made responsible for proclaiming the just deeds of God and blessing "all the men of God's lot who walk unblemished in all his paths" (1QS 2:1–2). The Levites recite the iniquities of the children of Israel and curse "all the men of the lot of Belial" (1QS 2:4–5). Both blessing and curse are highly scripturalized compositions which might be a strong indication of the strength and quality of their protective appeal.

If there are varieties of priestly identity reflected in varieties of cultic practice in the Second Temple period, then the diversity of priestly groups and interests within a movement like that reflected in the community compositions from Qumran might reflect a range of ideological stances which are held together in tension in changing patterns of prayer as the movement moves from one generation to another. One suspects that as the movement endured, so there were fewer actual priests recruited to it, since there are signs of the democratization of priesthood in such phrases as *miqdaš 'ādām* (4Q174), a term which seems to suggest that the whole community has access to the sanctuary to offer there as incense "deeds of thanksgiving" (*ma'aśê todāh*). In the movement of which the Qumran community was a part, thanksgiving as the overarching and fundamental category of prayer provided the background for both penitential and protective prayer whose common ground can be found in the shared space of blessings and curses. Such ideological tensions and combinations are also there in the prayer for Prince Louis of Cambridge.

Charlotte Hempel
The Apotropaic Function of the Final Hymn in the Community Rules

1. Introduction

From Ben Sira to 2 Baruch, the hymn constitutes one of the most attested forms of prayer, or address to God, in Second Temple Jewish literature. This genre of prayer is also attested among the Dead Sea Scrolls. The Final Hymn in a number of copies of the Qumran Community Rules, for example, is one of the most significant hymns from Qumran. It is most fully preserved in the Community Rules manuscript from Cave 1—1QS—and begins with an exhortation to bless God the creator at divinely ordained times embracing the celestial, liturgical, and eschatological spheres. Two manuscripts of the Community Rules from Cave 4—4QS^f and 4QS^j—constitute small-scale and perhaps portable scrolls that preserve remains of the Final Hymn.[1] The single fragment that survives of 4QS^j may belong to a liturgical anthology.[2] Jutta Jokiranta and Hanna Vanonen have problematized the identification of several manuscripts as copies of the Community Rules and cautioned against the assumption that texts that share material known from 1QS likely constitute parts of an assumed 1QS-shaped whole.[3] Making a distinctive and yet complementary point we have recently argued that the presence of portions of text in the Cave 4 manuscripts of the Community Rules that is not attested in 1QS or other S manuscripts should not be taken to suggest that such a composition is *not* a copy of the Community Rules.[4] To acknowledge distinctive representations of this work I employ the plural Community Rules. For the purposes of this essay we will include all manuscripts of the Community Rules that contain parts of the Final Hymn, though our argument does not depend on such an identification.

---

[1] Philip S. Alexander and Geza Vermes, *Qumran Cave 4.XIX: Serekh Ha-Yaḥad and Two Related Texts*, DJD 26 (Oxford: Clarendon Press, 1998), 154, 201.

[2] The Final Hymn or parts of it are preserved in the following manuscripts of the Community Ruless: 1QS 9:26b–10:22; 4QS^b 19:1–7; 20:1–7; 23:1–3; 4QS^d 8:10–10:8; 12:4; 13:1–3; 4QS^f 2:1–5; 3:1–3; 4:1–10; 5:1–7; and 4QS^j 1 1–10.

[3] Jutta Jokiranta and Hanna Vanonen, "Multiple Copies of Rules Texts or Multiple Rules Texts? Boundaries of the S and M Documents," in *Crossing Imaginary Boundaries: The Dead Sea Scrolls in the Context of Second Temple Judaism*, ed. Mika S. Pajunen and Hanna Tervanotko, PFES 108 (Helsinki: Finnish Exegetical Society, 2015), 11–60.

[4] Charlotte Hempel, *The Community Rules from Qumran: A Commentary*, TSAJ (Tübingen: Mohr Siebeck), forthcoming.

https://doi.org/10.1515/9783110624526-007

The Hymn is made up of a collection of disparate material[5] including a section that has been identified as a liturgical calendar.[6] One of the manuscripts of the Community Rules from Cave 4, 4QS[e], continues with a calendrical collection *Otot* ("Signs") where the Hymn is found in several other witnesses.[7] This article will examine the function of the Hymn in the manuscripts of the Community Rules against the background of recent research on apotropaic texts from Qumran. Before turning to the Hymn, however, we will draw attention to a number of statements beginning with the opening lines of 1QS and 4QS[a] that offer a valuable wider context within which the Hymn is embedded in those manuscripts of the Community Rules that preserve it.

2. A Programmatic Entreaty to Keep Away from All Evil in 1QS 1:1–7a and 4QS[a] 1 1–5[8]

The opening lines of the Community Rules as represented by 1QS and 4QS[a] foreground a programmatic entreaty to keep away from all evil in 1QS 1:4; 4QS[a] 1 5–6.

---

[5] Alfred R. C. Leaney, *The Rules of Qumran and Its Meaning*, NTL (London: SCM, 1966), 115, and Daniel K. Falk, *Daily, Sabbath and Festival Prayers in the Dead Sea Scrolls*, STDJ 27 (Leiden: Brill, 1998), 101.

[6] Compare already Józef T. Milik, *Ten Years of Discovery in the Wilderness of Judaea* (London: SCM, 1959), 107–18, and Leaney, *Rules of Qumran*, 17–26, 80–107. For the suggestion that we are dealing with "a series of hymns" see Arjen Bakker, "The Figure of the Sage in *Musar le-Mevin* and *Serek ha-Yahad*" (PhD diss., Katholieke Universiteit Leuven, 2015), 98.

[7] See Alexander and Vermes DJD 26:129–52; Shemaryahu Talmon, Jonathan Ben-Dov, and Uwe Glessmer, *Qumran Cave 4.XVI: Calendrical Texts*, DJD 21 (Oxford: Clarendon Press, 2001), 196–201; Jonathan Ben-Dov, *Head of All Years: Astronomy and Calendars at Qumran in Their Ancient Context*, STDJ 78 (Leiden: Brill, 2008), 147; Uwe Glessmer, "The Otot-Texts (4Q319) and the Problem of Intercalations in the Content of the 364-Day Calendar," in *Qumranstudien: Vorträge und Beiträge der Teilnehmer des Qumranseminars auf dem internationalen Treffen der Society of Biblical Literature, Münster, 25–26 Juli 1993*, ed. Heinz-Josef Fabry, Armin Lange, and Hermann Lichtenberger, Schriften des Institutum Judaicum Delitzschianum 4 (Göttingen: Vandenhoeck & Ruprecht, 1996), 125–64; Sarianna Metso, *The Textual Development of the Qumran Community Rules*, STDJ 21 (Leiden: Brill, 1997), 48–54; Józef T. Milik, *The Books of Enoch: Aramaic Fragments of Qumrân Cave 4* (Oxford: Oxford University Press, 1974), 62–64; James C. VanderKam, *Calendars in the Dead Sea Scrolls: Measuring Time* (London: Routledge, 1998), 80–84.

[8] We do not include here the remains of 4QS[c] 1 1–2 which breaks off before the material that is the focus of our attention here.

1QS 1	4QSª 1
1¹ To/for[ ] š/śym for his life [the Book of the Ru]le of the Community. (They are) to seek ²God with [all (their) heart] and with [all (their) soul; to] do what is good and right before Him according to that which ³He has commanded through Moses and through all His servants the prophets; to love all ⁴that which He favours and hate all that He despises; **to keep away from all evil ⁵but adhere closely to all good works;** לרחוק מכול רע ולדבוק בכול מעשי טוב to act truthfully, righteously, and justly ⁶in the land and **no longer** walk in the stubbornness of a guilty heart and prurient eyes ⁷and **perform all kinds of evil.** לעשות כול רע	1¹[ ] for his [lif]e the Book of the Rule of the Community. ²[(They are) to seek God with all (their) heart and with a]ll (their) soul; to do ³[what is good and right before Him according to that which] He has commanded through Moses ⁴[and through all His servants the prophets; to l]ove a[l]l [that which ⁵He favours and hate all that He despi]ses; **to k[eep away from all ⁶evil but adhere closely to all good works];** [...]

Much in 1QS 1:1b–7a and parallels is reminiscent of Deut 6:17–18 with its emphasis on obedience to God's commandments and the promise of the land. Of particular interest for the present discussion is the emphasis on keeping away from all evil which is not mirrored in Deuteronomy 6. The opening lines as preserved in 1QS contain two admonitions to keep away from or cease to perform "all evil" (כול רע) in lines 4 and 7. Only the first reference is preserved in 4QSª. Both references juxtapose admonitions to shun "all evil" with commending good deeds as part of a two-fold scheme that is attested more widely in Early Jewish and Christian literature (see, e. g., T. Ash. 1–3; Rom 12:9; 1 Thess 5:21–22).[9]

---

[9] Preben Wernberg-Møller, *The Manual of Discipline*, STDJ 1 (Leiden: Brill, 1957), 45–46, and Michael A. Knibb, *The Qumran Community*, Cambridge Commentaries on Writings of the Jewish and Christian World 200 BC to AD 200 (Cambridge: Oxford University Press, 1987), 80.

3. A Second Programmatic Admonition to Reject all Evil in 1QS 5:1–3a; 4QS^b 9 1–3 and 4QS^d 11–12

A second programmatic requirement to turn away from all evil occurs in 1QS 5 with corresponding yet distinctive material in 4QS^b 9 and 4QS^d 1.

1QS 5	4QS^b and 4QS^d (Composite Text)[10]
5^1 And this is the rule for the people of the community. **They shall be fervently committed to turn back from all evil and to hold fast to all that He has commanded** as His wish. They shall keep separate from the congregation of ^{2}the people of injustice to form a community with regard to law and property. They shall be accountable to the sons of Zadok, the priests who keep the covenant and to the multitude of the people of ^{3}the community who hold fast to the covenant.	9^1/1^1 Midrash for the Maskil over <u>the people of the law.</u> <u>**They shall be fervently committed to turn back from all evil and to hold fast to all**</u> 9^2 **that He has commanded.** 1^2 They shall keep separate from the congregation of the <u>people of injustice to form a community with regard to la[w] and property. They shall be accountable</u> 9^3 to the many ...

What is a second programmatic introduction in 1QS 5 above constitutes, in fact, the opening lines of 4QS^d.[11] A great deal of scholarly discussion has focused on the diverging headings as well as the striking absence of the sons of Zadok in the two shorter Cave 4 witnesses.[12] We have argued elsewhere for the need to pay due attention also to the shared elements between the otherwise divergent manuscripts.[13] In this contribution the Maskil heading in 4QS^b 9 1 and 4QS^d 1 1 and the

---

[10] Text preserved only in 4QS^d is indicated by double underline.
[11] The combination of turning back from (שוב) and evil (רע) occurs in Jer 44:5, see Wernberg-Møller, *Manual of Discipline*, 89
[12] See Philip S. Alexander, "The Redaction-History of *Serekh ha-Yaḥad*: A Proposal," *RevQ* 17 (1996): 437–53; Charlotte Hempel, *Qumran Rule Texts in Context: Collected Studies*, TSAJ 154 (Tübingen: Mohr Siebeck, 2013); Sarianna Metso, *Textual Development* and Alison Schofield, *From Qumran to the Yaḥad: A New Paradigm of Textual Development for the Community Rule*, STDJ 77 (Leiden: Brill, 2009). Further, more recently, compare also Ulrich Dahmen, "צדוק צדוק ṣādôq," *ThWQ* 3:379–83, and Nathan McDonald, *Priestly Rule: Polemic and Biblical Interpretation in Ezekiel 44* (Berlin: De Gruyter, 2015).
[13] Hempel, *Rule Texts in Context*, 109–16.

admonition to turn from all evil that follows across the manuscripts are of particular interest.

While the association of the Maskil with the spiritual and liturgical sphere is widely recognised, this figure also occurs in a number of contexts that emphasize obedience to the law in an environment influenced by malevolent forces.[14] Thus, the Teaching on the Two Spirits is associated with the Maskil in the heading.[15] It is illuminating to note the extent to which halakhic rectitude is ascribed to the influence of the Spirit of Truth in 1QS 4:2–3[16] by filling the heart of its followers with "respect for the commandments of God."[17] Moreover, the same spirit "engenders enthusiasm for righteous ordinances" according to 1QS 4:4; 4QS^c 5 1.[18] Obedience to the law recurs in the Statutes for the Maskil in the heading "These are the statutes for the Maskil to walk in them" in 1QS 9:12; 4QS^e 3 6–7.[19] In addition, we find references to the significance of God's commandments in 1QS 9:15; 4QS^e 3 11 and 1QS 9:24.[20] Finally, a number of references to statutes and commandments also occur in the Final Hymn which is associated with the Maskil. The latter is to be identified with the first-person speaker of the Hymn and is introduced at 1QS 9:26; with the instruction to "bless his maker." We take 1QS 9:26 as the transition between the Statutes for the Maskil and the Final Hymn.

---

14 In addition to the bibliography on the Maskil in Hempel, *Rule Texts in Context*, 239–51, see Joseph L. Angel, "Maskil, Community, and Religious Experience in the Songs of the Sage (4Q510–511)," *DSD* 19 (2011): 1–27; Torleif Elgvin, "מַשְׂכִּיל," *ThWQ* 2:802–806; Charlotte Hempel, "Wisdom and Law in the Hebrew Bible and at Qumran," *JSJ* 48 (2017): 155–81 (165–66); Judith H. Newman, "Speech and Spirit: Paul and the Maskil as Inspired Interpreters of Scripture," in *The Holy Spirit, Inspiration, and the Cultures of Antiquity: Multidisciplinary Perspectives*, ed. Jörg Frey and John R. Levison, Ekstasis 5 (Berlin: De Gruyter, 2014), 243–66, and Michael E. Stone, *Secret Groups in Ancient Judaism* (Oxford: Oxford University Press, 2018), 71–73.
15 For the text of the treatise see 1QS 3:13–4:26; 4QS^c 5 1–8, 12–14 and 6 2–5. The heading is preserved only in 1QS 3:13. For further discussion see Charlotte Hempel, "The Treatise on the Two Spirits and the Literary Development of the Rule of the Community," in *Dualism in Qumran*, ed. Geza Xeravits, LSTS 76 (London: T&T Clark, 2010), 102–20, and further literature cited there.
16 The are no preserved parallels in other manuscripts.
17 See Wernberg-Møller, *Manual of Discipline*, 73–74.
18 Cf. 1QS 3:1; 4QS^c 3 2 and 1QS 9:17; 4QS^d 8 2; 4QS^e 3 14–15.
19 Judith Newman has teased out the connection of the Maskil with the idea of engraved statutes in more detail in *Before the Bible: The Liturgical Body and the Formation of Scriptures in Early Judaism* (New York: Oxford University Press, 2018); see also Armin Lange, *Weisheit und Prädestination: Weisheitliche Urordnung und Prädestination in den Textfunden von Qumran*, STDJ 18 (Leiden: Brill, 1995), 146.
20 The pertinent words have been reconstructed but are not attested in 4QS^d 8 8; 4QS^e 4 6 and 4QS^f 1 2. See Alexander and Vermes, DJD 26:115, 150, 159.

In short, the Maskil's area of expertise comprises human conduct as an organic part of the spiritual make-up of community members in the Teaching on the Two Spirits, the Statutes for the Maskil, and the Final Hymn. It is therefore not out of place to find the Maskil in the heading of 4QS[d] 1 and 4QS[b] 9 at the point where all three manuscripts turn to the regulations that present the authors' vision of how members of the movement described here are to conduct themselves in harmony with the law. Finally, we observe that whereas the antonym to all evil was "good works" in 1QS 1:4–5 and 4QS[a] 1 5–6, the present passage contrasts all evil with holding fast to the divinely ordained commandments.

An emphasis on human conduct in the Rule texts is discernible elsewhere too. For example, the translation above takes the *hitpael* participle of נדב[21] in 1QS 5:1; 4QS[d] 1 1 and 1QS 5:6; 4QS[d] 1 4–5 as endorsing a fervent commitment to a particular course of action or behaviour rather than a self-designation for the community as the terminology is often understood.[22] A commitment to undertake a specific immediate course of action is expressed by the same verb in Exod 35:21 and 29. Moreover, in the present passage the participle does not represent a generic descriptor of the members of the community but rather a characteristic attribute of the latter. Its predicative syntactic function reflected in our translation is compatible to the *hiphil* participle of שוב, "they shall be answerable" (1QS 5:2; 4QS[d] 9 2) that occurs in the next line.[23]

Besides the use of the *hitpael* participle of נדב to speak of a commitment to a particular course of action or behaviour, the instruction "to turn back from all evil" is emphatically positioned as the first objective stated in 4QS[d] 1 1, at the very beginning of this manuscript, which lacks the material found in the first four col-

---

21 It occurs seven times in 1QS 5–6, five of which are also attested in manuscripts from Cave 4. The remaining two cases are conspicuous pluses in 1QS. The passages are as follows: 1QS 5:1; 4QS[d] 9 1; 1QS 5:6; 4QS[d] 1 5; 1QS 5:8 (a "plus" in 1QS); 1QS 5:10 (a "plus" in 1QS); 1QS 5:21; 4QS[d] 2 1; 1QS 5:22; 4QS[d] 2 2; 4QS[h] 1a–b 2; 1QS 6:13; 4QS[b] 11 8). We also have two occurrences in the *niphal* in 1QS 1:7, 11 (no 4QS text preserved).

22 See, e.g., Devorah Dimant, "The Volunteers in the Rule of the Community—A Biblical Notion in Sectarian Garb," *RevQ* 23 (2007): 233–45; eadem, "נָדַב nādab," *ThWQ* 2:879–83; Benedikt Eckhardt, "The Yahad in the Context of Hellenistic Group Formation," in *The T&T Clark Companion to the Dead Sea Scrolls*, ed. George J. Brooke and Charlotte Hempel (London: T&T Clark, 2018), 86–96; Aloysius Fitzgerald, "MTNDBYM in 1QS," *CBQ* 36 (1974): 495–502. Jacob Licht even designates the large segment of the Community Rule in 1QS 5:1–6:23 as "Statutes for the volunteers," rather than referring to the opening heading in 1QS 5:1. See Jacob Licht, *The Rule Scroll* (Jerusalem: Bialik, 1965), 19 (Hebrew); for discussion see Charlotte Hempel, "Rules," in *The T&T Clark Companion to the Dead Sea Scrolls*, 405–12 (408).

23 For a more detailed analysis of this terminology and the significance of the pronounced fervour of the laity in a cultic context in Num 35:21, 29 and 2 Chron 29:31 see Hempel, *The Community Rules*, 132–133.

umns of 1QS and parallels. This admonition is also prominently placed at a major juncture in 1QS 5:1 and 4QS[b] 9 1, the central section of the longer text of the Community Rules. Such an emphatic position of the instruction to turn back from all evil deserves more attention than it has received. In 1QS this warning comes immediately after the Teaching on the Two Spirits which is similarly concerned with opposing forces of light and darkness as well as the associated spheres of influence of good and evil.[24]

4. The Expanded Priestly Blessing in 1QS 2:1–4

Finally, the Priestly Blessing attested in the Covenant Ceremony as preserved only in 1QS 2:1–4 testifies to an expanded form over against Num 6:24–26.[25] The longer version attested here refers to being blessed "with all good things" and being "preserved from all things evil" alongside sapiential themes such as the granting of knowledge and insight.[26] The addition of the words "from all evil" (מכול רע) again illustrates the apotropaic force of blessings that also emerges elsewhere in the Community Rules.

In short, the dangers emanating from malevolent forces and the lure of wicked behaviour even *within* the community runs across disparate parts of the complex Rule tradition. In the remainder of this chapter we offer a reading of a number of features in the Final Hymn in light of the apotropaic liturgical collections 4Q510–511 (Songs of the Sage). This recently published liturgical material suggests an apotropaic potency for the prominence of blessing in the Hymn as well as its placement in the a number of manuscripts of the Community Rules.

---

[24] See also Jutta Leonhardt-Balzer, "Evil at Qumran," in *Evil in Second Temple Judaism and Early Christianity*, ed. Chris Keith and Loren T. Stuckenbruck, WUNT 2.317 (Tübingen: Mohr Siebeck, 2016), 17–33 (18–22).

[25] Further, George J. Brooke, *Exegesis at Qumran: 4QFlorilegium in Its Jewish Context*, JSOTSup 29 (Sheffield: JSOT, 1985), 295–301; Falk, *Daily, Sabbath and Festival Prayers*, 224–25; Steven Fraade, "Rhetorics and Hermeneutic in Miqṣat Maʻaśeh ha-Torah (4QMMT): The Case of the Blessings and Curses," *DSD* 10 (2003): 150–61 (157); Bilhah Nitzan, *Qumran Prayer and Religious Poetry*, trans. Jonathan Chipman, STDJ 12 (Leiden: Brill, 1994), 148–50, 357–58; James A. Loader, "The Model of the Priestly Blessing in 1QS," *JSJ* 14 (1983): 11–17, and Shani Tzoref, "The Use of Scripture in the Community Rule," in *A Companion to Biblical Interpretation in Early Judaism*, ed Matthias Henze (Grand Rapids: Eerdmans, 2012), 203–34, 218–19.

[26] See Tzoref, "Use of Scripture," 218–19, and Manfred Weise, *Kultzeiten und kultischer Bundesschluss in der "Ordensregel" vom Toten Meer*, SPB 3 (Leiden: Brill, 1961), 82–93.

5. A Wider Context of Apotropaic Texts from Qumran

There has been an influx of apotropaic texts from Cave 4 which gave rise to a large amount of scholarly discussion on malevolent forces and demonology in the Scrolls over recent years. This new material sheds fresh light on the role of blessing and praise in protecting individuals as well as the community from the latent threat of malevolent powers. Among the host of apotropaic texts to have emerged from Qumran are the Songs of the Maskil (4Q510–511), Apocryphal Psalms (11Q11), the Plea for Deliverance (11QPsalms[a] 19:15b–17a), 4QExorcism (4Q560), Incantation (4Q444), and 4QPhylactère T-U (4Q147 and 4Q148). Ariel and Faina Feldman have recently identified the latter manuscripts as amulets.[27] There is no doubt, therefore, that the Scrolls have increased the breadth of written material dealing with the influence and power of malevolent beings in the Second Temple Period. We have also learnt a great deal more about the kinds of beings whose power was being feared, probably unremittingly, as well as some indications of how it was hoped one might contain or combat them.[28]

The function of praise in the service of protection from evil forces is clearly attested in the Songs of the Maskil (4Q511). Thus, Bilhah Nitzan recognizes the apotropaic force of blessing in her discussion of 4Q511 and suggests,

---

[27] "Ariel and Faina Feldman, "4Q147: An Amulet?" *DSD* 26 (2019): 1–29; eidem, "4Q148 (4QPhylactère U): Another Amulet from Qumran?" *JSJ* 50 (2019): 197–222.
[28] For recent scholarly discussion see Philip A. Alexander, "'Wrestling against Wickedness in High Places:' Magic in the Worldview of the Qumran Community," in *The Scrolls and the Scriptures: Qumran Fifty Years After*, ed. Stanley E. Porter and Craig A. Evans, JSPSup 26 (Sheffield: Sheffield Academic Press, 1997), 318–37; idem, "The Demonology of the Dead Sea Scrolls," in *The Dead Sea Scrolls After Fifty Years: Volume II: A Comprehensive Assessment*, ed. Peter W. Flint and James C. VanderKam (Leiden: Brill, 1999), 331–53; Gideon Bohak, *Ancient Jewish Magic: A History* (Cambridge: Cambridge University Press, 2008); Esther Eshel, "Apotropaic Prayers in the Second Temple Period," in *Liturgical Perspectives: Prayer and Poetry in Light of the Dead Sea Scrolls*, ed. Esther Chazon with Ruth Clements and Avital Pinnick, STDJ 48 (Leiden: Brill, 2003), 69–88; Tupá Guerra, "Encountering Evil: Apotropaic Magic in the Dead Sea Scrolls" (PhD diss., University of Birmingham, 2007); Armin Lange, Hermann Lichtenberger, and K. F. Diethard Römheld, eds., *The Demonology of Israelite-Jewish and Early Christian Literature in Context of Their Environment* (Tübingen: Mohr Siebeck, 2003); Farah Mébarki and Émile Puech, *Les manuscrits de la mer Morte* (Arles: Éditions du Rouergue, 2002), 270–72; and Hanne von Weissenberg, "God(s), Angels and Demons," in *The T&T Clark Companion to the Dead Sea Scrolls*, 490–95, as well as further bibliography there.

> The songs of scroll 4Q511 are recited, as are other "conventional" songs, in order "to frighten and terrify" evil spirits. In other words, the conventional songs of praise serve a magical purpose, explicitly defined in the scroll.²⁹

Another particularly instructive statement is preserved in 4Q510 (Songs of the Maskil) 1 4–6 which refers to the power exerted by praise for God's majesty in the fight against malevolent forces,

> And I, the Instructor (ואני משכיל), proclaim the majesty of his beauty to frighten and to te[rrify] all the spirits of the destroying angels and the spirits of the bastards, the demons, Lilith, desert howlers and [the yelpers] they who strike suddenly to lead astray the spirit of understanding (רוח בינה) ... (Translation Bilhah Nitzan)³⁰

The reference to dangers facing even those benefitting from a spirit of understanding is noteworthy. The Community Rules, similarly, includes statements that make it clear the community is by no means a safe zone, and threats from insincere newcomers and groups such as "the people of injustice" are addressed repeatedly. Thus, a separation from "the people of injustice" is part and parcel of the community's formation in the Community Rules, which describe "the people of injustice" as potentially influential insiders with access to the hidden things, as well perceived figures of authority among some members of the movement.³¹ The authority of this group that is being challenged uses the same language of deference as is applied to the "sons of Zadok" and "the many" in 1QS 5 and parallels above. Thus 1QS 5:15b–16a prohibits honouring the authority of "the people of injustice" by "not being accountable to them with regard to any law or judgment" (שוב hiphil plus על פי). It seems clear that only a group of influential former insiders can hold such sway among community members. In this context we have argued elsewhere that the expansions of the Community Rules tradition with the additions of the Covenant Ceremony and the Teaching on the Two Spirits reflect an

---

29 Nitzan, *Qumran Prayer and Religious Poetry*, 193.
30 Nitzan, *Qumran Prayer and Religious Poetry*, 240.
31 On the separation from the people of injustice in the course of an account of the admission of new members by swearing an oath, see 1QS 5:7b–20a// 4QS^b 9 6b–13// 4QS^d 1 5b–13; cf. also the instruction to separate from the people of injustice at the point of community formation in 1QS 5 1c–2a; 4QS^b 9 2; 4QS^d 1 2. Further, Charlotte Hempel, "The Community and Its Rivals according to the Community Rules from Caves 1 and 4," *RevQ* 21 (2003): 47–81, and Jutta Jokiranta, "Black Sheep, Outsiders, and the Qumran Movement: Social-Psychological Perspectives on Norm-Deviant Behaviour," in *Social Memory and Social Identity in the Study of Early Judaism and Early Christianity*, ed. Samuel Byrskog, Raimo Hakola, and Jutta Jokiranta, NTOA/WUNT 116 (Göttingen: Vandenhoeck & Ruprecht, 2016), 151–74.

attempt to counter-act a crisis of commitment *within* the movement by means of promoting a much more polarised discourse.[32]

We will now turn to the Final Hymn and begin with a synoptic translation that highlights elements which deserve to be reflected on in light of the discussion of the larger apotropaic corpus to have emerged from Qumran.

6. The Final Hymn in the Community Rules: A Synoptic Translation

The translation of the Final Hymn that follows highlights especially words that point to the insights we have gained on the remit of the Maskil in the fight against demonic influences through praise and blessing (in **bold**), as well as an emphasis on the lawful conduct of individuals in a liturgical context associated with the Maskil (underlined).

Introduction (1QS 9:26–10:1a; 4QS^d 8 10–11a)

1QS 9–10	4QS^d 8
[26][ ] *qh* he shall **bless** his maker and re[count] everything that comes to pass [… with an offering of the] lips he shall **bless** Him [10][1a]at *vacat* the times which God has decreed (חקק).	[10][he shall **bless** his maker and re]count [everything that comes to pass … with an offering of the lips he shall] **bless** Him at [the times] [11a][which God has decreed.]

A Calendar for Praise (1QS 10:1b–8; 4QS^b 19 1–6; 4QS^d 8 11b–9 7a; 4QS^f 2 1–5)

1QS 10	4QS^d 8
[1b]At the beginning of the rule of light at its turning point and when it is gathered to its assigned place.	[11b][At the beginning of the rule of light a]t [its] turning [point and when] it is gathered to [its] assigned place.

---

32 See Charlotte Hempel, "The Long Text of the *Serekh* as Crisis Literature," *RevQ* 27 (2015): 3–24.

The Apotropaic Function of the Final Hymn in the Community Rules — 141

1QS 10	4QS^d 8	4QS^f 2
¹ᶜAt the beginning of ²the watches of darkness when He opens its storehouse and spreads it out over <the world> and at its turning point when it is gathered before the light when	¹¹ᶜAt the beginning of [the watches of ¹²darkness when He opens its storehouse and spreads it out over <the world> and at] its [turning point when it is gathered be]fore the light when	¹At the beginning of the w[at]ches of [darkness when He opens its storehouse and spreads it out over <the world> and together with] its turning point ²when it is gathered be-[fore the light when]

1QS 10	4QS^b 19	4QS^d 8	4QS^f 2
²the heavenly lights ³shine forth from the holy height and are gathered at the place of glory. At the onset of the appointed times on the days of the new moon at their turning point when ⁴one succeeds the other. The time of their renewal is a great day for the holy of holies and a sign *n vacat* for the outpouring of His eternal love at the beginning of ⁵the appointed times at all periods to come. At the beginning of months according to their appointed times and their established holy days	¹the heavenly lights [shine forth] from His holy height and are gathered at the place of glory. At the onset of the appointed times on the days of the new moon at ²their turning point when one succee[d]s the other. The time of their renewal is a great day for the holy of holies and a sign ³for the outpouring of eter[na]l lo[ve at the be]ginning of the appointed times at all periods to come. ⁴and [their established holy] days	¹²[the heavenly lights] shine forth [from the holy ¹³h]eight [and are gathered at the place of glory.] 9¹ The time of their renewal is a great day for the holy of holies and a sign for the outpouring of eternal love ²at the beginning of the appointed times at all periods to come. At the beginning of months according to their appointed times and their established holy ³days	²[the heavenly lights shine forth from the holy height and] are [gather]ed at the place of ³glory. When the [appointed times] arrive [on the days of the new moon together at their turning point when o]ne [succeeds] the other. ⁴The time of [their] renew[al is a great day for the holy of holies and a sign *vacat* (?) for the outpouring of] eternal [love] ⁵at the begin[in]g [of the appointed times at all periods to come. At the beginning of months according to their appointed times and their established hol]y [days]

1QS 10	4QS^b 19	4QS^d 9
⁵for remembrance, at their appointed times ⁶ (with**) an offering of the lips I will bless Him** according to the statute engraved forever. At the beginning of years and at the turning point of their appointed times when their established statute ⁷is fulfilled on each day according to its law one after the other. At harvest time until summer, *vacat* at sowing time until the time of growth, at the appointed times of years until their year weeks,	⁴[for re]membrance, at their appointed times (with) **an offering of the lips I will bless Him** according to the sta[tute] engraved forever. ⁵[At the beginning of years and at the turning] point of appointed times when their established statute is fulfilled on each day according to [its] l[aw one after the other. ⁶At harvest time until summer, at sowing time and the ti[m]e of growth, at the appointed times of ye[ars until their year weeks]	¹for remembrance, at [their] appointed times (with) **an [offering of] the lip[s] I will bless Him** according to the statute ⁴[en]graved forever. At the beginning of years and at the turning p[oint of their appointed times when their established statute [is ful]filed on each day according to its law one after the other. At [harvest] tim[e until summer, at so]wing [time] until the time of ⁶growth, at the appointed times of ye[ar]s until [their] year weeks,

1QS 10	4QS^d 9
⁸at the beginning of their year weeks until the time of release. For as long as I live a statute is engraved on my tongue **regarding the fruit of praise and the portion of my lips.**³³	⁶[at the beginning of] their [ye]ar weeks until the appointed time of release. ⁷ᵃFor as long as I live a statute is [en]graved on [my tongue **regarding the fruit of] praise and the por[tion of] my lips.**

Music and Praise of God (1QS 10:9–16a; 4QS^b 20 2–5a; 4QS^d 9 7b–10:5a; 4QS^f 3 1–3, 4 1–3a)

1QS 10	4QS^d 9
⁹Let me perform music with accomplishment, and all my music shall be for the glory of God.	⁷ᵇLet me perform music ⁸with accomplishment, and all my music shall be for the glory of God.

---

33 This reference to the role of prayer does not negate a role for sacrifices alongside prayer, as recent scholarship has emphasized, see, e. g., Falk, *Daily, Sabbath and Festival Prayers*, 218.

1QS 10	4QS^d 9	4QS^f 3
My lyre and harp (shall play) for His holy scheme, and I will raise up the flute of my lips in accordance with the measuring line of His fitting pattern[34]. ^10With the arrival of day and night I shall (re)enter the covenant of God and with the departure of evening and morning <u>I shall recount His statutes. And on the basis of them I shall set up</u>^11 <u>my boundaries so that there is no (scope for) turning back.</u>	**Let me play [my] harp** [for His holy] scheme, [and the flute of ^9my lips I will] raise up in accordance with the measuring [line of] His [fitting pa]ttern. Wi[th the arrival of] day [and] ni[gh]t I shall (re)enter the covenant of ^10[God and with the departure of evening and morning <u>I shall recount His statutes.</u>] And <u>on the basis of them I will re-establish</u> ^11[<u>my boundaries so that there is no (scope for) turning back</u>].	^1**Let me play [my] harp** for [His holy scheme, and the flute of my lips I will] raise up in accordance with the measuring line of His fitting pattern. ^2With [the arrival of day and night I shall (re)enter the covenant of God and wi]th the departure of evening ^3and morning <u>I shall re[count His statutes.</u> And on the basis of them I will re-establish (?) my boundaries s]o that there is no (scope for) turning back.

1QS 10	4QS^d 9–10
^11I will pronounce His judgment according to my corruption, <u>and my wrongdoing shall be engraved like a statute before my eyes.</u> To God I will call out "my righteousness" ^12and to the Most High "architect of my wellbeing, fountain of knowledge, spring of holiness, pinnacle of glory, almighty strength with eternal splendour." I will choose that which ^13 He teaches me and I will take delight in the way He disciplines me. Before I stir my hands and feet I will **bless** His name,	^11[I will pronounce His judgment according to my corruption, <u>and] my [wrong]doing [shall be engraved like a statute]</u> ^12before my eyes. [To God I will call out "my righteousness" and to the Most High "arch]itect of my wellbeing, foun[tain of ^13knowledge, spring of holiness, pinnacle of glory, almighty strength with eternal splendour." I will choose] 10^1 that which He teaches [me and I will take delight in the way He disciplines me. Before I stir my hands] ^2and feet I will **bless** [His name]

---

34 On the translation "fitting pattern" see Menahem Kister, "Physical and Metaphysical Measurements Ordained by God in the Literature of the Second Temple Period," in *Reworking the Bible: Apocryphal and Related Texts at Qumran*, ed. Esther Chazon, Ruth Clements and Devorah Dimant, STDJ 58 (Leiden: Brill, 2005), 153–76 (155).

1QS 10	4QS^b 20	4QS^d 10	
^{13}before going out and coming in, ^{14}settling or rising and while I lie on my bed I shall **rejoice** for Him. I shall **bless** Him with the **holy offering emanating from my lips** from among the lines of people ^{15a}before I raise my hand to taste the delights of the fruits of the earth.	^{2}[before going out and coming in, settling or rising and while I lie on my bed] I shall **rejoice** for Him. I shall [**bless** Him ^{3}with the **holy offering emanating from my lips** from among the lines of people before I raise my hand] to taste the delights of the fruits of ^{4}[the earth].	^{2}[and I shall **bless** Him] [before I raise my hand to taste] ^{3}the delights of the fru[its of the earth.]	

1QS 10	4QS^b 20	4QS^d 10	4QS^f 4
^{15b}**At the onset of fear and terror and in the place of distress (filled) with desolation** ^{16}I shall **bless** Him on account of performing **exceedingly marvellous acts**, I will ponder **His might** and lean on **His loving acts** all day long.	^{4}[**At the onset of fear and terror and in the place of distress (filled) with desolation** I shall **bless**] Him on account of performing **exceedingly marvellous acts**, [I will ponder] ^{5a}**His might** [and lean **on His loving acts** all day long.]	^{3}[**At the onset of fear and terror and in the place of distress**] ^{4}(filled) wi[th desolation I shall **bless** Him on account of performing **exceedingly marvellous acts**, I will ponder **His might** and] lea[n on ^{5}**His loving acts** all day long.]	^{1}[**At the on**]**set of fear and terror [and in the place of] distress** (filled) with desolation [I shall **bless** Him] ^{2}and (His) **exceedingly marvellous acts**, [I will] ponder [**His**] **mighty deeds** and [lean on **His**] **loving acts**, ^{3}all day long.

God's Judgment and the Hymnist's Restraint (1QS 10:16b–24b; 4QS^b 20 5b–7; 4QS^d 10 5b–8a; 4QS^f 4 3b–5 7)

1QS 10	4QS[b] 20	4QS[d] 10	4QS[f] 4–5
[16b]I know that the judgment of all the living [17]and the truth of all His actions lie in His hand. **When distress is set free I shall praise Him and on account of His salvation I shall exalt Him also.** I shall not recompense a person[18] with evil, but I shall pursue the individual with kindness. For with God lies the judgment of all the living and it is He who will render a person their reward.	[5b][I] know th[at] the judgment of all the living and the tru[th of all [6]His actions lie in] His [ha]nd. **[When distress is set free I shall praise Him and on account of] His [salvat]ion I shall [exalt Him also.** I shall] no[t recompense a person [7]with evil, but I shall pursue the individual with kindness. For with God lies the ju]dgment of all the living and it is He [who will render a person their reward.]	[5b][I know that the judgment of all the living and the truth of all His actions lie in His hand.] [6]**When [distress] is set [free I shall praise Him and on account of His salvation I shall exalt Him also.** I shall not re]compense [7][a person with evil, but I shall pursue the individual with kindness. For with God lies the judgment of all the living and it is He] [8]who will render [a person his reward.]	[3b]The judgment of all the living [and the truth of His ac]tions [lie in His hand]. **When distress [4]is s[et free] I shall praise Him and on account of [His] salvation [I shall exalt Him al]so.** I shall not recom[pense] [5]a person with evil, [but I shall pursue] the individual with kindness. F[or with God [lies the judgment of] [6]all the living and it is He who will render a per[son] their [rewa]rd.

1QS 10	4QS^f 4–5

1QS 10
^{18c}I shall not display jealousy in a spirit of ¹⁹wickedness, and my soul shall not desire property acquired through violence. I shall not seize (opportunities to) quarrel with a person (intent) on destruction until the day of vengeance. I shall not deflect ²⁰my anger from the people of injustice, and I will not be satisfied until He has dispensed judgment.
I will not bear a raging grudge against those who turn away from wrongdoing, but I will have no compassion ²¹with all those who rebel against the way, nor will I comfort the stricken until their conduct is perfect. I will not keep Belial/worthlessness in my heart. Frivolousness and sinful deception ²²shall not be heard in my mouth, treachery and lies shall not be found on my lips. Fruits of holiness shall be on my tongue, but abhorrent (words) ²³shall not be found on it. **With praise I shall open my mouth, and my tongue shall recount God's righteous deeds continually** alongside the treachery of humanity until the end of ²⁴their wrongdoing.
I will banish emptiness from my lips, impurities and distortions from the knowledge of my heart.

4QS^f 4–5
⁶I shall not display jealou[sy] in [a spirit of] ⁷wickedness, and my soul [shall not desire] property acquired through violen[ce]. I shall n[o]t seize (opportunities to) qua[rrel with ⁸a person (intent) on destruction un[til the day of venge]ance. I shall no[t deflect] my anger ⁹from the people of injustice, and I will n[o]t [be satisfied until He has disp]ensed judgment.
[I will not] ¹⁰bear a grudge against those who tu[rn] away from wrongdoing […] people of [and I will have no] 5¹[com]passion with all those who rebel against the way, nor will I comfort the stricken until their con[duct] ²is perfect. I will not keep Belial/worthlessness in my heart. Frivolousness and sinful deception ³shall not be heard in my mouth, [trea]chery and lies shall not be found on my lips. ⁴Fruits of holiness shall be on my tongue *vacat* but abhorrent (words) shall not be found ⁵on it. **With prai[se I shall o]p[en]** *vacat* **my mouth, [and] my tongue shall re[count] God's righteous** ⁶**deeds continu[ally]** alongside the treachery of] humanity un[til the e]nd of their wrongdoing. [I will banish ⁷emptiness from my lips, impurities and distortions] from [the knowledge of my heart.]

Secrecy (1QS 10:24c–11:2a)

1QS 10–11
10^{24c} With sound counsel I will recount knowledge, ²⁵with prudent knowledge I will fence […] *h* in with a firm boundary in order to preserve faithfulness and strong judgment for God's righteousness. I will prescribe ²⁶a statute according to the measuring line of the times. […] righteousness and devoted love towards the humble, but a firm hand against those who hast[en to make known] 11¹ insights to those whose spirits go astray and to teach those who grumble, to answer humbly in front of the haughty and with a broken spirit to the people of ^{2a}perversion who point (their) finger and spread wicked talk and acquire property.

The Psalmist's Relationship to God (1QS 11:2b–5b)

²ᵇAs for me, my justice lies with God, in His hand (He holds) the perfection of my conduct as well as the uprightness of my heart. ³Through His righteous acts he blots out my wrongdoing, for He set free His light from the source of His knowledge, and my eyes have seen His wonders, the light of my heart the mystery of ⁴being and happenings of eternity. My right hand is supported, and the path of my steps is on sound rock which will not tremble under any circumstances. For God's truth is ⁵the rock of my steps, and His strength is the support of my right hand. From the source of His righteousness emanates my justice, a light shines in my heart because of His marvellous mysteries.

The Psalmist's Access to Revelation (1QS 11:5c–7a)

My eyes have seen ⁶happenings of eternity, wisdom which is hidden from humanity, knowledge and prudent thoughts (concealed) from humankind, a source of righteousness and a reservoir of ⁷strength as well as a spring of glory (undisclosed to) the assembly of flesh.

A Community in Communion with the Heavenly Realm (1QS 11:7b–9a; 4QSᵈ 12 4)

Those whom God has chosen He has established as an eternal possession

1QS 11	4QSᵈ 12
⁷ᵇand He bestowed upon them as an inheritance a share in the lot of ⁸the holy ones.	⁴ [and he bestowed upon] them [as an inheri]tance a share in the lo[t of the holy ones.]

1QS 11
⁸And he united their assembly with the children of heaven to (form) a joint council, the foundation of a holy structure, and an eternal planting for all ⁹time to come.

The Speaker's Shortcomings Contrasted with Divine Providence and Righteousness
(1QS 11:9b–15b; 4QS^d 13 1–3; 4QS^j 1–3a)

But I belong to wicked humanity and to the assembly of unjust flesh. My trespasses, my wrongdoings, my sins as well as my perverted heart [10]belong to an assembly of worms and those who walk in darkness. For a human being does not determine its path, nor humankind its steps, but judgment belongs to God and from His hand [11]perfect conduct (is granted), on account of His knowledge everything has come into being. He arranges every event according to His plan and without Him nothing is achieved. As for me, when [12]I stagger God's loving acts are my salvation for ever, and if I stumble because of fleshly sinfulness my justice stands in perpetuity on account of God's righteousness. [13]And though He sets free my distress He will deliver me from destruction and guide my steps onto the path.

1QS 11	4QS^j
[13]With His kind acts He drew me close and through His loving acts my justice [14]will emerge. With His true righteousness He has judged me and with His abundant goodness	[1][With His kind acts He drew me close and through His loving acts my justice will emerge. With] His true [righteousness] He has judged me and with [His] abundant good[ness]

1QS 11	4QS^d 13	4QS^j
[14]He will atone for all my trespasses. With His righteousness He will cleanse me from human [15]uncleanness and (from) the sin of human beings **so that I may praise God for His righteousness**	[1][He will a]tone [2][for all] my [trespass]es. [With His righteousness He will cleanse me from human uncleanness and (from) the sin of hu]man be[ings] [3][**so that I may praise God for] His [ri]ghteousness**	[2][He will atone for all my trespasses. With His righteousness He will cleanse meから] hu[man uncleanness] and (from) the sin of human beings **so that I may praise God** [3]**for His righteousness**

1QS 11	4QS^j
and the Most High for His glory.	**and the Most High for His glory.**]

Final Blessing and Restatement of Humanity's Frailty (1QS 11:15c–22; 4QS^b 23 1–3; 4QS^j 3b–10)

1QS 11	4QS^j
^{15c}**Blessed** are You, my God, who unlocks the heart ^{16}of Your servant to knowledge. Prepare with righteousness all his deeds and raise up the child of Your handmaid according to Your satisfaction with the elect of humanity so that they may take their stand ^{17}before You forever. For without You no conduct is perfect and without Your approval nothing is accomplished. You have taught ^{18}all knowledge and every event has occurred with Your approval. There is no other apart from You to reply to Your counsel, to comprehend ^{19}all of Your holy plan, to look upon the depth of Your mysteries and to understand all **Your wonders along with the might of ^{20}Your strength. Who is able to grasp Your glory** and what, indeed, is the human being amongst Your wonderful works? ^{21}**What is one born of a woman to reply before You? One fashioned from dust, whose home is food for worms, one who is a splutter of spittle,** ^{22}**nipped off clay**	^{3b}[**Blessed** are You, my God, who unlocks] the heart of Your servant [to knowledge]. Prepare with [righteous]ness all [his] deed[s] ^{4}[and raise up the child of Your handmaid according to Your satisfaction with the elect of humanity so that they may take] their stand before You forever. For without You ^{5}[no conduct is perfect and without Your approval nothing is accomplished. You have] taught all knowledge and every event ^{6}[has occurred with Your approval. There is no other apart from You to reply to] Your [couns]el, to comprehend all of Your [holy] ^{7}plan, [to look upon the depth of Your mysteries and to understand] all **Your wonders along with the might of Your strength.** ^{8}[**Who is able to grasp Your glory** and what indeed is the human] being amongst Your wonderful works? [**What is**] ^{9}**one born of a woman** [**to reply before You? One fashioned from dust, whose home is food for worms, one who is a splutter of spittle, nipped off**] ^{10}**clay**

1QS 11	4QS^b 23	4QS^j
whose predilection is for the dust? What can clay reply and what counsel can one formed by hand convey? *Vacat*	^{1}[whose predilection is for the dust? What can clay reply? And] what [counsel can one formed by hand convey?] *Vacat* ^{2}[ ]according to everything wh[ich] ^{3}[ ] 1[ ]	[whose predilection is for the dust? What can clay reply?] And what counsel can [one formed by ha]nd convey? *Vacat*

7. Apotropaic Resonances in the Final Hymn

In this final section we will offer a reading of the Final Hymn that draws on the apotropaic practices that have emerged from the body of recently published texts from Qumran and reflect on the Hymn's purpose in its wider literary context as far as that is preserved. We will argue that we have not yet fully appreciated the implications of the plethora of primary sources and concomitant scholarly studies on the beliefs and fears that preoccupied the lives of Jews in antiquity.

7.1 Blessing and Praise

A number of scholars have emphasized the apotropaic function of praise in the literature from the Second Temple period. Thus, Loren Stuckenbruck has argued that the recital of hymns was one of the ways in which ancient Jews sought to "manage" the impact of malevolent forces afflicting humanity.[35] Moreover, Daniel Falk's has observed that,

> it needs to be considered whether this eschatological outlook and apotropaic function for praise contributes to the use of song more generally in the community. In the song of the Maskil at the end of the Community Rule, praise in affliction and distress is an expression of continuous praise (1QS 9:26; 10:15, 17; cf. 11:13).[36]

Given the centrality of praise[37] as a means to terrify spirits in the apotropaic Songs of the Maskil (4Q510–511),[38] as well as in the Hymn, it is significant that several manuscripts of the Community Rules end with the Final Hymn with its repeated and emphatic emphasis on praising and blessing.[39] Rather than simply offering protection by being recited as a stand-alone piece, we suggest that the literary

---

[35] Stuckenbruck, "Demonic World of the Dead Sea Scrolls," 69.

[36] Daniel K. Falk, "The Contribution of the Qumran Scrolls to the Study of Ancient Jewish Liturgy," in *The Oxford Handbook of the Dead Sea Scrolls*, ed. Timothy H. Lim and John J. Collins (Oxford: OUP, 2010), 617–51 (636); idem, "Material Aspects of Prayer Manuscripts at Qumran," in *Literature or Liturgy? Early Christian Hymns and Prayers in the Literary and Liturgical Context in Antiquity*, ed. Clemens Leonhard and Helmut Löhr (Tübingen: Mohr Siebeck, 2014), 33–87 (71).

[37] For an important broader study on the centrality of praise in the Second Temple period see also Mika Pajunen, "The Praise of God and His Name as the Core of the Second Temple Liturgy," *ZAW* 127 (2015): 475–88.

[38] Cf. Nitzan, *Qumran Prayer*, 268, and Angel, "Maskil, Community, and Religious Experience in the Songs of the Sage," 1–27.

[39] See also Asaf Gayer, "The Centrality of Prayer and the Stability of Trust: An Analysis of the Hymn of the Maskil in 1QS IX,25b–XI,15a," in *Ancient Jewish Prayers and Emotions: Emotions Asso-*

composition of those manuscripts of the Community Rules that end with the Hymn also exude a protective literary closure that is saturated with blessing and praise.

A number of other texts contain features that support a reading of the Final Hymn as serving apotropaic functions.

7.2 The Divine Statutes

As Tupá Guerra has noted, the "statutes of God" are another source of strength to draw on in the war against spirits of wickedness.[40] Thus, the Incantation 4Q444 includes the admonition to "strengthen yourself with the statutes of God and wage war against the spirits of wickedness (ותתחזק בחוקי אל ולהלחם ברוחי רשעה)."[41] Statutes, laws and regulations are a defining feature of the Community Rule and are, as we noted above, several times closely associated with the Maskil. Several references to statutes and commandments and the root "to engrave" (חקק) also occur in the Final Hymn and are underlined in the translation above.[42] This intertwining of the requirement of conducting oneself in line with God's will and commandments alongside blessing and praise offers a multifaceted arsenal of protection. Even the rules for admission and their reversal in the penal code which aims to identify and purge those whose conduct falls short play a part in keeping the community—at least literarily—in line with the statutes of God and His will.

7.3 The Lyre

The reference to a lyre (כנור) in 4Q511 10 8 is associated by Jeremy Penner and Guerra with widespread Ancient Near Eastern apotropaic connotations for this instrument. The gift of employing the lyre to combat a demonic episode is famously associated with David who is described as curing Saul of an evil spirit by playing the lyre.[43] We find a reference to the same instrument in the Final Hymn where the speaker's lyre and harp are played in the service of performing music for the glory of God. The apotropaic resonances of this instrument as well

---

ciated with *Jewish Prayer in and around the Second Temple Period*, ed. Stefan Reif and Renate Egger-Wenzel (Berlin: De Gruyter, 2015), 317–34.
40 Guerra, "Encountering Evil," 64.
41 See 4Q444 1–5 4.
42 For bibliography see section 5 above.
43 See 1 Sam 16:13–23 and Eva Mrozcek, "The Hegemony of the Biblical in the Study of Second Temple Literature," *JAJ* 6 (2015): 1–35.

as of praise alongside a range of shared features between the explicitly apotropaic texts and the Final Hymn are suggestive of an apotropaic significance for the reference to the lyre in 1QS 10:9.[44]

7.4 Self-Abasement[45]

In her recent contribution to a *Festschrift* for George Brooke Carol Newsom examines the "negative anthropology" in the Hodayot, the Final Hymn in some copies of the Community Rules, and the Songs of the Maskil in 4Q511.[46] Her particular focus is on the exegetical interplay with Genesis 2–3 and Job 33:6. For our purposes it is curious that the expressions of self-abasement in 4Q511—often referred to with the German term *Niedrigkeitsdoxologie*—are modified with dualistic elements. Thus, the speaker describes his lowly state as follows:

> I am a splutter of spittle,[47] moulded [from clay] and from darkness [my] sha[pe ...] and injustice (עולה) in the soft tissue[48] of my flesh. (4Q511 28–29 3–4; my translation)

---

[44] 1QS literally reads "the lyre of my harp." 4QS^d 9 8 reads a first-person impf. *hiphil* of נכה (אכה), "to play an instrument," with initial *aleph* damaged. This was noted already by József T. Milik, "Texte des variantes des dix manuscrits de la Règle de la Communauté trouvés dans la Grotte 4: Recension de P. Wernberg-Møller, The Manual of Discipline," *RB* 67 (1960): 410–16 (415); also Alexander and Vermes, DJD 26:124. The preserved first word of 4QS^f 3 1 may agree with 4QS^d 9 8; cf. Alexander and Vermes, DJD 26:162, and Elisha Qimron, *The Dead Sea Scrolls: The Hebrew Writings: Volumes 1–3* (Jerusalem: Yad Ben-Zvi, 2010), 1:228 (Hebrew).

[45] Heinz-Wolfgang Kuhn, *Enderwartung und gegenwärtiges Heil: Untersuchungen zu den Gemeindeliedern von Qumran*, SUNT 4 (Göttingen: Vandenhoeck & Ruprecht, 1966), 27–29.

[46] Carol Newsom, "Deriving Negative Anthropology Through Exegetical Activity: The Hodayot as Case Study," in *Is There a Text in this Cave? Studies in the Textuality of the Dead Sea Scrolls in Honour of George J. Brooke*, ed. by Ariel Feldman, Maria Cioată, and Charlotte Hempel, STDJ 119 (Leiden: Brill, 2017), 258–74 (268).

[47] Reading מצירוק as written continuously, as proposed already for 1QS 11:21 by Wernberg-Møller, *Manual of Discipline*, 43. Alexander and Vermes read מצוררק in 4QS^j 9 and translate "formed from semen," taking "spittle" as a euphemism (DJD 26:203–206).

[48] On the term תכמים see Nicholas A. Meyer, "תכמים *tkmjm*," *ThWQ* 3:1121–23. Newsom, "Deriving Negative Anthropology," 260, Noam Mizrahi, "תכמי בשר 'Body Parts:' The Semantic History of a Qumran Hebrew Lexeme," in *The Reconfiguration of Hebrew in the Hellenistic Period: Proceedings of the Seventh International Symposium on the Hebrew of the Dead Sea Scrolls and Ben Sira at Strasbourg University, June 2014*, ed. Jan Joosten, Daniel Machiela, and Jean-Sébestien Rey, STDJ 124 (Leiden: Brill, 2018), 123–57, and Elisha Qimron, "Notes on the 4Q Zadokite Fragments on Skin Disease," *JJS* 42 (1991): 256–59.

It is noteworthy that a reference to the realm of darkness and the speaker's character and conduct also occur in the Final Hymn,

> But I belong to wicked humanity and to the assembly of unjust flesh. My trespasses, my wrongdoings, my sins as well as my perverted heart belong to an assembly of worms and those who walk in darkness. (1QS 11:9–10).

As Newsom makes clear, "this wretched condition does not simply characterize a wicked subset of human beings [...] but represents the fundamental human condition...."[49] This interest in injustice and darkness as negative "poles" is again prominent in the Community Rules in a further *Niedrigkeitsdoxologie* in 1QS 11:21–22. As a counterpart to the apotropaic connotations of praise this negative anthropology, to use Newsom's terminology, occurs in liturgical contexts and appears to serve as "inverted praise" of God's majesty. By praising God and at the same time abasing the speaker the eminence of the deity—and by implication its protective power—is heightened.

8. Conclusion

We began by highlighting a series of statements in different parts of the Community Rules that admonish a turning away from all evil to illustrate how the movement is portrayed as establishing a clear rhetorical boundary between its members and those who pursue evil.[50] We then reviewed some of the compositions from Qumran Cave 4 that shed important fresh light on how malevolent forces were perceived and contained in an ancient Jewish milieu that almost certainly spanned much more widely than the movement associated with the scrolls from Khirbet Qumran. Recent scholarly engagement with this new cache of literature has shed fresh light on the apotropaic significance of blessing and praise.[51] Our analysis of the Final Hymn in light of these recent advances emphasized the recognition of the prominent role of blessing and praise in the Hymn.[52] In addition, we considered the shared penchant for self-abasement both on the part of the speaker of the Final Hymn and the apotropaic Songs of the Maskil. Such a self-abasement constitutes a kind of inverted praise that highlights the chasm between community members and the supreme divine glory and might even further it. We also drew attention to the evidence of 4QIncantation (4Q444) which

---

49 Newsom, "Deriving Negative Anthropology," 260.
50 See sections 2, 3 and 4 above.
51 See section 5 above and further literature listed there.
52 See, e.g., Nitzan, *Qumran Prayer*, 193.

suggests a conviction that divine statutes and, by implication, the regulations that facilitate appropriate conduct—a key concern in several copies of the Community Rules—are not devoid of apotropaic significance. The blending of divinely mandated conduct and paying emphatic liturgical homage to God and His power ensures members could feel safe within the bounded community. However, where members harbour a lack of commitment, they may be expected to live in fear of both divine and communal sanctions. In short, several copies of the Community Rules offer a powerful symbiosis between rules of conduct and a liturgical framework. Those manuscripts of the Community Rules signal protection to vulnerable members of the movement, as well as constitute a literary shield protecting from the menacing malevolence that loomed large in the lives and minds of ancient Jews.[53]

---

[53] Cf. further Hempel, "The Long Text of the *Serekh* as Crisis Literature," 3–24.

Molly M. Zahn
The Absence of Prayer in the Temple Scroll

1. Introduction

Prayer, it seems, is everywhere in Second Temple texts. Hundreds of texts containing prayers of various types were discovered among the Qumran Scrolls, from the famous Hodayot to prayers included in rituals of exorcism and purification, from collections of psalms resembling what we find in the biblical Psalter to hymns embedded in narrative or rule compositions and/or attributed to prestigious ancient figures.[1] Such a deposit in the literary record suggests that prayer played an equally important role in Second Temple religious practice: as Judith Newman puts it, "[j]udging by its ubiquity in all early Jewish texts that have been transmitted to us, praying became a central feature of Jewish practice in the centuries following the Babylonian Exile ...."[2]

Against this background in which prayer appears to pervade the textual record, the Temple Scroll (henceforth: TS) stands out for its nearly complete *disinterest* in prayer. This longest of Qumran scrolls barely mentions prayer anywhere in its sixty-six extant columns, a fact that raises intriguing questions both for our understanding of this particular composition and for our conceptualization of the role of prayer in early Judaism. If prayer was a foundational element of Second Temple culture, what are we to make of a text that shows no interest in prayer? How might such a text fit into this culture? Or does it fit in at all?[3] In what follows,

---

[1] I am grateful to Professors Feldman and Sandoval for their invitation to participate in the conference from which this volume originates. I regret that a last-minute family issue prevented me from being there in person, but I thank them for including me in the volume, and I appreciate the opportunity provided by the conference theme to think through an important issue that I had not previously considered.
An up-to-date overview is provided by Daniel K. Falk, "Hymns, Prayers, and Psalms," in *T&T Clark Encyclopedia of Second Temple Judaism*, ed. Daniel Gurtner and Loren T. Stuckenbruck (London: T&T Clark, 2019), 2:337–42.
[2] Judith H. Newman, *Before the Bible: The Liturgical Body and the Formation of Scriptures in Early Judaism* (New York: Oxford University Press, 2018), 9.
[3] The formulation begs the question of the date of TS. The best-preserved manuscript, 11Q19, and the closely-related 11Q20, date paleographically to the first century CE. The very fragmentary copy from Cave 4, 4Q524, which has been dated to the late second century BCE, is usually cited as providing a terminus ante quem for the composition, though it should be kept in mind that 4Q524 differs in substantial respects from 11Q19, thus indicating that the composition would have under-

https://doi.org/10.1515/9783110624526-008

after briefly presenting the meager data relating to prayer in TS, I will consider possible explanations for its absence, focusing especially on the literary genre of the scroll and the ideology of its composers.

This paper is part of a larger project in which I am concerned to understand TS in its broader literary and cultural setting. Previous research on TS (including my own) has focused largely on its redeployment of the Pentateuch and other compositions now part of the Hebrew Bible.[4] Important work has also been done on the scroll's halakhah in light of parallels in other Qumran materials and in rabbinic literature.[5] But the ideology of the TS, and in particular how it fits into the kinds of debates and discussions we see manifested in other Second Temple compositions, has been underexplored. To be fair, TS does not make it easy for us to access the worldviews of its authors: its framing as the direct speech of God from Sinai and its almost entirely prescriptive contents obscure the actual historical circumstances of its compilation in a remarkably effective way. Nevertheless, consideration of questions such as the one posed here, raising issues that appear not to be issues at all for TS, proves a useful way to read between the lines and begin to situate TS in relation to its Second Temple contemporaries.

2. Prayer in the Temple Scroll

The Temple Scroll, as preserved in 11Q19 (= 11QT^a), presents instructions for a gigantic temple complex, along with prescriptions for the various daily, monthly, and festival sacrifices to be offered on the temple's altar, as well as a range of

---

gone further development in the period between the dates of the two manuscripts. In terms of a terminus post quem, though some scholars have suggested dates as early as the Persian period, most (including myself) see strong allusions to Hasmonean-period events and issues in the scroll's Law of the King (cols. 57–59) and thus conclude that it was most likely compiled in the latter part of the second century BCE. For this position, see especially Lawrence H. Schiffman et al., eds., *Temple Scroll and Related Documents*, PTSDSSP 7 (Tübingen: Mohr Siebeck, 2011), 4–5. A convenient review of the manuscripts and their dates is provided by Sidnie White Crawford, *The Temple Scroll and Related Texts*, CQS 2 (Sheffield: Sheffield Academic Press, 2000): 12–14; see p. 24 for the range of scholarly suggestions on date of composition.

4 See Molly M. Zahn, *Rethinking Rewritten Scripture: Composition and Exegesis in the 4QReworked Pentateuch Manuscripts*, STDJ 95 (Leiden: Brill, 2011): 179–228; for an early, incisive critique (which has largely fallen on deaf ears) of the "biblicism" of most scholarship on TS, see Johann Maier, *Die Tempelrolle vom Toten Meer und das «Neue Jerusalem»*, 3rd ed., UTB 429 (Munich: Ernst Reinhardt, 1997): 28–35.

5 See in particular the extensive contributions of Lawrence H. Schiffman, now collected in *The Courtyards of the House of the Lord: Studies on the Temple Scroll*, ed. Florentino García Martínez, STDJ 75 (Leiden: Brill, 2008).

other laws pertaining to ritual purity and life in the land. These regulations draw in varying degrees on legal materials known to us from the books of Leviticus, Numbers, and Deuteronomy.[6] The entire scroll is presented as the direct revelation of God to Moses on Mt. Sinai. Since the beginning and end of the scroll are lost, it is impossible to know what sort of narrative framing might have originally been present, if any: where the text picks up, God is already speaking, with commandments to avoid contact with the inhabitants of the land that parallel those of Exodus 34. The salient features of the composition as we have it are thus its halakhic or legal nature, and its self-presentation as direct divine speech.[7]

The only actual text of a prayer in the Temple Scroll comes in col. 63, where the scroll presents the procedure for expunging the bloodguilt produced by a corpse found in the countryside:

11Q19 63:4–7[8]

4 וכול זקני העיר ההיא הקרובה אל החלל
5 ירחצו את ידיהמה על ראוש העגלה הערופה בנחל וענו ואמרו ידינו
6 לוא שפכו את הדם הזה ועינינו לוא ראו כפר לעמכה ישראל אשר פדיתה
7 יהוה ואל תתן דם נקי בקרב עמכה ישראל וכופר להמה הדם

4   And all the elders of that city nearest to the slain man
5   shall wash their hands over the head of the heifer whose neck was broken in the stream, and they shall declare: "Our hands
6   did not spill this blood, and our eyes did not see. Make purgation for your people Israel whom you ransomed,
7   O YHWH, and do not place innocent blood in the midst of your people Israel!"
    And the blood shall be purged for them.

These lines differ only in minor details from their precise parallel in Deut 21:6–8.[9] This means that the only actual prayer in TS is a preexisting text imported in the course of the scroll's extensive reuse of Deuteronomy. That it is reused essentially unchanged might reasonably be taken to imply that the scroll's composers were not particularly invested in its details.

---

6 For an overview of the use of scripture in TS, see Zahn, *Rethinking Rewritten Scripture*, 179–228.
7 See Alex Samely, "Observations on the Structure and Literary Fabric of the Temple Scroll," in *The Temple in Text and Tradition: A Festschrift in Honour of Robert Hayward*, ed. R. Timothy McLay, LSTS 83 (London: Bloomsbury, 2015): 233–77.
8 Transcriptions and translations of the Temple Scroll, and translations of biblical and Qumran texts, are my own.
9 The substantive variants from known versions are: line 4: הקרבים MT SP LXX 4QDeut^f] הקרובה 11Q19; line 5: על העגלה MT SP] על ראוש העגלה LXX 11Q19.

There is very little else in TS that can be construed as referring to prayer, even in broad terms. In a couple of cases, also with close parallels in Deuteronomy, the priests are described as being chosen "to bless in my name," though this seems less likely to refer to prayer directed *towards* God as to the conveyance of God's blessing to the people along the lines of the priestly blessing of Numbers 6.[10] The only other possible reference comes in the covenant curses of col. 59:

11Q19 59:2–7

2 ויבזרום בארצות רבות והיו שמ[ה] למשל ולשנניה ובעול כבד
3 ובחסור כול ועבדו שמה אלוהים מעשי ידי אדם עץ ואבן כסף
4 וזהב ובכול זה יהיו עריהמה לשומה ולשרקה ולחורבה והיו
5 אויביהמה שוממים במה והמה בארצות אויביהמה מתאנחים
6 ומזעיקים מפני עול כבד וקראו ולוא אשמע וזעקו ולוא אענה
7 אותמה מפני רוע מעלליהמה

2. And they shall scatter them among many lands, and they shall become there a proverb and a taunt, and with a heavy yoke
3. and with lack of everything, and they shall serve there gods made by human hands, wood and stone, silver
4. and gold, and in all this their cities shall become a horror and a hissing and a ruin, and
5. their enemies will be horrified at them, while they, in the lands of their enemies, groan
6. and cry out because of a heavy load. And they shall call, but I shall not hear, and they shall cry out, but I will not answer
7. them because of the wickedness of their deeds

Presumably it is fair to interpret the people's "calling" and "crying out" in line 6 as a reference to prayer.[11] In contrast to many other Second Temple compositions, however, this exilic supplication is in no way thematized or elaborated upon, an issue to which I will return below.

---

10 See 11Q19 63:3 (= Deut 21:5) and 60:11 (= Deut 18:5). In this latter instance in Deuteronomy there is no mention of blessing (לעמד לשרת בשם יהוה). The word ולברך was likely added in accordance with the formulation in Deut 21:5 and, possibly, 10:8. On the connection with the priestly benediction in Numbers 6, see Moshe Weinfeld, *Deuteronomy 1–11: A New Translation with Introduction and Commentary*, AB 5 (New York: Doubleday, 1991), 422; Jeffrey H. Tigay, *The JPS Torah Commentary: Deuteronomy* (Philadelphia: Jewish Publication Society, 1996), 106.

11 See Falk's comments on the roots of Second Temple penitential prayer lying in part in the emphasis on "confession of guilt" in, among other texts, the covenant curses of Leviticus 26 ("Hymns, Prayers, and Psalms," 338); the connection is also noted by Newman, *Before the Bible*, 56.

3. Possible Explanations

This very brief survey has shown that there is extremely little reference to prayer in TS, considering the length of the text. What possible explanations might be proffered for this absence?

3.1 Genre

First, we might consider whether there are issues of genre that might play a role—maybe the Temple Scroll is *not the type of text*, in some way, that would include prayer. Most salient in this regard might be the legal contents of the scroll. The near-exclusive focus on law means that any reference to prayer will be in the framework of behaviors that are being divinely prescribed. If we imagine a narrative text, we can think of plenty of examples where characters are depicted as praying and the texts of their prayers are included (e. g., the penitential prayers in Daniel 9; Ezra 9; Nehemiah 9). A pedagogical text like Ben Sira can refer to prayer and praise as key elements in the life of the ideal sage, as Newman has pointed out.[12] In a purely halakhic context, by contrast, natural opportunities to refer to prayer or include the texts of prayers will be somewhat constrained to situations where prayer is actually part of the halakhically required behavior. Within the legal corpora of the Pentateuch, such cases are rare: occasions for prayer or the wording of prayers are not typically legislated.[13] Besides the prayer regarding the unidentified corpse mentioned above (Deut 21:6–8), the only examples I could discover were in Deuteronomy 26, where presentation of firstfruits and the tithe is to be accompanied with fixed prayers addressed to God (Deut 26:5–10, 13–15).

Other prescriptive texts seem to be more interested in prayer: we have several examples from the Qumran scrolls where ritual instructions include "scripts" of prayers to be recited as part of the ritual described. For example, 4Q284 (4QPurification Liturgy) describes the appropriate processes for purification from ritual impurity, similar to what we find in the Temple Scroll, or in Leviticus for that matter (e. g., 4Q284 2 i 3–4, "when] his seven [days] are completed [ ] he shall wash [his] bo[dy in water ..."). But it *also* includes the text of blessings that are to be proclaimed at particular points in the process by the individual being purified (e. g., 4Q284 3 3–4, "he shall respond and say, 'Blessed are yo[u, God of Israel ...] you

---

12 *Before the Bible*, 24–27.
13 Noting this phenomenon with regard to the Priestly source, see Baruch A. Levine, *Numbers 1–20: A New Translation with Introduction and Commentary*, AB 4 (New York: Doubleday, 1993), 176.

engraved true purity for your people to]'"). In other words, the words of blessing have become part of the halakhah itself.¹⁴ This suggests that we should not attribute the absence of prayer in the Temple Scroll to the legal genre of the text *per se*.

The near-absence of legally mandated prayer in the Pentateuch, however, might suggest another possibility. Perhaps the issue is not law itself, but a desire on the part of the scroll's composers to make it resemble the Pentateuch.¹⁵ That is, one strategy for casting the Temple Scroll as "Torah" was to establish continuity with the Pentateuch, the paradigmatic example of Torah.¹⁶ If prayer is not typically legislated in the Pentateuch, the composers of TS may have felt that it had no place in their new presentation of divine law, even if prayer may have played an important role in their lived religious experience.

Such an explanation might make some sense, but is not completely satisfactory. In general, the Temple Scroll's composers seem to display considerable freedom and agency in their reframing of Pentateuchal law. They include new annual festivals, a plethora of new laws, and of course an apparently innovative blueprint for the utopian temple and its courts. So why not introduce or refer to prayers, if prayer was important to them? One might respond that the Temple Scroll's other innovations all continue forms or genres that are already well-represented in the Pentateuch: building instructions, sacrificial commands for feast days, purity laws, etc. This is true, but the composers' overall willingness to depart from the Pentateuch when it is in their interests to do so makes it difficult to imagine that they could not have found a way to incorporate prayer, if they had been so inclined.

---

14 See also 4Q414 (Ritual of Purification A) and 4Q512 (papRitual of Purification B).
15 See Bernard M. Levinson and Molly M. Zahn, "Revelation Regained: The Hermeneutics of כי and אם in the Temple Scroll," *DSD* 9 (2002): 295–346. I would no longer construe such imitation solely as an attempt to claim authority, but more in terms of the desire to participate in a genre of which the Pentateuch is a paradigmatic example. See Molly M. Zahn, *Genres of Rewriting in Second Temple Judaism: Scribal Composition and Transmission* (Cambridge: Cambridge University Press, 2020), 201–4, and the literature cited there.
16 This formulation indicates that I do not assume that "Torah" (even with a capital T) would be viewed as coterminous with the books of Genesis-Deuteronomy in the Second Temple period. For an overview of the issues, see Molly M. Zahn, "Torah, Traditioning of," in *T&T Clark Encyclopedia of Second Temple Judaism*, ed. Daniel Gurtner and Loren T. Stuckenbruck (London: T&T Clark, 2019), 2:783–85.

3.2 Ideological Factors

The previous section explored the possibility that, even if the scribes who composed the Temple Scroll were steeped in a culture in which prayer played an important role, the genre of the text might have placed constraints on their willingness to incorporate prayer into this particular composition. The fact that such a possibility does not appear particularly compelling raises another one: that prayer is simply not very important to the composers of TS. That is, there might also be *ideological* factors that inform the Temple Scroll's disinterest in prayer. Three data points stand out as potentially relevant, based on my preliminary work on the social location of TS: the lack of concern with exemplarity; the ambiguous attitude towards exile; and the particular brand of priestly interests on display in TS.

3.2.1 Exemplarity

In contrast to certain other key Second Temple texts, especially those that employ pseudepigraphy, the Temple Scroll shows no interest in exemplarity—it does not thematize the person or role of the scribe in any way, nor does it thematize the writing process or the written word.[17] If we think for the moment of the Temple Scroll not as a legal text but as a *revealed* text, we can see the contrast with other texts which claim to transmit divine revelation, in which the character who receives the revelation plays an important role. In Jubilees, for instance, Moses is depicted as writing down what the Angel of the Presence dictates to him from the heavenly tablets, and this writing is portrayed as a continuation of the scribal activities of Enoch, Noah, Abraham, and Jacob (Jub. 4:17–18; 10:13; 12:27; 21:10; 32:24–26). In Dan 12:4, Daniel is commanded to "keep the words secret and the book sealed until the time of the end." In 4 Ezra 14, Ezra famously dictates ninety-four books of revelation. Significantly, all of these figures—Moses in Jubilees, Daniel, and Ezra in 4 Ezra—are depicted as offering substantial prayers.[18] It seems to me that there is a possible connection between this attention to the characters who receive revelation and an interest in prayer—the exemplary status of

---

[17] On the idea of exemplarity, see especially Hindy Najman, "How Should We Contextualize Pseudepigrapha? Imitation and Emulation in *4 Ezra*," in eidem, *Past Renewals: Interpretative Authority, Renewed Revelation and the Quest for Perfection in Jewish Antiquity*, JSJSup 53 (Leiden: Brill, 2010): 235–42. On writing, see Najman, "Interpretation as Primordial Writing: *Jubilees* and Its Authority Conferring Strategies," in *Past Renewals*, 39–71; Eva Mroczek, *The Literary Imagination in Jewish Antiquity* (New York: Oxford University Press, 2016): 122–25, 139–55.
[18] E.g., Jub. 1:19–21; Dan 9:4–19; 4 Ezra 3:4–36.

these figures is partially manifested in their writing, but also in other aspects of their character, including the ways they address the divine. Of course, the idea of exemplarity implies that the scribes who produced these works saw something of themselves in these figures. Thus, Newman can read Daniel, and also Ben Sira and Baruch, and Najman can read Ezra, as reflections of what Second Temple religious elites imagined as the ideal scribe, sage, or visionary.[19]

The Temple Scroll stands in stark contrast to all this in its resolute elision of the human recipient of its revelation. Moses is not totally absent from the text, as earlier scholars sometimes claimed – there are two oblique references to him as the immediate addressee of God's words.[20] But there is no development of Moses's character, no reference to him writing or transmitting the text. There is nothing that matters except the direct word of God, and only the barest contextualization. Of course, this impression might be different if the opening column(s) of the scroll had been preserved.[21] But the point is, in TS as we have it, the lack of interest in prayer correlates with a lack of interest in the process of transmission of revelation, and the characters responsible for that transmission.

3.2.2 Exile and Restoration

The idea of exile and questions about when a true restoration and end of exile would take place loomed large in the imaginations of the composers of many Second Temple texts, as we see from works as disparate as Daniel, Baruch, and Words of the Luminaries. Strikingly, in all of these texts the dynamics of restoration apparently involve a role for prayer (e.g., Daniel 9; Bar 1:15–3:8). We even find a prediction of exile in the opening chapter of Jubilees, along with a petitionary prayer by Moses that this fate might be avoided. Exile and restoration is also a major theme of the book of Ezekiel, with which the Temple Scroll has much in common in terms of its theology of God dwelling amongst the people.[22] But when

---

19 See Newman, *Before the Bible*, esp. 45, 59–60, 66–70; Najman, "Imitation and Emulation."
20 See "the sons of Aaron your brother" in 11Q19 44:5, and "they [the children of Israel] shall not become impure by those things that I am telling you on this mountain," 11Q19 51:6–7.
21 Yadin surmised, largely on the basis of content, that only one column was missing from the beginning of 11Q19 (hence the designation of the first extant column as col. 2); see Yigael Yadin, *The Temple Scroll* (Jerusalem: Israel Exploration Society, 1977–83), 1:5; 2:1. There are reasons, however, to think this conclusion may be too hasty. The editors of the Princeton edition are more judicious, observing that "at least one" column is missing. See Schiffman et al., *Temple Scroll*, 3.
22 See Tova Ganzel, "The Reworking of Ezekiel's Temple Vision in the Temple Scroll," in *Law, Literature, and Society in Legal Texts from Qumran: Papers from the Ninth Meeting of the Interna-*

it comes to exile, TS appears to depart from the interests of Ezekiel and so many other Second Temple texts.

Exile and restoration are mentioned only once in TS, at the end of the Law of the King:

11Q19 59:9–13[23]

9 אחר ישובו
10 אלי בכול לבבמה ובכול נפשמה ככול דברי התורה הזואת
11 והושעתים מיד אויביהמה ופדיתים מכף שונאיהמה והביאותים
12 לארץ אבותיהמה ופדיתים והרביתים וששתי עליהמה
13 והייתי להמה לאלוהים והמה יהיו לי לעם

9. Afterwards they will return
10. to me with all their heart and with all their soul, according to all the words of this Torah,
11. and I will save them from the hand of their enemies, and I will ransom them from the grasp of those who hate them, and I will bring them
12. to the land of their ancestors, and I will ransom them and multiply them and I will rejoice over them,
13. and I will be their God and they will be my people.

In this scenario, cries to God are useless (59:6, ויקראו ולוא אשמע וזעקו ולוא אענה), but once the people return to God "according to all the words of this Torah," God will restore them to their land, "and I will be their God, and they shall be my people." Given the overall concerns of TS, it is rather striking that there is no mention in this passage of the fate of the temple.

The depiction of exile and restoration in col. 59 also stands in tension with the only other "predictive" or "covenantal" passage in TS, which comes at the end of the schedule of yearly sacrifices.

11Q19 29:4–10

4 כתורת המשפט הזה
5 תמיד מאת בני ישראל לבד מנדבותמה לכול אשר יקריבו
6 לכול נדריהמה ולכול מתנותמה אשר יביאו לי לרצון לה[מ]ה
7 ורציתים והיו לי לעם ואנוכי אהיה להם לעולם ושכנתי
8 אתמה לעולם ועד ואקדשה [את מ]קדשי בכבודי אשר אשכין
9 עליו את כבודי עד יום הברכה אשר אברא אני את מקדשי
10 להכינו לי כול הימים כברית אשר כרתי עם יעקוב בבית אל

---

tional Organization of Qumran Studies, Leuven 2016, ed. Jutta Jokiranta and Molly M. Zahn, STDJ 128 (Leiden: Brill, 2019): 230–52.

23 For the description of exile found earlier in col. 59, see Section 2 above.

4   ... according to the teaching of this ordinance,
5   perpetually from the children of Israel, apart from their free-will offerings, for everything that they present,
6   for all their vows and for all their gifts which they will bring to me for th[eir] acceptance.
7   And I will accept them, and they shall be my people and I shall be theirs forever, and I will dwell
8   with them forever and ever. And I will sanctify my [san]ctuary with my glory, upon which I will settle
9   my glory until the day of blessing when I myself will create my sanctuary
10 to establish it for myself for all time, according to the covenant that I made with Jacob in Beth-El

Here the same language as in 59:13 is used to describe the mutual possessive relationship between God and Israel ("they shall be my people and I shall be theirs," 29:7). But there is no hint in this passage of a past or future hiatus in that relationship: no mention of exile; no interruption in God's dwelling with the people at any time from the delivery of these words on Sinai up until the eschatological day of blessing.

Of course, it has long been postulated that the Law of the King (11Q19 57–59) originated independently and was used as a source by the compiler of TS.[24] This may explain the lack of mention of the temple in the exile scenario in col. 59, as well as the tensions noted above between this passage and the end of col. 29. Aside from col. 59, TS shows absolutely no interest in the dynamics of exile and restoration. Yet, returning to the main issue at hand, even col. 59 fits the pattern of the rest of TS when it comes to the absence of prayer. The role of penitential prayer in restoring or maintaining the relationship between God and Israel (bringing about the end of exile or avoiding similar punishment) is mentioned already in texts like Lev 26:40 and 1 Kgs 8:47–48, and the conceptual importance of penitential prayer appears only to grow during the Second Temple period.[25] Even though the curses and blessings in 11Q19 col. 59 use language familiar from Leviticus 26, there is no reference to penitential prayer or confession as a component of what is required for restoration. Instead, the focus is on covenant obedience alone: ישובו אלי ... ככול דברי התורה הזואת, "they shall return to me … according to all the words of this Torah."[26]

---

24 For a recent review, see Schiffman et al., *Temple Scroll*, 3–4.
25 See the essays collected in the three volumes edited by Mark J. Boda, Daniel K. Falk, and Rodney A. Werline, *Seeking the Favor of God*, EJL 21–23 (Atlanta: Society of Biblical Literature, 2006–2008).
26 A similar construal of restoration as predicated on covenant obedience alone, using many of the same key terms, is found in Deut 30:1–3, a passage with which TS may well be in conversation here.

The Temple Scroll's lack of explicit engagement with ideas about exile and restoration requires more sustained attention than is possible here. The entire project of promulgating divine, Sinaitic commands for a temple and a community organized around it implies a deep critique of the status quo and hints that the authors in fact had very strong feelings about current relations between God and Israel, concerns that were framed in other texts through the lens of exile and restoration.[27] In this context, I merely want to point out the prominence in many Second Temple texts of a connection between concern with exile/restoration and an imagined role for prayer. Given that exile does not seem to play a prominent role in the historical conception of the Temple Scroll, perhaps it is not surprising that prayer does not either.

3.2.3 Temple-Focused Priestly Ideology

Finally, a third ideological issue that could factor into TS's lack of interest in prayer is the specific brand of priestly commitments evident in the scroll. Newman notes that one of the reasons prayer grew in popularity during the Second Temple period is its democratic nature – communion with God could be achieved by anyone, not only by "ritual specialists" at the temple.[28] But the Temple Scroll is precisely a temple-oriented text: it finds the prerequisite for God's indwelling with the people in the construction of the temple according to divine specifications, and in the maintenance of the appropriate sacrificial cult and the ritual purity of

---

[27] See Lawrence H. Schiffman, "The Concept of Restoration in the Dead Sea Scrolls," in idem, *Qumran and Jerusalem: Studies in the Dead Sea Scrolls and the History of Judaism* (Grand Rapids: Eerdmans, 2010), 286–302 (294–98). Schiffman details various senses in which TS looks for "restoration in the present age," from the temple structure itself to the image of Israel as an independent polity and the extensive attention to the cultic calendar. Yet Schiffman leaves a major aspect of the idea of "restoration" in TS unexplored, in that he does not give sufficient attention in this context to the scroll's framing and self-presentation. Undoubtedly, were TS's vision somehow actually to be implemented, it would result in a "restoration" of people, land, and temple from the perspective of TS's Second Temple authors. Yet the text itself does not acknowledge this perspective—it does not thematize the idea of accumulated sin, corruption, or distance from God, much less physical exile or colonization as a consequence of such. It is unrelentingly original and primary—almost never looking out from Sinai and the imminent occupation of the land (56:12; 60:16, both quoting the *Landnahme* formula of Deuteronomy) into Israel's future. (Cols. 29 and 59 are the only exceptions.) Thus, its ideas about restoration can only be reconstructed obliquely, by figuring the gap between the Temple Scroll's Sinaitic vision and what we know of the reality of the authors' Second Temple context.
[28] Newman, *Before the Bible*, 10.

the temple city. It is a text, in other words, that reflects and serves the interests of sacrificial specialists.

Of course, temple cult and prayer are not mutually exclusive. Elsewhere in this volume, George Brooke explores how two broad categories of priestly ideology, which he designates as the "atoning" and the "apotropaic," might be reflected in the prayer texts from Qumran. The former ideology is focused primarily on addressing the effects of human sin (through sacrifice or other means, such as prayer), while the latter emerges in the image of the priest as transmitter of ancient lore that ensures Israel's protection from the demonic forces that threaten it.[29] From another perspective, the books of Chronicles show a strong interest in the temple cult, and in the role of prayer in particular. One of the main aspects of the expanded role given to the Levites in Chronicles is musical: they are to perform psalms and hymns in the temple, as exemplified by 1 Chronicles 16, where words known to us from Psalms 105, 96, and 106 are put in the mouths of the Levite Asaph and his kin.[30] Though the authors of TS are also concerned to enhance the position of the Levites, they take a completely different approach, most notably through granting the Levites a regular sacrificial portion (11Q19 60:6–9).[31]

The example of Chronicles (as well as that of Words of the Luminaries mentioned above) suggests that, were the authors of TS interested in prayer, good models were available for how one might include prayer in a temple-focused text. In this light, the sole focus on sacrificial ritual rather than prayer suggests that this silence is not accidental. Rather, we may be justified in inferring that its authors did not see prayer as a primary element in maintaining or restoring the covenant relationship between God and Israel. Thus, to return to Brooke's model, alongside distinguishing priestly ideologies that focus relatively more or relatively less on atonement vs. transmission of priestly apotropaic lore, we might also distinguish between different priestly views of how atonement may be effected: through the ritual actions of sacrificial cult alone (TS) or through ritual action accompanied by prayer (Chronicles).

---

[29] See, in this volume, Brooke, "Patterns of Priesthood and Patterns of Prayer in the Dead Sea Scrolls."
[30] See also 1 Chr 23:30–31 and Gary N. Knoppers, "Hierodules, Priests, or Janitors? The Levites in Chronicles and the History of the Israelite Priesthood," *JBL* 118 (1999): 49–72 (67–68).
[31] This difference in the role imagined for the Levites is one piece of evidence that TS is less closely related to Chronicles than has frequently been claimed; see Molly M. Zahn, "The Levites, the Royal Council, and the Relationship between Chronicles and the Temple Scroll," in *Law, Literature, and Society in Legal Texts from Qumran: Papers from the Ninth Meeting of the International Organization of Qumran Studies, Leuven 2016*, ed. Jutta Jokiranta and Molly Zahn, STDJ 128 (Leiden: Brill, 2019): 253–69.

4. Conclusion

Although I have proposed a number of possible explanations for the near-complete absence of prayer in TS, my purpose in doing so was not ultimately to adjudicate between them, as if that could be done with any confidence. It seems most likely that multiple factors might have been at play simultaneously: the genre of TS as divinely revealed law discourages the presentation of exemplars or scripts for prayer, at the same time as the ideological concerns of the scroll – its commitment to the efficacy of sacrificial-cultic action and ritual purity—leave less of a role for prayer. The result is a text that shows practically no interest in prayer. Thinking through the various possibilities has proved productive in that it highlights several promising avenues for further investigation of how the Temple Scroll fits into the larger landscape of Second Temple literary and religious culture. Its Sinaitic setting, divine voicing, and almost entirely legal content give the Temple Scroll a timeless quality, but between the lines it speaks to ongoing debates concerning issues such as exile and restoration, human sin and its consequences, access to God's blessings, and the ultimate course of history.

Ariel Feldman
On Amulets, Apotropaic Prayers, and Phylacteries: The Contribution of Three New Texts from the Judean Desert

1. Introduction

In an overview of liturgical texts from Qumran Daniel Falk calls for closer scholarly attention to these scrolls as physical artifacts.[1] Elsewhere, he observes that "the collections of liturgical prose prayers stand out among all other genres of texts found at Qumran as especially likely to be compact, personal copies."[2] This study, which explores the newly-deciphered miniature texts containing a language of prayer, is a contribution to the sort of mapping of the diverse forms of prayer and prayer texts from Qumran for which Falk calls.

Three recent studies draw attention to three small texts from the Judean Desert.[3] Two of them, 4Q147 and 4Q148, are from the fourth cave of Qumran, whereas the third, Mur5, is from Wadi Murabbaʻat. These three texts were assigned to Józef T. Milik for publication.[4] Unable to read them, he assumed that 4Q147 and 4Q148 are tefillin, while the somewhat thicker Mur5 is a mezuzah. As the editor of most of the tefillin and mezuzot found in the Judean Desert, Milik was thoroughly familiar with their peculiar features and his assessment of 4Q147, 4Q148, and Mur5 appeared to be highly plausible. Like other tefillin and mezuzot, these three were

---

[1] Daniel K. Falk, "Liturgical Texts," in *T&T Clark Companion to the Dead Sea Scrolls*, ed. George J. Brooke and Charlotte Hempel (London: T&T Clark, 2019), 423-34 (432).
[2] Daniel K. Falk, "The Contribution of the Qumran Scrolls to the Study of Ancient Jewish Liturgy," in *The Oxford Handbook of the Dead Sea Scrolls*, ed. Timothy H. Lim and John J. Collins (Oxford: Oxford University Press, 2010), 617–51 (628). See further his "Material Aspects of Prayer Manuscripts at Qumran," in *Literature or Liturgy? Early Christian Hymns and Prayers in Their Literary and Liturgical Context in Antiquity*, ed. Helmut Löhr and Clemens Leonhard (Tübingen: Mohr Siebeck, 2014), 33–87.
[3] Ariel and Faina Feldman, "4Q147: An Amulet?" *DSD* 26 (2019): 1–29; "4Q148 (4QPhylactère U): Another Amulet from Qumran?" *JSJ* 50 (2019): 197–222; "Is Mur 5 a Mezuzah?" *RevQ* 31 (2019): 291-98.
[4] Józef T. Milik, "Mur5," in Pierre Benoit et al., *Les grottes de Murabbaʻat*, DJD 2 (Oxford: Clarendon Press, 1961), 85; idem, "4Q147," "4Q148," in Roland de Vaux and Józef T. Milik, *Qumrân Cave 4.2: I. Archéologie, II. Tefilllin, Mezuzot et Targums (4Q128–4Q157)*, DJD 6 (Oxford: Clarendon Press, 1977), 79.

inscribed in a tiny script and folded.[5] However, an application of new imaging techniques to the photographs of these three texts reveals that none of them seems to contain passages from Exodus and Deuteronomy common to tefillin and mezuzot. Rather, 4Q147, 4Q148, and Mur5 appear to yield non-biblical texts. The best preserved of the three, 4Q147, features an address to God. A few legible words found in 4Q148 may also belong to a prayer.

The preliminary editions of 4Q147, 4Q148, and Mur5 propose that these might be amulets. Since no other written Jewish amulets from Second Temple period have yet been found, this identification relies first and foremost on the physical features of the three texts, such as their tiny script, miniature size, folding, and, in the case of 4Q148, fastening of the folded package. All these suggest that the three texts were not intended for reading. Surviving late antique Jewish amulets exhibit comparable features.[6] Moreover, a comparison between the three new texts and later written Jewish amulets, as known from the archaeological finds and rabbinic sources, yields several contextual affinities.

While preliminary editions of 4Q147, 4Q148, and Mur5 focused on one text at a time, this paper brings all the three texts together and asks three questions. First, assuming that they are indeed amulets, what are the differences between the three and the later Jewish amulets? Second, how does their tentative identification as amulets impact the classification of another miniature text from Qumran, 4QPhyl N (4Q141), containing portions from Deuteronomy 32? Third, can these three texts, along with 4QPhyl N, shed new light on a reference to "phylacteries" in Matt 23:5?

2. 4Q147, 4Q148, and Mur5—An Overview

2.1 4Q147

As Plate XXIV in the sixth volume of the DJD series indicates, Milik assigned some twelve tiny fragments to the "scroll" 4Q147. Apparently, he assumed that all of them belong to one and the same text, which he designated 4QPhylactère T. However, a scrutiny of the fragments suggests that they belong to two or perhaps even three discreet texts. First, the script of Milik's fragments 11 and

---

[5] Both 4Q147 and 4Q148 remain partially folded, awaiting further attention by the curators. In Mur5, the presence of multiple imprints suggests that it is a segment of a larger text that was tightly folded.

[6] Although none of the surviving ancient Jewish amulets is inscribed on leather, they are small, written in a miniature script (predominantly on one side of a thin metal sheet), and rolled.

12 (frags. 12, 12a, and 12b in Feldman and Feldman 2019) is clearly different from that of the other fragments. Second, the two largest fragments, Milik's frags. 1 and 2, may also have been inscribed by different hands, though the paleographic differences here are far less pronounced than in the case of frags. 11 and 12. Since the preliminary publication of 4Q147, an additional early image of 4Q147 has come to my attention. This photograph, PAM 42.604, does not appear along with other images of 4Q147 at the Leon Levy Dead Sea Scrolls Digital Library (fig. 1).[7]

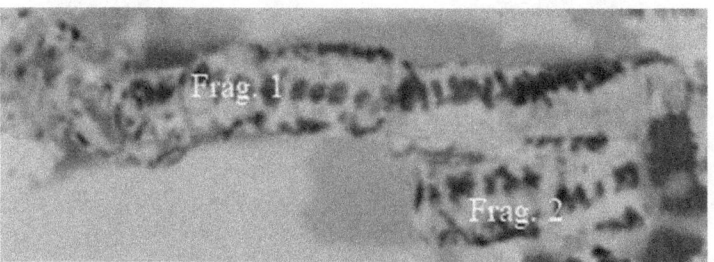

Fig. 1: 4Q147 1 and 2 (PAM 42.604)

Perhaps the earliest photograph of this text, it displays frags. 1 and 2 folded together as they might have been since antiquity.[8] Therefore, scribal differences notwithstanding, this study treats them as belonging to the same text. These are the two fragments that deserve our closest attention.

---

[7] https://www.deadseascrolls.org.il/explore-the-archive/manuscript/4Q147-1. All the images provided in this article are courtesy of The Leon Levy Dead Sea Scrolls Digital Library, Israel Antiquities Authority. I am very grateful to Dr. Pnina Shor, Mrs. Orit Rosengarten, and Mrs. Yael Barschak of the IAA for their assistance in obtaining these images.
[8] https://www.deadseascrolls.org.il/explore-the-archive/image/B-284015

2.1.1 Fragment 1

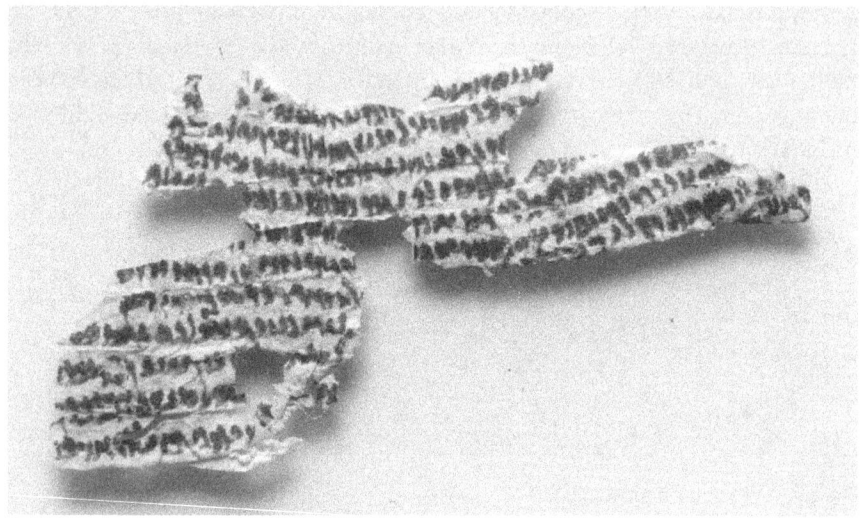

Fig. 2: 4Q147 1 (PAM 43.456)

The largest fragment, frag. 1, is 30 mm wide and 15 mm high (fig. 2). Its often highly cursive letters range in size between 0.6 and 0.9 mm (except for a few *lameds* and final letters). The fragment is partially folded. Its exposed area features a text in which an address to God (lines 3, 9, 12) intertwines with direct speech to a human addressee, both in singular and plural (lines 2, 4, 6, 8, 11), and a third person narrative (lines 2, 5, 7, 10, 11). One striking feature of its extant wording is an extensive use of Ps 36:8–9, 11 (lines 3–4). While this broken and partially concealed text leaves much uncertain, it seems to deal with several divine provisions, such as land (line 2), protection (lines 3, 5), abundance of food and drink (lines 3–4), rest (line 4), healing (line 7), strength (line 8), and blessing (lines 6, 8, 10).

2.1.2 Text and Translation[9]

]∘[ ]∘[ ]∘[	1
[חו בואו ורשו כי שומע]∘∘∘∘∘[]∘∘∘∘ [ו]	2
∘[ירויון כי בצל כנפיך יחסיון דשן ביתך ∘בֿםׄ [10]	3
[יתנך בנחל עדנים וישרי לב ירבצון]	4
[∘∘∘יסובבם כי ינגפו ושבו לפני כ]∘∘∘שםׄ [	5
[∘∘∘∘∘ישוב ויצווך לדרש את] כ]בודו ויברכו זכרו לדור דור [	6
[סוד אלוהי רום ו]∘∘נו֯דֿבֿב[∘ו֯]∘ב יהיו וֹבֿידו ירפא וחיו[	7
[∘∘∘ויתנך עוז רב ויברכך] [∘לבו יהיו בדרכך תלך ∘∘∘∘ vac]	8
9 ∘י֯ונו[∘ [ ]∘ ∘[∘ינו יענונו כי כצל לפניך מעט]
[ ]לׄ[[כ∘∘יה[פ]ל֯לו֯ ל[מ]כון שבת[ו֯] ויברכ]ם	10
[ ]∘[]צ[]∘[[בשוב שובבי צון]	11
[∘∘∘∘∘∘∘∘[ ]∘∘∘∘∘∘∘∘∘∘ל[∘∘ב∘∘] ∘[∘] [מו לפניך כי שח אדם]	12
[∘∘∘∘∘∘∘לכל אבות עלם vacat [ ] [vacat]	13
Bottom margin]	

2.].. come and take possession because he hears ....[].......[].[
3.]. they will drink their fill, for in the shadow of your wings they will take refuge. The fatness of your house ... [
4.]he will place you in the river of delights. And the upright of heart will rest [
5.]............ he will surround them for they will be smitten. And they will return before .[]..... [
6.].....he will restore. And he commanded you to seek[ ]his[g]lory. And they will bless his memory from generation to generation [
7.] council of lofty God and..[]... ...[ ].. (they) will be. And by his hand he will heal and they will live [
8.]... and he will give you great strength and he will bless you ..[ ]. his heart (they) will be. You will walk in your path .... *vac* [
9.].....[ ]. they will oppress us, for (we are) as a shadow before you. Few [

---

9 To assist the reader, intervals between the words have been introduced into the transcriptions of 4Q147 1 and 2, as well as 4Q148 verso. In some cases, they are supported by the presence of the final letters. In all other cases, the intervals reflect the editors' subjective interpretation of the text.
10 The preliminary edition, Feldman and Feldman, "4Q147," 6, reads בֿשׄוׄ. It seems, however, that *bet* is absent from the images. What might appear to be a base stroke (as in a *bet*) is probably a trace of an ink linking the *dalet* to the following *shin*. For a tendency to link letters see, for instance, ירבצו in line 4. The reading בֿיתך remains highly tentative, as explained in Feldman and Feldman, ibid., 8.

10.].[   ].... (they) will p[r]ay[to his]dwelling place and he will bless[them
11.   ]..[].[].[   ]...as backsliding ones of the flock return .[
12.].........[ ].........to you......[   ].. before you, because man will be humbled[
13.   ]......to all fathers of old.   *vacat*   [

2.1.3 Fragment 2

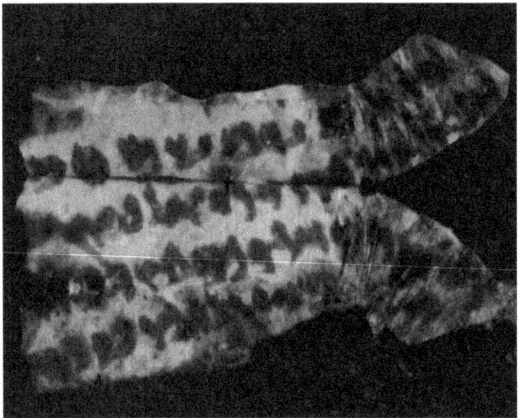

Fig. 3: 4Q147 2 (digital reconstruction based on new images, including B-480005; photographer: Shai Halevi)

The largest scrap that belongs to a conglomerate of fragments designated by Milik as frag. 2 is also partially folded. The digital unfolding presented on fig. 3 reveals a text employing a phrase שלט ב[, "(he) had a power over[" (line 2), and evoking the name of the angel Raphael (line 4). The latter is charged here with "frightening them," רפאל יפחׄידן (line 4). The unspecified feminine plural "them" may refer to רוחות, "spirits."[11]

---

[11] The preliminary edition, Feldman and Feldman, "4Q147," 16, reads in line 2 a name of another angel, Ḥ(e)iliel (or, alternatively, Raziel): וחׄיליאל יאסׄרן[, "and Ḥ(e)iliel will bind them[." The reading of the last word, however, remains uncertain, as it is unclear whether there are two overlapping letters (a correction?), an *aleph* and a *samekh*, or just one, an *aleph*, between the *yod* and the *resh*. It is similarly uncertain whether the last letter is a final *nun* or a final *kaph* (see ibid., "4Q147," 17). If the reading וחׄיליאל יארן[is adopted, one might assume that the fem. 3rd pl. suffix here refers to the same entities as יפחׄידן in the next line, while יארן could be understood as an imperfect of אר"ר, "to bind with a curse" (HALOT, 91).

2.2 4Q148

The fragment labeled by Milik as 4QPhylactère U is still partially folded.[12] It is 16.5 mm high and 24.5 mm wide, but once fully unfolded its width will be 44.5 mm. 4Q148 is an opistograph with the text inscribed on the one side being at 90° to that of the other (figs. 3 and 4).

Fig. 4: 4Q148 recto (PAM 43.456)

---

12 Although PAM images 43.456; 43.457 and plate XXV in DJD 6 exhibit two fragments, one large and one small (shaped as a triangle), earlier images of 4Q148, PAM 41.364; 41.365, make it clear that the small fragment became detached from the large one, leaving an easy to identify cavity. On the most recent images of 4Q148, e.g., B-498571, this small fragment is mistakenly attached at the top of the large one. See Feldman and Feldman, "4Q148," 200 (fig. 2).

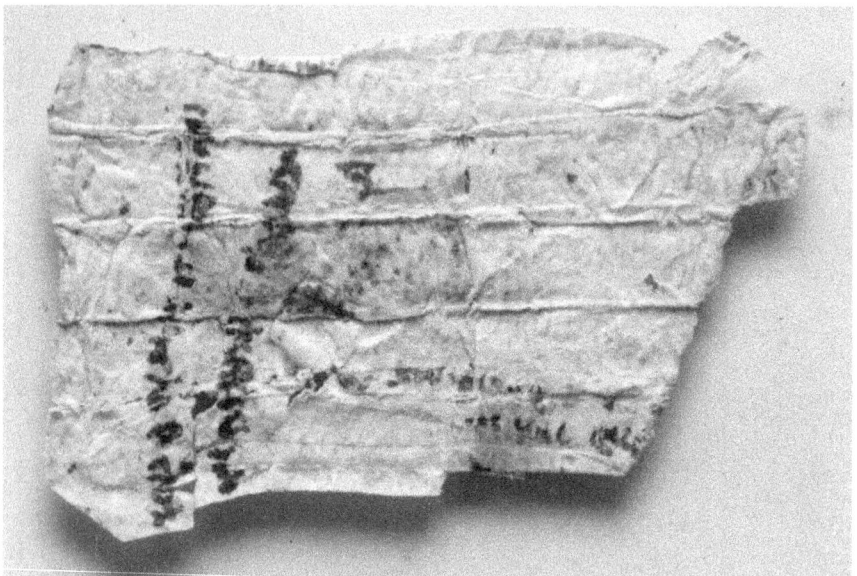

Fig. 5: 4Q148 verso (PAM 43.457)

The side with the three lines of text, 4Q148 verso (fig. 5), seems to be a legal document. Written in minuscule letters ranging between 0.6 and 1.2 mm (except for long *lameds* and final letters), it names a certain Yoḥai son of Ṣuri and indicates an amount of money, 20 silver *zuzin*, which he was apparently eligible to receive. Next, the fragment mentions either "my sons" or "sons of" someone whose name is difficult to read and states that they "will inherit all / money." The other side, 4Q148 recto (fig. 4), is barely legible. Some of it is folded, while the rest is tainted by imprints of letters, which could have resulted from folding the fragment before the ink had completely dried out. The script here appears to be slightly smaller than that of the verso, 0.6–0.9 mm (except for *lameds* and final letters). The hand seems to be more elegant (or trained?) and less cursive than that of the verso. The few legible complete words indicate that this is not a legal text, but rather a literary one. The phrase "they wrote before you" along with references to sin and forgiveness—typical motifs in penitential prayers—may suggest that this is a prayer.

Since the two sides of the fragment come from two different hands, one may wonder how a legal note and a prayer came to be inscribed on the same fragment. The legal text is missing several important elements: a name of the issuer, date, signature of the issuer and those of witnesses. Perhaps it was never completed and later reused to inscribe a literary text. Or maybe it was a part of a larger text which was cut into pieces and then recycled. Alternatively, though less likely, the literary text could have been written first and then folded, as is indicated by the imprints of letters which have not dried completely off before folding. Then someone unfolded it, inscribed a legal note, and folded it again.

One remarkable aspect of this fragment is that the creases left by the folding and tying, apparently with a hair of an animal, reflect a technique similar to the one utilized to fold and fasten tefillin slips from the Judean Desert.[13] These creases also allow us to calculate the size of the small package into which this fragment was carefully folded. It is approximately 3 x 5 mm. Of the multiple tefillin cases found in Qumran Cave 4, several feature compartments in which such a small bundle would fit perfectly well.[14]

2.2.1 4Q148 Recto: Text and Translation

1. and they will bless	1 וֹיְבָרְכוּ
2. in (the) water	2 בְּמַיִם
6. misdeed	6 עָוֺן
7. the sea	7 הים
9. they wrote before you	9 כתבו לפניך
10. (he) will consider the grace of	10 יתבונן בחן
(*or*: [he] will consider. Examine)	
11. Forgive (*or*: [he] forgave/will forgive)	11 סלח

2.2.2 4Q148 Verso: Text and Translation

Upper margin

1. To Yoḥai son of Ṣuri twenty silver z[	1 ליוֹחי בר צורי עשרים כסף ז]
2. sons of/my sons .... will inherit all[	2 בני ○○○ש ירשו מלוא]
3. silver	3 כסף

Bottom margin

2.3 Mur5

This narrow strip of leather, 6 mm wide and 46 mm high, contains 29 lines of text (fig. 6). The letters' height varies between 0.9 and 1.3 mm. Multiple imprints visible on the fragment indicate that it was folded. Given its somewhat thicker leather

---

13 For a detailed discussion see Feldman and Feldman, "4Q148," 201–205.
14 Compare Milik's (DJD 6:35) tefillin case #4 (four compartments, 5 x 5 mm each), case #7 (four compartments, 6 x 3 mm each), case #8 (four compartments, 6 x 3.5 mm each).

than one would expect in a slip of tefillin, Milik classified Mur5 as a mezuzah, while Hartmut Stegemann and Jürgen Becker insisted on its identification as a tefillah.[15] A few legible words suggest a use of the Exodus story, with Pharaoh being explicitly mentioned in line 27. There is also a phrase in line 9 lending itself easily for a reconstruction as an allusion to Exod 15:26.[16]

2.3.1 Text and Translation

7.]he will bring us[	7 [יְבִיאֲנוּ]
8.]to you in (the) lan[d	8 [לְדבָּאָרֶץ]
9. Y]HWH (is) [your] heal[er	9 יְ[הוָה רֹפֶ]אךָ
10.]his hand ..[	10 [ººידוֹ]
20.]swore (and?) because[	20 נ[שבעוכי]
25. Y]HWH..[	25 יְ[הוָהºº]
27.] Pharaoh[	27 [פרעה]
29.] and he went down[	29 [וירד]

Fig. 6: Mur5 (new image, photographer: Shai Halevi)

---

15 Milik, DJD 2:85; Hartmut Stegemann and Jürgen Becker, "Zum Text von Fragment 5 aus Wadi Murabbaʿat," *RevQ* 3 (1961): 443–48.
16 Michael O. Wise has argued at length that Mur5, along with a tefillin Mur4, was a part of an archive that belonged to Jesus b. Galgula, the commander of Herodium during the Second Jewish Revolt against Rome, who might have taken a cache of texts, both legal and literary, with him to the caves of Murabbaʿat. Still, he also admits that our text, which was not discovered *in situ* but rather acquired from Bedouins, could have been brought into the caves during the First Jewish Revolt. Michael O. Wise, *Language and Literacy in Roman Judaea: A Study of the Bar Kokhba Documents* (New Haven: Yale University Press, 2015), 107, 124, 418n4.

Tiny fragments, folding, marks left by tying (4Q148), and some of the smallest scripts attested in the scrolls from the Judean Desert—all these match rather well Milik's initial classification of these fragments as tefillin and mezuzah. And yet, their contents are strikingly different from tefillin and mezuzot as we know them both from the findings in the Judean Desert and rabbinic halakha. The rabbinic sources prescribe Exod 13:1–16; Deut 6:4–9; 11:13–21 for tefillin and Deut 6:4–9; 11:13–21 for a mezuzah.[17] Tefillin and mezuzot from the Judean Desert often include larger chunks of text from both Exodus (12:43–13:16) and Deuteronomy (5:1–6:9; 10:12–11:21).[18] If not tefillin and mezuzot, what might have 4Q147, 4Q148, and Mur5 been used for? The same physical characteristics that led to their preliminary identification as tefillin suggest yet another possibility—amulets. A brief excursus into the history of ancient written Jewish amulets will reveal several other shared features, as well as important differences.

3. Jewish Written Amulets: From the Iron Age to Late Antiquity

The Hebrew Bible sheds little light on the Israelites' use of amulets in general and written or lettered amulets in particular.[19] This is not to say that there have been

---

[17] David Nakman, "Tefillin and Mezuzot at Qumran," in *The Qumran Scrolls and Their World*, ed. Menahem Kister, Between Bible and Mishnah (Jerusalem: Yad Ben-Zvi Press, 2009), 143–55 (154; Hebrew).

[18] On the scriptural passages included in tefillin and mezuzot from the Judean Desert, see Yonatan Adler, "The Content and Order of the Scriptural Passages in Tefillin: A Reexamination of the Early Rabbinic Sources in Light of the Evidence from the Judean Desert," in *Halakha in Light of Epigraphy*, ed. Albert I. Baumgarten et al., JAJSup 3 (Göttingen: Vandenhoeck & Ruprecht, 2011), 205–29; David Nakman, "The Contents and the Order of the Biblical Sections in the Tefillin from Qumran and Rabbinic Halakhah," *Cathedra* 112 (2004): 19–44 (Hebrew); idem, "Tefillin and Mezuzot at Qumran," 143–55 (Hebrew); Yehudah B. Cohn, *Tangled Up in Text: Tefillin and the Ancient World*, Brown Judaic Studies (Providence: Brown University, 2008), 55–102; Emanuel Tov, "The *Tefillin* from the Judean Desert and the Textual Criticism of the Hebrew Bible," in *Is There a Text in This Cave: Studies in the Textuality of the Dead Sea Scrolls in Honour of George J. Brooke*, ed. Ariel Feldman, Maria Cioată, and Charlotte Hempel, STDJ 119 (Leiden: Brill, 2017), 277–92. This is not the place to address the curious problem of distinguishing between mezuzot and tefillin. See further Cohn, ibid., 60–62, who argues for a possibility that mezuzot from the Judean Desert may be, in fact, tefillin.

[19] Cf. Raphael Posner's remark summarizing the evidence: "It is not known whether amulets were used in the biblical period. Presumably they were, but there is no direct evidence to prove it" (Raphael Posner, Judith R. Baskin, and Theodore Schrire, "Amulets," *Encyclopaedia Judaica*, 2nd

no attempts to locate amuletic practices in the Jewish Scriptures. Thus, several items of jewelry have been understood as charms.[20] Among these are the High Priest's breastplate featuring gemstones with the names of the twelve tribes engraved upon them (Exod 28:15–21) and the golden ציץ bearing the inscription "Holy to YHWH" (Exod 28:36; 39:30).[21] Likewise, it has been suggested that Exod 13:9, 16; Deut 6:8–9; 11:18, 20, the four passages utilized by the Jewish tradition as proof-texts for tefillin and mezuzah practices, and Prov 3:1–4; 6:20–22 reflect a use of inscribed amulets or at least are informed by such a use.[22] However, none of the aforementioned jewelry items is explicitly presented in the Hebrew Bible as an amulet. Similarly, the purported references to amuletic practices may as well

---

ed., 2:121–23). On three broad groupings of amulets, "unlettered", "semi-lettered," and "lettered," see Roy D. Kotansky, "Textual Amulets and Writing Traditions in the Ancient World," in *Guide to the Study of Ancient Magic*, ed. David Frankfurter (Leiden: Brill, 2019), 507–54 (508–509). A good example of "semi-lettered" amulets, often including images along with a bit of text, are inscribed gems and rings. However, as Bohak indicates, very few of these can be classified as Jewish, which may suggest that late antique Jews were less attracted to these kinds of amulets. See Gideon Bohak, "The Use of Engraved Gems and Rings in Ancient Jewish Magic," in *Magical Gems in Their Contexts*, ed. Kata Endreffy, Árpád M. Nagy, and Jeffrey Spier (Budapest: L'Erma di Bretschneider, 2019), 37–45.

20 Among the items which have been understood by some as amulets are the "rings/earrings" which Jacob's household gave to him to be buried along with "the alien gods" in Gen 35:4, the gold earrings used to cast the Golden Calf in Exod 32:3, and the various pieces of jewelry listed in Exod 35:22 and Num 31:50. Just as these items can be easily explained as mere jewelry, so can the reference in Isa 3:18–21 to לחשים (v. 20). While it is often rendered as "amulets" (see, e.g., BDB, 538 and HALOT, 527; the latter tentatively suggests a "string of conch shells"), Menahem Zevi Kaddari, *Dictionary of Biblical Hebrew* (Ramat-Gan: Bar-Ilan University, 2006), 561 (Hebrew), prefers "an unknown piece of female jewelry." The "seal" of Song of Songs 8:6 has also been understood as an amulet and so were the various kinds of jewelry used by Midianites in Judg 8:21, 26. See David E. Aune, "Amulets," in *The Oxford Encyclopedia of Archaeology in the Near East*, ed. Eric M. Meyers (Oxfod: Oxford University Press, 1997), 1:113–15 (114). On the Song of Songs see Othmar Keel, "Review of *Ancient Seals and the Bible* by Leonard Gorelick and Elizabeth Williams-Forte," *JAOS* 106 (1986): 307–11. These identifications remain highly tentative.

21 Gideon Bohak, *Ancient Jewish Magic: A History* (Cambridge: Cambridge University Press, 2008), 117–18, 141. With regard to the amuletic use of the Tetragrammaton, Aune, "Amulets," 114, also lists Zech 14:20, envisioning horses bearing bells with an inscription "Holy to YHWH."

22 See Jeremy D. Smoak, *The Priestly Blessing in Inscription and Scripture: The Early History of Numbers 6:24–26* (Oxford: Oxford University Press, 2016), 39–41. On possible affinities between some of the biblical psalms and ANE amulets, see also Smoak's earlier study "May YHWH Bless You and Keep you from Evil: The Rhetorical Argument of Ketef Hinnom Amulet I and the Form of the Prayers for Deliverance in Psalms," *JANER* 12 (2012): 202–36. He suggests that there might have been more "fluidity between magical formulae and ancient Judahite prayer traditions than previously recognized" (203).

be understood figuratively or read with a common use of jewelry as their background.[23]

At the same time archaeology reveals a widespread use of amulets in Iron Age Palestine and its immediate neighbors, especially Egypt.[24] Hundreds of both lettered and unlettered amulets were unearthed in Israel/Judah. None of them bears distinct Israelite or Judahite features. Rather, they appear to be predominantly Egyptian.[25]

The only exception to this rule are the two silver scrolls from Ketef Hinnom.[26] Discovered in a burial cave, these two tiny rolled sheets of thin silver are inscribed in paleo-Hebrew, probably by two different hands.[27] Though their dating is somewhat controversial, with scholarly opinions ranging from pre-exilic to Hellenistic times, an extensive re-edition of the two scrolls appears to make a strong case for the earlier, First Temple, date.[28] The wording of the two amulets is not identical. However, they exhibit a similar structure and share some of the same language.[29]

---

23 See Cohn, *Tangled Up*, 39–48.
24 For an overview of the evidence, see Aune, "Amulets," 1:113–15. For the amulets from Syria and Palestine, see Angelika Berlejung, "There is Nothing Better than More! Texts and Images on Amulet 1 from Arslan Tash," *JNSL* 36 (2010): 1–42 (9–10).
25 See Christian Herrmann, *Ägyptische Amulette aus Palästina/Israel I–III*, OBO (Fribourg: Academic Press, 1994–2006). On the many figurines of the Egyptian goddess Mut found in Megiddo, Beth Shean, Lachish, and Gezer, see Christopher B. Hays, "The Egyptian Goddess Mut in Iron Age Palestine: Further Data from Amulets and Onomastics," *JNES* 71 (2012): 299–314. One might also mention here the hundreds of seals discovered in the Land of Israel. It has been suggested that not only have seals, bearing images and inscriptions, originated from amulets, but that they also continued to serve (among their other functions) as such. See Keel, "Review," 307–308. For seals themselves, see Nahman Avigad and Benjamin Sass, *Corpus of West Semitic Stamp Seals* (Jerusalem: The Israel Academy of Sciences and Humanities, 1997).
26 For the edition of the two scrolls, see Gabriel Barkay et al., "The Amulets from Ketef Hinnom: A New Edition and Evaluation," *BASOR* 334 (2004): 41–71. Nadav Na'aman, "A New Appraisal of the Silver Amulets from Ketef Hinnom," *IEJ* 61 (2011): 184–95, offered a few corrections to the readings proposed by Barkay et al. For a critique of his suggestions, see Shmuel Aḥituv, "A Rejoinder to Nadav Na'aman's 'New Appraisal of the Silver Amulets from Ketef Hinnom'," *IEJ* 62 (2012): 223–32.
27 Barkay et al., "The Amulets from Ketef Hinnom," 47. In the scroll designated by the editors as KH I, the top line, which presumably contains the name of the owner of the amulet, seems to have been inscribed by yet another scribe (ibid., 55).
28 Barkay et al., "The Amulets from Ketef Hinnom," 42. See an overview and discussion in Smoak, *Priestly Blessing*, 13–16.
29 Smoak, "May YHWH Bless You and Keep you from Evil," 211, suggests that the text of KH 1 features five elements: name of the owner or an opening blessing (lines 1–2), statement about the deity's character (lines 2–7), statement of the amulet's intended function (lines 8–10), statement of confidence (11–14), concluding blessing (14–18).

The two scrolls name God's attributes, refer to his protection from evil, and conclude with a blessing that is strikingly similar to the Priestly Blessing from Num 6:24–26.[30]

One of the most intriguing aspects of these two silver amulets is their uniqueness. While similar lamella-type amulets are well-attested in the neighboring cultures, no other specimen of such an Israelite/Judahite amulet is known from the pre-exilic times. In fact, archaeology suggests there would be no other Jewish written amulet for another millennium.[31] This is not to say that Jews did not use amulets in Second Temple times. There is literary and material evidence to the contrary. A passage from 2 Macc 12:39–42 reports that the fallen fighters of Judas Maccabeus lost their lives because they carried on their bodies pagan amulets.[32] The text clearly laments the idolatrous nature of the amulets, not the use of amulets per se.[33] The multicolored cords that Job gives to his daughters as their inheritance in the Testament of Job 46–50 have also been understood as amulets.[34] Finally, among the findings from the Cave of Letters were a child's linen shirt and a piece of cloth containing pockets created by placing shells, salt crystals, seeds, spices and, wax in the fabric and tying a string around the protrusion.[35] A mishnaic text (m. Shabbat 6:9) speaking of קשרים, "ties" or "bindings," led Yigael Yadin to suggest that these served an "apotropaeic purpose."[36] In light of these literary sources and artifacts, Gideon Bohak concludes that Second Temple Jews

---

30 Jacob Milgrom, *Numbers* (Philadelphia: JPS, 1989), 52, observes that such a use of the Priestly Blessing may reflect a literal interpretation of Num 6:27 (ושמו את שמי על בני ישראל), i.e., that this benediction should have been used as a prophylactic.
31 As Bohak, *Ancient Jewish Magic*, 114, puts it, "of all the artifacts which strike us by their apparent absence from the Jewish society of the Second Temple period, the absence of inscribed Jewish amulets is perhaps the most surprising."
32 Jonathan A. Goldstein, 2 *Maccabees*, AB (New York: Doubleday, 1983), 431, 448–49, argues that the Greek should be rendered as "objects which were consecrated to the idols of Jamnia." For him, the text refers to idolatrous objects taken from pagan temples (as in Achan's story), rather than to amulets. On the other hand, Bohak *Ancient Jewish Magic*, 120n145, insists that these are amulets, as the booty would be stored elsewhere and not worn into the battle.
33 Bohak, *Ancient Jewish Magic*, 121.
34 For a discussion of these in light of contemporary and later magic practices, see Rebecca Lesses, "Amulets and Angels: Visionary Experiences in the Testament of Job and the Hekhalot Literature," in *Heavenly Tablets*, ed. Lynn LiDonnici and Anrea Lieber (Leiden: Brill, 2007), 49–74 (56–59).
35 Yigael Yadin, *Bar-Kokhba: The Rediscovery of the Legendary Hero of the Last Jewish Revolt against Imperial Rome* (New York: Random House, 1971), 81; ibid., *The Finds from the Bar-Kokhba Period in the Cave of Letters* (Jerusalem: The Israel Exploration Society, 1963), 256–58.
36 Yadin, *Finds*, 256. See also Bohak, *Ancient Jewish Magic*, 122, citing b. Shabbat 66b; j. Shabbat 8b; j. Eruvin 26c.

indeed used amulets, though not written ones, which in itself is somewhat surprising, given what he describes as "the well-attested Jewish use of *tephillin* and *mezuzot*."[37]

Jewish written amulets resurface in Late Antiquity. In his 2008 study, Bohak identifies some forty (and counting) Jewish Aramaic and Hebrew amulets, both published and unpublished, from the pre-Muslim period.[38] Those found during organized excavations are mostly dated to the 5th–7th century CE.[39] They were often inscribed on tiny metal sheets (lamellae) of bronze, lead, silver, and (rarely) gold, predominantly on one side only, and then rolled or folded.[40] Some of these lamellae were placed in a container or wrapped around a cord so that they could be worn on one's neck.[41] Others appear to have been hidden in structures, including synagogues.[42] Yuval Harari observes that the extant Jewish amulets in Greek may precede the Aramaic/Hebrew ones by "about two centuries."[43] One such recently published lamella containing a Greek transliteration of Deut 6:4 is dated as early as the 3rd century CE.[44]

Diverse as they are, most of these amulets appear to have been intended, to use Bohak's formulation, for "medical purposes—either to exorcize demons which were deemed to be afflicting a specific patient, or to prevent any harm from

---

37 Bohak, *Ancient Jewish Magic*, 122–23. In light of the earlier and later evidence, Bohak considers various factors that might shed light on the absence of written amulets from Second Temple Jewish artefacts. For instance, he notes (ibid., 115) the Aramaic scroll 4Q560, yet discards it as an unlikely candidate for an amulet. While 4Q560 contains an incantation that could be used to produce an amulet, in itself it is not an amulet. It is relatively large and has no signs of folding. On this text see below. On the possibility that an ostracon (#53) from the Herodion containing the Hebrew alphabet is an amulet, see Joan Taylor, "4Q341: A Writing Exercise Remembered," in *Is There a Text in This Cave?*, 133–51 (146).
38 Bohak, *Ancient Jewish Magic*, 149–50.
39 Bohak, *Ancient Jewish Magic*, 151; and in more detail, Hanan Eshel and Rivka Leiman, "Jewish Amulets Written on Metal Scrolls," *JAJ* 1 (2010): 189–99 (196).
40 Yuval Harari, *Jewish Magic Before the Rise of Kabbalah*, transl. Batya Stein (Detroit: Wayne State University Press, 2017), 227. See further Eshel and Leiman, "Jewish Amulets Written on Metal Scrolls," 189–99.
41 Harari, *Jewish Magic*, 227.
42 See further Eshel and Leiman, "Jewish Amulets Written on Metal Scrolls," 197–98.
43 Harari, *Jewish Magic*, 229 and note 65. Kotansky dates a Jewish amulet in Greek (Amulet 2) from Segontium (Caernarvon, Wales) to 75–140 CE (though later periods are equally possible) and another Jewish amulet in Greek (Amulet 33) from Mazzarino, Sicily, to the 3rd to 4th centuries CE. See Roy Kotansky, *Greek Magical Amulets: The Inscribed Gold, Silver, Copper and Bronze Lamellae: Part I: Published Texts of Known Provenance*, Papyrologica Coloniensia 22,1 (Opladen: Westdeutscher, 1994), 3, 155.
44 Esther Eshel, Hanan Eshel, and Armin Lange, "'Hear, O Israel' in Gold: An Ancient Amulet from Halbturn in Austria," *JAJ* 1 (2010): 43–64.

such demons and from the evil eye."[45] Often naming their owners, these amulets commonly feature an adjuration requesting a demon(s) to leave the patient's body and/or not to enter it.[46] They also quote scriptural passages, evoke angelic and demonic names, include *charaktêres*, and *voces magicae*.[47]

Rabbinic literature, both tannaitic and amoraic, also contains multiple references to amulets, קמיע/קמיעין, denoting "something bound."[48] Rabbinic sources speak of several types of amulets, such as written amulets (or amulets of writing; קמיע של כתב) and amulets of roots (קמיע של עיקרין; t. Shabbat 4:9). In these texts amulets are not discussed as magical implements, but rather as a common item carried by a person.[49] Bohak observes that unlike the highly regulated tefillin and mezuzot, the rabbis did not attempt to "standardize the *contents* of written amulets," leaving such matters to practitioners.[50] In fact, besides noting that amulets contain scriptural passages and holy names, the many rabbinic references to amulets tell us very little about their contents.[51] Significantly, tefillin and amulets are sometimes mentioned together. For instance, m. Shabbat 6:2 prohibits going out on the Sabbath "with phylacteries, or with an amulet," unless the latter had "been prepared by one that was skilled."[52] Rabbinic tefillin and written amulets appear to have shared several features: both contained biblical texts (b. Shabbat 61b; 115b), were covered with leather (b. Shabbat 62a), and were bound to their owners (b. Shabbat 61a; b. Sanhedrin 22a).[53] A discussion of m. Eruvin 10:1 in

---

45 Bohak, *Ancient Jewish Magic*, 152.
46 Bohak, *Ancient Jewish Magic*, 152. Unlike most of these amulets, an amulet from Ḥorvat Marish was intended to subjugate others to its owner. See further Harari, *Jewish Magic*, 221–22.
47 See further Bohak, *Ancient Jewish Magic*, 141, 149–53; idem, "Hebrew, Hebrew Everywhere? Notes on the Interpretation of Voces Magicae," in *Prayer, Magic, and the Stars in the Ancient and Late Antique World*, ed. Scott Noegel, Joel Walker, and Brannon Wheeler (University Park: The Pennsylvania State University Press, 2003), 69–82; idem, "The Charaktêres in Ancient Jewish Magic," *Acta Classica Universitatis Scientiarum Debreceniensis* 47 (2011): 25–44.
48 Harari, *Jewish Magic*, 217–18, notes three definitions of קמיע: leather pouch or a small metal box in which amulet was placed, the contents of the pouch, or both the pouch/container and its contents. For a discussion of rabbinic references to amulets, see Julius Preuss, *Biblical and Talmudic Medicine*, transl. Fred Rosner (New York: Sanhedrin Press, 1978), 146–47, 149, 196; Catherine Hezser, *Jewish Literacy in Roman Palestine*, TSAJ 81 (Tübingen: Mohr Siebeck, 2001), 209–26; Bohak, *Ancient Jewish Magic*, 370–74.
49 Bohak, *Ancient Jewish Magic*, 370.
50 Bohak, *Ancient Jewish Magic*, 372–74 (the italics are original).
51 Bohak, *Ancient Jewish Magic*, 372–74, refers to b. Gittin 67b to suggest that they also included names of the demon(s) they were meant to exorcise.
52 Transl. Danby, 104–105. See also m. Mikvaot 6:4; m. Kelim 23:9.
53 Jeffrey H. Tigay, "On the Term Phylacteries (Matt 23:5)," *HTR* 72 (1979): 45–53 (50n26). T. Demai 2:17 (ed. Lieberman, 72) speaks of a woman who, having married a *haver*, is said to bind

b. Eruvin 96b raises a concern that a tefillin found on the road on the Sabbath may, in fact, be an amulet, suggesting that the two might have looked quite alike.⁵⁴ To highlight the physical similarities between the two, Tigay draws attention to Massekhet Tefillin referring to tefillin as קמיע (9, 12).⁵⁵ Similarities notwithstanding, the rabbis clearly differentiate between tefillin and amulets.⁵⁶

4. 4Q147, 4Q148, Mur5, and Late Antique Jewish Amulets: What Is Different?

The foregoing overview suggests two main lines of argument to support the aforementioned identification of 4Q147, 4Q148, and Mur5 as amulets, rather than tefillin. First, there is the remarkable physical resemblance between the three texts, especially 4Q148, and tefillin, a feature implied in the rabbinic sources. Second, there are several contextual similarities between the three texts and late antique Jewish amulets as we know them both from archaeological finds and rabbinic texts. These include:
- *Scriptural quotations.* Extant late antique Jewish amulets frequently utilize quotations from the Hebrew Bible, a feature noted also in rabbinic sources.⁵⁷ 4Q147 1 contains an extensive quotation from Ps 36:8–11 (lines 3–4), whereas

---

(קומעת) tefillin on his arm. Once married to a tax collector, she is said to tie to his arm קישורין. Meir Bar-Ilan, "Writing Torah Scrolls, Tefillin, Mezuzoth and Amulets on Deer Leather," *Beit Mikra* 30 (1985): 375–81 (380n22; Hebrew), suggests that the contrast implied in the passage indicates that קישורין is/are amulet(s).

54 B. Eruvin 96b asks whether anyone would "exert himself to fashion an amulet in the form of the phylacteries" (וכי אדם טורח לעשות קמיע כמין תפילין), whereas Masekhet Tefillin 2 disqualifies a tefillin which was crafted "in the form of an amulet" (כמין קמיע).

55 Tigay, "On the Term Phylacteries," 50; idem, *Deuteronomy* (Philadelphia: Jewish Publication Society, 1996), 442. On similarities between tefillin and amulets, see also Bar-Ilan, "Writing," 379–81, referencing medieval texts suggesting that one and the same scribe could have produced Torah scrolls, tefillin, and amulets.

56 Cf., e.g., the ruling that, although amulets may contain scriptural passages or holy names, they, unlike tefillin, are not to be saved from fire (b. Shabbat 115b). See further John Bowman, "Phylacteries," in *Studia Evangelica*, ed. Kurt Aland et al., Texte und Untersuchungen zur Geschichte der Altchristlichen Literatur 73 (Berlin: Akademie-Verlag, 1959), 523–38 (529).

57 Bohak, *Ancient Jewish Magic*, 141, names this feature as one of the three elements characteristic of Second Temple magical texts and practices, along with the use of the divine name and sacred objects, such as priestly vestments. On the use of Scripture in Jewish and Christian amulets, see Nils H. Korsvoll, "Bible Bible Everywhere? Reviewing the Distribution of Biblical Quotes in Ancient Amulets," *BN* 176 (2018): 89–110.

Mur5 9 seems to allude to Exod 15:26. The latter one is rather significant, as late antique Jewish amulets often feature this verse.[58]

- *Divine and angelic names.* Surviving Jewish amulets abound with divine and angelic names. The use of the holy names in amulets is also observed in rabbinic texts. Mur5 employs the Tetragrammaton (line 25), while 4Q147 2 names Raphael.[59] The latter appears quite often in late antique Jewish amulets.[60]
- *Historiolae.* Several late antique Jewish amulets feature *historiolae*, "mythical stories and precedents which are narrated or alluded to in order to tap their hidden powers for a specific magical ritual."[61] Mur5 seems to allude to the story of Exodus, as do also later magical texts.[62] Line 27 mentions Pharaoh, whereas lines 7–8 juxtapose a phrase "]he will bring us[" to a reference to the Promised Land. A form of יר"ד found in line 29 may point the Song of the Sea (Exod 15:5) depicting the fate of Pharaoh's armies using the same verb.

However, the comparison between the three new texts and late antique Jewish written amulets also reveals several significant differences. Though these may well be a result of the texts' poor state of preservation, they still deserve close attention:

---

[58] Joseph Naveh and Shaul Shaked, *Magic Spells and Formulae: Aramaic Incantations of Late Antiquity* (Jerusalem: Magnes, 1993), 22–23; Bohak, *Ancient Jewish Magic*, 57, 299, 309, 339, 377–79, 421. For examples of amulets utilizing this verse see Amulet 13, lines 12–20 in Joseph Naveh and Shaul Shaked, *Amulets and Magic Bowls: Aramaic Incantations of Late Antiquity*, 2nd ed. (Jerusalem: Magnes, 1987), 98. Cf. also Rabbi Akiva's famous dictum in m. Sanhedrin 10:1 denying the world to come to those who whisper this verse over a wound.

[59] It is also possible that the divine name Shaddai occurs in Mur5, line 16. See Feldman and Feldman, "Is Mur 5 a Mezuzah?" 291-98. For the use of Shaddai in late antique Jewish amulets, see, e.g., Amulet 12, line 27, in Naveh and Shaked, *Amulets and Magic Bowls*, 96.

[60] See the indices in Naveh and Shaked, *Amulets and Magic Bowls*, 282; Naveh and Shaked, *Magic Spells and Formulae*, 289.

[61] Bohak, *Ancient Jewish Magic*, 312–14.

[62] For a possible reference to God's fighting Egyptians in an amulet from Horvat Marish, see Gideon Bohak, "The Uses of Cosmogonic Myths in Ancient Jewish Magic," *Archiv für Religionsgeschichte* 13 (2011): 93–107 (101). On the Jewish background of the use of the Exodus story in early Christian magical texts, see See Pieter W. van der Horst, "'The God Who Drowned the King of Egypt': A Short Note on an Exorcistic Formula," in idem, *Jews and Christians in Their Graeco-Roman Context*, WUNT 196 (Tübingen: Mohr Siebeck, 2006), 280–84. In addition to the sources cited in these two studies, note a possible allusion to the story of Exodus in 11Q11 3:2-3: מי ע[שה את האותות] / ואת המופ[תים האלה ב[אָרץ, as observed by Florentino García Martínez, Eibert J.C. Tigchelaar, and Adam S. van der Woude in Florentino García Martínez et al., *Qumran Cave 11.II: 11Q2-18, 11Q20-31*, DJD 23 (Oxford: Clarendon Press, 1998), 194.

- *Lack of Personalization.* While a few of the extant late antique Jewish amulets do not include the names of the clients, most of them do.[63] Often the name would appear at the beginning of the amulet. Yet some evoke the name much later in the text,[64] whereas multiple amulets refer to the client several times.[65] In the case of 4Q147, 4Q148, and Mur5, it is unclear whether any of them preserve their incipits. Nevertheless, it seems important to point out that the surviving wording of 4Q147, 4Q148 recto, and Mur5 yields no names of their owners.[66]
- *Lack of Specifics.* Though some late antique amulets can be described as multi-purposed, most of them target clearly specified maladies.[67] That this was the case with incantations utilized already in late Second Temple times is indicated by the Aramaic spell 4Q560 detailing the diseases it was intended to heal ("fever and chills and the fire [or fever] of heart" [1 i 5]).[68] The extant text of 4Q147, 4Q148, and Mur5 has nothing of the kind.
- *Absence of an Adjuration.* Harari notes with regards to late antique amulets that "all amulets were meant to bind."[69] Hence, the vast majority of them contain adjurations commonly phrased as a second-person address to the adjured supernatural beings, who are commonly called by their names. The Dead Sea Scrolls yield several incantations containing such adjurations: the aforementioned spell 4Q560 (1 ii 5–6), the fragmentary 8Q5 (frag. 1), and the somewhat better preserved 11Q11 (4:1, 4–12; 5:6–8).[70] No such language of

---

[63] Thus the absence of the name in the bronze amulet against fever from Sepphoris suggests its generic character, a kind of amulet that "was 'mass produced' in advance." Bohak, *Ancient Jewish Magic*, 151–52; see also Harari, *Jewish Magic*, 219, 224–25.
[64] See Amulets 11 and 15 in Naveh and Shaked, *Amulets and Magic Bowls*, 90, 104, and Amulet 16 in Naveh and Shaked, *Magic Spells and Formulae*, 43. In the recently published amulet intended to secure a victory in a legal dispute the name of the client appears in line 56. See Shaul Shaked and Rivka Elitzur-Leiman, "An Aramaic Amulet for Winning a Case in a Court of Law," *JSQ* 26 (2019): 1–16 (6).
[65] E.g., Amulet 17, lines 1 and 17; Amulet 18, lines 2–3 and 9; Amulet 19, lines 5–6, 14, 26–27, 31–32; Amulet 26, lines 4–5, 11–12 in Naveh and Shaked, *Magic Spells and Formulae*, 50, 57, 61–62, 87–88.
[66] One may note a possibility that the legal note inscribed on 4Q148 verso might have served as a sort of a personalization for 4Q148 recto. I thank Prof. George Brooke for drawing my attention to this aspect of 4Q148.
[67] Bohak, *Ancient Jewish Magic* 152, 216.
[68] Joseph Naveh, "Fragments of an Aramaic Magic Book from Qumran," *IEJ* 48 (1998): 252–61 (257).
[69] Harari, *Jewish Magic*, 219.
[70] For 8Q5 1 see the new edition by Elisha Qimron, *The Dead Sea Scrolls: The Hebrew Writings, Between Bible and Mishnah* (Jerusalem: Yad Ben-Zvi, 2014), 3:246 (Hebrew).

adjuration is to be found in our three texts. On the contrary, 4Q147 2 refers to the actions of Raphael in the third person. The presumed objects of these actions, the spirits, are referred to in the third person as well.

The three aspects of the late antique amulets absent from 4Q147, 4Q148, and Mur5 are also missing from the two Ketef Hinnom silver scrolls.[71] It is not impossible that there were Second Temple amulets containing all these features. After all, the last two are attested to in 4Q560. Yet until they are found, the foregoing discussion confirms Bohak's observation about a significant gap between Second Temple magic texts and practices and later Jewish magical lore: "When we turn to late-antique Jewish magical texts, we find ourselves in a very different world."[72]

5. 4Q147 and Apotropaic Prayers

While the extant text of 4Q147 features no language of adjuration, its largest fragment includes a direct address to God, a prayer. Unlike early Christian amulets, Jewish late antique amulets rarely contain prayers, though some of them incorporate second-person blessings of God and even short addresses to God.[73] When the prayer-like formulations in frag. 1 are read along with Raphael's presumed actions against spirits in frag. 2, the two are reminiscent of contemporary apotropaic prayers.[74] Unlike incantations addressing demonic powers directly in order to

---

[71] On a possibility that KH 1 and KH 2 could have contained the name of their owner(s), see Barkay et al., "The Amulets from Ketef Hinnom," 55, 64.
[72] Bohak, *Ancient Jewish Magic*, 141.
[73] See Amulet 3, lines 18–20; Amulet 7, lines 13–16 (second person possessive pronoun in line 13 is reconstructed); Amulet 15, lines 23–25, in Naveh and Shaked, *Amulets and Magic Bowls*, 50–51, 68–71, 106, 107, and Amulet 16, lines 1, 3–6 in Naveh and Shaked, *Magic Spells and Formulae*, 43. For a longer address to God see Amulet 7a, lines 13–16, in Naveh and Shaked, *Amulets and Magic Bowls*, 70. An unusually extensive second-person address to God precedes the list of requests in the amulet published by Shaked and Elitzur-Leiman, "An Aramaic Amulet for Winning a Case in a Court of Law," 5–6. The Hebrew-Greek amulet from Evron includes what has been described by Bohak as "a pious prayer to God" in Greek. Roy Kotansky, "An Inscribed Copper Amulet from 'Evron," *Atiqot* 20 (1991), 81–87; Bohak, *Ancient Jewish Magic*, 231–32. On prayers in Christian amulets in Greek, see Roy Kotansky, "Incantations and Prayers for Salvation on Inscribed Greek Amulets," in *Magika Hiera: Ancient Greek Magic and Religion*, ed. Christopher A. Faraone and Dirk Obbink (Oxford: Oxford University Press, 1991), 107–37 (117–21); Christopher A. Faraone, *The Transformation of Greek Amulets in Roman Imperial Times* (Philadelphia: University of Pennsylvania Press, 2018), 177–197.
[74] On apotropaic prayer see David Flusser, "Qumrân and Jewish 'Apotropaic' Prayers," *IEJ* 16 (1966): 194–205; Philip S. Alexander, "'Wrestling against Wickedness in High Places': Magic in

force demons to do one's bidding, apotropaic prayers seek God's protection against demons.[75] Admittedly, 4Q147 does not contain a request for divine help against demons. Still, several phrases found in 4Q147 2 occur also in the primary examples of apotropaic prayer:
- the construction ‎של"ט ב-, "to have a power/dominion over." This collocation is used with a reference to "satan" both in Levi's prayer in Aramaic Levi Document (ALD 3:9: ‎[ו]אל תשלט בי כל שטן, "and let not any satan to have power over me")[76] and in Plea for Deliverance (11Q5 19:7: ‎אל תשלט בי שטן ורוח טמאה, "let satan have no dominion over me, nor an unclean spirit").[77] In both cases the

---

the Worldview of the Qumran Community," in *Scrolls and the Scriptures Fifty Years After*, ed. Stanley E. Porter and Craig A. Evans, JPSup 26 (Sheffield: Sheffield Academic Press, 1997), 318–37; Esther Eshel, "Apotropaic Prayers in the Second Temple Period," in *Liturgical Perspectives: Prayer and Poetry in Light of the Dead Sea Scrolls*, ed. Esther G. Chazon, STDJ 48 (Leiden: Brill, 2003), 69–88; Loren T. Stuckenbruck, "Pleas for Deliverance from the Demonic in Early Jewish Texts," in *Studies in Jewish Prayer*, ed. Robert Hayward and Brad Embry, JSSSup (Oxford: Oxford University Press, 2005), 55–73; Benjamin Wold, "Apotropaic Prayer and the Matthean Lord's Prayer," in *Das Böse, der Teufel und Dämonen—Evil, the Devil, and Demons*, ed. Jan Dochorn, Susanne Rudnig-Zelt, and Benjamin Wold (Tübingen: Mohr Siebeck, 2016), 101–12; Miryam T. Brand, *Evil Within and Without: The Source of Sin and Its Nature as Portrayed in Second Temple Literature*, JAJSup 9 (Göttingen: Vandenhoeck & Ruprecht, 2013), 198–217; Michael J. Morris, *Warding off Evil: Apotropaic Tradition in the Dead Sea Scrolls and Synoptic Gospels*, WUNT 2.451 (Tübingen: Mohr Siebeck, 2017), 51–147.

75 With the first category belong 4Q560, 8Q5, and 11Q11. The second includes Levi's prayer from Aramaic Levi Document (ALD 3), two psalms from 11QPsalms[a] (Plea for Deliverance [col. 19] and the so-called Syriac Psalm III [col. 24]), two prayers from the book of Jubilees (Noah [10:3–6] and Abraham [12:19–21]), 4Q444, 4Q510–511, 6Q18, 1QH[a] 22:25, and the Lord's Prayer in Matt 6:9–13. Eshel also discusses the Priestly Blessing from Numbers 6 and Psalm 91 (especially as preserved in 11Q11). Several other texts have been also classified as apotropaic prayers/hymns: Moses's prayer from Jub. 1:19–20, Abraham's blessing from Jub. 19:28, and Tobiah's prayer from Tob 8:4–8. On Tobiah's prayer see in detail Stuckenbruck, "Pleas for Deliverance from the Demonic in Early Jewish Texts," 69–72.

76 The Aramaic text is from Jonas C. Greenfield, Michael E. Stone, and Esther Eshel, *The Aramaic Levi Document: Edition, Translation, Commentary*, SVTP 19 (Leiden: Brill, 2004), 62–63.

77 On the translation "satan" in both ALD 3:9 and 11Q5 19:7 see Ryan E. Stokes, *The Satan: How God's Executioner Became the Enemy* (Grand Rapids: Eerdmans, 2019), 146–47. In addition to these two sources, see also Jub. 1:20 where Moses prays: "may the spirit of Belial not rule over them"; Jub 10:3, 6 where Noah asks: "may the wicked spirits not rule over them … may they not rule the spirits of the living … and may they not have power over the sons of the righteous"; Jub. 12:20 where Abraham prays that God will save him "from the power of the evil spirits who rule the thoughts of people's minds"; and Abraham's blessing of Jacob in Jub. 19:28: "May the spirits of Mastema not rule over you and your descendants" (James C. VanderKam, *Jubilees 1–21*, Hermeneia [Minneapolis: Fortress Press, 2018], 1:132, 394, 441, 584). On Abraham's prayer in Jubilees 12, see further Menahem Kister, "Body and Purification from Evil: Prayer Formulas and Concepts

formulation appears to be based on Ps 119:133: ואל תשלט בי כל און ("do not let iniquity dominate me" [NJPS]).[78]
- a transitive form of פח"ד, "to frighten." The closely related scrolls 4Q510 and 4Q511 (Songs of the Sage[a–b]) present the sectarian Maskil as entrusted with a task of scaring off demonic forces using a form of the same verb (admittedly a *piel*, and not a *hiphil*): לפחד ולב[הל] / כול רוחי מלאכי חבל ורוחות ממזרים שד^אים לילית והפוגעים פתע פתאום [ ]ן אחים, "in order to frighten and terri[fy] all the spirits of the ravaging angels and the bastard spirits, demons, Lilith, howlers and [...] and those who strike without warning" (4Q510 1 4–6; cf. also 4Q511 8 4; 35 6–8).[79]

While Esther Eshel suggests that apotropaic prayers/hymns constitute a discreet genre, Benjamin Wold, following on David Flusser's initial observation, proposes that they are better described as prayers/hymns incorporating apotropaic elements.[80] Flusser, in his initial exploration of some of the aforementioned texts, attempted to identify several themes that set apotropaic prayers apart, though these are not consistently present in all of them.[81] Still, following in his footsteps, it is of interest that 4Q147 1 shares several topics of concern with the same primary exemplars of apotropaic prayers, including some of Flusser's categories, such as "saving from troubles" and "salvation in the divine interest" broadly conceived:[82]
- divine protection (4Q147 1 3): ALD 3:11; Plea of Deliverance (11Q5 19:12 [=11Q6 4–5); Syriac Psalm III (11Q5 24:15)
- divine gift of strength (4Q147 1 8): ALD 3:6; Plea of Deliverance (11Q5 19:12–13)

---

in Second Temple Literature and Their Relationship to Later Rabbinic Literature," *Meghillot* 8–9 (2010): 243–84 (245–46; Hebrew).

78 Flusser, "'Apotropaic' Prayers," 197.

79 The English translation is from Joseph L. Angel, "Maskil, Community, and Religious Experience in the Song of the Sage (4Q510–511)", *DSD* 19 (2012): 1–27 (4). Qimron, *The Dead Sea Scrolls*, 2:316, reconstructs the lacuna (apparently with Isa 34:14) as following: אחים ו]ציים המשוטטים [והפוגעים. On the apotropaic features of this text(s), see Bilhah Nitzan, *Qumran Prayer and Religious Poetry*, STDJ 12 (Leiden: Brill, 1994), 227–72. She suggests that the praise of God is understood to scare away demons. On the list of demonic powers in this passage see Philip S. Alexander, "The Demonology of the Dead Sea Scrolls," in *The Dead Sea Scrolls After Fifty Years: A Comprehensive Assessment*, ed. Peter W. Flint and James C. VanderKam (Leiden; Brill, 1999): 331–53 (331–37).

80 Flusser, "'Apotropaic' Prayers," 202; Wold, "Apotropaic Prayer and the Matthean Lord's Prayer," 104.

81 Flusser, "'Apotropaic' Prayers," 203.

82 Flusser, "'Apotropaic' Prayers," 203. One might observe that, as in 4Q147 1, Plea for Deliverance also attests to rapid alterations from the second-person to third-person description of God (11Q5 19:5b–8a).

- God hears (4Q147 1 2, 10): Plea of Deliverance (11Q5 19:5–6)
- God heals (4Q147 1 7): Syriac Psalm III (11Q5 24:14)

While the suggestion that 4Q147 1 and 2 contained an apotropaic prayer(s) must remain tentative, in the event it did, then 4Q147 could have been classified as a "prophylactic" amulet, one that fends off threats, rather than deals with existing maladies.[83]

5. Is 4QPhyl N (4Q141) a Tefillin or an Amulet?

The identification of 4Q147, 4Q148, and Mur5 as amulets sheds new light on another miniature text from the Judean Desert regarded by Milik as tefillin, 4QPhyl N (4Q141). In several respects, the tefillin slips from the Judean Desert reveal a remarkable affinity to the later rabbinic tefillin.[84] At the same time, while rabbinic tradition insists on an extremely scrupulous and uniform execution of tefillin (m. Menachot 3:7), this small textual corpus is rather diverse.[85] Multiple tefillin from Qumran contain much larger portions from both Exodus and Deuteronomy than required by rabbinic halakha (see 2.4). Moreover, some Qumran tefillin feature a wide range of scribal phenomena, including lengthy omissions and additions.[86] Still, 4QPhyl N (4Q141) complicates the matters even further. According to Milik, this fragment is one of the three tefillin slips inscribed by the same scribe, 4Q139–141. He seems to have assumed that all three could have come from one and the same tefillin case. However, unlike any other tefillin known to us,

---

83 Perhaps one should mention here a fragmentary text 4Q444 (4QIncantation). It displays several significant affinities with the aforementioned Songs of the Sage[a–b] (4Q510–511). The sheet of leather on which 4Q444 is inscribed consists of three strips of leather (each containing four lines of text) sewn together. Esther Chazon, who edited this "prophylactic" text in Esther Chazon et al., *Qumran Cave 4.XX: Poetical and Liturgical Texts, Part 2*, DJD 29 (Oxford: Clarendon Press, 1999), 367–78, considered the possibility that its contents and codicological features suggest that this easy-to-fold manuscript was intended for magical use (368n3). I thank Prof. Chazon for drawing my attention to this text.
84 Cohn, *Tangled Up*, 56–79, offers the most exhaustive discussion of the evidence to date. He calls the tefillin from the Judean Desert the "Galapagos Islands" of the tefillin practice. See Yehudah B. Cohn, "Were Tefillin Phylacteries," *JJS* 59 (2008): 39–61 (40).
85 Cohn, "Were Tefillin Phylacteries," 41.
86 See George J. Brooke, "Deuteronomy 5–6 in the Phylacteries from Qumran Cave 4," in *Emanuel: Studies in the Hebrew Bible, Septuagint, and the Dead Sea Scrolls in Honour of Emanuel Tov*, ed. Shalom Paul et al., SVT 94 (Leiden: Brill, 2003), 57–70; Nathan Jastram, "Tefillin and Mezuzot," in *The Hebrew Bible: Volume 1B: Pentateuch, Former and Latter Prophets*, ed. Armin Lange and Emanuel Tov, Textual History of the Bible (Leiden: Brill, 2007), 105–11.

4QPhyl N contains Deut 32:14–20, 32–33.[87] To explain this anomaly, David Nakman suggests that 4Q141 is not a tefillah, but rather an amulet akin to those mentioned in the rabbinic sources.[88] At the same time, Yehudah Cohn, arguing against the tendency to interpret Second Temple evidence in light of rabbinic halakha, asserts that 4Q141 is a tefillin.[89] To support his argument, he points to the so-called excerpted scrolls found at Qumran that include passages commonly placed in tefillin (4QExod$^{d,\ e}$; 4QDeut$^{n,\ j,\ k1,\ q}$).[90] Given their affinity to tefillin and the rather small size of some of them (4QDeut$^{j,\ k1,\ n}$), these scrolls are often described as "special use" scrolls, devotional or liturgical.[91] One of these, 4QDeut^j (4Q37), includes, along with excerpts from Deut 5, 6, 8:5–10, and 11, also Deut 32:7–8.[92] An even more interesting case is the fragment 4QDeut^q (4Q44) containing Deut 32:9–10, 37–43. The scribe who produced this text did not continue beyond verse 43, and scholars suspect that it may have contained Deuteronomy 32 only. Partial stychometric arrangement of the verses (col. II and perhaps frag. 1, but not col. I) reflects, according to Falk, a liturgical use.[93] Alluding to the possibility that some of these excerpted scrolls (4QDeut$^{j,\ k1,\ n}$) are also tefillin, as is Papyrus Nash, Cohn uses their inclusion of Deuteronomy 32 as an indication of a scribal tradition associating this chapter from Deuteronomy with the passages placed in tefillin.[94] Moreover, he finds thematic affinities between Deuteronomy 11 and 32. And yet though Cohn prefers to classify 4QPhyl N as a tefillin, rather than amulet, his discussion of this text is a part of an overarching claim that tefillin are basically amulets intended to secure long life for their owners, a promise he finds both in Deut 11:21 and Deut 32:47.[95]

While the three newly deciphered texts do not fully resolve this enigma, they place 4QPhyl N in a new perspective. The very existence of written amulets closely resembling slips of tefillin lends weight to a proposal that 4QPhyl N is an amulet. In fact, several verses from Deuteronomy 32, one of the most often cited sections of Deuteronomy in the entire DSS corpus, have been used in later

---

[87] Milik, DJD 6:72–74.
[88] Nakman, "The Contents and the Order," 35–37.
[89] Cohn, *Tangled Up*, 76, 93–94.
[90] Cohn, *Tangled Up*, 67.
[91] Patrick W. Skehan and Eugene Ulrich in Eugene Ulrich et al., *Qumran Cave 4.IX: Deuteronomy, Joshua, Judges, Kings*, DJD 14 (Oxford: Clarendon Press, 1995), 138.
[92] Deut 5:1–11, 13–15, 21–33; 6:1–3; 8:5–10; 11:6–10, 12, 13; 11:21?+Exod 12:43–44; 12:46–13:5; Deut 32:7–8.
[93] Falk "The Contribution of the Qumran Scrolls to the Study of Ancient Jewish Liturgy," 633.
[94] Cohn, *Tangled Up*, 67, 68, 76, 96.
[95] Cohn, *Tangled Up*, 76, 93–94.

amulets and magical texts, Jewish, Christian, and Samaritan.⁹⁶ Most of them utilize the opening verses of Deuteronomy 32.⁹⁷ Interestingly, Deut 32:39, referring to YHWH's power to give life and heal, the very verse alluded to in 4Q147 1 line 7, is used in an amulet from the Cairo Genizah.⁹⁸

If this is correct, we seem to possess a Second Temple amulet that contains a plain scriptural text (4QPhyl N) and three non-scriptural amulets, some of which incorporate biblical quotations (4Q147; Mur5). If 4QPhyl N were indeed placed in a container along with two tefillin slips written by the same scribe, 4QPhyl L (=Deut 5:7–24) and 4QPhyl M (=Exod 12:44–13:10; Deut 5:33–6:5), as Milik seems to suggest, a question of differentiating between amulets and tefillin needs further attention.⁹⁹ This sets the stage for the discussion of Matt 23:5.

6. Matthew 23:5

Matthew 23:5 famously criticizes Pharisees for doing "all their works to be seen by people." In particular, "They broaden their phylacteries; they enlarge the fringes."¹⁰⁰ The Greek φυλακτήριον employed here by the Gospel denotes "means

---

96 See Armin Lange and Matthias Weigold, *Biblical Quotations and Allusions in Second Temple Jewish Literature*, JAJS 5 (Göttingen: Vandenhoeck & Ruprecht, 2001), 109–10; Ariel Feldman, "Deuteronomy in the Texts from the Judean Desert," *The Oxford Handbook of Deuteronomy*, ed. Don C. Benjamin (forthcoming).
97 In a forthcoming study on a recently published amulet in Greek citing Deut 32:1 (Gideon Bohak and Christopher A. Faraone, "'Pay Heed, O Heaven, and I Will Speak': A Greek Amulet with Biblical, Angelic and Female Names") Bohak and Faraone refer to Genizah 17 quoting Deut 32:1–3 in Naveh and Shaked, *Magic Spells and Formulae*, 184; Amulet 32 citing Deut 32:1–3 in Kotansky, *Greek Magical Amulets*, 126–54; and several Genizah texts referenced in Dorothea M. Salzer, *Die Magie der Anspielung: Form und Funktion der biblischen Anspielungen in den magischen Texten der Kairoer Geniza*, TSAJ 134 (Tübingen: Mohr Siebeck, 2008), 99, 404. I am grateful to Prof. Bohak for sharing with me a draft of this paper. On the inclusion of verses from Deuteronomy 32 in one of the late Samaritan amulets described by Bowman see his "Phylacteries," 532.
98 Salzer, *Die Magie der Anspielung*, 99 and note 309. The possibility that 4QPhyl N is an amulet is putting in new perspective David Lincicum's concern that Deuteronomy (well represented in liturgical texts from Qumran) does not seem to play a significant role in Qumran apotropaic prayers and incantations. David Lincicum, "Scripture and Apotropaism in the Second Temple Period," *BN* 138 (2008): 63–87 (87).
99 Milik, DJD 6:70.
100 Ulrich Luz, *Matthew 21–28: A Commentary*, transl. James E. Crouch, Hermeneia (Minneapolis: Fortress, 2005), 96. I am grateful to Prof. Warren Carter for his help with the relevant bibliography on Matthew 23.

of protection," a "safeguard," an "amulet."¹⁰¹ Most commentators, both ancient and modern, suggest that Matthew refers here to tefillin.¹⁰² Yet, why does he call them "amulets"? Several explanations have been proposed. First, some have argued that this is a misnomer reflecting a superficial familiarity with the Pharisaic practice. The passage misses the difference between a tefillin containing verses from Exodus and Deuteronomy and an amulet.¹⁰³ Indeed, the three newly deciphered texts indicate that the difference between a rolled tefillin slip and 4Q148 could have been a very fine one. Moreover, if 4QPhyl N was also an amulet, it would require an intimate knowledge of the opponents' views to know that the items in question contained other scriptural passages besides the customary Exodus 13 and Deuteronomy 6 and 11 and therefore were not amulets, but tefillin. A second proposal suggests that the Matthean word choice might be compared to the Rabbinic use of the noun קמיע utilized (though very rarely) to describe both tefillin and amulets, probably because of the physical similarities between the two.¹⁰⁴ In other words, the author knew rather well that Pharisees carried tefillin and not amulets, but for him both could be described by the same word.¹⁰⁵ For this argument, the three texts also provide support as they indicate that a similarity between amulets and tefillin dates back to Second Temple times. Third, it has been proposed that by describing tefillin as phylacteries, Matthew criticizes the Pharisaic custom of wearing tefillin.¹⁰⁶ One must note that if this is indeed a polemic against the practice itself, it is rather overshadowed by the main line of critique reflected in this passage, namely

---

101 Andrea Becker, "Phylakterion," *Brill's New Pauly Encyclopedia of the Ancient World* (Leiden: Brill, 2007), 11:206–207; Ruth Satinover Fagen, "Phylacteries," *ABD* 5:368–70 (370).
102 See a detailed discussion and pertinent bibliography in Tigay, "On the Term Phylacteries"; W.D. Davies and Dale C. Allison, *The Gospel according to Saint Matthew*, ICC (Edinburgh: T&T Clark, 1997), 1:17–19; 3:273; Luz, *Matthew 21–28*, 103–104; Cohn, *Tangled Up*, 109-11. On the interpretation of this passage in patristic sources and on the wider topic of the use of scriptural texts as amulets in early Christian communities, see Robert Matthew Calhoun, "The Gospel(-Amulet) as God's Power for Salvation," *Early Christianity* 10 (2019): 21–55. I am grateful to Dr. Calhoun for making his study available to me.
103 Fagen, "Phylacteries," 370, refers to the incorrect "view (of tefillin) of the Christian community in 70 to 90 C. E."
104 Tigay, "On the Term Phylacteries," 45–53.
105 Yonatan Adler, "Review of Yehuda B. Cohn, *Tangled up in Text: Tefillin and the Ancient World* (Brown Judaic Studies, 351), Brown Judaic Studies, Providence, RI 2008, xi+169 pp," *Zion* 76 (2011): 383–87 (387; Hebrew), offers a variation on Tigay's proposal and surmises that the Greek term was intimated by the physical similarity between the amulets and tefillin and a lack of a better word to describe the ritual to someone unfamiliar with it.
106 For G. George Fox, "The Matthean Misrepresentation of Tephillîn," *JNES* 3 (1942): 373–77 (374), it is either a mistake or a deliberate misrepresentation. Luz, *Matthew 21–28*, 104, suggests that it is a polemical description perhaps indicating Matthew's non-Pharisaic milieu. Daniel

the hypocritical broadening of tefillin. Still, once again, the three new texts might support this line of thinking because a polemical description of tefillin as amulets would only be possible if the readers were familiar with a contemporary Jewish use of amulets. Fourth, Matthean phylacteries might have indeed been amulets, not tefillin, a claim raised in particular by John Bowman, who, for a comparison, pointed to the written amulets used by Samaritans. He adduced several rather late (medieval) specimen which were made out of parchment, folded (in a desirable size, smaller or larger), and placed on one's hand without utilizing any kind of container.[107] This suggestion is dismissed by Tigay, who observes that a charge of a hypocritical exploitation of a religious symbol could only work with reference to a tefillin, not for an amulet.[108] Had Bowman had access to 4Q147, 4Q148, and Mur5, his case would have been much stronger, since these three appear to have belonged to a Jewish community and are dated to the late Second Temple times. As to Tigay's objection, it partially depends on an assumption that in the late Second Temple times tefillin had already attained the status of a religious symbol. However, one wonders whether the mere presence of miniature texts resembling later tefillin among the discoveries in the Judean Desert warrants such an assumption.

In light of our three new texts I would like to suggest that Matthew's wording reflects a well-informed Jewish non-polemical view that considers the objects Pharisees are said to enlarge to be *amulets*. This may appear to be a variation on Bowman's proposal, but it is one that grounds this claim differently than he does. All the interpretations cited above, including that of Bowman, assume a strict dichotomy between amulets and tefillin. However, such a dichotomy is borrowed from the later rabbinic sources and may well be anachronistic. Our three or four miniature texts blur the line between amulets and tefillin. They indicate that Matthean phylacteries could have included the so-called tefillin scriptural passages, non-scriptural texts like our three newly deciphered ones, Deuteronomy 32 or any combination of the three. We will probably never know. What I suggest is that whatever texts may have been associated with Matthew's "phylacteries," for Matthew, they were all amulets.[109]

J. Harrington, *Sacra Pagina: The Gospel of Matthew* (Collegeville: The Liturgical Press, 1991), 320–21, also assumes a polemical stance here.
107 Bowman, "Phylacteries," 523–38.
108 Tigay, "On the Term Phylacteries," 48. For a further, somewhat more favorable review, see Kenneth G. Newport, *The Sources and Sitz im Leben of Matthew 23* (Sheffield: Sheffield Academic Press, 1995), 84–88.
109 For a similar conclusion arrived at from a different set of arguments (unaware of 4Q147–148 and Mur5), see Cohn, "Were Tefillin Phylacteries," 56. The notion that phylacteries, i.e., amulets, are a "somewhat derogatory term" underlying Luz's interpretation, appears to be anachronistic

Whether Matthean Pharisees or other groups within Second Temple Judaism would share such a view of the items they were wearing, we have no way to ascertain. With reference to the findings from the Judean Desert, Philip Alexander cautiously observes that it remains unknown whether the individuals who used miniature excerpts from Exodus and Deuteronomy considered them "as protection against demons or simply as the literal fulfillment of the injunctions in *Deuteronomy* 6.8–9."[110] And yet, the history of tefillin practice in Judaism throughout the ages demonstrates that like amulets they were often believed to possess apotropaic qualities.[111] Moreover, in recent years multiple scholars have argued that tefillin originated and/or functioned as amulets.[112] The most detailed argument has been marshalled by Judah Cohn who suggests that the emergence of tefillin sometime during the Hasmonean period was influenced by the widespread use of amulets in the Greco-Roman world.[113] Searching for the origins of the custom,

---

(Luz, *Matthew 21–28*, 104). Compare Bohak's observation (*Ancient Jewish Magic*, 370) that "contrary to our own instinctive assumption that amulets are a magical implement, the rabbis saw amulets as a standard constituent of a person's daily garments. Thus, their many references to amulets have nothing to do with their discussion of magic, and do not even raise the question whether their use is forbidden or permitted, a question which their Christian contemporaries found so vexing, and so worthy of their pious ruminations."

110 Philip S. Alexander, "Magic and Magical Texts," in *Encyclopedia of the Dead Sea Scrolls*, ed. Lawrence H. Schiffman and James C. VanderKam (Oxford: Oxford University Press, 2000), 1:502–504 (502).

111 Tigay, "On the Term Phylacteries," 51, adduces ample evidence of amuletic use of tefillin, yet rejects the idea that they originated as amulets. In his Hebrew entry on tefillin he seems to be willing to entertain a possibility that rabbinic tefillin came to replace or to reshape an earlier apotropaic practice. Jeffrey Tigay, "Tefillin," in *Encyclopedia Biblica* (Jerusalem: Mosad Bialik, 1982), 8:883–95 (894; Hebrew). See also Davies and Allison, *Matthew*, 1:18.

112 For a detailed overview of tefillin scholarship, see Cohn, *Tangled Up*, 3–15. To supplement it, one may mention that Bowman, "Phylacteries," 529–30, suggested that tefillin "might have been a concession to the fairly common ancient practice of wearing amulets ... but they also represented an attempt to control rigidly, and under the framework of the Oral Torah, the tendency of the people to wear amulets." Satinover Fagen, "Phylacteries," 370, wonders whether "the very custom of wearing phylacteries might have emerged as a popular superstition, one which was then made normative by the leaders of Jewish community, who stripped the symbol of its original magical overtones and infused it with a more 'legitimate' religious significance. The choice of the term *tĕpillîn* seen as the plural of 'prayer,' would thus be part of the rabbinic polemic to replace the original prophylactic nature of phylacteries with the liturgical nature of *tĕpillîn*."

113 Cohn, *Tangled Up*, 93–95, 146–55. For a critique of his thesis, see, for instance, Adler, "Review of Yehuda B. Cohn, *Tangled up in Text*," 383–87. In light of 4Q147, 4Q148, Mur5, and 4QPhyl N, perhaps there is no need to over-emphasize outside influence in the development of the practice, as these indicate a presence of written amulets of an explicit Jewish nature. Interestingly, in his recent study of amulets from the Roman Imperial period, Faraone, *Transformation*, 178, attempts to explain the prevalence of amulets in part by "a growing desire among some

Cohn takes a closer look at the term tefillin. The widespread notion that it is a plural of תפילה and reflects the use of the two objects during prayer is hardly satisfactory, for rabbinic sources suggest that tefillin were worn throughout the day.[114] Cohn draws attention to the earliest and probably only use of the noun תפ(י)לה with reference to an object outside of the later rabbinic texts.[115] An Aramaic papyrus from Egypt, C 3.28 (P. Cowley 81), lists among items entrusted to a certain Jonathan twenty תפלה זי כסף. These have been understood to be silver amulets.[116] For Cohn, the name suggests a perception of an amulet as a sort of prayer.[117] However, in light of 4Q147 one might suggest that such silver amulets were called תפלה because they contained prayers.

7. Questions for Future Study

The proposed identification of 4Q147, 4Q148, Mur5, and 4QPhyl N as amulets poses several questions for further investigation. Of the many miniature texts from the Judean Desert, those containing a limited array of verses from Exodus and Deuteronomy, the tefillin passages, are the vast majority.[118] Looking at Qumran Cave 4 specifically, only two yield non-scriptural texts (4Q147, 4Q148), whereas one, 4QPhyl N, holds a "middle ground," featuring a scriptural text,

---

Greeks to imitate the scribal practices of older and presumably wiser eastern cultures, especially the Mesopotamian, the Egyptian, and the Jewish."

114 On the form תפילין, on the pattern of תהלים, see A.M. Habermann, "The Phylacteries in Antiquity," *Eretz-Israel* 3 (1954): 174–77 (174); Cohn, *Tangled Up*, 147–48. On wearing tefillin throughout the day see b. Sukkah 28a; b. Menahot 36b and Jeffrey H. Tigay, "Tefillin," in *Encyclopaedia Biblica* (Jerusalem: Mosad Bialik, 1982), 8:883–895 (884; Hebrew). On the traditional explanation, see Habermann, "The Phylacteries in Antiquity," 174, though he himself refers to the passage from b. Sukkah on page 175.

115 Cohn, *Tangled Up*, 147. Tigay, "Tefillin," 887, adduces also a text from Ugarit describing Baal as carrying תפלי on his head: ראשה תפלי, and suggests that the ending *yod* is an ancient feminine ending.

116 Bezalel Porten and Ada Yardeni, *Textbook of Aramaic Documents from Ancient Egypt, Volume 3: Literature, Accounts, Lists* (Jerusalem: Hebrew University, 1993), 260, 267, translate this phrase as "20 amulet(s) of silver" (267). So also Moshe Weinfeld, *Deuteronomy 1–11*, AB (New York: Doubleday, 1991), 335. He thinks that the word tefillin originally denoted amulet. These items are mentioned along with the "string(s) of beads" (line 105).

117 Cohn, *Tangled Up*, 147. Tigay's ("Tefillin," 887–88) use of this source seems to suggest that he reads it (with m. Megillah 4:8 prohibiting overlaying tefillin with gold) as referring to a case of tefillin.

118 Cohn, *Tangled Up*, 56, counts forty-four slips of tefillin/mezuzot and twenty-five housings. The numbers need to be adjusted to reflect the new identification of 4Q147, 4Q148, and Mur 5.

though not from one of the "tefillin" passages.[119] Are these numbers a mere coincidence? Do they testify to the popularity of the practice that rabbis will later call tefillin?[120] Was this apparent preference for miniature texts with Exodus and Deuteronomy specific to a particular community or does it represent wider Jewish circles?[121] Answers to these questions, which will continue to complexify our understanding of Second Temple Jewish practices, including those pertaining to prayer, must await further study, which hopefully will be informed by the forthcoming publication of the recently re-discovered unopened tefillin from Qumran.[122]

---

[119] Qumran caves feature both conservative and expansive approaches to Exodus and Deuteronomy tefillin passages. For a discussion of the distribution of these, see Adler, "Distribution," esp. 172–73. Since the Bar-Kochbah caves feature only a conservative approach to tefillin passages, he suggests, following others, the possibility of a diachronic development, from expansive to conservative approaches to tefillin passages.

[120] On the dating of tefillin practice, see Cohn's detailed discussion in his *Tangled Up*, 45–109. He suggests that our earliest unequivocal evidence of the practice in written sources is Josephus, *Ant.* 4.196. He doubts whether the reference to wearing "a sign on our hands" in Let. Aris. 159 implies a practice of donning tefillin, whereas Philo's discussion in *Spec.* 4:137–42 appears to him as implying only some kind of mezuzah practice. For a more positive view of the passage from Letter of Aristeas, see Satinover Fagen, "Phylacteries," 369. Weinfeld, *Deuteronomy 6–11*, 335, attempts to link Philo's description of "the rules of justice" as "shaking before the eyes" (4.137) as compatible with the tiny phylacteries from Qumran and the rabbinic prohibition of suspending the tefillin on the head below hairline. For Philo's wording based apparently on the LXX rendering of this verse, see Jeffrey H. Tigay, "On the Meaning of Ṭ(W)ṬPT," *JBL* 101 (1982): 321–31.

[121] On the hypothesis that Qumran tefillin exhibiting an expansive approach are sectarian, see Milik, DJD 6:37–47. His arguments are analyzed and discarded by Cohn, *Tangled Up*, 73–75.

[122] On these tefillin to be published by Yonatan Adler see meanwhile Ilan Ben Zion, "Uncovered in Jerusalem, 9 Tiny Unopened Dead Sea Scrolls," *The Times of Israel*, March 12, 2019 (https://www.timesofisrael.com/nine-tiny-new-dead-sea-scrolls-come-to-light/).

Matthias Henze
Prayer in 2 Baruch

The Syriac Apocalypse of Baruch, or 2 Baruch, is a Jewish text from the late first century CE.[1] That means that, strictly speaking, 2 Baruch falls outside the chronological borders of Second Temple Judaism, since it was composed after, and, in fact, in response to the destruction of Jerusalem. And yet, in form and content, 2 Baruch is very much part of the literature of the Second Temple period: it is an apocalypse of the historical type, much like the Enochic Apocalypse of Weeks (1 En. 93:1–10, 91:11–17), the Animal Apocalypse (1 En. 85–90), and the book of Daniel, all written well before the year 70 CE. And it picks up and continues to develop a host of apocalyptic themes and topics that are already found in earlier apocalyptic writings. While 2 Baruch responds to a major disruption in ancient Israel, the destruction of Jerusalem and its temple, it gives testimony to an intellectual continuity beyond the loss of the temple.[2]

2 Baruch survives in its entirety in a single Syriac manuscript, the Milan Bible or Codex Ambrosianus, a sixth or seventh century CE manuscript.[3] That Syriac text, which is a translation of a lost Greek version, will be the basis of this

---

1 Writing over a century ago, Robert H. Charles, *The Apocalypse of Baruch: Translated from the Syriac* (London: Adam and Charles Black, 1896), lxiv–lxv, proposed that 2 Baruch consists of several sources and reached its final form between 130 and 140 CE. Louis Ginzberg, "Apocalypse of Baruch (Syriac)," *Jewish Encyclopedia* (New York, 1902), 551–56, opted for a date "between the years 70 and 130" (555), which has since become the majority opinion. Rivka Nir, *The Destruction of Jerusalem and the Idea of Redemption in the Syriac Apocalypse of Baruch*, EJL 20 (Atlanta: Society of Biblical Literature, 2003), has attempted to demonstrate that 2 Baruch is a Christian book. And Martin Goodman, "The Date of 2 Baruch," in *Revealed Wisdom: Studies in Apocalyptic in Honour of Christopher Rowland*, ed. John Ashton (Leiden: Brill, 2014), 116–21 (120), has argued that we should "allow for the very real possibility that it [2 Baruch] was composed before 70 C. E." Both are minority positions, and neither is compelling.
2 Daniel R. Schwartz and Zeev Weiss, eds., *Was 70 CE a Watershed in Jewish History? On Jews and Judaism before and after the Destruction of the Second Temple*, Ancient Judaism and Early Christianity 78 (Leiden: Brill, 2012); see especially Daniel R. Schwartz, "Introduction: Was 70 CE a Watershed in Jewish History? Three Stages of Modern Scholarship, and a Renewed Effort," 1–19.
3 Antonio Maria Ceriani, ed., *A Facsimile Edition of the Peshitto Old Testament Based on Codex Ambrosianus (7a1). Translatio Syra Pescitto Veteris Testamenti: Ex codice Ambrosiano, Sec. fere VI* (Piscataway: Gorgias Press, 2013); Liv Ingeborg Lied, "2 Baruch and the Syriac Codex Ambrosianus (7a1): Studying Old Testament Pseudepigrapha in Their Manuscript Context," *JSP* 26 (2016): 67–107; Liv Ingeborg Lied, "2 Baruch: Syriac," in *The Textual History of the Bible: Volume 2B: Deuterocanonical Scriptures*, ed. Frank Feder and Matthias Henze (Leiden: Brill), 46–53.

https://doi.org/10.1515/9783110624526-010

study.⁴ Parts of the apocalypse have survived in other Syriac and Greek manuscripts. There is also a later Arabic version from the library of St. Catherine's Monastery, a "rather free rendering" of a Syriac text.⁵ A highly complex work, 2 Baruch offers an apocalyptic program intended for the post-70 CE Jewish community in and around Jerusalem that seeks to make sense of the time interval between the fall of the Second Temple and the arrival of the end times, which the author thought to be imminent.

1. Reading 2 Baruch as an Independent Text

Since its rediscovery by Antonio Maria Ceriani in the late eighteen-hundreds in the Ambrosian Library in Milan, 2 Baruch has been the stepchild and little sister of 4 Ezra, a widely studied apocalypse to which 2 Baruch is closely related. The exact nature of their relationship remains somewhat of a mystery.⁶ The first Western readers of 2 Baruch who wrote about it in the late nineteenth and early twentieth century were united in their verdict that 2 Baruch is the inferior of the two works.⁷ A recurring point of criticism leveled at 2 Baruch has been the book's apparent lack of a clear structure: whereas 4 Ezra is neatly divided into seven, easily identifiable parts with a discernable mid-point in the fourth part and a clear progression

---

4 A critical edition of the Syriac text, without the Epistle (2 Baruch 78:1–87:1), has been prepared by Sven Dedering, "Apocalypse of Baruch," in Sven Dedering and Raphael J. Bidawid, *Apocalypse of Baruch; 4 Esdras*, The Old Testament in Syriac according to the Peshiṭta Version 4.3 (Leiden: Brill, 1973), i–iv, 1–44; the English translation is by Matthias Henze, "2 Baruch," in Michael E. Stone and Matthias Henze, *4 Ezra and 2 Baruch: Translations, Introductions, and Notes* (Minneapolis: Fortress Press, 2013), 83–141.
5 Adriana Drint, "2 Baruch: Arabic," in *The Textual History of the Bible: Volume 2B: Deuterocanonical Scriptures*, 53–59 (53). For an edition and English translation of the Arabic text, see Frederik Leemhuis, Albertus F. J. Klijn, and G. J. H. Van Gelder, *The Arabic Text of the Apocalypse of Baruch* (Leiden: Brill, 1986).
6 "In fact, the existence of an intimate relationship is quite obvious, but the direction of dependence is very difficult to determine. If there were decisive arguments in one or the other direction, of course, the matter would not still be the subject of difference of opinion." Michael E. Stone, *Fourth Ezra: A Commentary on the Book of Fourth Ezra*, Hermeneia (Minneapolis: Fortress Press, 1990), 39; Matthias Henze, "*4 Ezra* and *2 Baruch*: Literary Composition and Oral Performance in First-Century Apocalyptic Literature," *JBL* 131 (2012): 181–200.
7 See, for example, Ernest Renan, *Les Évangiles et la seconde génération chrétienne* (Paris: Ancienne Maison Michel Lévy Frères, 1877), 517; Hermann Gunkel, "Das vierte Buch Esra," in *Die Apokryphen und Pseudepigraphen des Alten Testaments*, ed. Emil Kautzsch (Tübingen: Mohr, 1900), 331–402, 351; Ginzberg, "Apocalypse of Baruch," 555.

of thought, 2 Baruch does not appear to have any such features that give it a clear structure.

More recently, modern interpreters have come to the rescue of 2 Baruch and have argued that 2 Baruch, too, has a sevenfold structure. In the recent edition of his introduction to apocalyptic literature, for example, John Collins cautiously adopts a division into seven sections, though he warns that the matter is far from certain.[8] Lutz Doering is another defender of the heptadic structure. Well aware of the complexity of 2 Baruch's composition, Doering pays particular attention to the recurring motifs and their placement throughout the book, such as Baruch's seven-day fasts and his public convocations, and opts for seven parts, though he leaves the door open for a division of the book into five units.[9] The ongoing discussion about 2 Baruch's composition underscores the complexity of the issue. Surveying the various proposals that divide the apocalypse into seven sections, one is struck by how few proposals agree on the same demarcations between sections. The idea of a seven-part division is imported from 4 Ezra. It seems highly doubtful that any reader of 2 Baruch unfamiliar with 4 Ezra would have proposed such a structure.

When we leave the comparative reading of 4 Ezra and 2 Baruch aside for a moment and read 2 Baruch on its own terms, it turns out that 2 Baruch has its own, carefully designed composition. One way in which the author structures the text is through the use of literary genres. Apocalypses by definition are generic hybrids, texts that deploy the literary features of more than one genre.[10] 2 Baruch is an apocalypse of the historical type.[11] But its author also makes strategic use of several other literary genres to convey distinct aspects of 2 Baruch's apocalyptic program. Understanding the role of different genres in the text is of critical importance for understanding the book as a whole.

Apart from genres, another way in which the author structures the text, as Doering and others have pointed out, is through narrative markers. These markers

---

[8] John J. Collins, *The Apocalyptic Imagination: An Introduction to Jewish Apocalyptic Literature*, 3rd ed. (Grand Rapids: Eerdmans, 2016), 256–66.

[9] Lutz Doering, "The Epistle of Baruch and its Role in *2 Baruch*," in *Fourth Ezra and Second Baruch: Reconstruction after the Fall*, ed. Matthias Henze and Gabriele Boccaccini, JSJSup 164 (Leiden: Brill, 2013), 151–73 (155–56).

[10] On the genre of apocalyptic texts, see Carol A. Newsom, "Spying Out the Land: A Report from Genology," in *Seeking Out the Wisdom of the Ancients: Essays Offered to Honor Michael V. Fox on the Occasion of His Sixty-Fifth Birthday*, ed. Ronald L. Troxel, Kelvin G. Friebel, and Dennis R. Magary (Winona Lake: Eisenbrauns, 2005), 437–50; John J. Collins, "Introduction: The Genre Apocalypse Reconsidered," in *Apocalypse, Prophecy, and Pseudepigraphy: On Jewish Apocalyptic Literature* (Grand Rapids: Eerdmans, 2015), 1–20.

[11] Collins, *Apocalyptic Imagination*, 3–11.

take several forms: short phrases like "And after these [things]" (13:1; 22:1; 31:1), date formulae (1:1; 77:18), or a change of Baruch's location (20:6; 21:1; 35:1; 44:1; 47:2; 77:1). They can also take the form of literary motifs, such as a seven-day interval, often associated with fasting (9:1; 10:1; 12:5; 21:1; 43:3; 47:2–48:1), Baruch falling asleep (36:1; 52:8), waking up (37:1; 53:12), or becoming very weak (21:26; 48:25; 55:1), Baruch's fasts (5:6; 9:1; 12:5; 21:1; 43:3; 47:2), and the arrival of an angel (55:3). The deliberate employment of genres, in combination with narrative markers such as these, are the two most reliable indicators of 2 Baruch's composition.

With these observations in mind, 2 Baruch's structure can be outlined as follows.[12]

- 1:1–9:1   Narrative Prologue/Revelatory Dialogue
- 10:1–12:5 Baruch's Prayer
- 13:1–20:6 Revelatory Dialogue
- 21:1–26   Baruch's Prayer
- 22:1–30:5 Revelatory Dialogue
- 31:1–34:1 First public Address
- 35:1–5   Baruch's Prayer
- 36:1–43:3 Baruch's First Vision: Vision, Prayer (38:1–4), Interpretation
- 44:1–47:2 Second Public Address
- 48:1–25   Baruch's Prayer
- 48:26–52:8 Revelatory Dialogue
- 53:1–75:8 Baruch's Second Vision: Vision, Prayer (54:1–22), Interpretation
- 76:1–5   Revelatory Dialogue
- 77:1–17   Third Public Address
- 77:18-26   Narrative Epilogue
- 78:1–87:1 The Epistle

Following the prototypical format of early Jewish apocalypses, 2 Baruch has a narrative frame (*Rahmenerzählung*; 1:1–9:1 and 77:18–26). Both the narrative prologue and epilogue are introduced by a date formula in 1:1 and 77:18, the only such formulae in the book. Attached to the narrative frame at the end of the book is Baruch's Epistle (78:1–87:1). During 2 Baruch's reception history in Syriac Christianity, the epistle circulated independently of the rest of the apocalypse.[13] What

---

[12] Adopted from Matthias Henze, *Jewish Apocalypticism in Late First Century Israel: Reading Second Baruch in Context*, TSAJ 142 (Tübingen: Mohr Siebeck, 2011), 41–53.
[13] In the Codex Ambrosianus, the Epistle of Baruch occurs twice, once as an independent composition (176v–177v), located in between the Letter of Jeremiah and the book of Baruch, and again as part of the Syriac Apocalypse of Baruch (265v–267r). Mark F. Whitters, *The Epistle of Second*

holds 2 Baruch together is the revelatory dialogue (*Offenbarungsdialog*) between God and Baruch, which starts, rather abruptly, in 1:2 with the divine announcement of the impending destruction of Jerusalem and ends in 76:5, when, echoing the story of Moses's death, God tells Baruch to ascend a mountain and to prepare for his departure from this world in forty days. The dialogue is critically important in 2 Baruch: a genre with deep roots in the Hebrew Bible, both in the prophetic (e. g., Jeremiah) and the wisdom (e. g., Job) corpora, the dialogue steadily drives the action forward.[14]

2. The Prayers in 2 Baruch: Some Initial Observations

There are six prayers in 2 Baruch: in 10:1–12:5; 21:4–25; 35:2–5; 38:1–4; 48:2–24; and 54:1–22. The book's protagonist, Baruch, is the only person in 2 Baruch who prays. In the main manuscript, the Codex Ambrosianus, three of the six prayers are introduced with a brief superscription: in 21:1 "The Prayer of Baruch, Son of Neriah" (ܨܠܘܬܐ ܕܒܪܘܟ ܒܪ ܢܪܝܐ); in 48:1 "The Prayer of Baruch" (ܨܠܘܬܐ ܕܒܪܘܟ); and in 54:1 "The Prayer of Baruch" (ܨܠܘܬܐ ܕܒܪܘܟ). In the Syriac text, three of the six prayers are thus marked as distinct textual units in the book (no other subsection in the book is introduced by such a heading).[15] There is no way of knowing who first wrote these headings, whether they stem from the Syriac translator, whether they were introduced into the Greek text that underlies the Syriac, or whether they have always been part of 2 Baruch.[16] Violet says that they stem "probably from a later hand," without giving any reason; his view is

---

Baruch: A Study in Form and Message, JSPSup 42 (Sheffield: Sheffield Academic Press, 2003); Liv Ingeborg Lied, "Between 'Text Witness' and 'Text on the Page': Trajectories in the History of Editing the Epistle of Baruch," in *Snapshots of Evolving Traditions: Jewish and Christian Manuscript Culture, Textual Fluidity and New Philology*, ed. Liv Ingeborg Lied and Hugo Lundhaug, TU 175 (Berlin: De Gruyter, 2017), 272–96.
14 Mikhail M. Bakhtin, *The Dialogic Imagination: Four Essays*, University of Texas Press Slavic Series 1 (Austin: University of Texas Press, 2004); Karina Martin Hogan, *Theologies in Conflict in 4 Ezra: Wisdom, Debate, and Apocalyptic Solution*, JSJSup 130 (Leiden: Brill, 2008).
15 In personal conversation, Liv Ingeborg Lied has brought to my attention that ff. 258v–259r of the Codex Ambrosianus, which contain the first superscription, have wax stains and an erased title. The wax stain at least suggests that this passage was actively read.
16 The Arabic version has superscriptions in the same places, albeit with some variations: 21:1 "This is the Prayer of Baruch, the Son of Narkha"; 48:1 "Prayer of Baruch, the Son of Narkah"; and 54:1 "Prayer of Baruch, the Son of Narkah." See Leemhuis et al., *Arabic Text*, 36, 64, 80.

endorsed by Bogaert.[17] All six prayers are followed by a divine response. In most cases, the response takes the form of a dialogue that continues right after Baruch's prayer: God addresses the concerns Baruch has just voiced (13:2; 22:2; 39:1; 48:26). In chapter 36, Baruch receives a vision in response to his prayer, the Vision of the Forest, the Vine, and the Spring (36:1–37:1), which is followed by another prayer (38:1–4). In 38:1–4 and 54:1–22, Baruch prays for an explanation of the vision he has just seen. In both cases his prayer is answered, and Baruch receives a divine interpretation (39:1–43:3; 55:3–76:5).

As the superscriptions that introduce three of Baruch's prayers make clear, prayer and dialogue with God are distinct genres in 2 Baruch, at least in the Syriac text as we have it. The relationship between them presents the modern interpreter with a conundrum: if both prayer and dialogue are discrete speech forms in the apocalypse, representing distinct ways for Baruch to communicate with God, then how are they different from each other? Why interrupt the narrative and insert prayers into the text when Baruch is constantly in conversation with God anyhow? If prayer is a form of dialogue, or, perhaps more plausibly, dialogue is a form of prayer, then what are the distinct features and functions of the prayers in 2 Baruch? To answer these questions, we first have to turn to the prayers individually.

When reading the prayers in 2 Baruch, there are four aspects in particular that require consideration:

Context. The prayers in 2 Baruch are carefully embedded in their current narrative contexts. They cannot be understood without paying attention to their present locations. Whereas some prayers in Second Temple texts are so obviously ill-situated in their present narratives that it is quite obvious that they were not written by the same author but are later interpolations (an obvious example is the Prayer of Azariah in Old Greek Dan 3:24–45), this does not appear to be the case in 2 Baruch. There is nothing to indicate that any of the six prayers was originally an independent composition that was later inserted into the book.

Setting. All prayers in 2 Baruch are framed by brief narratives that set the prayers apart and mark them within their immediate contexts. These narrative frames serve to introduce the particular circumstances of the prayer and, at the end of the passage, form the transition to the next part of the book.

Genre. The prayers in 2 Baruch take two different forms: there are two laments of the individual (10:1–12:5; 35:2–5) and four petitionary prayers (21:4–25; 38:1–4; 48:2–24; 54:1–22).[18]

---

17 Bruno Violet, *Die Apokalypsen des Esra und des Baruch in Deutscher Gestalt* (Leipzig: J. C. Hinrichs'sche Buchhandlung, 1924), 232; Pierre-Maurice Bogaert, *Apocalypse de Baruch: Introduction, Traduction du Syriaque et Commentaire*, Sources chrétiennes 144–45 (Paris: Éditions du Cerf, 1969), 2:48.

18 Randall D. Chesnutt, "Prayer of a Convert to Judaism (Joseph and Aseneth 12–13)," in *Prayer from Alexander to Constantine: A Critical Anthology*, ed. Mark C. Kiley, et al. (London: Routledge,

The author of 2 Baruch has a tendency to return to the same topics multiple times throughout the book and gradually develop them further (e. g., Adam; the significance of the Torah; various divine attributes are mentioned repeatedly, such as God the Creator, God the Master over time). That means that some of the central themes Baruch brings up in his prayers are also found elsewhere in the book. Here, again, the author is genre-savvy: different genres lend themselves to the development of different aspects of the same topic.

Function. A prayer can have more than one function: there is the function of the prayer within the composition of 2 Baruch (here, the prayer reflects the needs of the narrative), and the function of the prayer for 2 Baruch's late first-century CE audience (here, the prayer reflects the needs of the intended audience). Methodologically, the latter is admittedly speculative, since we know little about that audience.[19]

3. Baruch's Prayers: A Closer Look

2 Baruch 10:1–12:5: Baruch's Lament

The first prayer in 2 Baruch is located between the book's narrative prologue in chapters 1–9 and the first extended dialogue section between God and Baruch in chapters 13–20. Having witnessed the destruction of Jerusalem, Baruch and Jeremiah lament and fast together for seven days (9:1). Then God sends Jeremiah away to the exiles in Babylon, whereas Baruch returns to the temple ruins (10:1–5), where he says his prayer (10:6–12:4). The author thus paints a vivid picture of the harrowing scene following the destruction of the city: Baruch and Jeremiah mourn, Jeremiah leaves, and Baruch, now left alone, says the book's first prayer while sitting on the ruins of the demolished temple. The focus of the scene is on Baruch's lengthy prayer. After Baruch is done, he continues his fast for another seven days (12:5).

1997), 65–72, includes in his list of petitionary prayers of the Second Temple period Jdt 9; 1 Macc 3:50–53; 4:30–33; 3 Macc 2:2–20; 6:2–15; Jub. 10:3–6; 2 Bar 48:2–24; 54:1–22; the Prayer of Manasseh; and Josephus, *Ant.* 2.334–337, and 4.40–50. Eileen Schuller, "Penitential Payer in Second Temple Judaism: A Research Survey," in *Seeking the Favor of God: Volume 2: The Development of Penitential Prayer in Second Temple Judaism*, ed. Mark J. Boda, Daniel K. Falk, and Rodney A. Werline (Leiden: Brill, 2007), 1–15. On supplications in the classical world, see Fred S. Naiden, *Ancient Supplication* (Oxford: Oxford University Press, 2006).
19 The social settings and *Sitze im Leben* of apocalyptic texts remain a matter of debate. See, e. g., Philip R. Davies, "The Social World of Apocalyptic Writings," in *The World of Ancient Israel: Sociological, Anthropological and Political Perspectives*, ed. Ronald E. Clements (Cambridge: Cambridge University Press, 1989), 251–71.

The seven-day fast just before the prayer is a recurring theme in 2 Baruch (9:1–10:1; 21:1). Here, as in other texts, fasting is a feature of mourning and repentance, an embodied practice associated with prayer (2 Sam 12:20; Neh 1:4; Dan 10:2–3).[20] It may be a way for Baruch to make himself available for more revelations and possibly induce further visions (4 Ezra 5:13; Ascen. Isa. 2:7–11), though this is not as clear.[21]

Baruch's first prayer in 10:6–12:4 is a lament over Jerusalem: "And I lamented this lamentation over Zion (ܡܐܠܝܬܐ ܐܘܠܝܬܐ ܗܕܐ ܥܠ ܨܗܝܘܢ)" (10:5; cf. Ezra's lament over Jerusalem in 4 Ezra 10:19–24). Bogaert regards the poem as one of the two *qinot*, or dirges, in 2 Baruch (of Hebr. קינה, "elegy, dirge;" cf. Amos 5:1; Jer 7:29).[22] The prayer itself can be broken down into the following four components:[23]

	Introduction: Call to Lament
10:6–7	Happy are the unborn, cursed the living
10:8	An invitation for demons to join in the lament
	Cessation of the Natural and Social Order
10:9–12	Call to the natural world to stop producing its fruit
10:13–17	A call for weddings to cease and for women no longer to bear children
	Return to God what is God's
10:18–19	A call to the priests to return the temple keys to God, and to the virgins to return their fine linen and silk to the Creator

---

[20] Carol A. Newsom, with Brennan W. Breed, *Daniel: A Commentary*, Old Testament Library (Louisville: Westminster John Knox:2014), 329–30.
[21] This aspect is clearer in 21:1, where Baruch says: i.e., "I sanctified myself (ܡܩܕܫ ܗܘܝܬ)." Michael E. Stone, "Apocalyptic Literature," in *Jewish Writings of the Second Temple Period*, ed. Michael E. Stone, CRINT 2.2 (Assen: Van Gorcum, 1984), 383–441 (430). An investigation of 2 Baruch's liturgical dimensions, and particularly of the rituals it includes as forms of communication, is still a *desideratum*; see Catherine Bell, *Ritual Theory, Ritual Practice* (New York: Oxford University Press, 1992), 69–117.
[22] Bogaert, *Apocalypse de Baruch*, 1:129–33. The other dirge is in 35:1–5.
[23] Violet, *Apokalypsen des Esra und des Baruch*, 214, claims that the prayer is a poem, whose seven parts are reminiscent of the seven parts of the book as a whole. Based on the Syriac text, neither claim is certain. Violet rightfully rejects as speculative the suggestion that the original poem was an acrostic.

	Babylon and Jerusalem
11:1–3	Babylon prospers, while Jerusalem is devastated
11:4–7	Happy are the deceased ancestors
12:1–4	Oracle against Babylon

In many respects, Baruch's lament over the fallen city is reminiscent of the book of Lamentations (Lam 1:1; 4:9), and, even more so, of Mattathias's lament over the defiled temple in 1 Maccabees ("Alas. Why was I born to see this, the ruin of my people, the ruin of the holy city?" [1Macc 2:7]). It has noticeably less in common with the individual laments in the biblical Psalter.[24] The main themes are divided into the four main parts of the prayer. First, Baruch praises the dead who, unlike the living, do not have to witness Jerusalem's destruction (cf. 4 Ezra 4:12; 5:35).[25] The blessing for the deceased is repeated in 11:7, so that 10:6 and 11:7 form an envelope structure around the prayer. Bogaert calls this the "*Leitmotiv*" of the prayer.[26] Second, Baruch calls on the natural and social order no longer to provide for the future: since no offerings will be brought into the temple, nature should no more bring forth its fruits; and since Jerusalem, the mother, has been laid waste, childbirth has become pointless. Third, Baruch calls on the priests and virgins to return to God what is God's: the keys and fine linen of the temple. These haunting lines stand at the center of the prayer.[27] And fourth, the prayer culminates in an oracle against Babylon, whose future punishment is assured (cf. 4 Ezra 3:28–31).[28]

Just like Jeremiah before him (e. g., Jer 4:11–14; 8:18–22; etc.), Baruch laments Jerusalem's plight and gives voice to the laments of the many who have been affected by Jerusalem's devastation.[29] Following Jeremiah's departure for exile,

---

[24] According to Claus Westermann, *The Psalms: Structure, Content and Message* (Minneapolis: Augsburg Publishing House, 1980), 59–60, the biblical psalms of lament consist of three parts: address, complaint, and petition, whereas Baruch's lament follows a different structure. See also Erhard S. Gerstenberger, *Psalms. Part 1: With an Introduction to Cultic Poetry* (Grand Rapids: Eerdmans, 1988); Davida H. Charney, *Persuading God: Rhetorical Studies of First-Person Psalms* (Sheffield: Sheffield Phoenix Press, 2015), 56–64.
[25] The numerous expressions of the sentiment that it were better to be dead than alive in biblical and post-biblical writings are listed by Stone, *Fourth Ezra*, 86.
[26] Bogaert, *Apocalypse de Baruch*, 1:130.
[27] On the parallels in rabbinic literature, see Ginzberg, "Apocalypse of Baruch (Syriac)," 553.
[28] Charles's claim that the prayer was originally an independent Sadducean fragment, "probably a Sadducean priest writing just after the fall of the temple" (Charles, *Apocalypse of Baruch*, 14), has rightfully been rejected by Ginzberg, "Apocalypse of Baruch," 555.
[29] Samuel E. Balentine, *Prayer in the Hebrew Bible: The Drama of Divine-Human Dialogue* (Minneapolis: Fortress Press, 1993), especially "The Lament Tradition: Holding to God against God," 146–98.

the prayer establishes Baruch in his new role as community leader and intercessor on behalf of Israel.

2 Baruch 21:4–25: Baruch's Petition

Baruch's second prayer follows on the heels of the long dialogue section in chapters 13–20. At the end of the exchange between God and Baruch, God promises Baruch further revelations about the future times (20:6). The dimensions of time are a prominent theme of the prayer (21:6, 9, 13, 17, 19, 25). Baruch sits in a cave in the Kidron Valley for seven days without eating or drinking (21:1–3). On the evening of the seventh day, he returns to the place where he had previously spoken with God, presumably Mount Zion (cf. 13:1; similarly, 47:2), and says his prayer (21:4–25). At the conclusion of the prayer, Baruch is overcome by a great weakness, and after an undetermined interval, the dialogue resumes (22:1–30:5).[30]

In the Codex Ambrosianus, Baruch's prayer is preceded by a short superscription: "The Prayer of Baruch, Son of Neriah."[31] The prayer itself can be broken down into the following three components:

21:4–8   Doxology: God the Creator (the past)
21:9–18 Doxology: God the Sustainer (the present)
21:19–25 Petition: Baruch asks God to inaugurate the apocalypse (the future)

According to Baruch's words in 21:8, the prayer is a petition: "Consider my petition" (ܫܡܥ ܒܒܥܘܬܝ).[32] The prayer falls into three parts, with each part culminating in a concluding petition: 21:8 "Consider my petition (ܫܡܥ ܒܒܥܘܬܝ)"; 21:18 "inform me" (ܐܘܕܥܝܢܝ) and "enlighten me" (ܢܗܪܝܢܝ); and 21:25 "quickly show your glory" (ܒܥܓܠ ܚܘܐ ܫܘܒܚܟ), and "do not delay" (ܠܐ ܬܘܚܪ).

---

[30] There is some debate whether what follows after 22:1 is a vision or the continuation of the dialogue. Baruch introduces the scene with the words: "See, heaven was opened and I saw (ܘܗܐ ܐܬܦܬܚ ܫܡܝܐ ܘܚܙܝܬ), and power was given to me, and a voice from on high was heard and said to me" (22:1). But there is no vision report that follows. Doering, "Epistle of Baruch," 154, writes: "This section then oscillates between dialogue—the predominant feature of the preceding section—and *visionary-enhanced* revelation." See also Martin Leuchtenberger, "Ort und Funktion der Wolkenvision und ihrer Deutung in der syrischen *Baruchapokalypse*," JSP 36 (2005): 206–46 (215).

[31] Bogaert, *Apocalypse de Baruch*, 2:48, observes that the superscription comes a few verses too early. It precedes 21:1, whereas the prayer proper only begins in 21:4. He suggests that this may be due to liturgical reasons, without further elaborating.

[32] Similarly, in 48:11: "Hear your servant and listen to my petition."

Baruch begins this prayer with a hymn, praising the Creator of heaven and earth (21:4–8).[33] At the moment of creation, God called the entire world into being, including future generations not yet born but known to God. Baruch focuses on the heavenly realm: God created the heavenly host "from flame and fire" (21:6; repeated in 48:8).[34] The opening doxology ends with the plea for God's attention, "look at my petition" (21:8). The doxology then continues in the second part of the prayer, where the focus shifts from creation to the transitory nature of all life (21:9–18). God alone sustains human life. And yet, life in this world is plagued by gradual decay. What was formerly is not what is now or what will be: strength turns into weakness, food of plenty into famine, and comeliness into ugliness. As a consequence, Baruch projects his hopes into the world to come and exclaims, "For if there were this life only, which is here for everyone, nothing could be more bitter than this" (21:13).[35] These first two doxological sections effectively serve as Baruch's *captatio benevolentiae*, a way of getting God's attention, and prepare Baruch now to turn from hymn to petition in the third and final part of his prayer (21:19–25). Baruch asks God how much longer this corruptible world will continue. Some interpret God's silence in the wake of Jerusalem's destruction as weakness. Reminding God of Israel's chosenness, Baruch calls on God to step in: to put an end to all death, to bring about the resurrection of the dead, and not to delay any further the final theophany.[36]

Baruch is concerned about the delay of the end times following Jerusalem's destruction. His petitionary prayer communicates an eschatological urgency we have not seen so far but that becomes an increasingly prominent theme in the book.[37] When will God put an end to death and devastation? It is also noticeable

---

33 Westermann, *The Psalms*, 81, speaks of "The Psalm of Descriptive Praise."
34 On the creation of angels from fire (cf. Ps 104:4), see Pieter W. van der Horst and Judith Newman, *Early Jewish Prayers in Greek* (Berlin: De Gruyter, 2008), 65; James L. Kugel, *Traditions of the Bible: A Guide to the Bible as It Was at the Start of the Common Era* (Cambridge: Harvard University Press, 1998), 75–76.
35 Baruch's sentiment that his hope cannot be for this world only has a close parallel in Paul's treatise on the resurrection in 1 Corinthians 15, "If for this life only we have hoped in Christ, we are of all people most to be pitied" (1 Cor 15:19).
36 Specifically, he asks God to reign in "the Angel of Death" (21:23); see Bogaert, *Apocalypse de Baruch*, 2:52–53.
37 Moshe Greenberg, *Biblical Prose Prayer as a Window to the Popular Religion of Ancient Israel* (Berkeley: University of California Press, 1983), 9, defines "petitionary prayer," including intercession, as "a petition one person makes on behalf of or for the good of another." Baruch is explicit that his concern is for Israel, "because for your name's sake you have called us the beloved people" (21:21).

how the nature of Baruch's concern has shifted: no longer complaining that God has delivered Jerusalem into the hands of the enemy, Baruch is now troubled that God delays the consummation of time.

2 Baruch 35:2–5: Baruch's Lament

This short prayer, Baruch's second lament, is as brief as it is poignant. Assembling the people in the Kidron Valley, Baruch has just made his first public statement. Upon his departure the people become worried that he might leave them for good, but Baruch assures them that he is only returning to the temple to ask God for further revelations (32:9–34:1). Baruch goes to the temple ruins, prays, falls asleep, and receives his first nocturnal vision (36:1).

The scene introduced by the narrative frame is similar to the scene of the first lament: once again Baruch goes to the destroyed temple, sits on its ruins, weeps, and prays (35:1; cf. 10:5). The prayer itself can be broken down into the following three components:[38]

35:2–3	Introduction: Lamentation over the inability to mourn adequately
35:4	The past: Sacrifices at the temple
35:5	The present: Dust and destruction

Baruch's second lament has much in common with the first (10:6–12:4): both prayers are lamentations, with language reminiscent of the book of Lamentations; both prayers are said on the ruins of the Jerusalem temple; and both contrast the former days, when the temple was flourishing, with the current situation, that is marked by devastation and loss. The parallelism in each verse (for example, "O that my eyes were springs // my eyelids a fountain of tears" in 35:2) suggests that this prayer is a poem, though its original form is beyond our reach.[39] The prayer is rich with scriptural echoes. The line in 35:2 just quoted, for example, closely follows Jeremiah's wording in his lament for the people of Jerusalem: "O that my head were a spring of water, and my eyes a fountain of tears" (Jer 8:23 [9:1]; also 9:17 [Engl. 9:18]). Similar language is also found in the book of Lamentations (Lam 2:11, 18; 3:48). Baruch's lament, "For *how* (ܐܝܟܢܐ) shall I groan over Zion"

---

38 Bogaert, *Apocalypse de Baruch*, 1:129.
39 Violet, *Apokalypsen des Esra und des Baruch*, 251–52, attempts to reconstruct the poem's original form.

(35:3) is an allusion to the opening verse of Lamentations, "How lonely sits the city" (ܐܝܟܢܐ; Lam 1:1).⁴⁰

This short prayer succinctly captures Baruch's precarious situation: because the temple lies in ruins, Baruch finds himself unable to lament adequately over the destruction of the city. The Jerusalem temple, source of Israel's "pride," has been turned into dust. Here, like in the first lament, it does not seem far-fetched to assume that Baruch's prayer seeks to capture the despair of the post-70 Jerusalem community. Robbed of the ability to atone, even to mourn properly, Baruch returns to "the holy place" (ܐܬܪܐ ܩܕܝܫܐ; 35:1) to give voice to the unspeakable.

2 Baruch 38:1–4: Baruch's Petition

This short prayer differs from the previous prayers in that it is embedded in Baruch's first vision account: Baruch has a vision of a forest, a vine, and a spring (36:1–37:1), he says a brief prayer in which he asks for an interpretation of the vision (38:1–4), and he is granted an interpretation (39:1–43:3).⁴¹ The purpose of the prayer, then, is to ask God for an explanation of what Baruch has seen. The prayer itself can be divided into the following two components:

38:1–2   Doxology: God enlightens those who have understanding
38:3–4   Petition: Baruch asks for an interpretation

The prayer neatly divides into two roughly equal parts, each consisting of two verses: in the first half, Baruch speaks to God about God ("O Lord, my Lord, *you are* the one …"; 38:1), and in the second half Baruch speaks about himself ("Let *me* know …"; 38:3). God enlightens those who strive for understanding (v. 1); understanding is here associated with God's life-giving Torah and wisdom (v. 2). Baruch asks for understanding (v. 3) and explains that he is a worthy recipient of such divine interpretation because all his life he has followed the Torah and has lived in compliance with God's wisdom (v. 4).

Torah and wisdom are recurring topics in 2 Baruch. Here they form a parallelism (also in 44:14; 48:24; 51:3–4, 7; 77:16): God will grant knowledge to those who follow the Torah and pursue wisdom. The centrality of the Torah in 2 Baruch's apocalyptic program for the post-70 community is noteworthy, not least because

---

40 Judith H. Newman, *Praying by the Book: The Scripturalization of Prayer in Second Temple Judaism*, EJL 14 (Atlanta: Scholars Press, 1999).
41 The same three-fold structure of vision report, prayer, and divine interpretation is repeated in the book's only other vision account in 53:1–76:5.

in this respect, at least, our author is in full agreement with rabbinic teaching of the time.⁴² Baruch himself is leading an exemplary life that focuses on the Torah.

2 Baruch 48:2–24: Baruch's Petition

This petition follows Baruch's second public address (44:1–47:2). Baruch leaves the crowd behind and, complying with God's command (43:3), returns to the place of revelation where God had previously spoken to him (47:2; the phrase is repeated from 21:2), presumably the temple ruins.⁴³ There he fasts for seven days, says his prayer, and upon its conclusion becomes very weak (48:25).

In the Ambrosian manuscript, Baruch's petition is prefaced by a short superscription (48:1): "The Prayer of Baruch." The prayer has the following three components:

48:2–11   Doxology: God's heavenly mysteries
48:12–19 Petition: Baruch asks God not to abandon God's people
48:20–24 Expression of confidence: Israel trusts in God and the Torah

Like Baruch's petition in 21:4–25, this petition, too, divides into three parts. The three parts are formally set apart from each other, with the first and second part each ending in petitions: 48:11 concludes the first part, "Hear your servant" (ܫܡܥ ܠܥܒܕܟ), and "listen to my petition" (ܘܨܘܬ ܠܒܥܘܬܝ); and 48:19 concludes the second part, "Look at the little ones ..." (ܚܘܪ ܒܙܥܘܪܐ), "redeem all" (ܦܪܘܩ ܠܟܠ), "do not cut off the hope of our people" (ܘܠܐ ܬܦܣܘܩ), and "do not cut short the times of our help" (ܘܠܐ ܬܩܛܢ). The third part begins in 48:20 with an emphatic statement of confidence in the election of Israel, "For (ܓܝܪ) this is the people you have chosen ...."⁴⁴

In addition to these formal division markers, the three parts of the prayer are also thematically distinct from each other. As in chapter 21, Baruch opens with a doxology (48:2–11), and also like in chapter 21, the focus of the doxology is on the heavenly realm that is heavily populated with angelic "armies without number"

---

42 Charles, *Apocalypse of Baruch*, lxxix–lxxxi; and, in greater detail, Ginzberg, "Apocalypse of Baruch," 552–53.
43 So already Charles, *Apocalypse of Baruch*, 37; see also Bogaert, *Apocalypse de Baruch*, 2:85–86.
44 Violet, *Apokalypsen des Esra und des Baruch*, 265, calls this petition the "long prayer" ("großes Gebet") and adds, "in the beginning hymn, at the end petition and reflection" ("am Anfang Hymnus, am Ende Bitte und Reflexion").

(48:10).⁴⁵ But whereas in the previous petition, Baruch praised God the Creator, here he speaks primarily about the divine "mysteries" (ܐܪܙܐ; 48:3). In particular, Baruch praises God, the Master over Time. Time appears to have agency: God calls "the advent of the times, and they stand before" God; God causes the ages to go by, "and they do not resist" God; God guides the seasons, and "they subject themselves" to God (48:2; similarly in 54:3).⁴⁶ The first part of the prayer ends with Baruch's plea that God may hear his prayer and listen to his petition (48:11; cf. 21:8).

In the second part of the prayer (48:12–19), the perspective shifts from the heavenly to the earthly realm. Baruch stresses that humans live at the mercy of God alone, "by your gift we come into the world" (48:15). We are not in control of when we are born or when we die, and we are not strong enough to bear God's anger. Therefore, Baruch concludes with an emphatic six-fold plea to God not to forget Israel: "protect us," "help us," "look at the little ones," "redeem all," "do not cut off the hope of our people," and "do not cut short the times of our help" (48:18–19). The cluster of imperatives, unparalleled in the other petitionary prayers, expresses the urgency of Baruch's request. His plea is most acute when he intercedes on behalf of Israel.

The reference to God's people ("the hope of our people") forms the transition to the third and final part of the prayer (48:20–24), in which Baruch's tone changes from plea to confidence. God has chosen Israel, therefore Israel trusts in God. As long as the faithful engage in the Torah, follow the divine statutes, and do not intermingle with the nations, Israel will not fall. Torah and wisdom, here like in chapter 38 set in parallelism, are present to assist the faithful.

Several similarities between Baruch's petitions in 21:4–25 and 48:2–24 are noteworthy. Each prayer consists of three parts, each begins with a doxology, and each uses imperatives to divide the parts formally from each other. There are also several themes that are repeated: God has spoken the world into being (21:4 and 48:8); the heavenly realm and all of creation obey God (21:4 and 48:2); God created the "holy beings" and "spirits" from fire (21:6 and 48:8); God is Master over "the course of the times" (20:6 and 48:2–3); Israel is God's chosen people (21:21 and 48:20); and Baruch asks God not to delay any further God's intervention in this world (21:25 and 48:18–19).

---

45 Van der Horst and Newman, *Early Jewish Prayers*, 233.
46 The constructions of time in Jewish apocalyptic thought remains an underexplored subject. On 2 Baruch and 4 Ezra, specifically, see Devorah Dimant, "*4 Ezra* and *2 Baruch* in Light of Qumran Literature," in *Fourth Ezra and Second Baruch: Reconstruction after the Fall*, ed. Matthias Henze and Gabriele Boccaccini (Leiden: Brill, 2013), 31–61; and Matthias Henze, "Dimensions of Time in Jewish Apocalyptic Thought: The Case of 4 Ezra," in *Figures of Ezra*, ed. Jan N. Bremmer, Veronika Hirschberger, and Tobias Nicklas (Leuven: Peeters, 2018), 13–34.

These similarities notwithstanding, we also see Baruch changing. He is increasingly turning into an eschatological Moses figure, who intercedes before God on behalf of Israel.[47] His pleas are becoming more intense, and he emphasizes Israel's chosenness in an attempt to appeal to God's mercy (48:20–23).[48] It is not difficult to detect the function of Baruch's prayer. 2 Baruch's apocalyptic program advocates for a Torah-based form of post-70 Judaism. This prayer wants to encourage the remnant community not to lose hope, while emphasizing the centrality of the Torah. In language that invokes the *Shema* (Deut 6:4), the prayer culminates in an expression of confidence that God's covenant with Israel, here recalled in terms of Israel's chosenness, remains intact, in spite of the recent devastation of Jerusalem:"For we all are one renowned people who received one Torah from the One. And that Torah that is among us helps us, and the surprising wisdom that is among us will help us" (48:24; repeated in 85:14).[49]

2 Baruch 54:1–22: Baruch's Petition

Like the prayer in chapter 38, this prayer is embedded in a tripartite vision that begins with the vision report (53:1–12), is followed by a petitionary prayer for divine interpretation (54:1–22), and ends with the dream interpretation (55:1–74:4). Unlike the prayer in chapter 38, this prayer is significantly longer and touches on several issues.

The prayer is preceded in the Codex Ambrosianus by a superscription (54:1): "The Prayer of Baruch." The narrative frame is minimal. Following Baruch's first-person account of his vision of the great cloud raining black and white waters, Baruch relates how he woke up and asked God for an interpretation (54:1). After the prayer, he sits under a tree to rest in the shade of its branches and ponders the significance of the dream (55:1–2), before the angel Remiel appears to provide the interpretation for which Baruch had asked (55:1–74:4). The prayer itself can be broken down into the following four components:

---

[47] Dale C. Allison, *The New Moses: A Matthean Typology* (Minneapolis: Fortress, 1993), 66, downplays the significance of Moses in the character development of Baruch. For a different view, see Henze, *Jewish Apocalypticism*, 102–7.

[48] Matthias Henze, "The Chosenness of Israel in the Apocrypha and Pseudepigrapha," in *The Call of Abraham: Essays on the Election of Israel in Honor of Jon D. Levenson*, ed. Gary A. Anderson and Joel S. Kaminsky (Notre Dame: University of Notre Dame Press, 2013), 170–98.

[49] Bogaert, *Apocalypse de Baruch*, 2:61–62. Charles's comment that 48:24 "is directed polemically against the Christians" (*Apocalypse of Baruch*, 2:76 n. 24) is hardly warranted.

54:1–6   God, who is omniscient, reveals what is hidden to those who fear God
54:7–11   Baruch has received revelations and praises God
54:12–19   Human beings choose their own fate
54:20–22   Baruch repeats his petition for an interpretation

Baruch begins once again with a doxology (54:1–6), praising the omniscient God, who makes future events known and reveals what is hidden to those who fear God. Like in the two previous petitionary prayers in 21:4–25 and 48:2–24, the first part, a doxology, ends with a direct petition, "reveal to me also [the vision's] interpretation" (ܓܠܝ ܠܝ; 54:6). In the second part of the prayer (54:7–11), Baruch reflects on his own standing. Even though others are more righteous than he, Baruch has received numerous revelations from God. He therefore will always praise God and tell of God's marvelous deeds. From here, Baruch moves into a reflection about those who will perish at the end of time (54:12–19). He emphasizes that their fate is justified and gives a quick summary of who they are: those who do not love God's Torah, those who do not subject themselves to God's power (54:14), and who reject the understanding of the Most High (54:17). At the center of his reflection is the figure of Adam. Even though all are affected by Adam's sin, the source of human mortality, human beings still have free will to make their own choices and hence determine their own fate. The passage ends with the memorable line, "each of us has become our own Adam" (ܠܐ ܗܘܐ ܐܢܫ ܐܢܫ ܡܢܢ ܗܘܐ ܠܗ ܐܕܡ; 54:19).[50] In the final part of the prayer (54:20–22), Baruch repeats his request for God to interpret for him the vision Baruch has just seen.

The petition for an interpretation of the vision, initially articulated at the conclusion of the first part (54:6) and then repeated in the last section (54:20), frames the prayer and is the reason why Baruch prays in the first place. But the prayer as a whole is considerably broader in scope than this petition. It is a probing meditation on God and human nature, on who receives divine revelations and who will be deemed righteous at the end of time. A continuous train of thought runs through the four parts of the prayer: it begins with a meditation on God, from

---

[50] This is one of several passages in 2 Baruch on Adam (4:3; 17:1–18:2; 23:4; 48:42–47; 54:15–19; 56:5–8). It has a close parallel in 4 Ezra 3:20–21, 26; 7:63–72, where we are told that Adam was "burdened with an evil heart," which he then passed on to all of his descendants. See Stone, "Excursus on Adam's Sin," in *Fourth Ezra*, 63–64. Whereas one can see how 4 Ezra's concept of the hereditary *cor malignum* might easily be used to absolve human beings of any ethical responsibility or guilt, 2 Baruch's position differs from that in 4 Ezra, in that Baruch emphasizes that each individual is accountable for their choices and that these choices will have consequences. Jason M. Zurawski, "Rethinking the Divide between 4 Ezra and 2 Baruch: Getting to the (Evil) Heart of the Matter," in *Wisdom Poured Out Like Water: Studies on Jewish and Christian Antiquity in Honor of Gabriele Boccaccini*, ed. J. Harold Ellens et al., DCLS 38 (Berlin: De Gruyter, 2018), 177–192.

whom nothing is hidden and who reveals the divine mysteries to those who fear him, then turns into a self-reflection, in which Baruch realizes that even though others are more excellent than he, God has revealed "marvelous things" to him (54:9), and it ends with the recognition that many choose to reject the Torah and thus bring desolation upon themselves.

As is true of the previous petition in chapter 48, the function of this prayer, too, is hortative, to exhort the community not to go down the wrong path and thus become their own Adam, but instead to make the right choice, to follow the Torah, and be guided by the understanding that only comes from God, so as to be granted entry into the world to come. To make sure that the point is not lost on the reader, the author adds a brief narrative episode immediately following the prayer (55:1–2), something we have not seen before. After Baruch has finished his prayer, he sits in the shade of a tree and ponders the blessings the sinners have knowingly spurned and the torment that awaits them as a consequence. A brief commentary on the main message of the prayer, this short meditative scene serves as a stern warning to the reader not to make the same mistake the sinners have made but to embrace God's goodness.

4. Conclusion

The nature and function of liturgies and prayers in Second Temple literature have long been understudied and underemphasized. This has changed in recent years. Prayers are now widely recognized to be pervasive in early Jewish texts. They are integral parts of the narratives in which they have come down to us and important carriers of the texts' theology. Prayers can also tell us a great deal about how the texts in which they are preserved function rhetorically and may even hint at the liturgical practices of the groups who composed, copied, and transmitted the texts. For example, Rodney Werline has argued that "ritualized speech forms" in the Book of the Watchers (1 Enoch 1–36) are designed to draw the reader into the imagined world of the authors. He has also observed that the prayers in the Enochic text lead to further revelations.[51] Similarly, the long prayer in Daniel 9, prompted by Daniel's reading of Jeremiah's oracles, is followed by an angelic revelation. In the words of Judith Newman, Daniel's prayer "marks a transformation of Daniel's cognition" more generally.[52]

---

[51] Rodney A. Werline, "Ritual, Order and the Construction of an Audience in *1 Enoch* 1–36," *DSD* 22 (2015): 325–41.

[52] Judith H. Newman, *Before the Bible: The Liturgical Body and the Formation of Scriptures in Early Judaism* (New York: Oxford University Press, 2018), 1. Newman's work is particularly impor-

In many ways, the situation in 2 Baruch is similar to that of other early Jewish apocalypses, such as the Book of the Watchers and Daniel. Prayers are plentiful, and they are carefully worked into the book's narrative. Baruch's prayers also lead to further revelations. And they play an important role for the author to develop an apocalyptic message for the post-70 community, in that they give hope and encourage the reader to follow the Torah.

Our reading of the prayers in 2 Baruch is complicated by the fact that the dominant literary genre of the book is the dialogue between God and Baruch. Prayer and revelatory dialogue are two distinct speech forms in 2 Baruch, two ways in which Baruch communicates directly with the divine. How, then, do they differ? The dialogue portions of the book are, for the most part, prosaic, with the occasional poetic moment, and they do not appear to follow any particular literary format. The dialogue runs freely through the entire book. It is occasionally interrupted when Baruch is exhausted or when God sends him away, only to be picked up again a few moments later. The primary rhetorical function of the dialogue is to hold the book's diverse sections together, to carry the action forward, and to give shape to the book as a whole. The dialogue is also instrumental for the apocalyptic message of the book. It is here that Baruch argues most forcefully with God, asks difficult questions, is argumentative, presses God for answers, and demands to know more about God's intention for Israel.

By comparison, prayers in 2 Baruch are more focused. In his laments, poignantly set on the ruins of the temple, Baruch gives voice to the unspeakable, the loss of the temple and of an intimacy with the divine. The devastation is so vast that Baruch wonders how he can possibly mourn adequately. The petitionary prayers combine doxologies, praises of God the Creator, Sustainer of life, and Master over Time, with petitions. They oscillate between prose and poetry, possibly an indication of their liturgical origin. Baruch's petitions have two foci. Baruch is asking for an interpretation of his visions, an explanation of what has been revealed to him. Baruch also petitions God on behalf of Israel and pleads with God not to terminate all hope: "Protect us in your mercy, and in your compassion help us" (48:18).

As one of Baruch's principal means of communicating with God, prayers form a critically important part of 2 Baruch. To grasp their significance, they have to be read within the context of the book as a whole, and of prayers in early Judaism in general.

---

tant in the significance it assigns to the role of individual and communal prayers for the transformation of literary texts into scriptures.

John R. Levison
The Prayers of Eve in the Greek Life of Adam and Eve

1. Introduction

The Apocalypse of Moses—typically referred to now as the Greek Life of Adam and Eve (GLAE)—contains fascinating stories that offer a fuller account of the life of Adam and Eve than Genesis 1–5. The Greek Life of Adam and Eve contains the tale of brother–murder (1–4), a heroic but failed quest to retrieve the oil of mercy from paradise to alleviate human pain (5–14), two wildly divergent autobiographical accounts of temptation and fall (Adam's [7–8] and Eve's [15–30]), and a vivid depiction of divine forgiveness, with the ascent of the soul and the washing of the body (31–43).[1]

The Life of Adam and Eve is preserved in several versions—Greek, Latin, Slavonic, Georgian, and Armenian—and its purpose differs according to which version is read. In fact, even within the Greek textual tradition, Marcel Nagel identified no less than three text forms of the Greek tradition,[2] while Jean-Pierre Pettorelli identified no less than two dominant Latin versions, which he labeled Latin-V and Latin-P.[3] Even within a single language, then, multiple text forms coexist, making it difficult to know which text to utilize. Several efforts have been made to trace the textual tradition of GLAE, including by Michael Eldridge,[4] Jan Dochhorn,[5] and Johannes Tromp.[6] The text that lies at the base of this study is the critical edition of Tromp, which, in many respects, is similar to Dochhorn's.[7]

---

[1] On the figure of Eve in GLAE, see Vita Daphna Arbel, *Forming Femininity in Antiquity: Eve, Gender, and Ideologies in the Greek Life of Adam and Eve* (New York: Oxford University, 2012); John R. Levison, "The Exoneration of Eve in the Apocalypse in of Moses 15–30," *JSJ* 20 (1989): 135–50.
[2] Marcel Nagel, "La Vie grecque d'Adam et d'Ève Apocalypse de Moïse. I–III" (Ph.D. diss., Université de Strasbourg, 1972; Université de Lille III, 1974). See as well John R. Levison, *Texts in Tradition: The Greek Life of Adam and Eve* (Atlanta: Scholars Press, 2000).
[3] Jean-Pierre Pettorelli et al., *Vita Latina Adae et Evae: Synopsis Vitae Adae et Evae Latine, Graece, Armeniace et Iberice* (Turnhout: Brepols, 2012).
[4] Michael Eldridge, *Dying Adam and His Multiethnic Family: Understanding the Greek Life of Adam and Eve* (Leiden: Brill, 2001).
[5] Jan Dochhorn, *Die Apokalypse des Mose: Text, Übersetzung, Kommentar* (Tübingen: Mohr Siebeck, 2005).
[6] Johannes Tromp, *The Life of Adam and Eve in Greek: A Critical Edition* (Leiden: Brill, 2005).
[7] See the review of Tromp's critical edition by Jan Dochhorn in "Review of J. Tromp, *The Life of Adam and Eve in Greek*," *JSP* 17 (2008): 313–19.

For this essay, it is important to note, at least in passing, that the question of whether GLAE reflects a Jewish or Christian provenance continues unresolved. For more than a century, GLAE has been deemed to be a Jewish composition, with views to the contrary emerging in the 1990s primarily from Dutch scholars Johannes Tromp, editor of the indispensable critical edition, and Marinus de Jonge.[8] Dochhorn, in his detailed commentary, has made the strongest case for the Jewish origin of GLAE. He argues in favor of a Jewish milieu, in large measure because of the alleged facility of the original author(s) of GLAE with Hebrew; many elements of GLAE, notes Dochhorn, represent solutions to conundrums in the Hebrew text.[9] Whether GLAE is of Jewish or Christian origin, there is consensus around its existence by the fourth century CE. The prayers of Eve analyzed in this study, therefore, should be included among the prayers of antiquity.

By way of introduction, it is essential also to note that GLAE can be divided into four parts, in each of which prayer features prominently:

(1) A scene in which Cain murders Abel and God promises Seth as a replacement for Abel, a promise to which Adam responds by wanting to give God glory and tender an offering (1:1–5:3; retelling Gen 4:1–5:5);

(2) With Adam on his deathbed, Seth and Eve return to paradise to weep and pray in order to retrieve the oil of mercy, with the aim of alleviating Adam's pain, though the archangel Michael denies this request (6:1–14:2);

(3) The testament of Eve, in which Eve recounts, in a flourish of biblical and unbiblical elements: the envy of the devil; the entrance of the serpent, the devil's tool, into paradise; Eve's inability to resist the devil's trickery; Eve's ability to persuade Adam to eat; God's awesome entry into paradise on a chariot; the curses; and the expulsion of the first pair from paradise, despite angelic pleas for mercy. Throughout this testament, Adam in particular prays to the angels that serve God (14:3–30:1; retelling Gen 3:1–24);

(4) The pardoning of Adam, the ascent of his soul, the heavenly visions of Eve interpreted by Seth, and the washing of Adam's corpse. Eve finds her voice in this final section of GLAE (31:1–43:4).

---

8 Johannes Tromp and Marinus de Jonge offer a summary of their arguments in *The Life of Adam and Eve and Related Literature* (Sheffield: Academic Press, 1997), 67–75. In contrast to Tromp and de Jonge, most scholars have interpreted GLAE as a Jewish composition. Some essential bibliography on the Jewish origin of GLAE includes: Carl Fuchs, "Das Leben Adams und Evas," in *Die Apokryphen und Pseudepigraphen des Alten Testaments,* ed. Emil Kautzsch (Tübingen: JCB Mohr/Paul Siebeck, 1900), 2:506–28 (510–11); Richard Kabisch, "Die Entstehungszeit der Apokalypse Mose," *ZNW* 6 (1905): 134; L.S.A. Wells, "The Books of Adam and Eve," in *The Apocrypha and Pseudepigrapha of the Old Testament in English,* ed. Robert H. Charles (Oxford: Clarendon, 1913), 2:123–154 (134); M.D. Johnson, "Life of Adam and Eve," in *The Old Testament Pseudepigrapha,* ed. James H. Charlesworth (Garden City: Doubleday, 1985), 2:249–296 (252).
9 Dochhorn, *Apokalypse des Mose,* 112–124; 152–72.

The dominant purpose of the Greek Life of Adam and Eve is to reinterpret Genesis 1–5 in order to provide hope for its readers by presenting Adam as a forgiven sinner who endures the pain of existence, faces mortality with uncertainty, but ultimately receives mercy after death. Prayer in GLAE is embedded in this tortured journey toward hope.

The prayers of Eve, however, do not play a role in each of these four sections of GLAE. In the first (1:1–5:3), Adam is the one who suggests that they give glory to God. In the second, as we shall see, Eve prays, but the archangel responds exclusively to Seth (6:1–14:2). In the third, which Eve delivers in her own voice (14:3–30:1), Adam prays and God responds. Eve does not pray; nor does God respond to her. Only in the fourth section (31:1–43:3) does Eve pray in her own voice. When it comes to prayer, then, Eve is a shadow figure in GLAE, though her prayers in the final section offer powerful testimony to the ways in which she is perceived in this illuminating reinvention of Genesis 1–5.

Perhaps this is the reason the prayers of Eve have received so little attention in scholarship. In his detailed commentary, Dochhorn devotes more space to the redactional layers of GLAE 32 than to the actual content of Eve's prayer. He considers the prayer in GLAE 32 a *Bußgebet* that underscores Eve's responsibility for sin. This emphasis, claims Dochhorn, belongs primarily to the final redaction of GLAE; with respect to the *content* of Eve's prayer of repentance, he has little to say.[10]

Vita Daphna Arbel's *Forming Femininity in Antiquity: Eve, Gender, and Ideologies in the Greek Life of Adam and Eve* offers only slightly more exploration of Eve's prayer. In her analysis of GLAE 31–42, Arbel naturally looks at Eve's prayers, though the focus of her analysis lies elsewhere, in funerary rites. Arbel does nonetheless note the association of Eve's prayer in GLAE 32–33 with atonement, the association of Eve's prayer with an ability to see visions, and the emotional aspects of Eve's prayer—signified by a tear-soaked face and swollen eyes. With respect to none of these, however, does Arbel attempt to do more than lightly pierce the surface of this text, since her interest lies less in Eve's prayers than in how "the account of Adam's death has appealed to persistent cultural conventions of women as esteemed, beneficial key bearers of practices related to the care of the dead."[11]

The present study offers a closer look at Eve's prayers. We will analyze those passages that contain the prayers of Eve and the prayers of Adam and Seth that

---

[10] Dochhorn, *Apokalypse des Mose*, 449–51.
[11] Arbel, *Forming Femininity*, 70–71; full discussion, 66–71. See also 88–92, where Arbel's concerns lie with Eve's visions more than with her prayers.

tell us, as readers, something significant about the prayers of Eve in the Greek Life of Adam and Eve.

2. Quest for the Oil of Mercy

After Adam falls into an unknown condition, he gathers his children around his deathbed in traditional testamentary fashion. Appalled by Adam's pain, Seth suggests that he should "place excrement upon my head, and I will weep and pray, and my Lord will hear me and will send his angel, and I will bring to you so that the pain will leave you" (GLAE 6:2).[12] Adam subsequently makes a similar proposal: "Get up and go with our son Seth to the vicinity of paradise," he orders Eve, "and place earth upon your heads and weep, begging God to have compassion upon me and send his angel into paradise and give to me from the tree in which the oil flows from it, and [so that] you may bring [it] to me and I may anoint myself and be free from my disease" (9:3).

Seth's and Adam's suggestions introduce an association between weeping and prayer, which permeates GLAE. Seth offers to place excrement on his head, to weep, and to pray (GLAE 6:2). Adam orders Seth and Eve to place earth on their heads, to weep, and to beg (9:3). Eve and Seth do this when they come to the vicinity of paradise to request the oil of mercy (13:1): "Seth went with his mother Eve into the vicinity of paradise. And they wept, begging God to send his angel and to give to them the oil of mercy."[13] Later, in the testament of Eve, while the couple is being driven out, Adam weeps and cries out, "Forgive me, Lord, what I have done" (27:3). At one moment during their expulsion, weeping substitutes for spoken words, Adam weeps, so the angels ask, "What do you want us to do for you, Adam?" (29:2). Finally, toward the end of GLAE, Eve weeps and prays to be buried alongside Adam (42:4).

Throughout this scene, Eve takes a subordinate position to Seth. When an animal attacks Seth, Eve is ineffective in her effort to forestall the attack (10:1–12:2). When they arrive in the vicinity of paradise, where "they wept, begging God to send his angel and to give to them the oil of mercy," God sends Michael the archangel, who speaks exclusively to Seth: "Seth, man of God, stop laboring,

---

[12] Translations of GLAE are from John R. Levison, "Life of Adam and Eve" in *Early Jewish Literature: An Anthology*, ed. Brad Embry, Ronald Herms, and Archie T. Wright (Grand Rapids: Eerdmans, 2018), 445–65.
[13] It is difficult to determine whether Eve and Seth are said to enter paradise itself or just the environs of paradise. On this question, see John R. Levison, "Terrestrial Paradise in the Greek Life of Adam and Eve," *JSP* 28 (2018): 25–44.

praying with this pleading about the tree in which flows the oil, in order to anoint your father Adam—which will not take place for you now" (13:1–3).

Despite the journey, the attack of the beast, and their earnest effort, the archangel Michael denies Seth's request. He and his mother return empty-handed, unable to relieve Adam's pain.

3. The Testament of Eve

In the wake of this failure, and the reality that death is inevitable, Adam orders Eve to narrate the story of the couple's sin. Her testament consists of exhortation, ending with, "Now therefore, my children, I have disclosed to you the way in which we were deceived. And you yourselves—guard yourselves so as not to disregard what is good" (GLAE 30). Although it is Eve's voice that dominates this section, surprisingly, she never depicts herself at prayer. Adam alone is the one who prays.

In an expansion of Gen 3:9, God calls to Adam, "Adam, where have you gone into hiding, thinking that I will not find you? A building will not be hidden from the one who built it, will it?" (23:1). Adam responds, "Not, my Lord, are we hiding from you because we think that we cannot be found by you, but I am frightened because I am naked, and I stood in awe of your power, Authoritative One" (23:2). God replies, "Who made known to you that you are naked, unless you disregarded my command—to keep it?" (23:3), prompting Adam to recall the words Eve spoke to him, "Free of danger from God I will make you" (23:4).

Later, the angels stop casting Adam and Eve out of paradise (27:1). Once again, Adam is front and center, with Eve consigned to the shadows. "While they were driving us out and wailing out loud, your father Adam begged the angels, saying, 'Allow me a little [time] so that I may beg God to have compassion and show me mercy, for I only sinned'" (27:2). As the angels stop driving the couple out of paradise, Adam cries out and weeps, "Forgive me, Lord, what I have done" (27.3). This is a simple penitential prayer, which comes on the heels of Adam's bearing full responsibility for the first sin (27:2). Still, Adam alone prays; Eve does not.

God's refusal to end the expulsion from paradise does not put an end to the interaction between God and Adam. Denied paradise, Adam begs, "Lord, give to me from the plant of life so that I may eat before I am thrown out" (28:2). It is difficult to miss the androcentric character of this prayer: Adam prays that God should give *him* the plant of life so that *he* may eat before *he* is thrown out of paradise. Eve is nowhere to be seen in the scope of Adam's prayer. Soon she will exist outside of paradise; for now, she exists beyond the purview of Adam's prayer.

God's response to Adam's prayer is partial but positive: "And having approached, the angels said to the Lord, 'Jael, eternal king, command that incenses of fragrance from paradise be given to Adam.' And God commanded that it be allowed to Adam that he should take fragrances and seeds for his sustenance" (29:4–5).

In the second and third narrative segments of GLAE, then, Eve is overshadowed by Seth and Adam, respectively. On their quest, she prays and weeps with Seth, but it is only Seth whom the archangel addresses. In her own testament, in which her voice rings out loud and clear—and, I have argued, in self-exoneration[14]—it is only Adam who prays and only Adam whom God and the angels address. Eve expresses no significant request to God in prayer. Only Seth and Adam do.

4. The Pardoning and Burial of Adam

4.1 The Confession of Eve

After she delivers her testament, which recounts the primeval pair's expulsion from paradise, Eve prays, though not of her own accord. She prays instead because Adam commands her to pray: "Pray to God until I give back my spirit into the hands of the one who has given it to me since we do not know how we will meet the one who made us, whether he will be angry with us or turn around to show us mercy" (31:4). Subservient to her husband, Eve:

> got up and went outside. And having fallen upon the earth, she said repeatedly,
> > I sinned, God,
> > I sinned, father of all,
> > I sinned against you.
> > I sinned against your chosen angels,
> > I sinned against the cherubim,
> > I sinned against your immovable throne,
> > I sinned, Lord,
> > I sinned much,
> > I sinned in your sight,
> > And all sin because of me has come about in the creation. (32:1–2)

Significant in this scenario is Eve's posture. For the first time in GLAE, prayer entails prostration. Prayer had entailed weeping. Prayer had even entailed the placement of dirt (or dung) on one's head. But prayer did not entail prostration—

---

[14] See Levison, "Exoneration of Eve," 135–50.

the position in which Eve prays. The prayer begins after Eve falls to the ground. It ends "while Eve was still praying," and "look, the angel of humanity came to her, and made her stand up, saying, 'Get up, Eve, from your penitence. For, look, Adam your husband has gone out from his body. Get up and see his spirit being carried up to the one who made him in order to meet him'" (32:3–4). The angel made Eve stand up, then told her, not once, but twice to get up.[15]

This prayer consists of untrammeled confession, which actually cuts against the grain of GLAE. Earlier, Adam had prayed, "Allow me a little [time] so that I may beg God to have compassion and show me mercy, for I only sinned" (27:2). *I only have sinned*. Adam offers a counterpoint to Eve, who now confesses, "all sin because of me has come about in the creation" (32:2). Eve addresses God in three ways in this prayer: God; father of all; and Lord. None of these is uncommon in the Second Temple period. Even the reference to God as *father* occurred already in Isa 63:16; 4Q372 16; 4Q460 5 i 4–5; Wis 14:3; 3 Macc 6:3, 8; and Sir 23:1, 4 (Greek).[16] In this final section, though nowhere else in GLAE, God is characterized as a father.

Eve's prayer, finally, offers a list of those against whom Eve claims to have sinned, which lends symmetry to her prayer. God is the object of the first three claims; Eve sinned against God, the father of all, and you (God). God is, generally speaking, also the object of the last three claims; Eve sinned against the Lord, she sinned much (this is the only line that is not explicitly a reference to someone or something), and she sinned "in your sight." The intervening three claims anchored by the words, *I sinned*, are directed toward elements that are featured elsewhere in GLAE: angels,[17] cherubim,[18] and the immovable throne.[19]

Capping these confessions is the climax of Eve's prayer: "And all sin because of me has come about in the creation." This confession is the apogee of indictments that have peppered GLAE up to this point. On his deathbed, Adam had

---

15 This posture in prayer is new but not unique; the angels, too, will adopt this position as they intercede on Adam's behalf (GLAE 33:5; 36:1).
16 After the washing of Adam's body in the Acherusian Lake and its transportation into paradise in the third heaven, "the archangel Michael cried out to The Father on account of Adam" (GLAE 38:1). The epithet, *the father*, without a genitive of any sort, is new, though in GLAE 31–43 God is also referred to as "father of all" (32:2), "father of the whole creation" (35:2; 37:4), and "the father of lights" (36:3); the doxology, which was probably appended to the narrative, concludes with a reference to "God the father."
17 Including references to archangels, see GLAE 6:2; 7:2; 9:3; 13:1; 14:1, 2; 22:1, 3; 27:1, 2, 4, 5; 29:1, 2, 3, 4, 6; 31:1; 32:2, 3; 33:2, 4, 5; 35:2; 37:1, 3, 6; 38:2, 3; 40:2, 5, 7; 42:2; 43:1, 3, 4.
18 GLAE 19:2; 28:3; 38:3; adjective in 22:3.
19 GLAE 19:2; 22:4; 37:4; 39:2, 3. The adjective, ασάλευτος, does not communicate that the throne is not mobile, which it is in GLAE, but that the throne is unshakable, strong, and sturdy.

attributed his own death to Eve: "When God made us, both me and your mother, through whom I am also dying, he gave to us every plant in paradise, but about one he commanded us not to eat from it, through which also we are dying" (GLAE 7:1). Later, the beast that attacked Seth attributed animal rebellion to Eve's greed: "Oh, Eve, your greed is not about us, nor your weeping, but about you, since the dominion of the wild animals came to be from you" (11:1). When they returned to Adam without the oil of mercy, Adam attributed death—not his death alone but the death of everyone—to Eve. "Oh, Eve, what did you bring about among us?" he said, "You have brought upon us enormous anger, which is death's exercise of dominion over all of our race" (14.2). According to her own testament, "when your father came, I spoke to him words of lawlessness, which brought us down from intense glory" (21:2). After she persuaded Adam to eat the fruit, Adam accused her again: "Oh, evil woman, what did you bring about among us?" he says, eyes now open, "You have estranged me from the glory of God" (21:6). Her action had caused Adam to die. Her greed had caused animals to rebel. Her action had given death its dominion. Her words had brought them down from great glory and alienated Adam from the glory of God. And now, claims Eve, her sin brought about all *sin* in the creation.

The significance of this claim can be grasped against the question of whether Adam and Eve brought death alone or sin as well into the world, which features in 2 Baruch and 4 Ezra. Ezra wonders whether Adam brought death to all. Baruch knows that each is the Adam of his or own soul; Adam and Eve did *not* bring death to all.[20] No such distinction features in GLAE, where Eve's actions bring death, the rebellion of the animal world, a loss of glory, even the glory of God, and now the entrance of sin into the created world.

Something else unique arises in Eve's prayer of confession. Eve had brought death to Adam, rebellion to the animals, death to the entire human race, and a loss of great glory. Those who felt the impact of Eve's sin include the animal and human races. In her confession, however, Eve expresses an understanding that her sin was principally against *God*. She does not even nod at other humans, including Adam, nor does she glance at the animal world. Eve's prayer reveals a heightened understanding that her sin is principally an affront to God. If sin has come about *in* the creation, those *against* which Eve sinned—the heavenly world, with its angels, cherubim, and throne—lie beyond the scope of creation.

From the standpoint of GLAE, this is a telling shift, which a corresponding shift in the narrative corroborates. From here on out, action moves from the

---

[20] For a brief discussion of this topic, see my *Portraits of Adam in Early Judaism: From Sirach to Baruch* (Sheffield: Academic Press, 1988), 113–44, 156–58.

earthly to the heavenly plane: the darkened sun and moon, the angels on their faces, the washing of Adam's corpse in the Acherusian Sea and its placement in paradise in the third heaven, and the instructions to Michael about how to bury the dead properly. The pivot for this shift from earth to heaven is Eve's confession, which acknowledges that she has sinned against God, against God's angelic company, even against God's throne. This shift is highlighted through narrative details. Eve had gone outside and fallen *upon the earth* (32:1). The angel, while she prayed, made her *stand up* and twice told her to *get up* and to watch Adam's spirit being *carried up* to the one who made him. So Eve rises from the earth and looks "closely into heaven" (33:2). Her attention turns from the earth, where she once lay, to a focus upon (ἀτενίζειν) heaven.

4.2 Eve's Prayer(s) to Be with Adam

Following the heavenly visions that would capture her attention (GLAE 33–37), Eve picks up where she left off, with anxiety over her being left without Adam and her burial (31:2). "And Eve prayed, weeping, that she would be buried in the place where Adam her husband was" (42:4). What follows evinces some literary unevenness, perhaps even as the result of an awkward fusion of two versions of the scene. "*And after she finished the prayer*" to be buried where Adam was, she apparently prayed to the same end, that is, not to be separated from her husband. She finished her prayer, in other words, only to pray similarly.

> Lord, Authoritative One, God of All Virtue, stop estranging me from the body of Adam, from which you took me up from his body parts, but consider even me—this worthless sinner—worthy to enter with his tent-dwelling. As I was with him in paradise, both of us, without being separated from one another, as in the (act of) sinful neglect, having been deceived, we sinfully neglected your command without being separated—so also now, Lord, stop separating us. (42:4–7)

This final, lengthy prayer introduces the epithet, "God of All Virtue." This is new to GLAE. Yet the prayer also reprises elements familiar from earlier in GLAE: the association of prayer with weeping; the theme of Eve's close earthly relationship with Adam, and Eve's sinfulness (7:1; 11:1; 14:2; 21:2, 6) and sinful neglect (30:1); their complicity in the first sin—a perspective *not* shared by Adam (GLAE 7–8), who blamed Eve entirely, but evident in Eve's testament (14:3-30:1); and epithets for God, including the "Authoritative One" (8:1) and "Lord" (32:2).

4.3 Eve's Final Prayer

In her last prayer, "having looked up into heaven, she groaned, beating her breast and saying, 'Oh, God of All, receive my spirit'" (GLAE 42:8). Similar to so many prayers earlier in GLAE, which were accompanied by weeping, this prayer is expressed by a groan (ἀνεστέναξεν). Adam had groaned deeply on his deathbed (9:1); Eve, like him, now groans as well. Her prayer is accompanied too by the beating of her breast—usually an act of funereal mourning performed by attendants, many of them female, but enacted here by Eve on her own behalf.[21] This final prayer, therefore, is an expression of funerary grief, an exclamation point of sorts on the decree of death, accompanied by perhaps the simplest words Eve expresses in GLAE, "Oh, God of All, receive my spirit."

This request situates Eve's prayer within the compass of her Jewish heritage. In Ps 31:5, the poet offers this prayer: "Into your hands I commit my spirit."[22] In Eccl 3:21, in reflecting upon the meaning of labor and the value of wisdom, Qohelet asks, "Who knows whether the human spirit goes upward and the spirit of animals goes downward to the earth?" (Eccl 3:21).[23] In final reflections upon the nature of aging and death, he ponders how "the dust returns to the earth as it was and the spirit returns to the God who gave it" (12:7).[24] Ps 31:5, Eccl 3:21, and Eccl 12:7 may provide the foreground to Eve's prayer, but GLAE contains none of the specific vocabulary that would allow us to anchor it in these texts from the Jewish scriptures.

Closer in time to the authorship of GLAE, Luke's gospel contains Jesus's words, which echo Ps 31:5: "Father, into your hands I commend my spirit" (Luke 23:46). Closer still is Stephen's final prayer at his martyrdom in Acts 7:59: "Lord Jesus, receive my spirit." Even the Greek phrase in Eve's prayer, δέξαι τὸ πνεῦμά μου (GLAE 42:8), precisely mirrors Acts 7:59. Eve's final prayer, like Stephen's— though without any visionary experience at this climactic point, even though Eve had magnificent and disturbing visions at the ascent of *Adam's* soul (GLAE 33–37) —is a simple and straightforward plea for God to receive her spirit. As such, it caps off a theme that permeates the final section of GLAE (31–42): her body will be buried next to her husband and, she hopes, God will receive her spirit.

---

[21] On this feature of funerals, see John R. Levison, "The Roman Character of Funerals in the Writings of Josephus," *JSJ* 33 (2002): 267–68.
[22] Translations of biblical texts are from the New Revised Standard Version.
[23] The verb in LXX Ecc 3:21 (ἀναβαίνει) differs from GLAE 32:4 (ἀναφερόμενον).
[24] The use of the same verb, δίδωμι, in Adam's statement in GLAE 31:4 may suggest a connection, but the verb is too frequently used to draw any certain inference from its occurrence in GLAE 31:4.

5. Conclusion

In her study of Eve, Arbel notes that "one finds in this single narrative a range of different Eves." One Eve is viewed as "a transgressor of God's way, as Satan's vessel, as a figure of illicit sexuality and desires, and as a culpable bringer of death to Adam and all humanity." The other Eve is "a moral figure committed to God's path, an ethical and wise teacher. She is Adam's devoted and dutiful wife, an esteemed performer of traditional funerary practices, and an elevated figure with spiritual abilities who is worthy of beholding divine visions."[25] What Arbel does not say, but might have, is that the nexus of these contrasting images of Eve is GLAE 32, where Eve prays in utter earnestness, in utter self-abnegation, and, as her truest self, in utter awareness of the damage she has done. Uncontrolled yet keenly aware, she prays a prayer that is cosmic in scope and unscripted in form.

Still, for all this prayer has to offer and for the nearly ubiquitous role she plays in GLAE, Eve's subordination to Seth and Adam with respect to prayer is salient. Eve has the first and only dream in the story, yet Adam is the one who suggests prayer (1:1–5:3). Eve travels with her son Seth to the vicinity of paradise to retrieve the oil of mercy. She weeps and prays and, presumably, places dirt on her head alongside Seth, but the archangel whom God sends addresses only Seth (6:1–14:2). Eve tells the story of the first sin in far greater detail, and with much more nuance, than Adam (14:3–30:1 in contrast to 7–8), but even in her version of that sin, which exonerates her, at least in part, Adam alone prays, the angels address Adam alone, and God responds alone to Adam, who, tellingly, asks to take out the plants of paradise primarily for himself: "Lord, give to me from the plant of life so that I may eat before I am thrown out" (28:2; see 29:4–5). Only in the final section does Eve find her voice in prayer—and then only because Adam commands her to pray (31:4).

Although Eve's prayers are overshadowed in GLAE by those of her husband Adam and her son Seth, her voice, when it does finally emerge, is effusive (32:1–2). Her confession is protracted—it is the longest prayer in GLAE—and detailed, with a litany of heavenly beings and realities against which she has sinned. It is also without reservation, as she claims that sin entered the creation through her, even if this claim conflicts with Adam's similar, if less effusive, claim to being the sole sinner in the story (27:2). Eve's confession is more than just an

---

25 Arbel, *Forming Femininity*, 113. For an earlier exploration of this contrast, noted in Arbel, idem, 7, see John R. Levison, "The Exoneration and Denigration of Eve in the *Greek Life of Adam and Eve*," in *Literature on Adam and Eve: Collected Essays*, ed. Gary Anderson, Michael Stone, and Johannes Tromp (Leiden: Brill, 2000), 251–75; earlier still, see Levison, "The Exoneration of Eve in the Apocalypse of Moses 15–30."

expression of her story, a solipsistic wringing of her hands; it marks the transition from earthly to heavenly realities. Her physical movements reflect the movement of the narrative as a whole: just as she gets up from the ground and lifts her eyes to heaven, so the story of GLAE shifts from the earthly plane to the heavenly, where the pardoning of Adam takes place.

If Eve's confession marks a climactic moment in GLAE, her prayers return, after this point, to more pedestrian concerns of someone about to lose a beloved spouse. Eve's final extended prayers focus upon her desire not to be left behind; she wants to join Adam, to be buried alongside him (42:4-7). She was created from him. She was inseparable from him in paradise. She was neglectful with him. She was deceived with him. Now she begs to be buried alongside him.

Her final prayer is simpler but no less profound for that reason. In fact, it is a prayer that reflects the prayers of the psalmists and the preoccupations of Ecclesiastes. It is a prayer that confronts the reality of death but affirms, too, life beyond death. Without the visions that attend the ascent of Adam's soul, Eve prays simply for God to receive her spirit. The narrator does not divulge God's response to this prayer, though perhaps the answer is implicit in God's response to her earlier plea: "And Michael came and taught Seth how to bury Eve. And three angels went and took her body up and buried it where the body of Adam—and of Abel—was" (43:1). Inseparable in life, inseparable in sin, Eve and Adam would now be inseparable in death.

Shelly Matthews
"I Have Prayed for You ... Strengthen Your Brothers" (Luke 22:32): Jesus's Proleptic Prayer for Peter and Other Gendered Tropes in Luke's War on Satan

1. Introduction

In Luke's distinctive version of the Last Supper, Jesus explains to Peter that he has offered up a prayer on his behalf, so that Peter might withstand Satan's attack. The passage reads: "Simon, Simon, listen! Satan has demanded to sift all of you (ὑμᾶς) like wheat; but I have prayed for you (περὶ σοῦ) that your own faith may not fail; and you (σύ) when you have turned back, strengthen your brothers" (Luke 22:31–32, NRSV). Readers with knowledge of the basic plot of the passion narrative will recognize the rhetorical function of this Lukan prayer, of course, as serving to foreshadow the apostles' abandonment of Jesus, Peter's denial of Jesus while Jesus is in custody, and Peter's eventual rehabilitation as first witness to the resurrection and chief spokesperson for the twelve apostles.[1]

But even though its rhetorical function is obvious, the prayer is yet part of a peculiar narrative scene. Here the Lukan Jesus discloses knowledge of something Satan has demanded. Differently from other pieces of information the reader gleans about the presence and movement of the devil at Luke 4:1–13, or of Satan at Luke 10:18 and Luke 22:3, no details are provided in this instance about how Jesus has come to possess this knowledge. Insofar as Satan's demand (ἐξαιτέω) is understood as a legal claim, it may be imagined that Jesus has knowledge of (or participated in?) the proceedings of a heavenly court, where Satan has legitimate standing.

Read in this way Jesus's words suggest a scenario of the sort found in Job 1:6–12. As in the case of Job, Satan has enough standing to receive what he demands. Jesus apparently cannot prevent the "sifting" (σινιάζω; for more on this term, see below), but he reassures Peter that he has prayed (δέομαι) for him that he might withstand the trial. Readers will find as the narrative unfolds that Peter does

---

[1] As indicated by the Greek insertions, the first instance of the pronoun "you" is plural presumably referring to the Twelve as a group, but the direct address is to Peter, and the prayer and the subsequent exhortation are in the singular and concern Peter alone.

https://doi.org/10.1515/9783110624526-012

indeed endure the sifting to assume a leadership role among the Twelve, and thus that Jesus's intercessory prayer is efficacious.

This essay attempts to clarify the function of this scene in Luke. First, we lay out some ground-clearing arguments concerning the mechanics of the prayer and the subsequent exhortation, in terms of rhetorical categories and Luke's rhetorical aims, as well as his compositional processes. Second, we engage recent scholarship which focuses more centrally on Satan's violence to clarify the specific meaning of Satan's demand upon Peter. In the final section, we situate this passage alongside other key Lukan passages concerning Satan and the demonic, using gender analysis as a lens. The argument here is that this proleptic prayer concerning Peter, along with the subsequent exhortation to "strengthen the brothers," shares with other references to Satan and the demonic in Luke the concern to frame the encounter with demonic forces as *a battle*, one that Luke casts in masculine, military tropes. Because Peter has withstood the dangerous confrontation with Satan, proof of not only his faith, but also his virility, he is then commissioned to "strengthen the brothers" for ongoing battles with Satan. That this commission is androcentric and exclusive is underscored by depictions of women in Luke, whose only postures vis-à-vis the demonic are as those whom the minions of Satan have inhabited.

2. Compositional Processes, Rhetorical Concerns, Literary Precedents

Luke's Last Supper narrative is distinctive among the Synoptic Gospels in attributing a relatively large amount of speech to Jesus during the meal. A widely recognized explanation for this is that Luke has modeled the scene on the form of a Greco-Roman farewell address, such as we have in Plato's *Phaedo* the Maccabean story of the patriarch Mattathias (1 Macc 2:49–70), or the Testament literature within Jewish Pseudepigrapha.[2]

Because Jesus's prayer is predictive, foreshadowing Peter's denial and subsequent rehabilitation, some commentators have regarded it as an instance of *vaticinium ex eventu*. But it may be more useful to think in terms of rhetorical categories

---

[2] For the argument that Luke draws from the literary trope of the farewell address here, see William S. Kurz, S.J., "Luke 22:14–38 and Greco-Roman and Biblical Farewell Addresses," *JBL* 104 (1985): 251–68. François Bovon agrees that the farewell address is a model, but also notes that Luke 22 is more dialogic than a typical farewell speech. See, François Bovon, *Luke 3: Commentary on 19:28–24:53*, Hermeneia (Minneapolis: Augsburg Fortress, 2012), 169.

rather than prophecy here. We have in this passage an instance of *prolepsis* or *procatalepsis*, in the technical sense of the term in ancient forensic rhetoric: Luke crafts a prebuttal, an argument that anticipates an objection concerning a particular defendant, in hopes of diminishing the strength of that objection. The objection, found in the Gospel of Mark's story of Peter, and retold with refinements in both Matthew and Luke, is that while Peter confidently vowed neither to desert nor to deny Jesus (Mark 14:29–31; Matt 26:33–35; Luke 22:33–34; cf. John 13:37–38), he does just that three times before the cock crows (Mark 14:66–72; Matt 26:69–75; Luke 22:54–62). Or, to say it another way, Peter does *not* stand by Jesus in his trials, a fact that suggests that Luke 22:28 ("You are those who have stood by me in my trials," NRSV) is part of Luke's prebuttal as well.

Because the prayer for Peter to endure Satan's attack is one of many distinct details within Luke's account of the Passover meal, some scholars hypothesize that Luke is drawing from his special written source, one available to no other gospel author, when he composes this scene.[3] But we agree instead with those who regard Luke's indisputable source—the Gospel of Mark—as containing sufficient materials from which Luke might build this saying. To state this in terms of the rhetorical nature of ancient historiography, on the one hand Luke is bound by the conventions of ancient rhetoric to acknowledge well known "events" of the recent past—such as the denial of Peter.[4] On the other hand, owing to the rhetorical practice of *inventio*—the aspect of rhetoric that Cicero defines as first and most important, involving, "the thinking-up of material true or truth-like, to make one's case plausible"—Luke has a considerable amount of freedom to craft the story of that denial in the best possible light.[5]

Equipped with the Gospel of Mark, in which Peter is portrayed as a coward and a moral failure, the rhetorical aim to present Peter in a more heroic light, and the rhetorical principle of *inventio*, Luke makes the following alterations to his source: while Luke 9:18–20 follows Mark 8:27–30 in assigning to Peter the correct identification of Jesus as messiah, he withholds the narrative of Jesus's rebuke of Satan

---

[3] Consider, for example, Bovon, *Luke 3*, 172.
[4] We do not argue here for the historicity of Peter's denial, but only for its secure place in pre-Lukan traditions about Jesus.
[5] Cicero, *Inv.* 1.9, cited in Cynthia Damon, "Rhetoric and Historiography," in *A Companion to Roman Rhetoric*, ed. Jonathan M. Hall and William Dominik (New York: Wiley & Sons, 2008), 439–50, esp. 440. For summary and analysis of arguments for Luke's use of an unknown, non-canonical written source of his passion, see Heather M. Gorman, *Interweaving Innocence: A Rhetorical Analysis of Luke's Passion Narrative (Lk 22:66–23:49)* (Eugene: Pickwick, 2015), 6–10. Gorman's argument aligns with the argument here that Luke's variations from Mark can be accounted for in terms of compositional techniques allowing for creative re-working of sources.

when Peter misapprehends Jesus's prediction of suffering (Mark 8:32–33). Instead of following Mark's sequence here, Luke reserves dominical speech concerning Satan's role in Peter's failings until immediately before the denial itself. This makes it possible to account for these failings within the window of time in which both Jesus and the rest of the disciples are also vulnerable to Satan's attacks (cf. Luke 22:3, 53; 23:44). Thus, Peter's widely known failings and Satan's intervention are introduced immediately before the denial itself, while being situated within a narrative that still affirms Peter's prominence and promises his swift rehabilitation.[6]

With respect to the question of analogues between Jesus's prayer here and other early Jewish literature, wide agreement exists that the prayer may be classified as "intercessory."[7] But there is no prayer quite like this, in which the intercessory prayer specifically concerns withstanding Satan's violent claim upon another. Joel Green suggests that the scene is a variation on the exhortations concerning future attacks of Satan in the Testament of the Twelve Patriarchs (T. 12 Patr.). Though the passages he cites contain both the prediction of future attack, and the promise of protection from Beliar, T. 12 Patr.'s generalized exhortations do not share the immediacy and specificity of Luke's direct personal address to Peter. Nor do the patriarchs express these predictions in the form of intercessory prayer.[8]

Michael Morris has noted that Jesus's prayer in Luke 22:32 shares certain features with "third party intercessory apotropaic petitions" found in Jubilees. As Moses intercedes on behalf of Israel against the spirit of Beliar (Jub. 1:20), and Noah intercedes on behalf of his progeny for protection against evil spirits (Jub. 10:3), so here Jesus intercedes for Peter in the face of Satan's demand. But Morris also notes that because Jesus's prayer is not for the fending off of Satan, but rather assumes

---

[6] This argument stands in basic agreement with Marc Rastoin, "Simon-Pierre entre Jésus et Satan: La théologie lucanienne à l'oeuvre en Lc 22,31–32," *Bib* 89 (2008): 153–72. Rastoin's characterization of Satan's demand to sift as an archaism (166), may not be precise, given that the Greek term employed for sifting is not attested before Luke. Yet, his more general proposal that Luke casts Satan in language that is exoticising, and thus might appeal to a Roman or Romanized reader who admires practitioners of so-called "eastern" religious rites for their strange and dramatic features, is suggestive. Consider the strange passage in Josephus concerning the exorcism Eliezar performs before Vespasian, *Ant.* 8.46–47.

[7] David Michael Crump, *Jesus the Intercessor: Prayer and Christology in Luke-Acts*, WUNT 2.49 (Tübingen: Mohr Siebeck 1992), 154–57.

[8] Joel B. Green, *The Gospel of Luke*, NICNT (Grand Rapids: Eerdmans, 1997), 771. Among the passages cited by Green from the testament literature (T. Benj. 3:3; T. Reu. 2:1–12; T. Dan 5:6, 10–12; T. Levi 18:12; T. Iss. 7:7), the closest match in terms of an exhortation by a dying patriarch concerning impending machinations of a demonic being (here, Beliar) may be this: "Even if the spirits of Beliar demand you for themselves for every evil affliction, they will not lord over you.... καὶ ἐὰν τὰ πνεύματα τοῦ Βελιὰρ εἰς πᾶσαν πονηρίαν θλίψεως ἐξαιτήσωνται ὑμᾶς, οὐ μὴ κατακυριεύσῃ ὑμῶν (my translation). For more on the verb for Beliar's demand, see below, n13.

Satan's interference, it is technically not apotropaic in function. Jesus advocates for Peter, but does not have the ability to shield him from the demonic.[9] We argue that the constraints of Luke's narrative prevent the inclusion of a truly apotropaic prayer of Jesus for Peter here. What Luke needs to account for are Peter's failings, which he does by pointing to Satan's presence. This constrains his account of Jesus's prayer, which can only be for Peter's conversion and rehabilitation, and not for the warding off of Satan altogether.

In what follows, Jesus's prayer for Peter is not considered in isolation from the larger saying of Jesus, in Luke 22:31–32. It is argued instead that the significance of the prayer is best understood through acknowledgment of Satan's demand as an act of violence on the one hand, and through analysis of Jesus's subsequent exhortation to Peter to "strengthen his brothers" on the other.

3. Satan the Executioner

Scholars have often turned to the book of Job, and to the traditional view that Satan's role in Job is the role of "the accuser" in a legal setting, to clarify the question of precisely what the roles of Satan and Jesus are in this saying addressed to Peter. Sometimes scenarios from modern courtroom proceedings are invoked, where judicial restraint presides, while the lawyers parry to score legal points. François Bovon, for example, has noted that Jesus's prayer suggests the "framework of a trial—a trial at God's court. On the one hand Satan 'demanded' and obtained the right to test Peter. On the other Jesus 'requested' as an attorney, and it was granted to him, that Peter's faith finally would prevail."[10]

While Luke might indeed be evoking a courtroom scene, we do well to remember the integral nature of violence to ancient Roman judicial procedure, and further to recognize the violent connotations that adhere to the figure of Satan in the ancient world.[11] Ryan Stokes has recently argued that while the term satan in Hebrew Scriptures is often translated as "accuser" or "prosecuting attorney," it commonly denotes physical attack. He concludes that in some instances the term might best be translated as "executioner."[12]

---

9 Michael J. Morris, *Warding Off Evil: Apotropaic Tradition in the Dead Sea Scrolls and Synoptic Gospels*, WUNT 2.451 (Tübingen: Mohr Siebeck, 2017), 242.
10 Bovon, *Luke 3*, 178.
11 See, for instance, Brent Shaw, "Judicial Nightmares and Christian Memory," *JECS* 11 (2003): 533–63.
12 Ryan E. Stokes, "Satan, YHWH'S Executioner," *JBL* 133 (2014): 251–70.

That Satan in Luke 22:31 is attacking rather than accusing, and thus that the scene invoked by the prayer might be a courtroom inhabited by an executioner—or even that the words are meant to evoke some ethereal battlefield—might be supported by the line's verbs, both of which are hapax legomena within the NT. The Greek verb ἐξαιτοῦμαι "to claim for oneself," when associated with Satan and the demonic, denotes violence against the one claimed.[13] Outside of the Gospel of Luke, σινιάζω is attested only in sources of a later date, from the patristic period and beyond. Because the word is associated with grain in Luke, and because this is how the word comes to be used in patristic sources, it is correctly translated in Luke 22:31 as "to sift, or filter." Yet, if it is recognized that this verb derives from the same family of terms as σίνομαι/σίνος, terms denoting violence, injury, ravishing or pillaging, the violence of that sifting is clear.[14] Satan's "claiming the apostles for himself," in order to "sift" them, is arguably a claim on their very lives.[15]

Stoke's understanding of the role of Satan in Zech 3:1–7, which he tracks as the movement from Joshua's status as sinner at the verge of execution by Satan to redeemed and commissioned high priest, may also help to clarify Luke 22:31. Stokes argues against the NRSV translation of Zech 3:1, in which Satan is understood as standing at YHWH's right hand *to accuse* Joshua the high priest, for not recognizing the violence implied in Satan's presence. He offers his own translation as, "Then he showed me the high priest Joshua standing before the angel of YHWH, and the Executioner standing on his right *to execute* him." The passage then offers up the following details: Joshua is guilty of some iniquity, as indicated by the filthy clothes he wears as he stands before the angel. But before the executioner can execute, the Lord rebukes him, and subsequently, the angel of the Lord intervenes to take away Joshua's guilt, re-clothing him in festal attire, and re-establishing him as high priest.

I suggest that the structure of the narrative that Stokes has outlined in terms of the high priest Joshua in Zech 3:1–7 conforms to the structure of Luke 22 with respect to Peter:[16]

---

[13] BAGD cites at the entry for ἐξαιτέω Plutarch's *Mor.* 417D: "But as Heracles laid siege to Oechalia for the sake of a maiden, so powerful and impetuous divinities, in demanding a human soul (ἐξαιτούμενοι ψυχήν) which is incarnate within a mortal body ... bring pestilences ... until they succeed in obtaining what they desire" (Babbitt, LCL). Cf. also T. Benj. 3:3: "And if the spirits of Beliar demand you for themselves for every evil affliction (εἰς πᾶσαν πονηρίαν θλίψεως ἐξαιτήσωνται ὑμᾶς)."
[14] LSJ, s.v. "σίνομαι," "σίνος."
[15] That sinners are appropriately handed over to Satan for execution seems also to be the understanding of Paul in 1 Cor 5:5.
[16] Stokes, "Satan," 262–66.

– Joshua's life is in peril on account of his guilt; Satan stands ready to execute (Zech 3:1–3)	– Peter's life is in peril on account of his guilt (guilt that is presumed by readers, and laid out later in the narrative of the denial, Luke 22:54–62); Satan demands the right to attack (Luke 22:31)
– the divine attendants remove Joshua's filthy clothes and the angel of YHWH declares that he has taken away Joshua's guilt (Zech 3:4)	– Jesus himself intercedes in order that Peter's "faith not fail," and signals proleptically Peter's repentance through the verb of returning (σύ ποτε ἐπιστρέψας) (Luke 22:32)
– Once his guilt has been removed and the danger eliminated, Joshua receives his commission to serve as high priest (Zech 3:7)	– once his guilt has been removed and the danger eliminated, Peter receives his commission to stand first among the Twelve, to "strengthen his brothers" (στήρισον τοὺς ἀδελφούς σου) (Luke 22:32)

In Peter's case, the consequence of having withstood the violent contest with Satan, is this charge from Jesus to Peter, cast in androcentric terms: "strengthen your brothers."

Recognizing that the contest with Satan is framed in these violent terms, and that Peter's survival of this attack results is the androcentric charge to strengthen his brothers, provides clarity on the workings of gender in Luke's Gospel, a point to which we now turn.

4. The Contest with Satan, Gender, and Authority in Luke

A significant body of feminist scholarship on the Gospel of Luke has recognized a redactional tendency both to privilege the male apostles and to shore up their authority on the one hand, while diminishing and silencing women in the *basileia* movement on the other.[17] The proleptic prayer for Peter, his rehabilitation and his

---

[17] See, for instance, Elisabeth Schüssler Fiorenza, "A Feminist Critical Interpretation for Liberation: Martha and Mary: Luke 10:38–42," *Religion and Intellectual Life* 3 (1986): 21–35, eadem, *But She Said: Feminist Practices of Biblical Interpretation* (Boston: Beacon, 1992), 51–76; Jane Schaberg and Sharon H. Ringe, "Gospel of Luke," in *Women's Bible Commentary*, ed. Carol A. Newsom, Sharon H. Ringe, and Jacqueline E. Lapsley, 3rd ed.(Louisville: 2012), 507–509; Barbara Reid, *Choosing the Better Part? Women in the Gospel of Luke* (Collegeville: Liturgical Press, 1996); Mary Rose D'Angelo, "Women in Luke-Acts: A Redactional View," *JBL* 109 (1990): 441–61; eadem, "The

commission to strengthen the brothers can be understood as part of that general redactional tendency.

But training our lens on the question of how gender functions specifically in relation to Luke's concerns with Satan and the demonic throughout his Gospel allows us to assess the gendered dynamics of this passage with more nuance. In this closing section, the argument is that Luke's rehabilitation of the morally compromised Peter as leader of the Twelve, while concomitant with his diminishment of women's place in the *basileia* movement, is not best explained as a simple contest concerning the sexes—one in which Luke prefers male over female characters because of a generic androcentrism. Rather, this proleptic prayer shares with other references to Satan and the demonic in Luke concern to frame the encounter with demonic forces as *a battle*, one Luke casts in military tropes, and thus one that requires virile male subjects as its generals and foot soldiers. Or, to say it another way, both the rehabilitation of Peter, anticipated in Jesus's words, and the suppression of traces of women's agency in the movement may be accounted for by Luke's concern to demonstrate that Jesus and his followers are engaged in a war of cosmic proportions to bring about the "demise of the devil"; and further, that the success of this mission proves that Jesus and his successors achieve a superior state of manhood, embodying Roman ideals of masculinity.[18] To make this argument, we situate the prayer of Jesus for Peter and the subsequent exhortation to strengthen the brothers alongside other key Lukan passages in which gendered tropes are utilized to characterize the battle with Satan and the demonic.

4.1 *Demise of the Devil* Reviewed and Expanded

Susan Garrett's monograph *Demise of the Devil* was a watershed contribution to Luke-Acts scholarship, demonstrating that Satan and the demonic play a larger part in the narrative of Luke-Acts than scholars had previously acknowledged.[19]

ANHP Question in Luke-Acts: Imperial Masculinity and the Deployment of Women in the Early Second Century," in *A Feminist Companion to Luke*, ed. Amy-Jill Levine FCNTECW (London: Sheffield Academic Press, 2002), 63–88; Marianne Sawicki, *Seeing the Lord: Resurrection and Early Christian Practices* (Minneapolis: Fortress, 1994), 149–81; Barbara Reid and Shelly Matthews, *Luke*, Wisdom Commentary 43 (Collegeville: Liturgical Press, 2021).

18 For the alternative view, that the gospel of Luke and the book of Acts do much to challenge Roman ideals of hegemonic masculinity, see Brittany E. Wilson, *Unmanly Men: Refigurations of Masculinity in Luke-Acts* (New York: Oxford, 2015).

19 Susan R. Garrett, *The Demise of the Devil: Magic and the Demonic in Luke's Writings* (Minneapolis: Fortress Press, 1989), esp. 37–60. Though scholarship on the demonic in the New Testament world has flourished since the time of this publication, Garrett's book well anticipates, and

These arguments include that Satan and his demonic forces have entered into and cause the suffering of countless persons, that Jesus battles these forces through exorcisms and other types of healings, and commissions his chosen leaders—the apostles and also the seventy (-two)—to do the same. Furthermore, Luke makes clear that Satan is active in the machinations of the Jewish leaders against Jesus, most explicitly in Satan's entering of Judas, who then conspires with the chief priests and temple police to bring him down (Luke 22:3–6).[20] Though Jesus and by extension his apostles, are temporarily weakened, during the "power of darkness" that reigns over his passion (Luke 22:53b; 23:44), he eventually triumphs over Satan, displacing him from the throne. After his resurrection and ascension, the Acts narrative demonstrates, with special focus on the heroism of Peter and then Paul, how the battle against the minions of Satan continues.

Building on Garrett's work, we demonstrate here that, as in Jesus's prayer for Peter, in key passages intimating the battle with, and ultimate defeat of, Satan by Jesus and his successors, gendered tropes are at play, manifesting themselves to authorize male leadership and de-authorize the women in the movement.

4.2. The Beelzebul Controversy / Subduing the Strong Man: Luke 11:14–22

In each of the Synoptic Gospels Jesus's refutation of the accusation that he casts out demons by the power of Beelzebul (Mark 3:22–26; Matt 12:22–28; Luke 11:14–20) is followed by a saying that likens Jesus to one who uses force against "the strong man" (Mark 3:37; Matt 12:29; Luke 11:21–22). Context makes clear that the strong man represents the demonic force of Beelzebul/Satan.[21] Luke raises the

---

stands in basic agreement with the best of this scholarship. For example, her recognition of Luke's argument that Jesus has essentially destroyed Satan and the demonic, but yet the demonic still exists in weakened form, to be battled again and again until the final eschatological judgment, lines up with Enochic and other Jewish traditions concerning the "already/not yet" of the divine triumph over the demonic that have recently been the subject of much scholarly attention. Consider here Loren T. Struckenbruck, *The Myth of the Rebellious Angels: Studies in Second Temple Judaism and New Testament Texts* (Tübingen: Mohr Siebeck, 2014), 161–84.

20 For analysis of how Lukan redaction serves to heighten the role of the Jerusalem leadership in Jesus's death, see Peter Rice, "The Rhetoric of Luke's Passion: Luke's Use of Common-place to Amplify the Guilt of Jerusalem's Leaders in Jesus' Death," *BibInt* 21-3 (2013): 355–76.

21 For the argument that the Strong Man is a cipher for the demonic power of the Roman empire in the Gospel of Mark, see the classic argument of Ched Myers, *Binding the Strong Man: A Political Reading of Mark's Story of Jesus*, 20th Anniversary Edition (Maryknoll: Orbis, 2018); Rodney A. Wereline, "The Experience of Prayer and Resistance to Demonic Powers in the Gospel of Mark,"

stakes of the battle with the strong man by using military tropes, as can be noted by comparing the distinctive features of Luke's strong man saying against his synoptic counterparts:

Matt 12:29	Mark 3:27	Luke 11:21–22
Or how can one enter a strong man's house and plunder his property, without first tying up the strong man? Then indeed the house can be plundered. (NRSV)	But no one can enter a strong man's house and plunder his property without first tying up the strong man; then indeed the house can be plundered. (NRSV)	When a strong man, **fully armed, guards his castle**, his property is safe. But when **one stronger than he attacks him and overpowers him, he takes away his armor** in which he trusted and divides his plunder. (NRSV)
ἢ πῶς δύναταί τις εἰσελθεῖν εἰς τὴν οἰκίαν τοῦ ἰσχυροῦ καὶ τὰ σκεύη αὐτοῦ ἁρπάσαι, ἐὰν μὴ πρῶτον δήσῃ τὸν ἰσχυρόν:; καὶ τότε τὴν οἰκίαν αὐτοῦ διαρπάσει.	ἀλλ' οὐ δύναται οὐδεὶς εἰς τὴν οἰκίαν τοῦ ἰσχυροῦ εἰσελθὼν τὰ σκεύη αὐτοῦ διαρπάσαι, ἐὰν μὴ πρῶτον τὸν ἰσχυρὸν δήσῃ, καὶ τότε τὴν οἰκίαν αὐτοῦ διαρπάσει.	ὅταν ὁ ἰσχυρὸς **καθωπλισμένος φυλάσσῃ τὴν ἑαυτοῦ αὐλήν**, ἐν εἰρήνῃ ἐστὶν τὰ ὑπάρχοντα αὐτοῦ· **ἐπὰν δὲ ἰσχυρότερος αὐτοῦ ἐπελθὼν νικήσῃ** αὐτόν, **τὴν πανοπλίαν αὐτοῦ αἴρει** ἐφ' ᾗ ἐπεποίθει καὶ τὰ σκῦλα αὐτοῦ διαδίδωσιν.

To list the most significant aspects of Lukan redaction:

1) the strong man is described as a combatant fully outfitted with weapons of war —καθωπλισμένος

2) the strong man has not merely a "house" that can be entered, but rather, a castle or estate (αὐλή) to be guarded; thus suggesting a territory, rather than a neighborhood setting

3) the stronger man does not merely bind, but rather gains victory (νικάω), and as a result is able to strip the weapons from the adversary.

In short, Luke transforms the Markan saying about a thief, one who breaks and enters a house in order to restrain the owner and burgle the house, into a military engagement involving a fully armed lord and his castle, with the victorious stronger man taking possession of the armaments. While all three versions of the say-

---

in *Experientia, Volume 1: Sites for Inquiry for Religious Experience in Early Judaism and Christianity*, ed. Frances Flannery, Colleen Shantz, and Rodney A. Werline (Atlanta: SBL Press, 2008), 59–71.

ing imply that Jesus, through his exorcisms, gains the upper hand against the demonic, Luke ups the ante by moving from the analogy of burglary to that of war.[22] This heightens the gendered nature of the conflict, for as Joy Connolly puts it in her study of Roman masculinity, war, along with "virtue, action, substance and integrity … constitute the ideal values of Roman manliness in its most archaic form—the purest expression of Rome's collective cultural fantasy."[23] Luke taps into that cultural fantasy of Roman manliness in this pericope.

4.3 The Commissioning of the Seventy (-Two): Luke 10:1–20[24]

Preceding the Beelzebul and strong man sayings in Luke is another passage that is distinctively Lukan, pertaining to the appointment by Jesus of the seventy (-two) sent out in mission. The story begins: "After this the Lord appointed seventy others and sent them on ahead of him in pairs to every town and place where he himself intended to go" (Luke 10:1, NRSV). Pointing to Luke's special interest in depicting Jesus as a Prophet like Moses (cf. Acts 3:22; 7:37), and also to the fact that both narratives assume that the spirit possessed by the Prophet can be transferred to those he commissions, Susan Garrett has argued that Luke's story is modeled on Moses's appointment of seventy elders from Num 11:16–25:[25]

> And the Lord said to Moses, "Gather me seventy men from the elders of Israel, whom you know to be the elders of the people, and their scribes … and I will take of the spirit that is upon thee, and will put it into them (Num 11:16–17a, LXX [Brenton]).

While agreeing with Garett's argument that the commissioning story from Numbers is evoked by Luke here, we underscore further that the gendered features of the narrative may also be important to Luke.[26] The leaders upon whom a share of Moses's own spirit are cast are men, elders, and scribes (ἀνδρές, πρεσβύτεροι,

---

[22] See John Nolland, *Luke 9:21–18:34*, WBC (Dallas: Word, 1993), 641.
[23] Joy Connolly, "Virile Tongues: Rhetoric and Masculinity," in *A Companion to Roman Rhetoric*, ed. Jonathan M. Hall and William Dominik (New York: Wiley & Sons, 2008), 83–97 (84).
[24] The manuscript tradition of Luke is divided over whether the number here is 70 or 72. See Bruce M. Metzger, "Seventy or Seventy-two Disciples?" *NTS* 5 (1958–59): 299–306, and the discussion of Garrett, *Demise of the Devil*, 46–49.
[25] Garrett, *Demise of the Devil*, 47–48.
[26] For the alternate view that the commissioning of the seventy (-two) symbolizes the story of the seventy (-two) nations established after the flood in Genesis 10:2–31, and thus prepares for the universal mission that will unfold in the book of Acts, see Bovon, *Luke 2*, 26; Joel B. Green, *The Gospel of Luke* NICNT (Grand Rapids, MI: Eerdmans, 1997), 412. Given that narratives may be multivalent, it is possible that allusions to both stories are operative.

γραμματεῖς, Num 11:16 LXX). The Greek ἀνδρές denotes men exclusively, and as Mary Rose D'Angelo has shown, concern to designate the protagonists of his narrative as ἀνδρές is signaled throughout Luke-Acts.[27] Further, elders and scribes suggest a group of men in public leadership positions. And while feminist linguists have taught us that in every instance of androcentric language one needs to "adjudicate in light of contextual clues whether wo/men are meant or not," both the casting of exorcism as a binding of the strong man by the "stronger man" at 11:21–22, and the other gendered clues concerning the battle with demons we take up below, suggest that Luke evokes the commissioning story from Numbers in order to establish a leadership group of seventy (-two) men in the gender exclusive sense.[28]

The conclusion of the pericope also crafts the seventy (-two) as the dominant force in a hierarchical, and thus gendered, struggle. The appointed group returns to celebrate the fact that the demons submit to them (ὑποτάσσω; Luke 10:17). Jesus responds by narrating a vision of Satan falling from heaven and the further authorizing of the seventy (-two) with respect to the demonic. They are empowered to "tread (πατέω) on snakes and scorpions, and over all the power (δύναμις) of the enemy" (Luke 10:19, NRSV). In short, in addition to singling out the Twelve—the male apostles—and granting them power and authority for an exorcising ministry in 9:1–6, Luke supplies in Luke 10:1–20 what might be considered an extra layer of offense in the virile army of those who battle demons and disease.[29]

4.4 Women, the Demon's Entry, and Sexual Shame

As we have seen above, Luke's descriptions of how his protagonists engage Satan and his minions utilize masculine tropes of warfare.[30] The lord of the castle may be a fully armed strong man, but Jesus is "the stronger man" who wrests from him

---

27 D'Angelo, "The ANHP Question in Luke-Acts."
28 Elisabeth Schüssler Fiorenza, *Wisdom Ways: Introducing Feminist Biblical Interpretation* (Maryknoll: Orbis, 2001), 115.
29 Even in terms of the commissioning of the Twelve, in Luke 9:1–6, Luke emphasizes force more than Mark or Matthew, telling that the twelve had not just authority (ἐξουσία, Matt 10:1; par. Mark 6:7); but "power and authority" (δύναμις καὶ ἐξουσία).
30 For gender analysis of Luke's descriptions of actual warfare, with reference to the siege and ultimate defeat of Jerusalem, see Caryn A. Reeder, *Gendering War and Peace in the Gospel of Luke* (Cambridge: Cambridge University Press, 2019). This book was made available to me too late to incorporate fully into the arguments here.

his weapons of war and thus attains the victory (νικάω). The seventy (-two) bring the demons to postures of submission, and Jesus grants them authority over the enemy's power (δύναμις). Peter survives a harrowing attack on his life by Satan himself, and in turn is granted the authority to strengthen his fellow apostles. These masculine contests in which Jesus, Peter, the male apostles, and the seventy (-two) male leaders engage Satan and his minions help to set in relief Luke's redaction of traditions that women held prominent places among Jesus's companions. Women might finance the mission, as they are said to have done in Luke 8:2–3; they might sit at Jesus's feet within private homes and listen, as Mary does in Luke 10:38–42. But the traces of women's prominence in the *basileia* movement that one finds in the other canonical gospels, as well as in Pauline literature, and extra-canonical sources such as the Gospel of Mary or the Acts of Thecla, are muffled or eliminated in Luke's Gospel.[31] Furthermore, in Luke's gendered construction of the battle against the demonic under consideration here, women are not exorcists or spiritual "soldiers" of any sort.[32]

Given that in the ancient Roman world, sexual roles and accompanying gender identities were centrally organized around questions of insertion and reception, "where those with more power ideally and phallically penetrated those with less," it is noteworthy that the only posture vis-à-vis the demonic for women in Luke is that of the stereotypical feminine posture of having been penetrated by demons.[33] Consider, especially the sweeping characterization in Luke that *all* of the women providing for Jesus were once inhabited by demons:

---

[31] See here most recently Reid and Matthews, *Luke*.

[32] That women in the ancient world were engaged in practices of healing, including healings of those considered under the power of the demonic, may be gleaned primarily from reading against the grain ancient sources denigrating women as witches, or as otherwise engaged in practices of magic. See Elaine M. Wainwright, *Women Healing/Healing Women: The Genderization of Healing in Early Christianity* (London: Equinox, 2006), 71–97; Kimberly B. Stratton, *Naming the Witch: Magic, Ideology and Stereotype in the Ancient World* (New York: Columbia University Press, 2007).

[33] For this quotation, see Jason Edwards, *Eve Kosofsky Sedgwick*, Routledge Critical Thinkers (New York: Routledge, 2009), 21. For an important analysis of ancient Roman gender ideology, with attention to issues of penetration, see Bernadette Brooten, *Love Between Women: Early Christian Responses to Female Homoeroticism* (Chicago: University of Chicago Press, 1996). Loren T. Stuckenbruck (*The Myth of Rebellious Angels: Studies in Second Temple Judaism and New Testament Texts* [Tübingen: Mohr Siebeck, 2014], 174–76) notes that demonic possession in the Synoptic Gospels is primarily assumed to involve entry into the body, and that this sets these gospels apart from the more widespread tendency to depict demonic activity as "affliction or attack" rather than as entry. My argument here requires some tweaking of Stuckenbruck's observation. For women and others outside of the masculine circle in Luke, demons penetrate, but neither

> The twelve were with him, as well as some women who had been cured of evil spirits and infirmities (γυναῖκές τινες αἳ ἦσαν τεθεραπευμέναι ἀπὸ πνευμάτων πονηρῶν καὶ ἀσθενειῶν): Mary, called Magdalene, from whom seven demons had gone out (ἀφ' ἧς δαιμόνια ἑπτὰ ἐξεληλύθει), and Joanna, the wife of Herod's steward Chuza, and Susanna, and many others, who provided for them out of their resources (Luke 8:1b–3a, NRSV).

Luke does not explicitly associate this demonic inhabitation with sexual penetration, but this conceptual cluster is recognized in near contemporary texts and may be implicit in Luke's characterization here. Consider that the temptation of Eve by Satan is widely assumed to be a form of sexual "seduction" (LAE 9–11; 4 Macc 18:7–8; 2 En. 31:6; 2 Cor 11:3) and that the story of the demon-possessed woman in the Acts of Thomas 42–46, to be discussed further below, is also a story of sexual violation. The conceptual overlap between the shame of sexual violation and corporeal inhabitation by demons might help to explain what comes to be a pervasive tradition in early Christian tradition, that Mary Magdalene, once possessed of seven demons, was a prostitute.[34]

A further implication of this assertion that all of the women who provided for Jesus and the Twelve had been exorcised by him may be drawn from recent scholarship on ancient demonology. Both Loren Stuckenbruck and Joel Marcus note that exorcism is typically a matter of relocation, rather than of the destruction of demons, and that bodies once inhabited by a demon or demons are thus vulnerable to a repossession.[35] Connections between demon penetration, sexual violation, and the threat of repossession are nicely illustrated in the story of the demon exorcised from a woman in the Acts of Thomas 42–46. Here the demon's entrance into the woman is described as violent intercourse.[36] While the demon is driven out by the presence of the Apostle Thomas, he threatens to enter her again, once

---

Jesus nor his commissioned warriors (the apostles, the seventy) are said to be entered into. Instead, they attack and are attacked.

34 Luke 8:3 along with the Markan appendix, 16:9, are the sources for the tradition that Mary Magdalene was once possessed of seven demons. With Jane Schaberg, I take this not as historical reminiscence, but rhetorical character defamation. See Jane Schaberg, *The Resurrection of Mary Magdalene: Legends, Apocrypha, and the Christian Testament* (New York: Continuum, 2004), 77.

35 Stuckenbruck, *Myth of Rebellious Angels*, 181–85; Joel Marcus, "The Beelzebul Controversy and the Eschatologies of Jesus," in *Authenticating the Activities of Jesus*, ed. Bruce Chilton and Craig A. Evans (Leiden: Brill, 1999), 247–77.

36 Acts of Thomas 43: "In that night he [the demon] came in to me and made me share in his foul intercourse.... According to his wont, he came at night and abused me.... I have been tormented by him for five years, and he has not departed from me." John K. Elliott, *The Apocryphal New Testament: A Collection of Apocryphal Christian Literature in an English Translation* (Oxford: Clarendon, 2005), 465.

the Apostle departs.[37] Readers who share this general understanding of the vulnerability of those once possessed might assume that all of these women mentioned in Luke 8:1–3 are damaged goods, susceptible to a demon's reentry. This vulnerability is most pronounced in the case of Mary Magdalene, singled out as having been possessed by no less than seven demons (!) a condition of grave depravity, and one that ominously mirrors the Lukan saying of the return of the unclean spirit with his seven additional evil companions (Luke: 11:24–26).[38]

5. Conclusion

While concerns with Satan and the demonic are expressed in a myriad of ways within the New Testament and related literature, there is no direct analogue for such a specific claim upon a follower of Jesus by Satan like we find in Luke 22:32. Consequently, there is no direct analogue to this intercessory prayer of Jesus on behalf of the one who has been turned over for the "sifting." In addition to recognizing the prayer as part of Luke's rhetorical efforts to rehabilitate Peter —an instance of prolepsis—we have suggested that the prayer, along with the accompanying exhortation to "strengthen the brothers" may be fruitfully subject to gender analysis. Peter's confrontation with Satan (Luke 22:31–32), along with the strong man saying (Luke 11:21–22) and the commissioning of the seventy (-two) (Luke 10:1–20), are three instances in Luke's Gospel where struggles with the demonic are cast in masculine tropes of violent warlike combat. To be sure, these are tropes of war on a spiritual/ethereal plane; references to earthly warfare in Luke concern primarily the siege and subsequent destruction of Jerusalem by the Romans. Luke's protagonists take no part in warfare of this type. But still, this spiritual warfare requires men to assume positions of agency and leadership.

In contrast to these virile warriors, women in Luke are never said to battle demons. Several women in Luke's narrative have been entered by demons; all of the women within the inner circle have been so possessed; Mary Magdalene, who takes prominent roles as witness and proclaimer of the resurrection in other

---

[37] Acts of Thomas 46: "And lifting up his voice [the demon] said, 'Remain in peace since you have taken refuge with one greater than I. I will go away, and seek one like you; and if I find her not, I shall return again to you." Elliott, *The Apocryphal New Testament*, 466.

[38] Luke 11:24–26 (NRSV): "When the unclean spirit has gone out of a person, it wanders through waterless regions looking for a resting place, but not finding any, it says, 'I will return to my house from which I came.' When it comes, it finds it swept and put in order. Then it goes and brings seven other spirits more evil than itself, and they enter and live there; and the last state of that person is worse than the first!"

sources,[39] was once according to Luke, the most demon possessed of them all (Luke 8:2–3).

Within this gendered framing, Jesus's description of Satan's claim on Peter in Luke 22:32 can be understood as a violent threat on his life, and Jesus's intercession through prayer along with Peter's "return" prove that Peter has withstood this violent confrontation. That his confrontation results in an increase in virility is suggested in the commission that follows the prayer. Surviving the attack, Peter becomes uniquely qualified to "strengthen the brothers." It is impossible to fully appreciate Jesus's proleptic prayer for Peter concerning his contest with Satan, without considering the virile commission that follows in its wake.[40]

---

39 See especially John 20:1–18, and the Gospel of Mary.

40 The exclusive, androcentric nature of this commission has been sensed by Pope John Paul II, who justifies definitively the exclusion of women from the priesthood, on the basis of this verse, writing:

> "Wherefore, in order that all doubt may be removed regarding a matter of great importance, a matter which pertains to the church's divine constitution itself, in virtue of my ministry of confirming the brethren (cf. Luke 22,32), I declare that the church has no authority whatsoever to confer priestly ordination on women and that this judgment is to be definitively held by all the church's faithful." (*Ordinatio Sacerdotalis* § 4)

Cited in Peter De Mey, "Authority in the Church: The Appeal to Lk 22, 21–34 in Roman Catholic Magisterial Teaching and in Ecumenical Dialogue," in *Luke and His Readers*, ed. Reimund Bieringer, Gilbert Van Belle, and Jozef Verheyden, BETL 182 (Leuven: Leuven University Press, 2005), 307–23 (317n49).

Warren Carter
Praying the Lord's Prayer in (Some Sort of) *Tameion* (Matt 6:6)

1. Introduction

Matthew 6:6 reads, "But whenever you pray, go into your room—your ταμεῖον (*tameion*)—and shut the door and pray to your Father who is in secret; and your Father who sees in secret will reward you" (NRSV). I ask in this paper—what is the space that the term ταμεῖον (*tameion*) designates and how might it influence the praying of the Lord's Prayer?

In a significant article, former esteemed colleague at Brite Divinity School, Lyn Osiek, examined the meaning of the term ταμεῖον (*tameion*), translated here in the NRSV as "room."[1] Osiek seeks to determine the type of room and what functions were appropriate to it. She notes the struggles and flights of fancy of some commentators in making sense of the term, and then turns to its uses in Septuagintal and classical texts. Positing an urban, Roman-influenced house in the east and not a Palestinian farmhouse, for example, she identifies three uses of *tameion*: a safe place for keeping valuables (both a public or private treasury), a storeroom, and an inner room or chamber or bedroom.[2] Then she discusses the use of the term's Latin "equivalent," *cubiculum*, equivalent at least in Jerome's eyes who translated *tameion* in Matt 6:6 with the Latin *cubiculum*. By Jerome's late fourth, early fifth century context (d. 420 CE), a meaning of treasury or storing valuables has dropped away, and the rooms so designated are not necessarily "inner" or "private," but somewhat more public in being accessible to at least some special guests.

Osiek draws on the research of Andrew Riggsby to note six uses of a *cubiculum*. From the nearly four hundred or so literary uses of the term *cubiculum* up to the second century CE, Riggsby, attending to the "moral topography" of the house, details six main uses of the space referred to as *cubiculum*: as a bedroom for rest or sleep, a place for sex, a place for adultery (a common association), a place to display art works (both paintings and sculpture) that signify luxury, a place for murder and suicide, and a reception area for special invited

---
[1] Carolyn Osiek, "'When You Pray, Go into Your ταμεῖον' (Matt 6:6): But Why?" *CBQ* 71 (2009): 723–40.
[2] Osiek, "'When You Pray'," 726–28.

guests.³ Katrina Sessa highlights the moral ambivalence of these activities, "some public, some private, others egregious and still more exemplary."⁴ She adds to Riggsby's list some further "morally suspect and illegal practices" in the *cubiculum*, namely "the practice of magic, and other illicit religious activities," as well as positive activities of philosophical and poetic reading and writing.⁵

Of course, we are in the world of elite houses here and not the *insulae* or tenements or the streets where most of the population and most of those addressed by the Gospel lived. This multi-functional *cubiculum* was usually located "off the *atrium* and later the peristyle."⁶ Access to it was not confined to household members or slaves. For the Roman architect Vitruvius (*De Arch.* 6.5.1), *cubicula* were not among the most common public areas (*atrium, peristyle, tablinum*) into which even the uninvited could enter. But like dining rooms (*triclinia*) and baths, *cubicula* were spaces reserved for invited guests and friends.

Riggsby emphasizes that the *cubiculum* was a place of concealment for secret activities such as sex or business interactions or sensitive conversation, a place free of surveillance and accessible only to those invited and sympathetic to its particular interactions.⁷ "It is characterized as a place where one can speak words that would be too indiscrete (Apul. *Metam.* 3.15) or too obscene (Apul. *Apol.* 78) to utter elsewhere."⁸ It is a place where some public rules are "relaxed," a place of "inappropriate" meetings, where "questionable actions" and "stigmatized" activ-

---

3 Andrew Riggsby, "'Public' and 'Private' in Roman Culture: The Case of the *Cubiculum*," *JRA* 10 (1997): 36–56; also Kristina Sessa, "Christianity and the *Cubiculum*: Spiritual Politics and Domestic Space in Late Antique Rome," *JECS* 15 (2007): 171–204. From archaeological perspectives, Andrew Wallace-Hadrill (*Houses and Society in Pompeii and Herculaneum* [Princeton: Princeton University Press, 1994], 17, 219n2; 58) identifies a place "not only for rest ('bedroom') but for the reception of intimate friends and the conducting of confidential business." Yet in his glossary on 230, he glosses *cubiculum* as "bedroom." Penelope Allison (*Pompeian Households: An Analysis of the Material Culture*, Monograph 42 [Los Angeles: Cotsen Institute of Archaeology at UCLA, 2004], 43–48, 166) emphasizes that the attempt to identify *cubicula* as bedrooms based on supposed "bed recesses" is quite unconvincing. She highlights the difficulty of naming a room's function/s from a label and understands the term *cubicula* as "a generic term" designating various uses and not restricted to a monolithic function of a bedroom (166–67). In addition to Riggsby's six uses derived from literary uses, Allison proposes the space's function for storage for personal activities (171).
4 Sessa, "Christianity," 177.
5 Sessa, "Christianity," 178.
6 Riggsby, "'Public' and 'Private'," 42.
7 Riggsby, "'Public' and 'Private'," 44.
8 Riggsby, "'Public' and 'Private'," 44. Riggsby cites James Scott's work on public and private transcripts ("publicly unacceptable speech and behavior"); see below.

ities are concealed.⁹ Such a space was requisite because, as is well recognized, a significant proportion of elite houses were public spaces and open to public scrutiny.¹⁰ Riggsby comments that the "relative openness of the Roman elite house made it a stage for the theatre that was aristocratic public display."¹¹

Within this stage of display, *cubicula* both permitted and enabled, yet also confined and restricted, any threat to societal norms. These ambiguities of permission yet confinement, of secrecy yet enabling countered and reduced "the power of (*tameion/cubiculum*) as sites of resistance to behavioral norms."¹² As places of inappropriate behavior, behaviors were not forbidden but contained by being confined to this space. The effect was, thereby, to protect and secure cultural norms and hierarchies, and to keep aristocratic competition in check.

In discussing Matt 6:6, Osiek particularly focuses on the last of Riggsby's six functions—a reception area for guests. She points out that the space was used for guests of relatively equal status and intimate friends, and for conducting business. She explains that the Roman house is not a place of retreat but the center of business and receiving guests and petitioners there is normal practice. She borrows Riggsby's distinction of "private" and "secret" whereby the *cubiculum* can be a place of both private *and* secret activity. While linked, the difference between "private" and "secret" is that private activity restricts access, while in the midst of public scrutiny secrecy is an act of deliberate concealment for activities, both honorable and shameful (sex, business, conversation).¹³

Osiek concludes that for Matthew the *tameion* is a place of secrecy, of "deliberate concealment" away from other humans who might bestow honor; it functions as "an exhortation ... to receive one's most important guest," namely God the Father.¹⁴

---

9 Riggsby, "'Public' and 'Private'," 47.
10 Kate Cooper, "Closely Watched Households: Visibility, Exposure and Private Power in the Roman 'Domus'," *Past and Present* 197 (2007): 3–33; Andrew Wallace-Hadrill, "The Social Structure of the Roman House," *Papers of the British School at Rome* 56 (1988): 43–96 (46), "A public figure went home not so much to shield himself from the public gaze, as to present himself to it in the best light."
11 Riggsby, "'Public' and 'Private'," 53.
12 Riggsby, "'Public' and 'Private'," 51.
13 Osiek, "'When You Pray'," 735–37; Riggsby, "'Public' and 'Private'," 43–44.
14 Osiek ("'When You Pray'," 737–39) notes that subsequently among early church writers there are several developments in understandings of the term. The *cubiculum* becomes for some both a literal place for, as well as a symbolic or metaphorical expression of, intimate encounter with God marked by solitude and separation from the world. For others, the *cubiculum* was a place of worship of idols that is renovated by Christians in removing the idols.

Osiek's discussion is helpful and certainly moves understanding of the *tameion/cubiculum* space away from the stereotypical dark, dusty, and overstuffed storerooms and windowless inner rooms favored by some commentators to foreground the space's flexible uses and especially its reception of intimate guests and friends. In this contribution, however, I want to expand the discussion by questioning two aspects of her analysis. One concerns matters of social status. Where or what are the *tameion* or the *cubiculum* spaces available to non-elites? By non-elites I refer to those in levels 5–7 on the Friesen-Longenecker scales which map a seven-tiered socio-economic hierarchy comprising three graduated tiers of elites (2-3% of the population), a middling group (7–15%), and three graduated tiers of the poor (approx. 80% of the population).[15] And second, I wonder about the identity of "the most precious guest" that Osiek posits as being invited into the *tameion/cubiculum*. Osiek identifies this guest as God the Father who is encountered in the *tameion/cubuiculum* in prayers. But given that the *tameion/cubiculum* was a place to receive friends and guests for numerous purposes, both honorable and shameful, I am not convinced that the identity of the guest should be so restricted, individualized, spiritualized, and confined to God alone. Perhaps the image of *tameion/cubiculum* points to spaces for praying with other people, other Jesus-followers. "Where two of three are gathered in my name, I am there among them (Matt 18:20)."

Osiek opens the door for such a reading when she declares that Matthew's scenario is "an exhortation *not to be alone* but to receive one's most important guest" (emphasis added). But she ignores her own words in focusing on God alone as the guest and overlooks the option of human guests who, as Riggsby's work establishes, clearly frequented *cubicula*. I want to inquire into what takes place for a small group of non-elite Jesus-followers in gathering to perform group prayer, the designated Lord's Prayer (6:9–13), in such a space. What might such a gathering for prayer of two or three Jesus-followers in a *tameion/cubiculum* accomplish beyond not gaining honor? What other impact might praying in a *tameion/cubiculum* have on a small group of two or three Jesus-followers?

---

15 Steven Friesen, "Poverty in Pauline Studies: Beyond the So-called New Consensus," *JSNT* 26 (2004): 322–61 (341, 347); Bruce Longenecker, "Exposing the Economic Middle: A Revised Economy Scale for the Study of Early Urban Christianity," *JSNT* 31 (2009): 243–278 (244–251).

2. Initial Objections

Two objections might be immediately lodged against this proposal that in Matt 6:6 group prayer in the *tameion/cubiculum* is in view. The first objection is linguistic since verse 6 abounds in singular, not plural, language. We have a second person singular verb "when you pray" (ὅταν προσεύχῃ), a second person singular imperative "go" (εἴσελθε), six second person singular pronouns (1 nominative; 4 genitives; 1 dative), and an aorist nominative masculine singular participle "shut" or "close" the door (κλείσας).

I suggest, however, that the singular forms do not specify a one-person audience for this instruction. That would be quite inconsistent with the multiform audiences of crowds and disciples identified for the Sermon at its beginning in 5:1–2 and in 7:28–29 at its close. The section of 6:1–18 is introduced with a plural imperative (προσέχετε), a plural indicative (ἔχετε), and three plural personal pronouns (ὑμῶν [2x], αὐτοῖς). And verse 5 introduces the topic of prayer—after a section on almsgiving expressed in the singular—by employing two second-person plural verbs (προσεύχησθε, ἔσεσθε) and a plural second-person pronoun (ὑμῖν). The switch of topic and number at verse 5 underscores a focus on group or communal prayer. Verse 7 also employs plural forms including its opening nominative masculine plural participle for the verb "pray" (προσευχόμενοι) translated as "when you (pl.) pray," and a negative second person plural imperative, "do not babble" or "heap up empty phrases" (βατταλογήσητε). The plural continues in verses 8–15. The choice of the singular in verse 6, then, would seem to be a rhetorical strategy to personalize or individualize the instructions to the audience of crowds and disciples to participate in communal prayer. It allows, not prevents, prayer by a group of two or three gathering in the *tameion/cubiculum*.

A consideration of the size of the *tameion/cubiculum* also mitigates the force of the objection that Matt 6:6 envisions only an individual, rather than a plurality of persons, who ought to retreat for private prayer. How many people can gather in the *tameion/cubiculum* to pray? It depends, in part, on the size of the space and in part on the social relationships or networks in view. Wallace-Hadrill comments that the topography of the elite house enacted degrees of social intimacy where the master uses the atrium for general reception and entertaining a large group "in his grandest room, a small group in his triclinium, or ones or twos in his cubiculum."[16] This claim of one or two coheres with Jesus's assurance that "where two or three gather in my name, I am there in the midst of them" (Matt 18:20).

---

16 Wallace-Hadrill, *Houses and Society*, 58.

A second possible objection to the proposal that Matt 6:6 exhorts more than a single individual to pray in a *tameion/cubiculum* concerns whether most of the hearers of Matthew's Gospel would have had access to such a space, and if so, whether it would be large enough to accommodate multiple individuals. Osiek's and Riggsby's discussions of *tameion* and *cubiculum* rely on data concerning elite houses. Osiek says, for example, that the conducting of secret business in the *cubiculum* "is well documented for elite houses," and then her discussion moves to "more modest houses" then back to "larger houses" that had a "a number of cubicula."[17] Riggsby says at the outset of his survey that he focuses on "large, urban, elite houses."[18] It is most unlikely that most of those hearing the Gospel lived in such houses, perhaps a few inhabited more modest houses where public sightlines and scrutiny had some importance, and/or lived in higher-status apartments. But most probably lived in small tenements.

What were the *tameion/cubiculum* options, if any, for non-elite/poor/poorer folks? Did non-elites have access to a literal *tameion/cubiculum*, or to some sort of equivalent and substitute, confined, secretive yet permissive space in elite houses? Did a couple of slaves who were Jesus-followers in larger houses have the option of popping into (one of) the master's *cubicula* for a quiet word of prayer or did slaves substitute their *cella* for a *tameion/cubiculum*? Were there a few folks in the Matthean audience, perhaps at levels 4 or even 5 on the Friesen-Longenecker poverty and economic scales, who owned smaller houses or areas in an *insula* to host other Jesus-believers for prayer in a *tameion/cubiculum*?[19] And as Zhenya Gurina-Rodriguez would ask, given her recently completed Brite PhD dissertation in which she reads this chapter out of a beggars-centric perspective, how might beggars who had no room of any sort but who lived on dung-heaps or under bridges or on the street understand this term?[20] Is the Gospel's instruction to pray in a literal *tameion/cubiculum* impractical or impossible for some or most of the Gospel's hearers, or is the language open to redefinition whereby the term *tameion* might evoke alternative, substitute spaces?

Several factors suggest that most of the hearers of the gospel had the necessary cultural knowledge or experience to at least make some sense of this teaching about a concealing yet dignifying space for two or three to pray. One source of such knowledge comprises the ever-present "public gaze" that passers-by had into elite houses, both the more extravagant and the more modest houses. Non-

---

17 Osiek, "'When You Pray'," 733.
18 Riggsby, "'Public' and 'Private'," 36, 52.
19 Friesen, "Poverty," 341, 347; Longenecker, "Exposing the Economic Middle," 244–51.
20 Zhenya Gurina-Rodriquez, "Begging for Their Daily Bread: Beggars-Centric Interpretations of Matthew 6" (PhD diss., Brite Divinity School, 2019).

elites were part of the public audience for the performance of both the house and its occupants.[21] They knew that some parts of houses were visible and some parts, like *tameion/cubiculum*, were more concealed. In buildings that contained multiple dwellings, and multi-levels with rented apartments upstairs, where living quarters were closely aligned, public scrutiny, impact, and observation were pervasive so knowledge of happenings within a house and its inhabitants could be widespread.

Moreover, as various scholars have emphasized, elite dwellings were not just visible spaces but public-access spaces. Houses included public areas where even the uninvited might enter as well as areas that were differentiated or were off-limits with privileged access, requiring invitation and different types of social interactions. Non-elites, like elites, were familiar with degrees of access to areas in houses reserved for only the most honored guests such as a *tameion/cubiculum*.

Furthermore, some of these passers-by moved from audience to performers in these onstage houses in performing roles as clients, tradespeople, suppliers, laborers, and slaves. And as scholars have indicated, the inhabitants of more elite houses did not comprise mum and dad and two kids plus a dog. There are various inhabitants, prompting Wallace-Hadrill to use the term "housefuls" to describe the multi-status inhabitants of houses that included slaves, the freed, clients, relatives, heirs, business associates, and guests, all of whom had cultural knowledge of the workings of houses and their varying circles of public and private spaces.

A consideration of the living spaces of non-elites also suggests that most of the hearers of Matthew's Gospel would have possessed the requisite cultural knowledge to make sense of the teaching of Matt 6:6. Work on non-elite housing in areas such as Ostia, Pompeii, and Herculaneum has identified a variety of dwellings including spaces identified as *cubicula*. In Pompeii and Herculaneum, Packer identifies living space comprising single rooms, rooms behind shops, combined workshops and living spaces, and small houses with a central *atrium* or hallway and eight to ten rooms including spaces he identifies as *cubicula*.[22] He also examines apartment blocks in Ostia and concludes that given vertical social hierarchy, above the first or ground floor in Ostia and Rome, "the great majority of these people must have inhabited one-and two-room apartments ... the average

---

21 Dominic Perring, "Domestic Architecture and Social Discourse in Roman Towns," in *Roman Working Lives and Urban Living*, ed. Ardle MacMahon and Jennifer Price (Oxford: Oxbow Books, 2005), 18–28.
22 James Packer, "Middle and Lower Class Housing in Pompeii and Herculaneum: A Preliminary Survey," in *Neue Forschungen in Pompeji*, ed. Bernard Andreae und Helmut Kyrieleis (Recklinghausen: Aurel Bongers, 1975), 133–42, with photos and floor plans.

Roman domicile must have served only as a place to sleep and store possessions," with people doing much of their living "outside the apartment."[23] Such buildings were often of poor quality and marked by overcrowding and poor sanitation.[24] De Laine notes a range of living options in Ostia from single rooms through to "apartments of different sizes and degrees of refinement."[25] Pirson identifies upstairs, independent rented apartments (*cenaculum*) in various *domus* in Pompeii of varying sizes but doubts that their inhabitants who lacked urban property lived in "surprising comfort" as Packer had claimed.[26] Wooden partitions perhaps marked off subspaces in small apartments.[27] Oakes identifies the pervasive small living areas of poorer inhabitants of Pompeii.[28] Given this variety, and if Packer's claim is correct that inhabitants of such spaces did much of their living outside on the street, there were some opportunities and spaces for two or three to gather for prayer.

Other spaces might also be understood to function as some kind of *tameion/cubiculum*, as a space for several Jesus-followers to pray. Spaces such as shops (*tabernae*) and workshops might function as a *tameion* for small group prayer.[29] Likewise Balch draws attention to taverns, outdoor gardens, and peristyle gar-

---

[23] James Packer, "Housing and Population in Imperial Ostia and Rome," *JRS* 57 (1967): 80–95 (85, 87).

[24] Andrew Wallace-Hadrill ("*Domus* and *Insulae* in Rome: Families and Housefuls," in *Early Christian Families in Context: An Interdisciplinary Dialogue*, ed. David Balch and Carolyn Osiek [Eerdmans: Grand Rapids, 2003], 3–18 [14–15]) surveys the four floors of the *Insula Araceoli* in Rome, moving from shops on the ground floor with living space on the first floor, to the generously sized apartments of the second floor, while the third floor comprises suites of three rooms, perhaps slave quarters (though Wallace-Hadrill is not convinced) with one room as the living space and the others variously for sleeping or utility purposes.

[25] Janet de Laine, "Housing Roman Ostia," in *Contested Spaces: Houses and Temples in Roman Antiquity and the New Testament*, ed. David Balch and Annette Weissenrieder (Tübingen: Mohr Siebeck, 2012), 327–51 (340–44).

[26] Feliz Pirson, "Rented Accommodation at Pompeii: The Evidence of the *Insula Arriana Polliana* VI.6," in *Domestic Space in the Roman World: Pompeii and Beyond*, ed. Ray Laurence and Andrew Wallace-Hadrill, Journal of Roman Archaeology Supplementary Series 22 (Portsmouth: Journal of Roman Archaeology, 1997), 165–81; Wallace-Hadrill, *Houses and Society*, 108–13; Packer, "Middle and Lower Class," 142. See also Bradly Billings, "From House Church to Tenement Church: Domestic Space and the Development of Early Urban Christianity—The Example of Ephesus," *JTS* 62 (2011): 541–69.

[27] This is the suggestion of Alex Scobie, "Rich and Poor in the Roman World (BC 50–A.D. 150)," *The Classical Outlook* 60 (1982–83): 44–46 (46).

[28] Peter Oakes, *Reading Romans in Pompeii: Paul's Letter at Ground Level* (Minneapolis: Fortress, 2009).

[29] MacMahon and Price, *Roman Working Lives and Urban Living*.

dens as possible gathering spaces for non-elites.[30] These spaces also might function as *tameion/cubiculum* for two or three to pray.

Like their elite counterparts, non-elites of the Roman Mediterranean world thus also knew the experience of public scrutiny. They lived in crowded spaces, both buildings and streets. In these contexts where they experienced in their own ways constant public scrutiny, they also found ways to gather "out of sight," whether in literal *tameion/cubiculum* or in substitute, non-literal *tameion/cubiculum* spaces in the sight of all.

In other words, from observing elite and more modest housing, as well as their own living and urban spaces, many non-elites would know the significance of entering a *tameion/cubiculum* with a host and shutting the door, as well as the experience of finding their own equivalent spaces. This space and action signified a special or intimate meeting, involving something either honorable and/or shameful, secret yet recognizable, permitted yet questionable, commonly practiced yet perhaps somewhat societally inappropriate, socially sanctioned yet perhaps a site of resistance, maintaining cultural norms even while bending them—an ambivalent space and act. Subsequently, it is safe to conclude that many non-elite hearers of the Gospel had access to spaces that might function in equivalent ways as a *tameion/cubiculum* and could be used for group prayer.

The instruction of Matt 6:6, then, to withdraw with others into a *tameion/cubiculum* to pray employs a well-established cultural ritual of privileged yet secretive meetings that is not dependent on accessing a literal *tameion/cubiculum* in an elite house. The teaching borrows the ritual and requires hearers to identify their own *tameion/cubiculum* space for prayer.[31] This prayer will not—in a disparaging and highly generalized description—imitate the "empty phrases" or the babbling of the Gentiles which Matt 6:7-8 immediately reject, but will comprise the succinct and well-focused prayer supplied in verses 9-13, a prayer that has of course come to be known as the Lord's Prayer or the "Our Father."

---

30 David Balch, "The Church Sitting in a Garden (1 Cor 14:30; Rom 16:23; Mark 6:39–40; 8:6; John 6:3, 10; Acts 1:15; 2:1–2)," in *Contested Spaces*, 201–35.

31 In their surveys, both Osiek and Riggsby downplay the use of *cubiculum* for religious observances. It is not one of Riggsby's six uses. Osiek ("'When You Pray'," 730, 739) recognizes the room "could even contain images of the *Lares*, the household gods," and concedes "there is some evidence of religious worship in *cubicula* from the earlier period," yet she minimizes the import of the observation by claiming the "primary place for household worship was in a more open space." That is true but it deflects attention from the use of the *tameion/cubicula* here for socio-religious practices. See Sessa, "Christianity," 178 and following, for its key role in subsequent centuries in the development of Christian traditions.

3. The Social Function of Praying the "Our Father" in a *Tameion/Cubiculum*

Why press the functions and types of spaces represented by *tameion/cubiculum*? Why does it matter? I suggest that, among other things, it invites us to consider how praying the Lord's Prayer in such a space, a prayer full of plural pronouns, might function for a gathering of two or three pray-ers? What might a gathering of a small group of Jesus-followers to pray this prayer in (some sort of) *tameion/cubiculum* accomplish for the pray-ers beyond not gaining honor? What impact might praying in a *tameion/cubiculum* have on a small group of Jesus-followers?

I employ two theoretical frameworks to formulate responses to these questions about the social function of the performance of the Lord's Prayer in a *tameion/cubiculm* where two or three have gathered.

3.1 James Scott's "Hidden Transcript"

One theoretical framework that in part explains the social function of praying the Lord's Prayer in a *tameion/cubiculm* is James Scott's much used and well-known theory of a "hidden transcript." I employ it with some caution as I will explain shortly. It nevertheless provides a starting point since Riggsby cites selected parts of Scott in his discussion of secrecy. Riggsby, however, parts company from Scott in that while Scott emphasizes the political strategies and roles of non-elites, Riggsby largely dismisses non-elites or "ordinary citizens" as posing no problem for elite-controlled society.[32] Scott, attentive to the "arts of resistance" among powerless groups, of course suggests otherwise.

Scott argues that "every subordinate group creates, out of its ordeal, a 'hidden transcript' that represents a critique of power spoken behind the back of the dominant ... a backstage discourse consisting of what cannot be spoken in the face of power ... they insinuate a critique of power while hiding behind anonymity or behind innocuous understandings of their conduct."[33] This hidden transcript is "contrapuntal, dissident, subversive discourse."[34] This "critique of power" can be articulated "in disguised form ... in rumors, gossip, folktales, songs, gestures,

---

[32] Riggsby, "'Public' and 'Private'," 52–53.
[33] James Scott, *Domination and the Arts of Resistance: Hidden Transcripts* (New Haven: Yale University Press, 1990), xii–xiii.
[34] Scott, *Domination*, 25.

jokes, and theater of the powerless."[35] I suggest here it is also articulated in prayer.

Only in "rare moments," Scott argues, is this "hidden transcript ... spoken directly and publicly in the teeth of power."[36] Rather, the transcript "is specific to a given social site or space, and to a particular set of actors ... [it is] elaborated among a 'restricted' public that excludes—that is hidden from—certain specified others ... [it comprises not] only speech acts but a whole range of practices."[37] Hidden transcripts are formulated and articulated in sequestered, autonomous social sites or spaces out of the supervision of the dominant, where like-minded folks might gather, and key figures or carriers or galvanizers exist.[38] Scott recognizes that hidden transcripts can remain hidden in part because their direct expression would bring harsh reprisals from authorities. So he calls the hidden transcript a "repository of the assertions whose open expression would be dangerous."[39] They are contained because of circumstances of "great peril" and function as "a substitute for an act of assertion directly in the face of power."[40]

3.2 A "Public" Word of Caution

Scott's theoretical framework is helpful for thinking about the social significance of two or three Jesus-followers gathered to pray the Lord's Prayer in (some sort of) *tameion/cubiculum*. Yet I am cautious in pursuing the analysis here in the light of the recent critique of Christoph Heilig who, in a discussion of the use of the notion of the hidden transcript in Pauline scholarship, urges greater care and precision.[41] Heilig dismisses, for example, the relevance of Scott's claims that the hidden transcript must remain hidden for NT texts because its exposure would bring reprisals in the form of persecution or sanction—for which there is no credible evidence for the early Jesus movement.[42] This critique, especially if official persecutions are in view, is well taken.

But that claim does not disqualify a recognition that critiques of power can remain unspoken publicly or disguised in articulation for a variety of reasons

---

35 Scott, *Domination*, xiii.
36 Scott, *Domination*, xiii.
37 Scott, *Domination*, 14.
38 Scott, *Domination*, 120–24.
39 Scott, *Domination*, 40.
40 Scott, *Domination*, 115, 199.
41 Christoph Heilig, *Hidden Criticism? The Methodology and Plausibility of the Search for a Counter-Imperial Subtext in Paul*, WUNT 392 (Tübingen: Mohr Siebeck, 2015).
42 Heilig, *Hidden Criticism?*, 57, 88, 129.

other than to avoid persecution. For example, they might remain hidden or disguised in order to ensure smooth "surface" social relations at a very local level, or perhaps by a realistic recognition of overwhelming odds and the pointlessness of public speaking. Alternatively, a transcript might remain hidden because of a sense that those embedded in and who serve as protectors of the system will not understand, be moved, or persuaded by any critique even if there was access to speak it. Likewise, a sense of hopelessness or pointlessness, or a conviction that only divine intervention can change matters, and survival is the only human option in the meantime, may keep a transcript hidden. It is also possible that the critique entailed by a hidden transcript might fund small acts of disguised dissent or function much more as an intra-group source of dignity than promote public confrontations. Pressures to not speak the transcript publicly, for keeping to oneself perspectives known to be unwelcome, do not have to involve persecution.

Heilig is particularly exercised over the use of Scott's theory to discuss NT texts as public documents when they are not written for public consumption but for in-house or intra-movement communication.[43] Some of Scott's analysis certainly concerns ways in which the hidden transcript is veiled or disguised in expression yet still seeks to infiltrate the public discourse in order to be accessible to the dominant powers. Heilig protests this use, however, because Paul's letters (the focus of his discussion) are written "for *other Christians*" (emphasis original) and are not coded communications for outsiders of "the dominating class."[44]

Again, Heilig's point is well taken. No public officials of the dominating class are reading NT texts including Matthew's Gospel; they are in-house documents. But the usefulness or otherwise of Scott's attention to expressions of the hidden transcript is not exhausted by, nor does it stand or fall on, this question of audience. Scott's discussions of the expression of the hidden transcript is not restricted to public encounters nor to how disguised forms of expression might enter public discourse. While that issue is one concern, fundamentally, as Scott recognizes in the preface to *Domination and the Arts of Resistance*, this discourse is secret, "behind the scenes ... offstage dissent ... spoken behind the back of ... [it] cannot be openly avowed."[45]

Heilig's emphasis on the in-house nature of the NT texts though well placed is too restrictive. It overlooks the possibility that what is expressed in in-house documents might filter into the public arena at micro levels of societal interaction through other means of speaking or doing. The documents' claims might shape the

---

[43] Heilig, *Hidden Criticism?*, 54–58, 66.
[44] Heilig, *Hidden Criticism?*, 57.
[45] Scott, *Domination*, xi–xii.

attitudes, practices, and actions of group members in various social contexts and interactions after the text has been read in private contexts. In such interactions, combinations of disguise and dissent will be necessary and part of the communication process. Scott's sixth chapter in *Domination* on the "Voice under Domination: The Arts of Political Disguise" thus has relevance in relation to how expressions of the worldview, identity, and practices prompted by a transcript—like one embedded in a NT document—might be performed in some local contexts.[46]

Informed by Heilig's cautions concerning the absence of reprisals and of public audiences, it is nonetheless warranted to suggest that praying the Lord's Prayer in (some sort of) *tameion/cubiculum* functions as a secret transcript, one deliberately concealed to borrow Osiek's definition. In an autonomous space, away from elite eyes and among sympathetic pray-ers, it constructs a critique, yet one that is ambivalent in simultaneously lusting for and imitating or replicating the dominating power that elites exercised. As such it is representative of any colonized context as postcolonial discussions have highlighted. To be clear, however, even if the praying of the Lord's Prayer in a *tameion/cubiculum* might secondarily impact public contexts, the practice itself is not for public consumption; it is not intended for a public official to overhear; it is not prayed in a secret place to avoid persecution.

3.3 The "Dignity" of a Hidden Transcript

Why, then, might the "Our Father" be prayed in (some sort of) space functioning as a *tameion/cubiculum*? Scott emphasizes the importance for powerless groups of reasserting dignity in the face of "slights to human dignity." In this Matthean context these slights are not engendered by persecution, but rather by an imperial system that benefits elites and exposes the rest to various, daily indignities of expressed elite disdain and rebukes.[47] The indignities are levied on people through the performance of deference expected of clients, those of low-status, and slaves;[48] it emerges in struggles for economic resources to counter food insecurities and poor living conditions, the failure of parents to supply what their children need, or in the social shame brought on by a failed business or limited resources.[49] In Scott's paradigm, when prayed in a *tameion*, "a social site apart

---

46 Scott, *Domination*, 136–82.
47 See the "lexicon of snobbery" in Ramsay MacMullen, *Roman Social Relations 50 B.C. to A.D. 284* (New Haven: Yale University Press, 1974), 138–41.
48 On deference, Scott, *Domination*, 23–25.
49 Scott, *Domination*, 7, 111–15.

from domination" and comprising "comparative safety," the Lord's Prayer constitutes a powerful "discourse of dignity, of negation, and of justice."[50] And this discourse of dignity is variously embedded in and in competition with, reinscribes and contests, some central imperial-cultural realities.

For example, the opening address to "our Father in the heavens" constructs the pray-ers as children of a particular father. They are differentiated from being children of father Zeus/Jupiter, or being children in the empire-wide, imperial household presided over by the father emperor, the *pater patriae* ("father of the fatherland"), and even from their own human fathers.[51] They are, first and foremost in the prayer, children of Israel's father-God made present by Jesus Immanuel, God with us (1:23). The prayer co-opts this God for these pray-ers and provides access to an alternative and what should prove to be a more fundamental set of kinship relations through its use of the rhetoric of "us" and "our" community. The affirmation does not disqualify other fatherhoods but it certainly decenters and relegates them. Locating God "in the heavens" empowers this father in a cosmic sphere even as he is "with us," his children. It provides cohesion, even momentary social redefinition for the pray-ers in constructing an undifferentiated household in which its members are placed on the same footing before their common cosmic father regardless of social status, gender, ethnicity, or roles in the everyday, hierarchical, imperial world.

Significantly, Riggsby points out that one receives guests "ordinarily of (roughly) equal or slightly lower status" in the *cubiculum*. "There are no cases of demonstrable social superiors being invited in."[52] Moreover, the *cubiculum* was not "a strongly gendered space" but is connected to men, women, and couples.[53] And it was adult space; "no *cubicula* are attested as belonging to children."[54] Praying the Lord's Prayer in some sort of *tameion/cubiculum* space to "our Father" thereby utilizes and redefines adult space in constructing a distinct identity of the pray-ers as equals in social status, without male privilege, and as children of one heavenly father. Ironically a space not associated with children is now redefined as the place of the powerless and vulnerable who are divinely-favored with divine

---

50 Scott, *Domination*, 114.
51 Warren Carter, "God as 'Father' in Matthew: Imperial Intersections," in *Finding a Woman's Place: Essays in Honor of Carolyn Osiek*, ed. David Balch and Jason Lamoreaux (Eugene: Pickwick, 2011), 81–102; Julian Sheffield, "The Father in the Gospel of Matthew," in *A Feminist Companion to Matthew*, ed. Amy-Jill Levine and Marianne Blickenstaff (Cleveland: The Pilgrim Press, 2004), 52–69.
52 Riggsby, "'Public' and 'Private'," 41.
53 Riggsby, "'Public' and 'Private'," 42.
54 Riggsby, "'Public' and 'Private'," 42.

presence—something made possible by its private, secret character. The culturally contestive space and the rhetoric of the prayer are mutually reinforcing. This dignity-enhancing work contests the corrosive effects of structural dominations.

The Gospel's construction of the father who is prayed to in one's *tameion/cubiculum* is also indiscriminately good. He makes the sun shine and sends rain on all (Matt 5:45; 7:11) but also treats harshly all those who do not obey (Matt 6:16; 7:21–23). The prayer centers on and elevates him. His name is to be hallowed. The pray-ers request that his kingdom or empire is to come, his will is to be done on earth as in heaven—truly a cosmic patriarchal household and empire to which the pray-ers belong (Matt 6:9–10). Interpreters have debated whether these petitions ask God to act or whether the petitioners answer their own petitions in their own actions, or a combination of both. I understand the petitioners to expect, ultimately, an eschatological response from the father God, but in the meantime Jesus-followers themselves, like the wise man of Matt 7:24–27, are to hear and do Jesus's teaching; they are to live as the household of Jesus's brothers and sisters and mothers in doing the will of this father (Matt 12:46–50). The prayer performs its dignity-enhancing work by commission, moving the pray-ers to find purpose in supreme commitments and an orientation to life that transcends the indignities of their everyday life.

The prayer that is prayed in a *tameion/cubiculum* concludes with children asking this father for what they need. They are dependent on this father for daily bread in an imperial world in which many struggled with food insecurity.[55] They seek forgiveness for debt.[56] They seek God's intervention so as not to experience eschatological woes. They seek deliverance from the evil one whose wicked ways are worked out through various agents, including the structures, personnel, and practices of the Roman empire whom the devil controls according to Matt 4:8. If there remained the expectation that the divine would respond eschatologically to such petitions, how, or if, such petitions were also answered among non-elites challenged by poverty on a daily basis is another matter.

Praying the prayer in (some sort of) *tameion/cubiculum*, thus, emerges in Scott's framework as a dignity-bestowing act. The site both permitted and enabled, yet also confined and restricted, any threat to societal norms. It allowed for the

---

[55] Peter Garnsey, *Food and Society in Classical Antiquity* (Cambridge: Cambridge University Press, 1999); Greg Aldrete and David Mattingly, "Feeding the City: The Organization, Operation, and Scale of the Supply System for Rome," in *Life, Death and Entertainment in the Roman Empire*, ed. David S. Potter and David J. Mattingly (Ann Arbor: University of Michigan Press, 1999), 171–204.

[56] Giovanni Bazzana, "*Basileia* and Debt Relief: The Forgiveness of Debts in the Lord's Prayer in the Light of Documentary Papyri," *CBQ* 73 (2011): 511–25.

expression of deviant norms (i.e., deviant in relation to the imperial order) even as it contained them, thereby reducing the site's power as a place of resistance and securing dominant cultural norms and hierarchies.

Yet how does this work happen in a small group of Jesus-followers praying this prayer in some sort of a *tameion/cubiculum*? I take a second pass at this question by using Social Identity Theory.[57]

3.4 Social Identity Approaches

Social Identity approaches (SIA) emerged in the 1970s and 1980s in the work of Henri Tajfel and his student John Turner (Self-Categorization Theory, SCT). Their approaches have been developed subsequently in the work of numerous scholars. The focus of the approach concerns inter-group relations and intragroup dynamics.[58] Tajfel defined social identity as "that part of an individual's self-concept which derives from (their) knowledge of (their) membership of a social group (or groups) together with the value and emotional significance attached to that membership."[59] Social Identity approaches engage questions such as: What happens when people join groups? How do individuals become a group, and what consequences follow for the identity of individuals, for intergroup interactions, and for intragroup or in-group practices and interactions? I mention four insights from this approach that alert us to some of what might happen when two or three pray the Lord's Prayer in (some sort of) the *tameion/cubiculum*.

First is the work of self-categorization. Fundamental to Social Identity approaches is the recognition that belonging to a group alters the way people see themselves and treat others. From the outset, Tajfel recognizes that group membership creates differentiation from or comparison with other groups.[60] A process of what his student John Turner calls self-categorization moves individualist identities away from interpersonal patterns toward the intergroup patterns of a posi-

---

57 While much social identity work has researched actual group experiences, we do not have the opportunity to do field work on the pray-ers of the Lord's Prayer in a *tameion/cubiculum*. Hence I explore the possible function of the textual construction without assuming a reflection of actual social circumstances.
58 Philip Esler, "An Outline of Social Identity Theory," in *T&T Clark Handbook to Social Identity in the New Testament*, ed. J. Brian Tucker and Coleman Baker (London: Bloomsbury, 2014), 13–39.
59 Henri Tajfel, "Social Categorization, Social Identity, and Social Comparison," in *Differentiation between Social Groups*, ed. Henri Tajfel (London: Academic, 1978), 61–76 (63).
60 Tajfel (ed.), *Differentiation*; Esler, "Outline," 17–22.

tive social or group identity.⁶¹ Group members recognize similarities among ingroup members, distinctive group practices and perspectives, boundaries, and comparisons with outgroups. Ingroup members learn to favor other ingroup members and gain bias against, and competition and conflict with, outgroups. Turner names this process "depersonalization" or "self-stereotyping" as people define their place in society by coming to see themselves as representing or cohering with, and benefitting from, particular group understandings, practices, behaviors, and members to which they are attracted; they thereby differentiate their own group from others.

In this perspective, praying the Lord's Prayer in (some sort of) *tameion/cubiculum* with one or two others can be seen as self-categorization work. It secures the identity of pray-ers as children of God their father and elevates that identity above all other identities. It aligns the individual with the group through its rhetorical focus on the plural language of "us" and "our" with plural pronouns occurring nine times. The "us/our" language signifies the divinely-favored status of the special ingroup, reinforces group belonging and differentiates the ingroup from an unspecified outgroup.

A second insight from Social Identity Theory that helps explain the exhortation to pray the Lord's Prayer in one's *tameion/cubiculum* concerns the process whereby members conform to group norms. As Hogg and Reid note, group norms are the "attitudes and behavior that characterize a social group and differentiate it from other social groups."⁶² Group members share common perspectives and behaviors and a sense of what makes group members special and different. Norms construct a world by which group members can make sense of the world. Norms guide behaviors and express and secure group identity. Social support and personal need-satisfaction are crucial to this internalization of group identity. Hogg and Abrams identify conforming to ingroup norms as the second and third stages in a three-stage process of self-categorization that involves i) identifying with a group; ii) discovering ingroup norms from other group members; and iii) embracing those norms in their own behavior and attitudes.⁶³

---

61 John Turner, "Social Categorization and the Self-Concept: A Social Cognitive Theory of Group Behavior," in *Advances in Group Processes*, ed. Edward Lawler (Greenwich: JAI Press, 1985), 77–122; John Turner et al., *Rediscovering the Social Group: Self-Categorization Theory* (Oxford: Blackwell, 1987); Esler, "Outline," 22–26.
62 Michael Hogg and Scott Reid, "Social Identity, Self-Categorization and the Communication of Group Norms," *Communication Theory* 16 (2006): 7–30 (7).
63 Michael Hogg and Dominic Abrams, *Social Identifications: A Social Psychology of Intergroup Relations and Group Processes* (London: Routledge, 1988), 172.

Praying the "our Father" constructs and secures group norms that comprise a world consisting of a communal identity turned toward God and other group members. The second person pronoun "your" occurs three times in the prayer along with four second-person imperatives ("give," "forgive," "do not bring," and "deliver"). The first three petitions construct a world where the divine name, the divine kingdom or empire, and the divine will are central concerns before the text's focus moves on to articulate benefits for "us." Moreover, this identity oriented to God is reinforced as the most powerful in the world by depicting God as the ultimate cosmic power embracing heaven and earth, the one who can rescue the pray-ers from the evil one or the devil. This cognition is linked with the pray-ers' volition and behaviors—they are to live in a way that is aligned with and reflective of this divine empire and divine will. This cognition entails an implicit contrast: group norms are not constituted by other fathers, other empires, other wills, nor by the evil one, the devil; nor are they established by those who withhold daily bread and who indebt the pray-ers (that is, the upper levels 1–4 of the imperial structures).[64] Praying with a small group of other Jesus-followers in some sort of *tameion/cubiculum* reinforces the ingroup norms in a context of competing options and contest for their allegiance. The confined, secretive yet permissive physical space and companionship of Jesus-group pray-ers reinforce these ingroup norms and identity.

Third, Social Identity theorists speak of ingroup prototypes.[65] A prototype is a construct that coalesces and represents what is central to a group's norms and which manifest the group's distinctive identity. Contexts of conflict mean that prototypes polarize group norms away from out-groups and increase conformity to ingroup identity among group members. Prototypes might be prescriptive in explicitly setting out "do's and don't's" of group norms and identity; or they can be descriptive in being exhibited or performed by group members. People or literary characters might function as prototypes in that they embody central group norms for other group members to emulate. In the Gospel, for example, Jesus is a prototype of the group's norms and identity of early Christians. Peter is to some extent also a prototype, but because of his shortcomings not completely nor consistently so—though his failures, ironically, highlight central understandings and behavior for early Jesus-followers. In addition to characters like Jesus and Peter, stories and explicit sections of teaching in Matthew prescriptively set out prototy-

---

[64] I refer to levels 1–4 of the poverty and economic scales developed by Friesen, "Poverty in Pauline Studies," and Longenecker, "Exposing the Economic Middle."
[65] Eliot Smith and Michael Zarate, "Exemplar and Prototype Use in Social Categorization," *Social Cognition* 8 (1990): 243–62 (244–46); Hogg and Reid, "Social Identity," 11.

pical behaviors and understandings.⁶⁶ The Beatitudes provide an example, as do the five big blocks of Jesus's teaching: the Sermon on the Mount (chs. 5–7), the mission (ch. 10), the parables (ch. 13), the community (ch. 18), and the eschatological discourses (chs. 24–25).⁶⁷

The Lord's Prayer, prayed by two or three in (some sort of) *tameion/cubiculum*, likewise serves a prototypical function. It centers the pray-ers in relation to their father God and other community members ("*our* Father"). It orients their identity and practice to God's name, to God's empire/kingdom, and to God's will. It seeks divine blessing in matters of daily societal justice—notably daily food and debt-forgiveness, in being spared eschatological woes, and in being delivered from the devil. These are prototypical practices or group norms.

And fourth, Social Identity theory, notably the work of Daniel Bar-Tal, has recognized the importance of beliefs for group identity.⁶⁸ Beliefs comprise a group's shared convictions about the world and about group members. They define the nature of the group, differentiate insiders from outsiders, as well as shape and judge consistent behaviors and norms. Beliefs embrace group norms to guide behavior, values (what is preferable), goals (for a valued or desired future), and ideology (the group's interrelated set of beliefs).

Similarly, the Lord's Prayer, prayed by two or three in (some sort of) *tameion/cubiculum*, functions to foreground group beliefs concerning: God as its father; the presence of God's reign/empire in its midst; its desired future in the full and final establishment of God's reign/empire and will; the centrality of knowing and doing God's will revealed in Jesus in the present; the notion of divine benevolence in providing for human needs; as well as the recognition of a cosmic binary between God and the devil yet with the affirmation that God is more powerful than the devil and able to deliver pray-ers from the power of the devil, which the Gospel recognizes is the power that controls the Roman empire (Matt 4:8).

These four insights are but a few of the insights that Social Identity theory has surfaced on inter- and intra-group experiences. They help us think about what might happen in praying the Lord's Prayer with one or two other Jesus-followers in (some sort of) *tameion/cubiculum*, whether a literal *tameion* or an equivalent space. Doing so secures the self-categorization and in-group differentiated iden-

---

66 Hogg and Reid, "Social Identity," 13.
67 Philip Esler, "Group Norms and Prototypes in Matthew 5:3–12: A Social Identity Interpretation of the Matthean Beatitudes," in *T&T Clark Handbook to Social Identity in the New Testament*, 147–71.
68 Daniel Bar-Tal, *Group Beliefs: A Conception for Analyzing Group Structure, Processes and Behavior* (New York: Springer, 1990).

tity of Jesus-followers; it foregrounds this group's norms, sets forth a prototype of central commitments, and expresses foundational group beliefs.

4. Conclusion

To conclude, in this paper, I have built on the work of Lyn Osiek and Andrew Riggsby concerning the functions of the room or space known as the *tameion/cubiculum* as a place for receiving one's special guest. But instead of arguing that this guest must be God and assuming that the *tameion/cubiculum* must be that of an elite house, I have argued that it is (some sort of) place or space for two or three non-elite Jesus-believers to gather to pray. And I have argued that praying the Lord's Prayer in this space functions to bestow dignity on individual Jesus-followers even as it imitates and contests cultural and imperial commitments. What is more, praying the prayer functions for Jesus-followers to secure their identity through self-categorization and through the rehearsal of group norms and beliefs. The prayer prayed in (some sort of) *tameion/cubiculum* thus functions as a prototype in expressing and reinforcing these aspects of group identity.

Ancient Sources Index

Hebrew Bible

Genesis
Gen 1:1–2:3 127
Gen 3:1–24 220
Gen 3:9 223
Gen 4:1–5 220
Gen 4:17 98, 99
Gen 5:18–27 99
Gen 20:3–6 81
Gen 25:14 85
Gen 28:9 56
Gen 35:4 180
Gen 49:2–27 50
Gen 50:20 81

Exodus
Exod 12:27 45
Exod 12:43–44 192
Exod 12:44 193
Exod 13:8, 14–15 45
Exod 13:1–16 179, 180
Exod 15 39, 41
Exod 15:1–18 49
Exod 15:5 186
Exod 15:21 7
Exod 15:26 56, 186
Exod 20:7 62
Exod 28:15–21 180
Exod 28:34–35 62
Exod 28:36 180
Exod 39:30 180
Exod 32:3 180
Exod 32:5–6, 18 46
Exod 34:6–7 35
Exod 35:21 136
Exod 35:22 180

Leviticus
Lev 5, 6, 26 17
Lev 16:21 122
Lev 21:23 79
Lev 26:40 164

Numbers
Num 6:24 137, 182
Num 6:27 182
Num 11:16–25 241, 242
Num 12:13 86
Num 22:5 99
Num 22:9–12 90
Num 22:20 90
Num 22:38 90
Num 22:23 91
Num 22:23–35 91
Num 23:3, 16, 26 90
Num 23:7 90
Num 23:18 99
Num 23:19 100
Num 23:24 50
Num 23:3, 16, 26 90
Num 24:1–3 90
Num 24:3–4 99
Num 24:3, 15 90, 99
Num 31:50 180
Num 35:21–29 136

Deuteronomy
Deut 4, 30 17
Deut 5:1–11 192
Deut 5:6–8 192
Deut 5:7–24 193
Deut 5:11 62
Deut 5:33 193
Deut 6:4 179, 183, 214
Deut 6:4–9 179
Deut 6:8–9 180
Deut 6:17–18 133
Deut 6:21–25 45
Deut 11:18, 20 180
Deut 11:21 192
Deut 18:5 158
Deut 21:5 158
Deut 21:6 157, 159
Deut 21:6–8 159
Deut 26:5 44, 45, 159
Deut 26:5–9 44, 45

Deut 26:5-10, 13-15 159
Deut 26:13-15 44, 45
Deut 30:1 164
Deut 30: 1-3 164
Deut 32:1 50, 193
Deut 32:1-3 193
Deut 32:1-43 50
Deut 32: 7-8 192
Deut 32:9-10, 37-43 192
Deut 32:14-20, 32-33 192
Deut 32:39 193
Deut 33:2-29 50
Deut 33:3 89

Joshua
Josh 1:1-43 63
Josh 1:8 111
Josh 24:2-13 45

Judges
Judg 1:26 64
Judg 8:21, 26 180
Judg 11:34 57

1 Samuel
1 Sam 2:1-10 32, 50
1 Sam 10:5 57
1 Sam 12:8 45
1 Sam 16:13-23 151
1 Sam 22:1 54

2 Samuel
2 Sam 6:5 57
2 Sam 6:6-7 62
2 Sam 7:18-29 45
2 Sam 12:20 206
2 Sam 15:17 54
2 Sam 22 49, 50
2 Sam 22:2-51 50
2 Sam 23:1-7 50, 90

1 Kings
1 Kgs 5:11 54
1 Kgs 8 45
1 Kgs 8:23-53 45
1 Kgs 8:37 56
1 Kgs 8:47-48 164

1 Kgs 12:25-13:6 46
1 Kgs 23:13 104

2 Kings
2 Kgs 14:25 32
2 Kgs 17:7-23 64
2 Kgs 20:11-12 32
2 Kgs 23:15-20 46
2 Kgs 25:30-45 64

Isaiah
Isa 1:11-12 62
Isa 2:7-11 206
Isa 3:18-21 180
Isa 8:19 106
Isa 31:4 111
Isa 34:14 190
Isa 38:7-39:1 32
Isa 38:9-20 111
Isa 38:10-20 50
Isa 38:14 111
Isa 38:20 45, 51
Isa 40:12-14 96
Isa 40:28-30 96
Isa 45:1 81
Isa 59:3 111
Isa 63:16 225

Jeremiah
Jer 2:22 56
Jer 4:11-14 207
Jer 7:29 206
Jer 8:23 210
Jer 8:18-22 207
Jer 9:17 210
Jer 10:22 104
Jer 33:11 45
Jer 39:4 30
Jer 44:5 134
Jer 51:51 79
Jer 52:7 30

Ezekiel
Ezek 17:2 90
Ezek 24:3 90
Ezek 21:7 79

Hosea
Hos 11:12 88
Hos 12:11 88

Amos
Amos 5:1 206
Amos 5:21–22 62
Amos 5:22–23 46
Amos 5:23 45, 47
Amos 7:10–13 46

Jonah
Jonah 2:3–10 20, 21, 27–42, 50
Jonah 2:8 51

Habakkuk
Hab 3:1 56
Hab 3:19 53

Zechariah
Zech 3:1–3 237
Zech 3:1–7 236
Zech 3:4 237
Zech 3:7 237
Zech 7:1–4 17
Zech 8:18–22 17
Zech 14:5 89
Zech 14:20 180

Psalms
Ps 1:1 75
Ps 1:2 111
Ps 3:1 54
Ps 3:3 62
Ps 6:4 65
Ps 7:1 50, 56
Ps 8:2 58
Ps 9:1 56, 57, 59
Ps 10:4 61
Ps 10:11 86
Ps 13 4
Ps 13:2–3 65
Ps 14:1 61
Ps 14:2 55
Ps 15:1–2 60
Ps 17:1 55
Ps 18 49, 50

Ps 27:4–6 80
Ps 31:5 228
Ps 31:23 36
Ps 32 76, 77
Ps 34:1 54
Ps 34:12–14 60
Ps 35:28 112
Ps 36:8–9 172
Ps 36:8–11 185
Ps 36:8–13 80
Ps 37:1–3 60
Ps 37:25 74
Ps 39:1 58
Ps 40:7 62
Ps 41: 2 55
Ps 42 36, 37
Ps 42:8 35, 36, 39
Ps 45:1 58
Ps 45:2 128
Ps 46:1 56, 57
Ps 46:11 62
Ps 48:15 57
Ps 50:5, 7–15, 16–23 62
Ps 50:8–13 62
Ps 51:18–19 62
Ps 53:3 55
Ps 57:1 54
Ps 60:1 55
Ps 62:4 65
Ps 63:1, 7 112
Ps 63:3 80
Ps 68:36 79
Ps 70:1 56
Ps 71:24 112
Ps 73 21, 22, 69–82
Ps 74:3–8 49
Ps 74:10 65
Ps 75:3–5, 11 62
Ps 77:1 58
Ps 77:12–13 112
Ps 78:1 74
Ps 78:1–3 74
Ps 79:1 49
Ps 80:1 55
Ps 80:5 65
Ps 81:2 58
Ps 81:7–15 62

Ps 82:1–7 62
Ps 82:2 65
Ps 83:2 86
Ps 86:1 55
Ps 89:4–5 62
Ps 89:6, 8 89
Ps 90:1 55
Ps 90:13 65
Ps 91:14–16 62
Ps 92:1 59
Ps 94:3 65
Ps 95:8–11 62
Ps 100:5 45
Ps 102 54, 55
Ps 104:4 209
Ps 106:1 45
Ps 107:1 45
Ps 110:1 81
Ps 115:2 61
Ps 118:1, 29 45
Ps 118:19–20 80
Ps 119:1–7 61
Ps 119:133 190
Ps 132:8 47
Ps 132:8–10 47
Ps 132:14–18 62
Ps 136:1 45
Ps 143:5 112
Ps 145:1 55
Ps 145:8 35
Ps 146–150 5

Job
Job 1:6–12 231
Job 1:20 75
Job 4:8 73
Job 4:12–21 73
Job 5:1 89
Job 11:13 74, 75
Job 11:14 75
Job 15:17 73
Job 15:18–20 72
Job 22:21–27 75
Job 33:6 152
Job 38:21–39 97
Job 42:2–6 66
Job 46:50 182

Proverbs
Prov 1:10–15 75
Prov 3:1 180
Prov 3:1–4 180
Prov 4:3 73
Prov 4:14, 24 75
Prov 4:10–11 73
Prov 6:20–22 180
Prov 9:10 88
Prov 15:8, 29 83
Prov 18:14 56
Prov 21:3 62
Prov 24:22 83
Prov 30:1–3 20, 22, 83–114
Prov 30:1–14 83
Prov 30:4 84, 96–99
Prov 30:5–14 84
Prov 30:7–9 83
Prov 30:8 75
Prov 30:15–33 83
Prov 31:1 85

Song of Songs
Song 8:6 180

Ecclesiastes
Eccl 3:21 228
Eccl 11:9 66
Eccl 12:1 66
Eccl 12:7 228

Lamentations
Lam 1:1 207, 211
Lam 2:11 210
Lam 2:11–18 210
Lam 4:9 207

Daniel
Dan 3:24–45 204
Dan 5:6–10 234
Dan 8:24 89
Dan 9 17
Dan 9:4–19 161
Dan 10:2–3 206
Dan 12:4 161

Ancient Sources Index

Ezra
Ezra 2:65 47
Ezra 3:4–36 161
Ezra 3:8–9 53
Ezra 3:10–11 47, 58
Ezra 3:20–21 215
Ezra 3:28–31 207
Ezra 4:12 207
Ezra 5:13 206
Ezra 9 17
Ezra 10:24 47
Ezra 10:19–24 206

Nehemiah
Neh 1:4 206
Neh 10:29 47
Neh 11:17 58
Neh 11:22–23 47
Neh 12:47 47

1 Chronicles
1 Chr 15:16 58
1 Chr 15:20–21 57, 58
1 Chr 16:4–6 47
1 Chr 16:8–36 47
1 Chr 16:41–42 47
1 Chr 23:4 53
1 Chr 23:30–31 166
1 Chr 25:3–6 58
1 Chr 25:7 53

2 Chronicles
2 Chr 2:1, 17 53
2 Chr 5:12 58
2 Chr 5:13 47
2 Chr 6:28 56
2 Chr 6:41–42 47
2 Chr 7:3–20 47
2 Chr 11:18–33 56
2 Chr 15:14 57
2 Chr 34:12, 13 53
2 Chr 36:22–23 48

Jewish Apocrypha and Pseudepigrapha

1 Maccabees
1 Macc 2:7 207
1 Macc 2:49–70 232
1 Macc 3:50–53 205
1 Macc 4:30–33 205

2 Maccabees
2 Macc 12:39–42 182

3 Maccabees
3 Macc 2:2–20 205
3 Macc 6:2–15 205
3 Macc 6:3, 8 225

4 Maccabees
4 Macc 18:7–8 244

Baruch
Bar 1:15–3:8 162

Tobit
Tob 3:12 14
Tob 8:4–8 189

Judith
Jdt 9 205

Prayer of Manasseh
Pr Man 205

Sirach
Sir 23:1, 4 225

Wisdom of Solomon
Wis 6:3, 8 225

1 Enoch
1 En. 1:2–3 99
1 En. 81:1–2 99
1 En. 81:5 99
1 En. 82:9–20 104
1 En. 85:90 199
1 En. 91:11–17 199
1 En. 93:1–10 199

2 Enoch
2 En. 31:6 244

2 Baruch
2 Bar. 10:1–12:5 203, 205–208
2 Bar. 21:1 203
2 Bar. 21:4–25 203, 208
2 Bar. 35:2–5 203, 210, 211
2 Bar. 38:1–4 203, 211, 212
2 Bar. 48:1 203–10
2 Bar. 48:2–24 203, 212–14
2 Bar. 54:1 203
2 Bar. 54:1–22 203, 214–16

4 Ezra
4 Ezra 3:4–36 161
4 Ezra 3:28–31 207
4 Ezra 4:12 207
4 Ezra 5:35 207
4 Ezra 14 161
4 Ezra 3:20–21, 26 215
4 Ezra 7:63–72 215
4 Ezra 10:19–24 206

Jubilees
Jub. 1:19–20 189
Jub. 1:19–21 7, 161
Jub. 1:20 189, 234
Jub. 2:21 14, 127
Jub. 4:17–18 161
Jub. 6:1–3 117
Jub. 7:1–6 117
Jub. 7:3 117
Jub. 7:7–19 117
Jub. 7:20 117
Jub. 7:20–33 117
Jub. 7:37–38 117
Jub. 10:1–6 117
Jub. 10:3 234
Jub. 10:3–6 189, 205
Jub. 10:13–14 117, 161
Jub. 12:19–21 189
Jub. 12:20 189
Jub. 12:27 161
Jub. 19:28 189
Jub. 21:10 189
Jub. 32:24–26 161

Aramaic Levi Document (ALD)
ALD 2:5 14
ALD 3:1 14
ALD 3:2 14
ALD 3:6 190
ALD 3:11 190

Letter of Aristeas
Let. Aris. 159 198

Testaments of the Twelve Patriarchs
T. Ash. 1–3 133
T. Dan 5:6, 10–12 234
T. Benj. 3:3 234
T. Iss. 7:7 234
T. Levi 18:12 234
T. Reu. 2:1–12 234

Testament of Job
T. Job 46–50 182

Greek Life of Adam and Eve (GLAE)
GLAE 6:2 222
GLAE 9:3 222
GLAE 9–11 244
GLAE 11:1 226
GLAE 13:1–3 222
GLAE 14:2 226
GLAE 21:2 222
GLAE 21:6 222
GLAE 23:1–4 223
GLAE 27:1–3 223
GLAE 27:2 225
GLAE 27:3 222
GLAE 29:2 222
GLAE 29:4–5 224
GLAE 31:1–2, 4 224
GLAE 32:1 227
GLAE 33:2 227
GLAE 32:2 225
GLAE 32:3–4 225
GLAE 42:4 222, 227
GLAE 42:4–7 227, 230
GLAE 42:8 228

Ancient Sources Index

Dead Sea Scrolls

Damascus Document (CD; Geniza)
CD 1:8–9 122
CD 9:16–10:3 126

Cave 1
Genesis Apocryphon (1QapGen ar; 1Q20)
1Q20 7:2 104
1Q20 20:12 14

1QWar Scroll (1QM; 1Q33)
1QM 10:8–12:16 9
1QM 13:2–14:1 9
1QM 14:4–17 9
1QM 18:6–19:8 9

Thanksgiving Hymns (Hodayot; 1QH[a])
1QH[a] 9:2–15 104
1QH[a] 10–17 11
1QH[a] 20:7–14 13
1QH[a] 20:9 105
1QH[a] 22:25 189
1QH[a] 26 11

Pesher Habakkuk (1QpHab)
1QpHab 7:5 128

Serek Ha-Yaḥad (1QS)
1QS 1 8, 107, 122, 126, 127, 132, 133, 136
1QS 1:1 132
1QS 1:2 8, 126, 127
1QS 1:4 132
1QS 1:4–5 136
1QS 1:7–11 136
1QS 1:11 133
1QS 1:18–19 107
1QS 1:22–23 122
1QS 1:24–25 122
1QS 2:1–2 128
1QS 2:1–4 107, 123, 137
1QS 2:2–4 109
1QS 2:4–5 128
1QS 2:5–9 123
1QS 2:10 123
1QS 2:13–14 123
1QS 3:5 135
1QS 3:13–4 135
1QS 4:2 135
1QS 5:1–3a 134
1QS 5:1 136, 137
1QS 5:1–6:23 136
1QS 5:2 136
1QS 5:6 136
1QS 5:6–7 111
1QS 5:8 136
1QS 5:10 136
1QS 5:21 136
1QS 5:22 136
1QS 5:23 126
1QS 5:23–6:1 126
1QS 5:51 134
1QS 6:4–6 14
1QS 6:6 101, 102, 111
1QS 6:6–8 101, 102
1QS 6:7 105, 107, 108, 111
1QS 6:7–8 14, 105–108, 110, 114
1QS 6:8 107, 109
1QS 6:13 136
1QS 8:15 107
1QS 9:10–26 140
1QS 9:12 135
1QS 9:15 135
1QS 9:17 135
1QS 9:24 135
1QS 9:26 135, 150
1QS 9:26–10:1a 140
1QS 9:26–10:17 13
1QS 9:26b–10:22 131
1QS 10:1b–8 140
1QS 10:9 152
1QS 10:9–16a 142
1QS 10:14–15 14
1QS 10:24c–11:2a 146
1QS 11:2b–5b 147
1QS 11:5c–7a 147
1QS 11:7b–9a 147
1QS 11:9b–15b 148
1QS 11:15c–22 149
1QS 11:9–10 153
1QS 11:21 152
1QS 11:21–22 153

Rule of the Community (1QSa)
1QSa 2:17–21 14
1Q25 13
1Q27 101
1Q30 13
1Q34 11
1Q34+1Q34^{bis} 11
1Q36 13

Cave 2
2Q21 1 7
2Q22 7

Cave 3
3Q6 13

Cave 4
4QDeut^j (4Q37) 192
4QDeut^q (4Q44) 192
4QPs^f (4Q88) 13
4QPs^f (4Q88) 10:5–6 104
4QCant^{a,b} (4Q106–107) 124

4Q141 170, 191–93
4Q147 138, 170–98
4Q148 138, 170–98
4Q160 4 i+5 8
4Q160 2+6+10 8
4Q171 4:26–27 128
4Q174 128
4Q174 1 i 3–7 119
4Q196 6 8 14
4Q213 1 i 9 125
4Q213a 1 3, 7, 9 14
4Q255 (4QS^a) 1 5–6 132, 136
4Q256 (4QS^b) 9 136
4Q256 9 1 137
4Q256 9 1–3 134
4Q256 19 1–6 140
4Q256 20 2–5a 142
4Q256 20 5b–7 144
4Q256 23 1–3 149
4Q257 (4QS^c) 3 2 135
4Q257 5 1–8, 12–14, 6 2–5 135
4Q258 (4QS^d) 1 136
4Q258 1 1 136
4Q258 1 4–5 136

4Q258 8 10–11a 140
4Q258 8 11b–9 7a 140
4Q258 9 2 136
4Q258 97b 97b–10:5a 142
4Q258 10 5b–8a 144
4Q258 11 136
4Q258 11–12 134
4Q258 12 4 146
4Q258 13 1–3 148
4Q259 (4QS^e) 3 6–7 135
4Q259 3 11 135
4Q260 (4QS^f) 2 1–5 140
4Q260 3 1–3, 4 1–3a 142
4Q260 4 3b–5 7 144
4Q264 (4QS^j) 1–3a 148
4Q264 3b–10 149
4Q266 8 109
4Q266 11 7–14 109
4Q266 11 8–14 8
4Q284 8
4Q284 1 3–6 125
4Q284 2 i 3–4 159
4Q284 3 3–4 159
4Q285 9
4Q285 8 9
4Q286 8, 9, 125, 126
4Q287 8, 126
4Q290 8, 125
4Q291 13
4Q292 13
4Q293 13
4Q299 101
4Q334 14
4Q341 125
4Q365 6a ii+6c 1–7 7
4Q369 13
4Q370 1 1–2 14
4Q371 7
4Q372 1 16–31 7
4Q372 16 225
4Q373 7
4Q373a 7
4Q374 13
4Q375 7
4Q376 7
4Q378 8
4Q379 8

4Q382 104 ii 8
4Q381 12
4Q382 8
4Q393 13
4Q400–407 10
4Q400 89
4Q401 14 ii 17 89
4Q402 4 6 89
4Q402 4 11 89
4Q403 1 i 44 93
4Q405 14 15 i 3 95
4Q408 7, 13
4Q408 2 7
4Q408 3+3a 7
4Q408 3+3a 5–11 104
4Q409 14
4Q414 8, 125, 160
4Q414 7 8 125
4Q416 2, 2a–c 4 93
4Q417 111
4Q417 1 i 102, 105
4Q417 1 i 6 101, 103, 106, 111, 113, 114
4Q417 1 i 16–17 92
4Q417 2 i 10–12 95
4Q417 1 i 6 101
4Q418 95, 96
4Q418 43 101, 113
4Q418 43, 44, 45 i 4, 9 113
4Q418 43–45 4 101
4Q418 55 93, 94
4Q418 55 8–11 93
4Q418 69 96
4Q418 69 ii 13 93
4Q418 69 ii + 60 10–14 94, 96
4Q418 76 3 93
4Q418 81+81a 1, 11–12 93
4Q418 164 2 93
4Q427–432 11
4Q427 7 11
4Q433 11, 13
4Q433a 11
4Q434–438 12
4Q440 11
4Q440a 11, 13
4Q442 13
4Q443 13
4Q444 12, 124, 138, 153, 189, 191

4Q444 1 5–4 151
4Q446 13
4Q448 12
4Q449 13
4Q450 13
4Q451 13
4Q452 13
4Q454 13
4Q457b 13
4Q460 5 i 4–5 225
4Q468i 13
4Q471c 13
4Q481c 13
4Q491 8+9 9
4Q492 1 1–8 9
4Q495 2 1–4 9
4Q496 9
4Q499 13
4Q500 13
4Q501 13
4Q502 8
4Q502 27 3 104
4Q503 10, 105
4Q503 7–9 3–4 104
4Q503 33 i+34 21 105
4Q503 40 ii–41 3 105
4Q503 51–55 10 105
4Q504 9
4Q507–509 11
4Q508 13
4Q510 12, 124, 137–39, 150, 189–91
4Q510 1 4–6 139, 190
4Q511 12, 104, 124, 138, 139, 151, 152, 190
4Q511 2 i 8 104
4Q511 8 12
4Q511 8 4 190
4Q511 35 6–8 190
4Q511 10 8 151
4Q511 28–29 3–4 152
4Q512 8, 125, 160
4Q512 7–9 3 125
4Q512 33+35 1–3 125
4Q512 42–44 6 14
4Q524 155
4Q542 2:12 117
4Q560 12, 19, 124, 138, 183, 187–89

Cave 5
5Q13 8

Cave 6
6Q18 12, 124, 189

Cave 8
8Q5 12, 124, 187, 189
8Q5 1 187

Cave 11
11QPs^a (11Q5) 13, 52
11QPs^a 19 13, 189–91
11QPs^a 19:5 191
11QPs^a 19:5–6 191
11QPs^a 19:5b–8a 190
11QPs^a 19:7 189
11QPs^a 19:12 190
11QPs^a 19:12–13 190
11QPs^a 19:15b–17a 138
11QPs^a 24 13, 82
11QPs^a 24:14 191
11QPs^a 24:15 190
11QPs^a 27 14
11QPs^b (11Q6) 13
11QPs^b 4–5 190

11Q11 12, 19, 124, 138, 189
11Q11 3:2–3 186
11Q11 4:1, 4–12; 5:6–8 187
11Q14 9
11Q14 1 ii 9
11Q15 13
11Q16 13
11Q17 10
11QTemple Scroll^a (11Q19; 11QT^a)
11Q19 155, 156, 162
11Q19 29 163
11Q19 29:4 163
11Q19 29:4–10 163
11Q19 44:5 162
11Q19 51:6–7 162
11Q19 57–59 164
11Q19 59:2–7 158
11Q19 59:6 163
11Q19 59:9–13 163, 164
11Q19 60:6–9 166
11Q19 63:3 158
11Q19 63:4–7 157
11Q20 155

Texts from Other Sites in the Judean Desert

Mas 1k 10
Mur4 178
Mur5 170–98
XḤev/Se 6 17

Ancient Jewish Writers

Josephus
Ant. 2.334–37 205
Ant. 4.40–50 205
Ant. 4.196 197

Philo
Spec. 4:137–42 198

New Testament

Matthew
Matt 1:23 260
Matt 4:8 261
Matt 5:1–2 251
Matt 5:45 261
Matt 6:1–18 251
Matt 6:6 25, 247–66
Matt 6:7–8 255
Matt 6:9–13 189, 255
Matt 6:16 261
Matt 7:11 261
Matt 7:21–23 261
Matt 7:24–27 261
Matt 7:28–29 251
Matt 12:29 240
Matt 12:46–50 261
Matt 18:20 251
Matt 23:5 23, 193–97
Matt 26:33–35 233
Matt 26:69–75 266

Mark
Mark 3:27 240
Mark 8:27–30 233

Mark 8:32–33 234
Mark 14:29–31 233
Mark 14:66–72 233

Luke
Luke 4:1–13 231
Luke 8:1–3 245
Luke 8:2–3 243
Luke 9:1–6 242
Luke 9:18–20 233
Luke 10:1–20 241
Luke 10:18 231
Luke 10:38–42 243
Luke 11:14–22 239–41
Luke 11:24–26 245
Luke 22:3 231
Luke 22:3–6 239
Luke 22:28 233
Luke 22:31–32 25, 231–46
Luke 22:53b 239
Luke 23:46 228

John
John 13:37–38 233

Acts
Acts 7:59 228

Romans
Rom 12:9 133

2 Corinthians
2 Cor 11:3 244

1 Thessalonians
1 Thess 5:21–22 133

Rabbinic Works

Mishnah
m. Berakhot 5:1 74
m. Shabbat 6:2 184
m. Mikvaot 6:4 184
m. Shabbat 6:9 182
m. Tamid 7:5 59
m. Kelim 23:9 184

Tosefta
t. Shabbat 4:9 184

Babylonian Talmud
b. Menahot 36b 197
b. Sanhedrin 22a 184
b. Shabbat 61a–62a 184
b. Shabbat 115b 184
b. Sukkah 28a 197

Massekhtot Qetannot
Massekhet Tefillin 9, 12 185

Early Christian Writings

Acts of Thomas 42–46 244–45

Greco-Roman Literature

Vitruvius, *De Arch.* 6.5.1 248
Apuleius, *Metam.* 3.15 248
Apuleius, *Apol.* 78 248

Subject Index

Aaron 116, 124, 127, 162
    Aaronic 22, 109, 110, 116, 123
    Aaronide 127
Abel 220, 230
Abihu 7
Abimelech 54, 81
Abraham 7, 117, 118, 126, 161, 189, 214
Acherusian (Sea) 225, 227
Achimelech 54
Achish 54
Acrostic 35, 206
Adam 9, 19, 24, 26, 116, 186, 199, 205, 215, 216, 219–30
Adjuration(s) 23, 184, 187, 188
Admonition 75, 133–35, 137, 151, 153
Adoration 5, 113
Advice 75, 76, 82
Affliction 54, 77, 104, 111, 126, 150, 183, 234, 236, 243
Agency 33, 39, 71, 81, 82, 108, 120, 160, 213, 238, 245
Agur 73, 83–98, 100, 102, 110
Alexander 3, 12, 121
Almsgiving 251
Altar(s) 46, 121, 156
Ambiguity 35, 88, 93, 98, 161, 249
Ambivalence 248, 255, 259
Amulet(s) 19, 20, 23, 103, 125, 138, 169–171, 173, 175, 177, 179–89, 191–97
Ancestors 22, 63, 163, 207
Angel(s), angelic 10–12, 88, 89, 91, 93–95, 99, 100, 104, 105, 107, 114, 135, 138, 139, 150, 161, 174, 182, 184, 186, 190, 193, 202, 209, 212, 214, 216, 220, 222–27, 229, 230, 237, 239, 243, 244
    cf. Archangels
Anger 35, 123, 146, 213, 224, 226
Animal(s) 45, 69, 127, 177, 199, 222, 226
Anthropology 2, 18, 73, 82, 103, 120, 121, 152, 153, 205
Apocalypse(s) 24, 199, 200–202, 204, 206–10, 212, 214, 217, 219, 229

Apocalyptic 104, 199, 200, 201, 203, 205, 206, 211, 213, 214, 217
Apocrypha(l) 1, 7, 13, 15, 17, 124, 138, 143, 214, 220, 244, 245
Apostle(s) 231, 237, 239, 242–45
Apotropaic 12, 14, 19, 22–25, 104, 115, 117, 119, 121, 123–25, 127, 128, 131–33, 135, 137–41, 143, 145, 147, 149–54, 166, 169, 171, 173, 175, 177, 179, 181, 183, 185, 187–91, 193, 195, 197, 234, 235
Aramaic 7, 9, 12, 14, 17, 19, 87, 95, 100, 117, 125, 128, 132, 183, 186–89, 197
Archaeology 23, 45, 63, 170, 180–85, 248, 254
    Excavating, Excavations 34, 181, 183
Archangel 220–25, 229
    cf. Angel(s), Angelic
Asaph 47, 54, 58, 166
Asmodeus 124
Astronomical, Astronomy 104, 105, 132
Atonement 11, 22, 71, 116, 117, 119–23, 126–28, 148, 166, 211, 221
Authority, Authoritative 13, 52, 57, 70, 107, 108, 139, 160, 161, 171, 223, 227, 237, 239, 242, 243, 246
Azariah 204

Baal 197
Babylon(ian) 29, 45, 48, 74, 155, 205, 207
Balaam 84, 89–91, 99, 100
Balak 91, 100
Bar Kokhba 178, 182
Basileia 237, 243, 261
Battle(s) 25, 182, 232, 238, 239, 240, 242, 243, 245
Beelzebul 239, 241, 244
Beggars, Begging 222, 223, 252
Belial 123, 128, 146, 189
Beliar 234, 236
Belief(s) 70, 73, 79, 80, 94, 102, 109, 150, 265, 266
Benediction(s) 19, 110, 123
Benevolence 265
Beor, son of 91, 99

https://doi.org/10.1515/9783110624526-015

Bethel 46
Bless, Blessing 4, 6, 8–12, 14, 24, 50, 63, 66, 95, 101, 106–10, 112, 113, 115, 117, 120–24, 126–29, 131, 135, 137, 138, 140, 142–44, 149–51, 153, 158–60, 164, 172–74, 180–82, 188, 189, 207, 216, 265
Blood, Bloodguilt 125, 157
Body, Bodies 11, 18, 70, 74, 82, 102–105, 135, 152, 155, 182, 184, 189, 216, 225, 227, 228, 230, 236, 243, 244
Burial 180, 181, 222, 224, 227, 230

Cain 98, 99, 220
Calendar(s) 13, 14, 120, 125, 132, 140, 165
Canon, Canonical 13, 15, 44, 52, 53, 64, 66, 67, 72, 233, 243
Celebrate, Celebration 8, 117, 242
Celestial 98, 104, 105, 131
Ceremony, (Covenant) 8, 110, 122, 123, 126, 128, 137, 139
  Marriage 8
  Expulsion 6
Chosen, Chosenness 94, 147, 158, 209, 212–14, 224, 239
Christology 234
Cicero 233
Class (economic) 253, 254, 258
Classification 6, 12, 13, 18, 25, 60, 189
  of prayers in Qumran Scrolls 6–23
  of Amulets 180, 191
Cognition, Cognitive 19, 21, 69, 73, 74, 76–82, 107–10, 216, 263
Collection(s) (Prayers and Psalms) 6, 9, 11–13, 53–54, 60, 121, 137, 155, 169
  Amulets and Mezuzot 125
  Calendrical (Otot) 132
  Manuscripts 4, 29
  Proverbial Sayings 83
Colonization, Colonized 165, 259
Combat 25, 31, 138, 151, 245, 240
Commands, Commandments 101, 117, 133, 134, 161, 173, 212, 223, 224, 226, 227, 229
  Divine 36, 40, 61, 63–65, 119, 133–36, 151, 157, 160, 161, 165, 173, 212, 223, 224, 226, 227

Compassion 146, 217, 222, 223, 225
Complaint(s) 51, 54, 64, 65, 72, 78, 102, 114, 207, 210
Confession 8, 9, 13, 17, 23, 25, 75, 76, 122, 158, 164, 224–27, 229, 230
Congregation 76
  Prince of 11
  Qumran 10, 134
  Rule of 102
Consumption 41, 258, 259
Cosmic, Cosmos 97, 104, 108, 110, 113, 186, 229, 238, 260, 261, 264, 265
Court, Courtroom 16, 88, 187, 188, 231, 235, 236
Covenant, Covenantal 3, 8, 23, 47, 63, 107, 110, 122, 123, 126, 128, 134, 137, 139, 143, 158, 163, 164, 166, 214
Creation 9, 25, 63, 70, 72, 92, 126, 127, 209, 213, 224–26, 229, 230
Creator 65, 66, 131, 205, 206, 208, 209, 213, 217
Cubiculum/a 25, 247–66
Cult, Cultic 21, 43, 45, 46, 48, 50–52, 62, 63, 113, 121, 128, 136, 165–67, 207
Culture(s), Cultural 34, 38, 69–71, 73, 79, 120, 135, 155, 156, 161, 197, 203, 221, 241, 248, 252, 253, 255, 260, 262, 266
Curse(s) 8, 63, 66, 108, 109, 117, 121–6, 128, 129, 137, 158, 164, 174, 206, 220

Darkness 104, 123, 137, 141, 148, 152, 153
David, Davidic 12, 14–16, 29, 45, 47, 49, 50, 53–55, 58, 64, 67, 71, 72, 75, 112, 122, 151, 179, 180, 188, 190, 192, 193, 234–55, 260, 261
Death 24, 56, 57, 59, 87, 95, 203, 207, 209, 219–23, 226, 228–30, 234, 239, 261
Deborah 32, 49, 50
Debt(s) 116, 261, 265
Deity 4, 8, 12, 18, 24, 46, 59–66, 73, 83, 90, 94, 104, 110, 112, 113, 153
Deliverance, 21, 28, 40, 41, 111, 112, 123, 148, 180, 190, 210, 261, 264, 265
Demon(s), Demonic 12, 19, 25, 118, 124, 138–40, 150, 151, 166, 183, 184, 188–90, 196, 206, 232, 234–36, 238, 239, 242–46

Desire(s) 60, 94, 146, 160, 195, 196, 229, 230, 236, 265
Despair 77, 81, 211
Destruction 59, 128, 244,
   Temple/Jerusalem 16, 24, 25, 49, 199, 203, 205, 207, 209, 211, 245
   Eschatological 123, 146, 148, 210,
Deuteronomic, Deuteronomistic 17, 19, 48, 49
Didactic, Didacticism 21, 61, 65
Dirge 206
Disciples 78, 234, 241, 251
Discourse(s) 4, 5, 19, 50, 51, 60, 62, 64, 70, 72, 73, 75, 83, 84, 89–92, 94, 97, 99, 100–102, 111, 113, 127, 140, 253, 256, 258, 260, 265
Diurnal (prayer) 13
Domestic, Domicile 253, 254
Doxology, Doxological 50, 63, 67, 208, 209, 211–13, 215, 225

Earth, Earthly 28, 59, 96, 97, 99, 144, 209, 213, 222, 224, 227, 228, 230, 245, 261, 264
Economics 66, 250, 252, 259, 264
Egyptian(s) 181, 186, 197
Elders 157, 241, 242
Elect, Election 12, 93, 119, 120, 127, 149, 212, 214
Eliezar 234
Elihu 74
Eliphaz 73
Elisha 7, 152, 187
Elite(s) 25, 162, 248–53, 255, 256, 259, 261, 266
Embodying, Embodied 25, 206, 238, 264
Emotion(s) 11, 14, 15, 59, 64, 70–73, 77–82, 150, 221, 262
Empire(s) 20, 66, 239, 260, 261, 264, 265
Enemy, Enemies 5, 61, 158, 163, 189, 210, 242
Enneateuch 45, 47–49, 50, 51, 63–66
Enoch, Enochic 7, 22, 84, 89, 98–100, 116, 117, 125, 132, 161, 199, 216, 239
Entreat, Entreaty 123, 132
Epistemology, Epistemological 65, 84, 89, 92–94, 97
Esoteric 22, 84, 88–92, 94, 95, 97, 99, 100, 102, 103, 106, 110, 113, 124, 128

Epistle 200–203, 208
Epithet(s) 95, 225, 227
Eschatology 6, 11, 12, 22, 51, 84, 88, 89, 92, 95, 99–102, 113, 131, 150, 152, 164, 209, 214, 239, 244, 261, 265
Eternal, Eternally 47, 89, 94, 95, 108, 109, 123, 141, 143, 147, 224
Ethics, Ethical 78, 84, 215, 229
Eve 19, 24, 26, 208, 219–30, 243, 244
Evening 7, 10, 105, 143
Evil, Evildoers 12, 22, 48, 60, 61, 65, 91, 113, 115–23, 124, 126–28, 132–39, 145, 151, 153, 180–82, 184, 189, 215, 226, 234–36, 244, 245, 261, 264
Execution, Executioner 189, 191, 235, 236
Exhausted 28, 54, 85, 87, 88, 92, 101, 217, 258
Exhortation(s) 106, 113, 131, 216, 223, 231, 232, 234, 235, 238, 245, 249, 250, 252
Exile, Exilic 9, 17, 21, 23, 27, 29, 30, 39, 45, 48, 49, 66, 67, 71, 155, 158, 161–65, 167, 181, 182, 205, 207
Existence 2, 24, 49, 53, 83, 120, 192, 200, 220, 221
   Mystery of 95, 101
   cf. *Raz Nihyeh; Mystery, Mysteries*
Exorcism(s) 119, 124, 155, 183, 186, 234, 239, 241–44
Experience(s) 11, 12, 21, 36, 66, 69, 70, 72–82, 95, 111, 119, 120, 135, 150, 160, 182, 228, 239, 240, 252, 255, 261, 262, 265
Eyes, Eyelids 14, 64, 79, 99, 111, 124, 133, 143, 147, 157, 198, 210, 221, 226, 230, 247, 259

Faith, Faithfulness 30, 45–47, 58, 60, 61, 65, 107, 115, 116, 146, 213, 231, 232, 235, 237, 246
Fasting, Fasts 17, 19, 103, 201, 202, 206, 212
Fate 24, 79, 162, 163, 186, 215
Fatigue 83, 87, 94, 95, 100, 102, 106, 112, 114
Favor (divine) 107, 108, 110, 123, 133, 205, 260
Fear 24, 40, 86, 138, 144, 150
   of God 11, 60, 64, 88, 154, 215, 216
Feast (days, of Weeks) 117, 160

Feeling(s) 69, 70, 72–74, 77, 78, 165
Female 180, 193, 228, 238, 243
Feminine, Femininity 219, 221, 229, 243
Feminist 20, 237, 238, 242, 260
Festival(s) 8, 11, 14, 46, 59, 132, 137, 142, 156, 160
Figurines (Mut) 181
Fire 123, 185, 187, 209, 213
Firstfruits 159
Fish 20, 30, 31, 38, 40, 41
Flood (waters) 40, 241
Folly 28, 113
Food 149, 172, 209, 259, 261, 265
Forgiveness 24, 75, 76, 116, 122, 123, 128, 176–78, 219, 221–23, 261, 264, 265
Formula(e) (of Prayer and Psalms) 8, 16, 35, 38, 39, 46, 47, 50, 52, 62, 121, 123, 124, 153, 180, 186–90, 193
Friends 25, 248–250
Funerals, Funerary 221, 228, 229

Gabriel 181
Gamaliel 16
Gender 20, 25, 221, 231, 232, 237–39, 241–43, 246, 260
Genealogy, Genealogies 19, 71, 99, 117
Genizah 193
Genre(s) 5, 15, 23, 24, 43, 46, 50, 51, 64, 72, 73, 75, 82, 116, 118, 131, 156, 159–61, 167, 169, 190, 201–205, 217
Gentiles 61, 255
Gideon 54
Gift(s) 151, 164, 190, 213
Glory 81, 93, 94, 113, 141–43, 147–49, 151, 153, 164, 208, 220, 221, 226
Gospel(s) 12, 20, 124, 189, 193–95, 228, 232–39, 241–46, 248, 252, 253, 255, 258, 260, 264, 265
Grace (before meals) 14, 38
Grace, Gracious (of God) 35, 108, 109, 123, 177
Greed 226
Guilt 17, 76, 122, 133, 158, 215, 236, 237, 239
Gunkel, Herman 43, 51, 200

Halakhah, Halakhic 23, 101, 102, 110, 117, 122, 135, 156, 157, 159, 160, 179, 191, 192

Hands 14, 74, 75, 77, 97, 109, 112, 113, 119, 143, 157, 158, 171, 176, 181, 198, 210, 224, 228, 230
Hannah 50
Hasmonean 156, 196
Healing 116–18, 124, 172, 173, 178, 187, 191, 193, 239, 243
Heart 28, 30, 33, 61, 76, 77, 81, 108, 123, 133, 135, 146–49, 153, 163, 173, 187, 215
Heaven(s) 93–99, 147, 193, 208, 209, 225, 227, 228, 230, 242, 260, 261, 264
Heavenly, heavenward 10, 84, 87–89, 91, 93, 94, 96, 97, 99, 102, 104, 112, 115, 141, 147, 161, 182, 209, 212, 213, 220, 226, 227, 229–31, 260
Hegemony, Hegemonic 151, 238
Hellenistic 83, 136, 152, 181
Heracles 236
Herculaneum 248, 253
Herodian (period) 29
Herodion, Herodium 178, 183
Heroic, Heroism 31, 50, 233, 239
Hezekiah 8, 49, 51
Hierarchy, Hierarchies 124, 249, 250, 253, 262
Hokmah 88, 92, 100
    cf. Wise, Wisdom; Sapiential
Holocaust 65, 67
Holy 22, 28, 36, 88, 89, 92, 93, 96–100, 109, 116, 119, 135, 141, 143, 144, 147, 149, 180, 184–86, 207, 211, 213
Homoeroticism 243
Honor 14, 28, 31, 67, 81, 82, 120, 126, 139, 201, 214, 215, 249, 250, 253, 255, 256, 260
Hope 24, 128, 209, 212–14, 217, 221, 228, 233
Hopelessness 258
House(s) 25, 45–47, 51, 58, 99, 119, 156, 173, 182, 207, 240, 245, 247–49, 251–55, 258, 266
Household 81, 180, 248, 255, 260, 261
Hybridity, Hybridization 50, 75
Hymn(s) 1–6, 10-13, 15, 17, 19, 20, 23, 24, 26, 29, 44–47, 50, 51, 61, 83, 105, 118, 121, 124, 131–37, 139–41, 143, 145, 147, 149–53, 155, 158, 166, 169, 189, 190, 209, 212

Subject Index

Identity, identities 3, 7, 11, 25, 26, 71, 119, 121, 124, 128, 139, 243, 250, 259, 260, 262–66
Ideological 2, 15, 20, 23, 25, 34, 35, 40, 116, 117, 127, 128, 161, 165, 167
Ideology, Ideologies 15, 23, 35, 84, 102, 116, 118, 119, 121, 126–28, 156, 165, 166, 219, 243, 265
Idols, Idolatry 123, 182, 249
Imperial 182, 188, 196, 238, 254, 257, 259–62, 264, 266
Impure, Impurities 125, 146, 162
Incantation(s) 6, 12, 19, 44, 104, 124, 138, 151, 183, 186–88, 193
Incense 128, 224
Inherit, Inheritance 147, 176, 177
Iniquity, Iniquities 61, 75, 122, 123, 128, 190, 236
Injustice 60, 75, 117, 134, 139, 146, 153
Insiders 101, 139, 265
Inspired 84, 102, 108, 109, 116, 135
Instruction 44, 61, 72–76, 90, 96, 106, 107, 117, 125, 135–37, 139, 156, 159, 160, 227, 251, 252, 255
Intercession 123, 208, 213, 214, 225, 232, 234, 235, 237, 245
Interiority 70–72, 75
Intertestamental 66
Intertext(s), intertextual 22, 35, 83–85, 87, 89–93, 96, 98–100
Introspection, Introspective 19, 21, 22, 69, 71–73, 76, 77, 82
Irony 33, 40, 91, 92, 260, 264
Israel 10, 21, 23, 34, 45, 55, 58, 61, 63–65, 76, 90, 102, 104, 110, 122, 123, 126, 128, 157, 159, 162, 164–66, 171, 181–83, 197–99, 202, 205, 208, 209, 212–14, 217, 234, 241
Israelite 27, 29, 30, 32, 33, 35, 39, 41, 43, 44, 60, 63, 66, 67, 71, 73, 81, 138, 166, 181, 182
Ithiel 84–86

Jealous, Jealousy 60, 146
Jehoiachin 48
Jerusalem 7, 9, 16, 24, 40, 45, 49, 110, 152, 156, 162, 165, 179, 182, 186, 187, 196–200, 203, 205–207, 210, 211, 214, 239, 242, 245
Jesus 25, 26, 45, 115, 178, 228, 231–35, 237–39, 241–45, 250, 252, 254, 256, 257, 260–62, 264–66
Jewelry 77, 180, 181
Joachim 43, 75, 78
Josephus 15, 198, 205, 228, 234
Joy 46, 58, 95, 241
Judah 8, 13, 27, 88, 89, 104, 112, 180–82
  Judahite 180, 181, 182
Judas 182, 239
Judean 15, 23, 27, 169, 177, 179, 191, 193, 195–97
Judgment(s) 29, 61, 66, 77, 78, 82, 139, 143–46, 148, 239, 246
Justice 12, 60, 80, 96, 113, 147, 148, 198, 260, 265

Kerygma 29, 30
Ketef Hinnom (amulets from) 180, 181, 188
Keys (temple) 206, 207
King 8, 12, 23, 32, 45, 47–50, 54, 55, 63, 74, 111, 156, 163, 164, 186, 224
Kingdom 28, 45, 49, 261, 264, 265
Knowledge 22, 80, 84, 88, 89, 91–103, 106, 108–11, 113, 123, 124, 137, 143, 146–49, 194, 211, 231, 252, 253, 262
Korah 54

Lament(s), Lamentation 4, 17, 24, 30, 36, 54, 55, 65, 71–73, 102, 112, 182, 204–207, 210, 211, 217
Land 12, 40, 45, 60, 63, 64, 117, 126, 127, 133, 157, 158, 163, 165, 172, 181, 186, 201
Law(s) 7, 23, 38, 61, 101, 102, 108, 110, 126, 134–36, 139, 140, 142, 151, 156, 157, 159, 160, 162–64, 166, 167, 187, 188
Lawlessness 80, 226
Lazy, Laziness 93, 94
Leader(s), Leadership 53, 196, 208, 232, 238, 239, 241–43, 245
Legal 23, 101, 157, 159–162, 166, 167, 176–78, 187, 231, 235
Levites, Levitical 44, 47, 58, 62, 107, 121–23, 128, 166
Literacy 178, 184

Liturgy, Liturgical 3–6, 8–19, 24, 42–45, 51, 52, 57–61, 63, 67, 102, 103, 105, 113, 118–22, 124, 126, 131, 132, 135, 137, 138, 140, 150, 153–55, 159, 169, 189, 191–93, 195, 196, 206, 208, 216, 217, 237, 238, 243
Love 35, 60, 115, 124, 133, 141, 146, 215, 243
 God's Loving Acts 144, 148
Luminaries 9, 10, 13, 16, 99, 105, 162, 166
Lying 118, 122, 158

Magic, Magical 6, 108–10, 124, 138, 139, 180–88, 191, 193, 196, 238, 243, 248
Malevolent, Malevolence 22, 24, 61, 121, 135, 137–39, 150, 153, 154
Marriage 8, 184, 185
Martyrdom 228
Mary 23, 165, 237, 242–46
Masculine, Masculinity 25, 232, 238, 241–43, 245, 251
Maskil 10–13, 18, 134–36, 138–40, 150–53, 190
Masoretic 13, 52, 53, 64, 84
Mattathias 232
Meal(s) 14, 46, 125, 232, 233
Memory 59, 69, 106, 128, 139, 173, 235
Mercy, Merciful 24, 35, 41, 123, 128, 213, 214, 217, 220–26, 229
Mesopotamian 81, 197
Metacognition 21, 69, 70, 73, 74, 78
Metaphors, Metaphorical 31, 64, 77, 79, 249
Method, Methodology 18, 19, 30, 32, 36, 37, 43, 44, 257
 Postcolonial 259
 Postmodern 37
 cf. *Theory*
Methuselah 99, 117
Mezuzah, Mezuzot 23, 125, 169, 178–80, 183–86, 197, 198
Military 25, 81, 232, 238, 240
Mind, Mindset 24, 70, 71, 74, 77–82, 108, 109, 112, 121, 154, 189
Moon 10, 105, 141, 227
Moral 17, 22, 33, 39, 76–78, 82, 84, 89, 91–93, 101, 122, 229, 233, 238, 247, 248
Mortal, Mortality 24, 95, 221, 236
Moses 7, 11, 23, 50, 54, 58, 64, 126, 133, 157, 161, 162, 189, 214, 219, 229, 234, 241

Mourning 95, 205, 206, 210, 217, 228
Murder(s) 219, 220, 247
Music 38, 45–47, 53, 55–58, 67, 142, 151
 Instruments: Cymbals 47, 58; Lyre(s) 57, 58, 143, 151, 152; Trumpeters, 47; Woodwind 59
 Musicians 47, 57, 58
 cf. *Tunes*
Mut 181
Mystery, Mysteries 59, 95, 101, 110, 128, 147, 149, 200, 212, 213, 216
 that is to be, to come 88, 95
 cf. *Raz Nihyeh*; *Existence*
Myth(s), Mythological 31, 38, 40, 88, 89, 186, 239, 243, 244

Nadab 7
Nathan 35, 134, 191
Niedrigkeitsdoxologie 152, 153
Ninevites 31
Noah 7, 22, 116, 117, 125, 161, 189, 234
Nocturnal 10, 103–105, 210

Obedience 24, 133, 135, 164, 213, 261
Oil (of mercy) 220, 222, 223, 226, 229
Oracle(s), Oracular 84, 85, 90, 99, 106, 107, 207, 216
Oral 11, 21, 29, 51, 53–55, 196, 200
Outsiders 139, 258, 265

Pain 24, 77, 79, 220, 221–223
Parables 91, 265
Paradise 220, 222–227, 229, 230
Parody, Parodic 20, 21, 27, 34, 35, 39–42
Passion (Jesus's) 25, 231, 233, 239
Passover 233
Pastiche 20, 21, 27, 29, 31, 33, 35, 37–42, 47
Patience 115, 116
Patient (medical) 78, 183
Patriarch(s), Patriarchal 82, 232, 234, 261
Paul, Pauline 49, 71, 86, 120, 122, 135, 191, 220, 236, 239, 243, 246, 250, 257
Peace 46, 60, 108, 123, 126, 127, 242, 245
Pentateuch 23, 34, 43, 48, 156, 159, 160, 191
Perception(s) 34, 39, 46, 54, 65, 76, 80, 82, 104, 109, 116, 126, 139, 153, 197

Subject Index — **285**

Perform, Performance 74, 106, 133, 141, 142, 151, 228, 229, 234, 250, 253, 259, 261, 264
  of Psalms, Prayer 2, 18, 46, 44–47, 51, 53–59, 63, 67, 77, 83, 103, 106, 108, 110, 116, 121, 126–28, 166, 200, 250, 253, 256
Persecution(s) 257–59
Peter 25, 231–239, 243, 245, 246, 254, 261, 264
Petition(s) 4–6, 9, 17, 18, 24, 41, 59, 83, 112, 115, 162, 204, 205, 207–209, 211–17, 234, 261, 264
Petitioners 1, 2, 15, 19, 20, 22, 24–27, 249, 261
Pharaoh 178, 186
Pharisees, Pharisaic, 193–196
Phylacteries 18, 23, 125, 169, 171, 173, 175, 177, 179, 181, 183–85, 187, 189, 191, 193–98
Pious 16, 21, 40, 41, 76, 77, 188, 196
Plant (of Life) 223, (of Paradise) 226, 229
Planting (Eternal) 147
Plea(s), Pleading 12, 13, 21, 54, 59, 61, 112, 138, 189–91, 209, 213, 214, 217, 220, 223, 228, 230
Poem(s) 6, 30, 32–34, 59, 124, 206, 210
Poetry 1, 4, 7, 9, 16, 29, 30, 32, 34, 37, 39–41, 46, 47, 49, 50, 59, 71, 86, 108, 120, 123, 137–39, 189–91, 207, 217, 248
Poet(s) 1, 2, 15, 19, 20, 22, 24–27, 32, 228
Politics 66, 92, 117, 121, 165, 205, 239, 248, 256, 259
Pollution 128
Pompeii 248, 253, 254
Poor, Poverty 186, 250, 252, 254, 259, 261, 264
Possession, Possessed
  by Demon(s) 243–46
  of Knowledge 93–94
  of Land 173
  of Spirit of Prophecy 241
  God's Eternal Possession 147
  Strongman Taking Possession 240
Postexilic 27, 29
Power 9, 66, 71, 73, 80, 85, 116, 117, 126, 138, 139, 153, 154, 174, 186, 188, 189, 193, 194, 208, 215, 221, 223, 236, 239, 242, 243, 249, 256–60, 262, 264, 265
Powerless(ness) (social) 121, 256, 257, 259, 260
Practice(s) 4, 13, 16, 18, 21, 22, 32, 37, 46, 47, 70–75, 79, 82, 84, 101–107, 110, 111, 113–17, 119, 120, 124, 125, 127, 128, 150, 155, 180, 182, 184, 185, 188, 191, 194, 196–98, 206, 216, 221, 229, 233, 234, 237, 238, 243, 248, 249, 255, 257, 259, 261–63, 265
Praise(s) 4, 5, 7, 9, 10, 14, 17, 18, 24, 37, 47, 51, 55, 58, 61, 65, 66, 72, 76, 95, 105, 107, 109, 110, 112–14, 127, 138–40, 142, 145, 146, 148, 150–53, 159, 190, 207, 209, 215, 217
Precepts 109
Priest, Priesthood 10–12, 22, 23, 44, 45, 48, 54, 58, 107–10, 115–19, 121, 123–25, 127–29, 134, 137, 158, 159, 161, 165, 166, 180–82, 185, 189, 206, 207, 236, 237, 239, 246
Prince(s) 11, 22, 58, 115, 117, 129
Prohibition 64, 198
Prophet(s), Prophecies 7, 8, 27, 29, 31, 32, 34, 36, 39, 41, 45, 47, 49–51, 60, 62–66, 84, 90, 96, 108, 128, 133, 191, 201, 203, 233, 241
Prosper, Prosperity 21, 63, 65, 76, 77
Providence 34, 125, 148, 179, 194
Pseudepigrapha, Pseudepigraphical 1, 6, 15, 17, 24, 26, 161, 199, 200, 214, 220, 232
Psychology, Psychological 21, 72, 73, 78, 79, 139, 263
Punishment 77, 164, 207
Pure 61, 76, 77
Purity, Purification 44, 102, 123, 125, 128, 155, 157, 159, 160, 165, 167, 189

Quote(s) Quotation(s) 27, 30, 35–38, 40, 41, 45, 46, 50, 61–63, 67, 92, 165, 184, 185, 193, 210, 243

Rabbi(s), Rabbinic 16, 17, 23, 74, 75, 103, 170, 179, 184–86, 190–92, 194–98, 207, 212
Raphael 119, 124, 174, 186, 188

Raz Nihyeh 95, 100, 101, 111, 113
  cf. Existence; Mystery, Mysteries
Rebuke(s) 77, 233, 236, 259
Recitation 10, 12, 44, 76, 104–106, 122, 123, 128, 139, 150, 159
Redaction, Redactor(s) 27–29, 33, 49, 84, 90, 100, 134, 221, 237–39, 240, 243
Redemption, Redeemed 119, 199, 236
Request 4, 65, 98, 106, 115, 184, 188, 189, 213, 215, 220, 222–24, 228, 261
Resurrection 209, 231, 238, 239, 244, 245
Revelation(s), Revelatory 23, 37, 95, 102, 110, 119, 147, 160–62, 202, 203, 208, 210, 212, 215–17
Reward(s) 66, 80, 93, 145, 247
Rhetoric 31, 64, 71, 84, 87, 89, 90, 92–94, 96, 98, 99, 101, 103, 113, 233, 239, 241, 260, 261
  Rhetorical 24, 30, 33, 40, 65, 72, 77, 78, 94–98, 109, 118, 153, 180, 207, 216, 217, 231, 232–45
Righteous, Righteousness 61, 65, 66, 72, 74, 99, 112, 117, 128, 135, 143, 146–49, 189, 215
Rite(s) 22, 120–22, 125, 126, 221, 234
Ritual(s) 2, 6, 8, 9, 10, 14, 15, 18, 19, 44, 47, 59, 104, 105, 108–10, 116, 118–120, 122, 124–27, 155, 157, 159, 160, 165–67, 186, 194, 206, 216, 255
Rome, Roman(s) 3, 25, 56, 86, 178, 182, 184, 186, 188, 196, 228, 232–35, 238, 239, 241, 243, 246–49, 253–55, 259, 261, 265

Sabbath, Sabbatical 5, 9, 10, 14, 56, 59, 89, 95, 105, 127, 132, 137, 142, 184, 185
Sacred 19, 88, 103, 108, 185
Sacrifice(s), Sacrificial 5, 9, 10, 28, 31, 41, 44–46, 60, 62, 63, 89, 95, 103, 105, 116–18, 121, 127, 142, 156, 160, 163, 166, 167, 210
Sadducean 207
Sage(s) 10, 12, 24, 91, 93, 95, 101, 124, 132, 135, 137, 150, 159, 162, 190, 198, 232, 234
Salvation 61, 84, 145, 148, 188, 190, 194
Sanctuary(ies) 28, 36, 44, 45, 47, 50, 79, 80, 128, 164

Sanhedrin 184, 186
Sapiential 18, 21, 22, 72, 74, 75, 82, 93, 137
Sarah 7, 81,
  in Tobit 124
Satan 25, 189, 231–39, 242–46
Satire, Satirical 20, 21, 27, 30, 32, 34, 35, 39, 41
Saul 34, 54, 151
Scale(s) 96
  Small scale scroll 131
  Economic 261
  Friesen-Longenecker 250, 252, 264
Scribe(s) 24, 99, 125, 128, 160–62, 171, 181, 185, 191–93, 197, 241, 242
Script(s) 10, 78, 105, 131, 132, 134, 159, 167, 170, 176, 179, 200, 257
Scripture(s), Scriptural 3, 7, 11, 13, 14, 18, 19, 36, 38, 52, 72, 91, 102, 103, 107, 108, 111, 125, 127, 128, 135, 137, 155–57, 179, 180, 184, 185, 189, 193–95, 197, 199, 200, 210, 211, 216, 217, 228, 235
Secret(s), Secrecy 59, 124, 135, 146, 161, 247–49, 252, 255, 256, 258, 259, 261, 264
Sect, Sectarian(ism) 3, 5, 8, 9–12, 14–17, 101, 102, 104–106, 119, 122, 123, 136, 190, 198
Self 6, 11, 13, 19, 22, 33, 43, 69–80, 82, 83, 97, 101, 115, 119, 121, 136, 152, 153, 157, 165, 216, 224, 229, 258, 262, 263, 265, 266
Semantic, Semantics 55, 56, 95, 126, 152
Sepphoris 187
Septuagint (LXX) 7, 29, 51, 52, 57, 59, 67, 86, 88, 95, 157, 191, 198, 228, 241, 242
Servant(s) 128, 133, 149, 208, 212
Service 16, 45, 46, 51, 53, 55, 60, 61, 63, 138, 151
Seth 220–222, 224, 226, 229, 230
Sex, Sexuality 81, 229, 242–44, 247–49
Shaddai 186
Shame 242, 244, 259
  Shameful 249, 250
Silence 38, 45, 56, 59, 166, 209
  Silencing (of women) 237
Simon (Peter) 231
Sinai, Sinaitic 156, 157, 164, 165, 167

Subject Index — **287**

Singers, Singing 19, 45–48, 53, 55, 57, 58, 62, 109, 123, 138, 166
  cf. Music, Musicians
Sin 9, 12, 17, 22, 25, 71, 75, 76, 81, 116, 119–22, 126–28, 146, 148, 153, 165–67, 176, 189, 215, 221, 223–27, 229, 230, 242
Sinner(s) 17, 24, 216, 221, 227, 229, 236
Sinfulness 148, 227
Slave(s) 248, 252–54, 259
Sleep, Sleeping 81, 103, 104, 247, 254
Society 8, 31, 33, 37, 49, 69, 110, 125, 131, 132, 158, 162, 164, 166, 182, 185, 199, 248, 251, 254, 256, 261, 263
Sociology, Sociological 2, 20, 122
Solomon 16, 45, 47, 54, 58, 124
Soul 133, 146, 163, 219, 220, 226, 228, 230, 236
Speech 2–4, 10, 40, 43, 45, 69, 72–74, 76–78, 87, 90, 105, 108, 113, 126, 128, 135, 156, 157, 172, 204, 216, 217, 232, 234, 248, 257
Spell(s) 108, 125, 186–88, 193
Spirit(s) 28, 82, 92, 93, 96, 104, 106, 107, 117, 135–139, 146, 150, 151, 174, 188–90, 213, 224, 225, 227, 228, 230, 234, 236, 244, 245
Spiritual 21, 76–78, 92, 93, 120, 126, 127, 135, 136, 229, 243, 245, 248
Status 11, 51, 89, 91, 94, 100, 104, 121, 161, 165, 195, 236, 249, 250, 252, 253, 259, 260, 263
Statute(s) 135, 136, 142, 143, 146, 151, 154, 213
Structuralism 38
Subversive (words, discourse) 78, 256
Suffering 21, 57, 65, 76, 112, 234, 239
Sunrise 13, 105
Supernatural 95, 103, 104, 125, 128, 187
Symbol(ism), Symbolic 11, 30, 32, 39, 41, 80, 81, 92, 109, 119, 121, 195, 196, 241, 249
Synagogue(s) 48, 53, 63, 183
Synoptic 12, 23, 124, 140, 189, 232, 235, 239, 240

Tameion 25, 26, 247, 249–57, 259–66
Tannaitic 184
Targum(s) 95, 96, 169

Teacher(s), Teaching 11, 22, 36, 39, 55, 60, 73, 74, 82, 91, 96, 106, 107, 125, 128, 135–37, 139, 143, 146, 164, 212, 229, 246, 252, 253, 255, 261, 264, 265
Tefillin 18, 23, 125, 169, 170, 177–80, 183–85, 191–98
Temple(s) 1–8, 10, 12–24, 26, 27, 33, 41–51, 53, 55, 57–59, 63, 67, 69–71, 79, 81–85, 88, 89, 92, 95, 96, 99–107, 111, 113–16, 119, 122, 127, 128, 131, 137, 138, 143, 150, 151, 155–67, 170, 181–83, 185, 187–90, 192–96, 198–200, 204–207, 210–12, 216, 217, 225, 239, 243, 254
Terror, Terrify 123, 126, 139, 144, 150
Tetragrammaton 180, 186
Thanks, Thanksgiving(s) 6, 10, 21, 28, 30, 36, 40, 41, 45–47, 51, 58, 61, 63, 67, 72, 73, 75–77, 108, 110, 111, 115, 119–21, 127, 129
Theodicy 21, 66, 67
Oil of mercy 219
Theology, Theological 2, 4, 19, 65–67, 116, 118, 120, 126, 127, 162, 203, 216
Theory 19, 20, 25, 37, 39, 44, 70, 92, 107–10, 206, 256–58, 262–65
  cf. Method, Methodology
Thomas 28, 90, 244, 245
Throne 224–27, 239
Tobias 124, 213
Torah 23, 24, 44, 45, 64, 84, 95, 102, 106, 111, 114, 137, 158, 160, 163, 164, 185, 196, 205, 211–17
Transformation 11, 36, 39, 75, 76, 81, 82, 93, 122, 126, 188, 196, 217, 240
Transgression(s), Transgressor 65, 75, 76, 109, 229
Truth, Truthful 40, 60, 70, 93–95, 109, 110, 113, 115, 135, 145, 147, 233
Tunes 46, 55, 58
  cf. Music

Ukhal 84, 85
Unclean, Uncleanness 148, 189, 245
Urban 247, 250, 252–55

Victory(ies), Victorious 25, 62, 107, 187, 240, 243

Vigilance 104, 105, 114
Vindication 112
Violence, Violent 25, 80, 126, 146, 232, 234–237, 244–246
Virgin(s) 206, 207
Virile, Virility 25, 232, 238, 241, 242, 245, 246
Virtue, Virtuous 40, 66, 227, 241, 246
Vision(s), Visionary 24, 99, 116, 117, 136, 162, 165, 182, 202, 204, 206, 208, 210, 211, 214, 215, 217, 220, 221, 227–30, 242

Warriors 64, 244, 245
Wash, Washing 14, 77, 157, 159, 220, 225, 227
Watchers 7, 89, 99, 100, 104, 216, 217
Water(s) 28, 33, 35, 38, 40, 41, 96, 97, 159, 177, 210, 214, 215
Weariness 22, 79, 83–87, 91, 92, 94–96, 100–102, 110, 111, 114
Weep, Weeping 18, 19, 210, 220, 222–24, 226–29

Wicked, Wickedness 21, 61, 65, 66, 72, 76–78, 80, 91, 111, 123, 128, 137, 138, 146, 148, 151, 153, 158, 188, 189, 261
Wise, Wisdom 22, 60, 64, 65, 73–75, 84, 87–93, 95–97, 99, 100, 102, 109, 113, 115, 116, 125, 135, 147, 178, 197, 199, 201, 203, 211–15, 228, 229, 238, 242, 243, 261
Woman, Women 15, 50, 66, 149, 184, 206, 221, 226, 232, 237–39, 242–46, 260
Wonders (divine) 110, 112, 113, 147, 149
Worship, Worshippers 18, 19, 21, 28, 31, 41, 47, 53, 61, 62, 67, 80, 81, 102–105, 120, 255
Wrongdoing 126, 143, 146, 147

Yael 171
Yahad 82, 132, 136
Yakeh, son of 84, 85
Yavneh 16

Zadok, Zadokite 11, 110, 116, 134, 139, 152
Zion 54, 194, 198, 206, 208, 210
Zophar 74, 75, 82